THE JAMAICA MOVEMENT,

FOR PROMOTING

THE ENFORCEMENT

OF

THE SLAVE-TRADE TREATIES,

AND THE

SUPPRESSION OF THE SLAVE-TRADE;

WITH STATEMENTS OF

FACT, CONVENTION, AND LAW:

PREPARED AT THE REQUEST OF

THE KINGSTON COMMITTEE.

"Hear it, ye Statesmen! hear this truth sublime:
He who allows oppression— shares the crime!"

DARWIN.

NEGRO UNIVERSITIES PRESS
NEW YORK

HT 1162
T 85
1969

Originally published in 1850
by Charles Gilpin

Reprinted 1969 by
Negro Universities Press
A DIVISION OF GREENWOOD PUBLISHING CORP.
NEW YORK

SBN 8371-1569-8

INTRODUCTORY STATEMENT.

WHEN the public mind has been prepared, by a long course of events, to view any given subject in a particular light, it requires but a trifling circumstance, something which, in common parlance, would be called an accident, to rouse it from a state of apparent lethargy, and impart to it a vigorous, or even vehement action.

It was the interruption of a dinner party, in the beginning of the last year, which overthrew a dynasty, and, by a series of revolutionary movements, shook to their foundations the most ancient thrones in Europe. And, to compare great things with small, it was the success of a dinner party, on a narrower scale, which, although it met with no interruption, has happily led to the great moral, social, and economical movement, which it is the business of these pages to record.

Nor are our present proceedings to be undervalued because of their humble and modest origin. In the end, if followed up with suitable energy, near the great centres of civilisation and progress, the results may prove more important, more permanent, and more beneficial to the great family of mankind, than the mightiest of those political eruptions,

> "—— With fear of change
> Distracting monarchies."

For the sake of doing an act of simple justice to a reverend and learned divine, who is no longer in Jamaica, but whose too short visit to our health-giving shores has been blessed in the restoration from the brink of the grave

of one who was nearest and dearest to him, the fact is not to
be withheld, that it is to his clearness of conception, and
earnestness of purpose, we are mainly indebted for fixing
the time, and settling the form and manner of that first step
in this movement, which, according to the well-known
French proverb, is the most important of all.

It was at a casual interview, in the hospitable halls of our
excellent Governor, that the Editor of these papers had
first the advantage of meeting and making the acquaintance
of his distinguished countryman, the Reverend Dr. King,
of Glasgow, who, although belonging to one of those
branches of the universal church which has too often been
charged with narrow-mindedness and bigotry, is possessed
of as catholic and pure a spirit, and as deeply imbued with
Christian charity, as the best of those who, in these our
days, have added their personal dignity to that of the mitre,
or have adorned the surplice with the subdued lustre of
their pastoral virtues.

When two men meet for the first time, with some pre-
disposition to think well of each other, it does not require
much inquiry, or discussion, to discover the points on which
they hold opinions and sentiments in common.   On the
present occasion, the duty of inflicting " a heavy blow, and
a great discouragement," on the practice of slavery and the
slave-trade, was the tie which bound the new acquaintances
to each other.   During a visit which the stranger found
leisure to pay to his resident countryman, in May last, a few
friends were invited to meet him for the 14th of the month;
and it was before the party had risen from table, on that
occasion, that Dr. King drew the attention of the company
to that peculiar system of slave-trade suppression, which,
under the auspices of Viscount Palmerston, had long been
identified with the name of the host.

In the course of conversation, it was suggested by one of

the guests that the subject was fit, and the season appropriate, for its consideration at a meeting, greater in point of numbers, in a place more public, and of a character more deliberative, than was possible on an occasion so casual and unexpected; and thereupon it was proposed that ground should be taken at once, and a day fixed for the purpose.

Between Kingston and Spanish Town, as the *locus in quo*, there was at first some difference of opinion; but the point was speedily settled in favour of the less populous locality, because it is at once the cathedral city, the seat of the Legislature, and the abode of her Majesty's representative. Thanks to the loyal suggestion of Mr. Justice Macdougall, her Majesty's birth-day, the 24th of the month, was adopted, without hesitation, as in every way the best that could be chosen; without consulting the convenience of Dr. King, who had made his arrangements for leaving the island in the packet appointed to sail on the previous day. In that retiring, unselfish, and truly social spirit, which forms one of the charms of the character of that admirable person, he took no notice of his own engagements; but having readily acquiesced in the peculiar fitness of the day, he agreed at once to lend us his assistance. And it will presently be seen how well he kept his word; although it made it necessary for him to alter his route, and to detain a vessel expressly, at a heavy charge, till the morning of the 25th, to carry himself and his family to one of the American seaports. This was all done so quietly, and in such undeniable good taste, that it deserves to be told at the expense of a little circumlocution.

Well! The requisition came on with the coffee!—and, in less time than we have taken to tell it, received the signatures which are seen at the head of the list, and which, from their influential character, secured its completion the following morning, at the expense of a single turn through the streets of Kingston and Spanish Town by two of the number. Here it is, as it appeared forthwith in the newspapers:—

"*To the Hon. William Dutton Turner, Chief Magistrate, and Custos Rotulorum of St. Katherine.*

"Kingston, May 14, 1849.

"We, the undersigned, request that your Honour will be pleased to allow the gentlemen, whose names are hereunto annexed, to have the use of the Public Rooms of Spanish Town, for the purpose of inviting the inhabitants of Jamaica to consider the effect produced on this country by the non-observance of the treaties for the suppression of the slave-trade, by which Spain and Brazil are bound to her Majesty; and of devising such a measure as may tend to promote at once the great interests of humanity, and the relief of the intertropical possessions of the Crown from the deep distress in which they are now involved.

"Aubrey G., Jamaica
A. L. De Santa Anna
Dowell O'Reilly
The Vice-Chancellor
W. C. Macdougall
C. M. Farquharson
James M. Facey
Leonard Howe Valpy
Samuel Rennalls
Richard Panton
Hector Mitchel
A. Barclay
Nathl. R. Darrell
Robert Osborn
Edward Jordon
Charles Lake
James Taylor
Peter Harrison
Wm. Irving Wilkinson
Samuel Oughton

Philip Henry Cornford
P. Lawrence
James Porteus
Wm. Titley
David King, LL.D.
Richard Hill, S.J.P.
W. W. Mackeson, J.P.
W. T. March
Jasper F. Cargill
George Freer
S. Magnus
John R. Hollingsworth
Edward Lucas
L. Gibson
F. Singleton
J. Leaycraft
James H. M'Dowell
Alex. Nathan
David Ramos
M. Ramos

D. Hart	R. J. C. Hitchins
M'Whinney, Hendrick,	J. H. Beuling
& Co.	Thomas Cargill
W. Wemyss Anderson	William Girod."

"With much pleasure I grant the use of the Rooms within-mentioned on Thursday, the 24th May, being her Majesty's birth-day.

" W. D. TURNER,
" Custos Rotulorum for St. Katherine."

Before entering more at large on the details of the history of a movement, which, in spite of the intervening dissolution of the Colonial Legislature, and the excitement which naturally arises from a general election, has been attended with a degree of unanimity, and a concurrence of public sentiment and opinion, which has very rarely been witnessed in modern times, or recorded in any era of our island annals, let us place in the front of the battle we propose to wage with the Moloch of the slave-trade, the plan of operations, in itself so simple, which had only to be clearly enunciated, to assure to us the benefit of universal assent.

The actual state of our international relations with the only two countries in the world in whose territories, and for whose supposed benefit, the abhorrent practices of the slave-trade are still carried on, must first be briefly stated, in order to bring more clearly and definitely under the eye of the reader the amount of the power of repression which has already been conceded to us; after which, it will be more easy to estimate the extent of the further powers which we need, to make those we already possess more practical and effective, for the accomplishment of the humane objects which our existing treaties had in view.

The countries which still resort to the coast of Africa, for the purpose of obtaining cheap labour, with which to carry on a more successful competition with others in the markets of the world, in the production of the intertropical staples, are now, happily, reduced in number to TWO. And, surely, this fact alone ought to be sufficient to raise some little doubt as to the soundness of the conclusion at which a most respectable class of persons seem to arrive, *per saltum*, that universal suppression is utterly impossible ; and that the cause, which has engaged the attention of the greatest statesmen and philanthropists the world has ever produced, ought, in this eminently practical and enlightened age, to be abandoned in despair.

The whole process has hitherto been gradual. It is not much less than half a century since Denmark, Great Britain, and the United States, abandoned their share in this source of profit. The Netherlands, Mexico, Sweden, and Norway, followed successively in the train of self-denial. And it is no more than justice to one of the most enlightened monarchs of modern times,—who erred, in the eyes of his people, by postponing the gratification of their wishes to the personal interests of his children ; the extension of his family connexions ; and the secure establishment of his dynasty on the throne,—to record the acknowledgment, that, in the first year of the reign of Louis Philippe, the practice of the slave-trade was vigorously and effectively abolished, in every portion of the French territory.

Then, with regard to Portugal,—who, although the last to persevere in covering this horrid traffic with her national ensign, long after she had lost the vast empire in America, for which alone it was really valuable, and which continues to derive a disgraceful advantage from it to the present hour,—it becomes equally a duty to acknowledge that this, the most ancient of our allies, has, at length, in all frankness and sincerity, resolved, not only to abandon the official perquisites, and the mercantile benefits which were formerly derived from it, but to co-operate zealously with her

Majesty's Government in impeding its successful prosecution by her cousins of Brazil, on the shores of the two continents which suffer, and which profit by it.

We come back, then, to Spain and Brazil, which have hitherto succeeded in defeating our efforts, because, in the struggle between individual interests and the demands of humanity, it has not yet been possible to bring the force of public opinion to bear on the subject with sufficient energy and decision. It is true, that before this final and practical abandonment of the trade by Portugal was realised, she resisted the renewal of the treaty which had furnished the most efficient of the suppressive machinery employed against it; and that it was only under the coercion of an act of Parliament, against the operation of which every form of diplomatic protest had been launched without success, followed by the actual capture of slavers, carrying on the traffic under the flag of Portugal—the confiscation of the slave ships in our own Courts of Admiralty, and the consequent liberation of the victims—that the Government of that country, finding it hopeless to persevere, or, perhaps, yielding to the sense of shame, and to that power of opinion which must, after all, be the supreme arbiter, in the practical decision of this question, consented, in the year 1842, in consideration of the repeal of the British statute complained of, to enter, with truth and sincerity, into a fresh engagement, which she continues to observe in a manner in perfect accordance with the glorious title of " her most faithful Majesty."

The success which attended the adoption of a coercive system, in the case of Portugal, has induced her Majesty's Government to pursue the same course with reference to Brazil. And, surely, the conclusion is not very logical or legitimate, that, because the Government of his imperial Majesty are either not virtuous enough to desire, or not strong enough to enforce, the execution of the obligations by which they are bound to us, we should, all at once, throw up in despair the great object for which we have striven so perseveringly and successfully ; and, sitting down with our arms across, wait, with what patience we may, until our own intertropical possessions are irretrievably ruined, and until the Spanish and Brazilian markets are glutted with human victims. Yet, this is the sort of advice we receive from certain wise legislators, gallant officers, and learned civilians, in the face of a measure of success, which, considering the enormousness of the profits which the traffic commands, and the smallness of the risks attending it, is all but miraculous.

With the Spanish and Brazilian Governments we have still subsisting treaties, giving us the clearest and most ample title to demand their effective fulfilment. The original Spanish treaty is dated in 1817, and came into operation in 1820. The treaty with Brazil is coeval with our recognition of the independence of the empire, and came into operation in 1830.

The Spanish treaty not having proved effectual, the Government of her Catholic Majesty was induced, in the year 1835, after a long course of negotiation, most skilfully conducted by the distinguished statesman who has been entrusted with the administration of Irish affairs during a period of great difficulty, to enter into a further treaty with Great Britain, in which a new principle was introduced, and fresh machinery supplied for giving effect to it.

The treaty of 1817 provided for the establishment of two Mixed Courts of Justice, to be composed of an equal number of individuals of the two nations, one to be held on the coast of Africa, the other in one of the colonial possessions of Spain : and, in virtue of this stipulation, two such Courts were then established, and still remain in operation, the one at Sierra Leone, the other at the Havanna.

By this treaty a mutual right of visit was conceded, under which the ships of war of the one nation became entitled to detain, and carry before the Mixed Courts, the merchant vessels of the other, provided slaves should actually be found on board at the time of the capture. And, by an explanatory article, negotiated by Lord Heytesbury, in 1822, it is declared, that if there shall be clear and undeniable proof that a slave or slaves had been put on board a vessel, for the purposes of illegal traffic, in the particular voyage on which the vessel had been captured, then, and on that account, according to the true intent and meaning of the stipulations of the treaty, such vessel should be detained by the cruisers, and condemned by the Commissioners.

The Clarendon convention, concluded at Madrid in 1835, again declared, on the part of Spain, the slave-trade to be totally and finally abolished in all parts of the world. And the Spanish Government engaged, that immediately after the exchange of the ratifications of that treaty, and from time to time afterwards, as it might become needful, they would take the most effectual measures for preventing the subjects of her Catholic Majesty from being concerned, and her flag from being used, in carrying on, in any way, the trade in slaves; and especially that, within two months after the said exchange, they would promulgate throughout the dominions of her Catholic Majesty a penal law, inflicting a severe punishment on all those of her Catholic Majesty's subjects who should, under any pretext whatsoever, take any part whatever in the traffic in slaves.

By the third article it was stipulated that the captain, master, pilot, and owner of a vessel, condemned as good prize by virtue of the stipulations of the treaty, should be severely punished, according to the laws of the country of which they were subjects; as also the owner of the condemned vessel, unless he proved that he had no participation in the enterprise. Succeeding articles concede the reciprocal right of search; fix the mode of exercising it; establish penalties in case of arbitrary or illegal detention; and declare that from the decisions of the Mixed Courts there shall be no appeal.

But what especially distinguishes the Clarendon treaty from that negotiated by Lord Cowley, in 1817, is to be found in article 10, better known by the name of the " equipment clause," which stipulates that every vessel visited in virtue of the treaty might lawfully be detained, and sent for adjudication before the Mixed Courts, if in her equipment there should be found—1st. Hatches with open gratings, instead of the close hatches which are usual in merchant vessels. 2nd. Divisions, or bulk-heads, in the hold, or on deck, in greater number than are necessary for vessels engaged in lawful trade. 3rd. Spare planks, fitted for laying down as a second, or slave deck. 4th. Shackles, bolts, or handcuffs. 5th. A larger quantity of water, in casks or in tanks, than is requisite for the consumption of the crew of the vessel, as a merchant vessel. 6th. An extraordinary number of water-casks, or of other vessels for holding liquid, unless the master shall produce a certificate from the Custom-house of the place from whence he cleared outwards, stating that a sufficient security had been given by the owners of such vessel, that such extra quantity of casks, or of other vessels, should only be used to hold palm oil, or for other purposes of lawful commerce. 7th. A greater number of mess-tubs, or kids, than are requisite for the use of the crew of the vessel, as a merchant vessel. 8th. A boiler of an unusual size, and larger than is requisite for the use of the crew of the vessel, as a merchant vessel ; or more than one boiler of the ordinary size. 9th. An extraordinary quantity either of rice, of the flour of Brazil, of manioc or cassada (commonly called farina), of maize, or of Indian corn, beyond what would probably be requisite for the use of the crew ; such rice, flour, maize, or Indian corn, not being entered on the manifest as part of the cargo for trade.

By this article it was also stipulated, that any one or more of these several circumstances, if proved, should be considered as *primá facie* evidence of the actual employment of the vessel in the slave-trade; and the vessel should thereupon be condemned, and declared lawful prize, unless satisfactory evidence, upon the part of the master or owners, should establish that such vessel was, at the time of her detention or capture, employed in some legal pursuit.

The next article declares, that if any of the things thus specified should be found in any merchant vessel, no person interested in her equipment, or cargo, should be entitled to compensation for loss or damage, although the Mixed Court should not pronounce any sentence of condemnation. And the 12th article provides for the breaking up of the condemned vessel, and for her sale in separate parts, immediately after condemnation.

Under the original treaty of 1817 it was provided, by the regulations annexed to it, that in case of the condemnation of a vessel with slaves on board, the slaves should receive from the Mixed Commission a certificate of emancipation, and should be delivered over to the Government on whose territory the Commission which should have so judged them should be established, to be employed as servants or free labourers. And each of the two Governments expressly bound itself to guarantee the liberty of such portion of those individuals as should be respectively consigned to it.

But as it was found, in the year 1835, when the second treaty was negotiated, that the slaves which had been taken on board Spanish vessels, captured by British cruisers, and consigned, in pursuance of this stipulation, to the care of the Spanish Government, were not by any means in the posses-

sion of their personal freedom, it was stipulated, by the 13th
article of the Clarendon treaty, that the negroes found on
board of a vessel detained by a cruiser, and condemned by
the Mixed Courts of Justice, should be placed at the
disposal of the Government whose cruisers had made the
capture.

The remaining articles of the second Spanish treaty, containing regulations for the good treatment of liberated
negroes, are more elaborate in detail than the corresponding
clauses in the first; but, in fact, they are only explanatory
and declaratory of the meaning and intention of the high
contracting parties, as will be seen at once by bringing them
into juxta-position. By Lord Cowley's treaty we have seen
that the emancipated slaves were to be delivered over to the
Spanish Government, by whom a clear and distinct guarantee
of their personal liberty, as free labourers or servants, was
solemnly undertaken; and by the corresponding regulations,
annexed to the Clarendon treaty, it is more specifically
declared, that their object is to secure to the liberated negroes
personal good treatment, and a full and complete emancipation, in conformity with the humane intentions of the two
Governments; that, immediately after sentence, all negroes
found on board the condemned vessel, having been brought
there for the purpose of traffic, should be delivered over to
the Government to whom the cruiser belonged which made
the capture. If the capturing cruiser were English, the
British Government engaged that the negroes should be
treated in exact conformity with the laws in force in the
British colonies for the regulation of free apprenticed
negroes. If the cruiser which made the capture· was
Spanish, then the negroes were to be delivered to the
Spanish authorities of the Havanna: and the Spanish
Government solemnly engaged that they should be there
treated strictly according to the regulations which had then

been recently promulgated with respect to the treatment of emancipated negroes, which regulations were declared to have the humane object of securing, honestly and faithfully, to the emancipated negroes the enjoyment of their acquired liberty; good treatment; a knowledge of the tenets of the Christian religion; their advancement in morality and civilisation; and their sufficient instruction in the mechanical arts, in order that the said emancipated negroes might be put in a condition to earn their subsistence, whether as artisans, mechanics, or servants.

By the fifth article of these regulations, annexed to the Clarendon treaty, it is expressly provided that there shall be kept, in the office of the Captain-general at the Havanna, a register of all the emancipated negroes, in which was to be entered, with scrupulous exactness, the names given to the negroes; the names of the vessels in which they were captured; the names of the persons to whose care they had been committed; and any other circumstances likely to contribute to the end in view. And it was further declared that the register, thus referred to, was to form a general return, which the Captain-general at the Havanna was to be bound to deliver, every six months, to the aforesaid Mixed Commission, in order to show the existence of the negroes emancipated, the decrease of such as had died, the improvement in their condition, and the progress made in their instruction, both religious and moral, as also in the arts of life.

And, finally, by the seventh article, it was most anxiously stipulated that, as the principal object of the treaty was no other than that of improving the condition of these unhappy victims of avarice, the high contracting parties, animated with the same sentiments of humanity, agreed, that if, in future, it should appear necessary to adopt new measures for obtaining the same benevolent end, in consequence of

those thus laid down turning out inefficacious, the high contracting parties would consult together, and agree upon
other means better adapted for the complete attainment of
the object proposed.

Such, then, is a brief outline of the solemn obligations by
which the Government of Spain is at present bound to that
of our most gracious Sovereign, in this matter of the slave-
trade. If these treaties had related to the cession of some
distant island, or some petty fortress, would any one of the
various administrations which have succeeded each other in
England since the year 1817, have sat down contentedly
under the imputation, which, in that case, would have been
unavoidable—that, in their hands, the national honour had
suffered, and that they were not fit to remain entrusted with
its guardianship?

As long as the sugar and the coffee consumed in England
were known to be produced in our colonies by the labour of
slaves, the British people would take no rest to themselves,
but laboured, night and day, until, in 1833, they had brought
about the act of negro emancipation, because they felt that
the national honour was involved, and that every day's delay
in wiping out the stain made the disgrace more indelible.
Since the accomplishment of that great object, and the successful issue of the last struggle, in 1838, to bring the system
of negro apprenticeship to a close, the public mind appears
to have sunk into a state of apathy, from which it is the just
and reasonable object of these proceedings in Jamaica to
rouse it, and to awaken the latent sensibility of the people of
England from the lethargy and indifference in which they
have too long indulged.

When the public voice was raised to its highest pitch, in
order to enforce the measure of abolition, whatever may
have been the feelings of the colonists at the time, there is
no man now living in Jamaica who would think of ascribing

the national enthusiasm to any but the purest motives. But now, unfortunately for the dignity of the English character, the case is somewhat altered. When Mr. Canning was spurred on to present his celebrated resolutions — when Brougham thundered, and Wilberforce and Clarkson pleaded —it was not quite apparent that any one was to suffer by pressing on the measure of emancipation but the owners of slaves and of sugar plantations; nay, it was conscientiously believed by many of the most active abolitionists that the cheapness of free labour, as compared with slave labour, was as true as any axiom in Euclid, and that, therefore, they were not likely either to enhance the price of sugar at home, or to do any damage to the colonists by persevering in the course which every sentiment of humanity appeared to prescribe.

The premises, however, on which this reasoning was founded are now essentially changed. It is demonstrated, as the result of the most disastrous experience, that in countries so thinly peopled as Jamaica, Guiana, and Trinidad, the planter, who attempts to cultivate the sugar cane by the labour of free men, is utterly unable to send his produce to market at such a price as will enable him to carry on his cultivation, and to persevere in sustaining a competition, on equal terms, with the sugar which results from slave labour, so long at least as the price of the thinking machine is kept down in the slave market by an unlimited supply from the coast of Africa.

The question is no longer doubtful. The abandonment of all but the very best estates, possessing every advantage of soil and climate, and a near proximity to the place of embarkation, affords, of itself, the most incontestible evidence that the West India colonies have been placed in a false position; and that, without reference to their other claims on the mother country, if they are not to be suffered to sink into a state of heathen barbarism; if the missionaries are not to desert them for the want of the means of subsistence; if the capital which still serves to maintain a few of the best estates in cultivation is not to fly away, with its proverbial timidity; and if these colonies are henceforth to furnish any demand for the productions of British industry, one of two things must be done:—either the exploded system of protection, which no man ventures to ask for, must be restored, or the level must be adjusted, which the slave-trade disturbs, by the vigorous and effective enforcement of the treaties, and the definitive extinction of the traffic which produces and perpetuates these disastrous results.

We come now to the point to which we were desirous of conducting the attentive reader.

The two treaties with Spain, which we have examined in some detail, having proved entirely ineffectual, in consequence of the signal bad faith, not only of the Government at Madrid, by whom they had been entered into, but of the Spanish authorities in Cuba and Porto Rico, to whom their execution was entrusted, it became necessary to consider whether any other system of suppression, short of an actual resort to the *ultima ratio regum*, would have any practical effect in recalling them to a sense of their duty.

It was in pursuance of a suggestion to this effect, that Viscount Palmerston, in his untiring zeal to accomplish the object which a perfidious ally had hitherto succeeded in defeating, determined, in the month of May, 1840, to open a new negotiation with the Government of her Catholic Majesty, for the concession of further powers to the Mixed Court already established at the Havanna. The principle of the measure thus proposed was entirely new. It left the power of dealing with vessels taken at sea, either with slaves on board, or with such an equipment as manifested a design to engage in the slave-trade, exactly as it stood under the treaties of 1817 and 1835; and, adopting the presumption already recognised by Spanish law, although not by Spanish practice, that a human being, of whatever complexion, was entitled to the enjoyment of his personal freedom, unless it could be proved that he was legally held in servitude, it proposed to throw on the person who assumed the right of possessing another as a chattel, the burthen of proving his legal title to the pretended property, to the satisfaction of the Mixed Court already established at the Havanna.

The expected effect of the recognition of this principle would be, that no man would be willing to pay a remunerating or profitable price to the importer, or other dealer in slaves, unless he were furnished with such evidence as would be sufficient to satisfy the Mixed Court of Justice that his proposed acquisition had a lawful and valid origin,—just as the purchaser of a horse would hesitate to pay the price if he suspected it to be stolen.

It was expected that in this way the cultivators of the soil, the practical consumers of the stolen commodity, would be effectually deterred from entering the market as purchasers; that if there were no buyers there would soon cease to be sellers, and that, in this way, the practical extinction of the slave-trade would be brought about by the application of one of the simplest principles recognised in the science of political economy.

The simplicity of this idea attracted the attention of Viscount Palmerston, who found it brought forward in a work on Cuba, forming one of a projected series of volumes on the British and Foreign West Indies, published by the Longmans in 1840. The book had scarcely got into circulation when the author received a letter from Earl Granville, at that time Under-secretary of State for Foreign Affairs, desiring him to present his views on this subject in such a condensed form as to admit of their being brought under the official notice of her Majesty's Government.

A suitable answer to this communication having been promptly returned, the principle it disclosed was at once embodied, at the Foreign Office, in the form of the draft of a convention, conceived in the following terms :—

Draft of Convention between Great Britain and Spain on the Slave-trade.

PREAMBLE.

Her Majesty the Queen of the United Kingdom of Great Britain and Ireland, and her Majesty the Queen Regent of Spain, having reason to believe that, notwithstanding the stipulations of the treaty concluded on the 23rd of September, 1817, and the further stipulations of the treaty concluded on the 28th June, 1835, between Great Britain and Spain, negroes are, from time to time, imported from Africa into the colonial possessions of her Catholic Majesty, and are there held in bondage, contrary to the letter and to the spirit of the said treaties, and in violation of the decrees which have been promulgated in Spain for carrying the said treaties into effect :

Their said Majesties have named and appointed, as their plenipotentiaries, to devise and agree upon further measures for preventing the violation of the said treaties in the manner abovementioned :

Who, having exchanged their full powers, &c., have agreed upon the following articles :—

ARTICLE FIRST.

The Mixed Court of Justice established at the Havanna is hereby authorised to receive information upon oath, to the effect that grounds of suspicion exist, that negroes recently arrived from Africa are detained as slaves in the the transatlantic dominions of Spain ; and the said Mixed Court, upon receiving such information, is hereby empowered and enjoined to summon before it such negroes, and the persons assuming to be owners of such negroes, and all other individuals apparently concerned in, or having knowledge of the transaction in question.   And the said Mixed Court is further empowered and enjoined to examine all such persons on oath touching the said transaction; and if, upon examination, it shall not be clearly proved, to the satisfaction of the said Court, that the negroes alleged to have been recently imported from Africa, were born in the transatlantic dominions of Spain, or were imported from Africa into those dominions before the 30th October, 1820, the said Court shall declare such negroes to be free, and such negroes shall be set free accordingly.

ARTICLE SECOND.

If the owner or owners of the negroes, said to be wrongfully held in bondage, shall, upon the first summons of the Court, refuse or demur to appear before the Court, either by themselves, or by others in their behalf, the Court shall summon the parties a second time; and if this second summons should not be effectual, the Court shall, after the expiration of a proper interval of time, summon the parties a third time; and if the parties do not obey either of the three summonses, the Court shall, notwithstanding the absence of such owner or owners, or other persons in their behalf, proceed to adjudge the cause, and to decide whether or not the negroes, who are alleged to be wrongfully held in bondage, shall be set free; and the decision of the Court in such case shall be held good and valid, notwithstanding the absence of the parties, and shall be carried into effect accordingly.

ARTICLE THIRD.

Her Catholic Majesty shall, within —— weeks after the exchange of the ratifications of this Convention, promulgate a decree, giving authority to the Mixed Court of Justice to enforce the execution of its decisions, in accordance with the provisions contained in the preceding articles.

The draft thus prepared, and which has been described somewhat prematurely, by the late Mr. Bandinel, for many years the chief of the slave-trade department at the Foreign Office, in his evidence before the Committee of the House of

Commons on the slave-trade, which sat during the session of
1848, as the "Turnbull Convention," was transmitted on
the 25th of May, 1840, by Lord Palmerston to Mr. Aston,
then her Majesty's Minister at Madrid, enclosed in the
following despatch :—

Viscount Palmerston to Mr. Aston.

Foreign Office, May 25, 1840.

SIR,—Although the slave-trade, under the Spanish flag,
has been, in a great measure, suppressed by means of the
treaty of June, 1835, between Great Britain and Spain, yet
slave traders have hoisted other flags to protect their vessels,
and thus the island of Cuba has continued to be supplied
with fresh importations of negro slaves from Africa. It has,
however, been suggested that these abuses might be stopped
by investing the Mixed Court of Justice, established at the
Havanna, with authority to investigate the cases of negroes
who are held in slavery in the island; and to declare whether
such negroes have, or have not, been imported into that
island since the 20th October, 1820, and whether, therefore,
they ought, or ought not, to be restored to freedom.

I have prepared a draft of convention with this view, and
I transmit it herewith to you, and I have to desire that you
will take an early opportunity of proposing it to the Spanish
Ministry.

I have received from Mr. Turnbull a letter at some length
upon this subject, and I herewith transmit to you a copy of
it, in order that you may avail yourself of the arguments
contained in it, in discussing with the Spanish Minister the
accompanying draft of convention.

I am, &c.,

(Signed)   PALMERSTON.

The communication thus referred to by Lord Palmerston
is extracted from the papers on slave-trade presented to
Parliament, by her Majesty's command, in the year 1840,
and is to the following effect :—

Mr. Turnbull to Viscount Palmerston.

London, March 13, 1840.

MY LORD,—In consequence of Lord Leveson's letter of the 10th March, 1840, the undersigned has the honour to submit the following statement to your lordship, in elucidation of the ᵖlan he has conceived for the suppression of the African slave-trade :—

From the great and increasing amount of this trade, the evils of which have only been aggravated by the various attempts that have hitherto been made to restrain it, the undersigned submits he is entitled to assume, that the true principle on which an effective measure of abolition should be based, has not yet been disclosed. He will not assert that the plan he has now to bring forward is free from all difficulty; but he confidently maintains that there is no difficulty attending it which cannot be easily surmounted, if the Government will consent to apply to it the mere moral force at its disposal.

The lever, with which it is proposed to overthrow this colossal grievance, is to be found among the simplest elements of economical science. It is by cutting off the demand for victims that the supply is to be suppressed. It is by making the purchaser and possessor of an African slave insecure in the enjoyment of his unlawful acquisition, that he is to be deterred from paying the price. It is by demonstrating to the slave dealer that imported Africans will no longer be a marketable commodity, and that by that process alone he will willingly abandon a trade which has ceased to be profitable.

The great consumers of African slaves are the empire of Brazil, and the colonial dependencies of Spain.

The white inhabitants of the Brazilian empire begin to be sensible of the imminent danger to which they will expose themselves, if they persevere much longer in adding to the disproportionate amount of their negro population, by the toleration of the African slave-trade. With St. Domingo before their eyes, we have a reasonable guarantee of the sincerity of the professions of his imperial Majesty's Government in favour of a system of absolute suppression.

The case is somewhat different with regard to the colonial dependencies of Spain. In Cuba the white and colonial portions of the population are nearly balanced in numerical strength. In Porto Rico the negroes are far outnumbered by the inhabitants of European descent. In both islands, but especially in Cuba, the natural desire for independence has of late years been stimulated into passion, by the intolerable burthen of the fiscal exactions, which have been levied for the purpose of defraying the charges of a war in another hemisphere, in which they feel no interest.

It is in consequence of this state of things that the sincerity of the professions of the Government of her Catholic Majesty, on the subject of the suppression of the slave-trade, is liable to reasonable suspicion. The planters of Cuba and Porto Rico, wherever their estates are fully and properly peopled, with a just proportion between the sexes, in place of desiring the continuance of the slave-trade, have a direct and obvious interest in its suppression.

On the neighbouring continent, within two days' sail of the Havanna, the average value of a field slave is, at least, a thousand dollars. In Cuba, the effect of the competition of the slave dealers with each other is to reduce the value of an imported African to less than the third part of that amount.

The high prices of slaves in those States of North America which adjoin the Gulf of Mexico is still maintained, in spite of the well-known fact, that in the breeding districts of Maryland and Virginia the negro population is found to increase in a duplicate ratio, as compared with the inhabitants of those regions of European descent.

The planters of Cuba are aware that the negro population of Virginia has long been doubling itself every twelve years and a half, while the white inhabitants require twenty-five years to accomplish the process of duplication.

There is nothing in the climate of Cuba to prevent a similar rate of increase of the negroes. There is nothing, in short, but the cheapness of labour, arising from the toleration of the African trade, which prevents the proprietors of old plantations in Cuba from throwing themselves with confidence on th_ principle of propagation.

Here the undersigned desires respectfully to guard himself against the supposition of his being the apologist of slavery under any circumstances, or with any degree of modification. His present business is to deal with the African slave-trade, and to suggest a practicable mode of accomplishing its suppression. In the proper place, and at the proper period, he does not despair of being able to demonstrate, that by a resort to sound principles, the practice of slavery itself may be rooted out, in those very countries whose social and political institutions are now so intimately blended with it.

The undersigned has not engaged in this conflict without endeavouring to measure the strength of the adversaries with whom he will have to contend. Of these he perceives there are several classes.

The mere dealer in slaves, the man who invests his capital in the building and outfit of fast-sailing clippers—in manning them with their ruffian crews, in loading them with cargoes of rum or gunpowder, and in devoting himself to the study of international treaties and preventive laws, for the sole purpose of evading them, is not by any means to be regarded as a very formidable antagonist. The terms of coward and capitalist were never more truly convertible, than in the person of the trafficker in slaves. He may hire the hands of ruffians and outcasts to hazard their lives in his service; but his money he will not peril without the assurance of a profitable return. That object he finds the means of accomplishing, either by spreading the risk over a sufficient number of separate adventures, or by abandoning a portion of the gain he contemplates, in the shape of premiums of insurance, to joint-stock companies or private underwriters.

Another class of opponents will be found among the ministerial and judicial servants of the Spanish Government. Their superiors in the mother country have ingeniously made it the interest of a great number of these public functionaries to evade the execution of the laws, and convert that evasion into a fruitful source of profit, the better to secure the retention of the island in her Catholic Majesty's dependence.

Inasmuch, however, as the existence of the Court of Mixed Commission at the Havanna, with all its acknowledged imperfections, has had the effect, during the twenty years elapsed since its creation, of disappointing the cupidity of these venal functionaries to a very considerable extent, the undersigned sees no reason to doubt, that with the improved machinery he proposes to introduce, this iniquitous source of profit will be completely dried up and extinguished.

Before entering on the specification of the nature of this machinery, it may not be inconvenient to indicate the first and most important steps of the process he proposes to follow.

It is asserted by many of our most eminent philanthropists, that according to the spirit of our existing treaties with Spain, we are entitled to demand the instant liberation of every individual consigned to slavery in any part of the Spanish dependencies since the date of the first of these conventions. To this argument it would not be easy to offer a satisfactory reply. For the present, however, the undersigned is content to cut off the source of future importation, and to leave this an open question, to be agitated by others. Should the humble voice of the undersigned be ever entitled to share in the decision, he trusts he need not say with what cordiality he would give it in the affirmative.

Let us not embarrass ourselves, however, with too much work at a time. The most convenient moment for discussing it will be after the channels of importation shall have been cut off, and after the enormous masses of capital, at this moment engaged in the trade to Africa, shall have been finally drawn off, to find their due level in the great money markets of the world.

According to the views of the undersigned, the Courts of Mixed Commission at the Havanna and Rio de Janeiro, which, under the operation of existing treaties, have gradually been sinking into a state of listless inactivity, will at once be raised to a degree of efficiency and vigour, which they have not possessed at any period of their existence.

The plan of the undersigned is, by the negotiation of new conventions, or of additional clauses to existing treaties, to confer on these Courts the power of enforcing the law of the country in which they sit, by declaring that A, B, or C, the inmate of a barracoon, or a labourer on a plantation, is not a native creole, but has been introduced into the country in violation of law and treaty. He would further propose that the *onus* of proving a lawful dominion over the slave should be thrown on the party claiming it; that, in short, there should be a legal presumption in favour of freedom; and there can be the less objection to introduce and recognise this principle in the treaty he recommends for negotiation, inasmuch as he has been informed, by the eminent Spanish jurisconsults with whom he has advised on the subject, that the presumption of freedom, in the absence of proof to the contrary, is already the right of every inhabitant of her Catholic Majesty's dominions. Happily, however, for the cause of humanity, it is a matter of notoriety among persons conversant with the subject, that a fresh imported or *bozal* negro can, for many years after his arrival in America, be distinguished at a glance from the native creoles. The distinction is, in fact, so clear, that the mere presentation of the individual in Court, without a word of evidence as to the place of his birth, would, in most cases, be sufficient to determine his condition.

Should her Majesty's Government be induced to enter on such a negotiation, the true grounds and motives for the opposition to be expected from the Government of her Catholic Majesty will not, in all probability, be openly avowed. It will never be admitted, that a clandestine encouragement of the worst practices of the slave-trade is rendered necessary, by a sort of political necessity, in order to repress the aspirations of the creole population of Cuba for that sort of independence which the other Spanish provinces of America have already achieved.

Neither will it be pretended, that the continuance of the slave-trade is necessary to the successful cultivation of the soil, in presence of the facts already alluded to, of the rapid increase of the negro population in the neighbouring States of the North American Union.

The ostensible ground of opposition will probably be confined to a pretended fear of discontent and insurrection, on the part of those slaves who will not be entitled to a declaration of freedom in their favour, in consequence of the place of their birth, or the date of their introduction. Her Catholic Majesty's Government have constantly professed as ardent a desire as our own, to concur in all the measures of suppression already proposed; and yet the fact is undeniable that, in place of being diminished or modified by any of the measures of restraint which have hitherto been resorted to, the evil is actually on the increase—a position satisfactorily established by the progressive nature of the official returns of the amount of the slave population. The arguments that may be drawn from a pretended fear of discontent and insurrection, may be answered by the fact, that it is the wild and savage African alone whose removal we propose, and that it is no part of our plan to disturb the condition of the comparatively civilised creole. It is besides by *units*, not by cargoes, that the process of liberation will take place; so that the proceedings under the new treaty will be much less alarming in their general aspect, or their individual amount, than those already sanctioned by existing conventions.

As the proceedings of the Court of Mixed Commission, however, have hitherto been conducted in strict conformity with the Spanish principle, of closed doors, written pleadings, and secret deliberations, it might possibly be advisable to adhere to the established practice, inasmuch as opposition would thereby be disarmed, and the presence of a British prosecutor, and one or more British judges, would afford a sufficient guarantee for their perfect regularity. The mere existence of the Court for upwards of twenty years, in the course of which discussions have frequently arisen, affecting the freedom of entire cargoes of Africans, without producing a single practical evil, to give the Captain-general or the Government any substantive cause of complaint, appears to the undersigned to afford a broad basis, on which the demand for the enlargement of the powers of the Court may be conveniently founded. The great advantage of proceeding by *units*, and not by masses, is, that every individual liberation would amount to the assertion of a vital principle, without affording any reasonable pretext for apprehension or alarm.

It may not be easy to suggest any better expedient than that already recognised by treaty, for the case of a difference of opinion between the two Commissary Judges. It is true that in doubtful cases a decided leaning has been observed, on the part of the Spanish members of the Court, towards the acquittal of the prizes brought up for condemnation, and there may, therefore, be some reason to apprehend a corresponding disposition to resist the liberation of the negro clients of the British prosecutor, as often as a sufficient air of doubt can be thrown over the case to justify the hesitation of the Spanish Commissary Judge. On the very worst supposition which it is possible to conceive, the drawing of lots for the choice of the arbitrator would be resorted to in every case, without a single exception. The past practice of the Spanish judges, however indefensible in many particular instances, has never yet been carried to this systematic extreme; and, in fairness, it cannot be said there is any just reason to anticipate such an unheard-of degree of pertinacity for the future. But suppose, for a moment, that a Spanish judge and a Spanish arbitrator were to be for ever deaf to the calls of duty and the evidence of fact, it results from the mere doctrine of chances, which, when applied to thousands of cases, becomes infallible, that one half of the whole of those to be thus presented to the Mixed Court for adjudication would be decided in favour of the liberty of the slave. Now, the systematic liberation of one half only of the future importations would be perfectly sufficient to prevent the planter from paying a remunerating price to the dealer or importer; and hence it is demonstrated that the system of the undersigned must be fatal to the trade.

Objections of a dilatory nature may, of course, be expected on the part of her Catholic Majesty's Ministers, at the outset of this negotiation. The necessity or convenience of consulting the Governors and Captains-general of their transatlantic possessions, will probably be urged as a reason for withholding their immediate assent to a proposition which is calculated to affect the future interests and prosperity of the Spanish West India colonies.

To render this pretence unavailing, the undersigned is strongly of opinion that the past and future importations of slaves into these colonies should be separated from each other by a broad line of distinction, and that the object of the proposed negotiation should be exclusively confined to the case of *future* importations. The most convenient *terminus à quo* would probably be the date of the first official note of the British Ambassador, directing the attention of her Catholic Majesty's Government to the subject.

Were it consistent with the duties or the dignity of a Cabinet Minister to undertake such a mission, the undersigned would respectfully suggest, that the well-earned popularity of the Lord Privy Seal * with the Spanish nation, would convert, in his lordship's hands, a tedious and difficult task into an easy and instantaneous operation. Before his lordship's arrival the mind of the Spanish people might be prepared for his reception through the medium of the Peninsular press. His re-appearance in Madrid would become a sort of triumphal entry, and the great and interesting object of his embassy would be accomplished under the influence of the first burst of national enthusiasm. In hazarding this prediction, the undersigned has not spoken without some knowledge of the Spanish character, nor without an intimate personal acquaintance with the machinery of the Peninsular press. It was his fortune to be a resident in Madrid during the period of the negotiation of the treaty of 1835.

Before closing this paper, the undersigned entreats your lordship's indulgent attention to a few of the collateral

* The Earl of Clarendon.

advantages which are destined to result from the adoption of his plan.

1. The whole of the naval force, so unprofitably, so injuriously employed in the ineffectual blockade of a whole continent on one side, of two large islands and a vast empire on the other, would be liberated from duties involving great loss of human life, and a heavy charge to the State, without any corresponding benefit, in the shape of honour or profit; and would either be rendered disposable for services more useful to the country, or would produce a proportional saving of the national expenditure.

2. The commercial interests of the country are deeply injured by this toleration of a trade, with the practice of which her Majesty's subjects refuse to pollute themselves.

The honour of her Majesty's crown is grievously tarnished by the habitual disregard of the solemn treaties which her Majesty and her royal predecessors have concluded and ratified for its suppression. These interests will be protected, that honour will be saved, by the adoption of a sound system of abolition.

3. In the department of Foreign Affairs, a vast amount of labour would be saved to the principal Secretary of State, by rendering it unnecessary to continue those widely ramified negotiations throughout the civilised world, the object of which is to create a universal league for the suppression of the slave-trade. The unprofitable labour of our foreign embassies and legations would equally be spared, and a similar saving would be effected in the colonial departments of the Government.

4. The state of our relations with Spain would be greatly improved. The suppression of the slave-trade, and the progressive civilisation of the creole negroes, to the total exclusion of any intermixture of savage Africans, would liberate the greater part of the overgrown garrisons of the Havanna, and of the outports of Cuba and Porto Rico; and would thus go far to enable the Spanish Government to satisfy their foreign creditors. If any serious difficulty presented itself in the course of the negotiation, the undersigned

submits that the incalculable importance of the object would justify the Government, either in threatening, on the one hand, to recognise and guarantee the independence of Cuba, in case of refusal, or in undertaking, on the other, as the price of her consent to an effectual and *bonâ fide* suppression, to secure the mother country in the possession of this valuable dependency, as long as it remained practically free from the stain of slave-trading.

5. The existing differences with Portugal, our ancient ally, arising out of the infringement of our slave-trade treaties, would be adjusted in the simplest and most satisfactory manner by the total extinction of the original cause of quarrel.

6. A fruitful source of discord with the United States of America would likewise be extinguished by the peaceful mode of suppression which the undersigned recommends. The law of last session (with reference to Portugal) is evidently destined to throw the whole of the carrying trade in slaves, directly or indirectly, into the hands of the Americans. The discussions which are sure to arise out of this state of things will serve to embitter the boundary question, uniting the inhabitants of the Southern States and of the Atlantic cities with the belligerents of Maine and the manufacturing interests of New England, in their no longer latent desire of an open rupture with Great Britain.

7. But the crowning advantage to arise from the peaceful solution of this *quæstio vexata* ought rather to be regarded as direct than collateral. The introduction into the interior of Africa of habits of peace and order, Christianity and civilisation, will be the inevitable result of suppression. A taste for foreign luxuries is already implanted in the mind of the native African. To obtain the enjoyment of them he resorts to war and rapine—to the capture and sale of his fellow-creatures. The taste will remain after the medium of exchange has lost its value; the arts of peace will take the place of deeds of violence; and the humanising influence of lawful commerce will follow in the steps of the man-stealer.

In laying this statement before your lordship, the under-

signed disburthens his mind of the high responsibility which
has never ceased to press on it, from the moment that his
views have reached a reasonable degree of maturity. That
responsibility he respectfully transfers to your lordship, and
with it the immortal honour of accomplishing the extinction
of the greatest practical evil that ever afflicted mankind.

The British Minister who shall accomplish an object which
has engaged the attention of statesmen and philanthropists
for the last half century, defeating the ingenuity of the one,
and disappointing the zeal of the other, will be hailed by his
contemporaries as the benefactor of his race, and will send
down his name with glory to the latest posterity. The
British Minister who should lightly reject the first practical
remedy that has ever been brought forward, if its soundness
and efficacy should afterwards be demonstrated, would not
only throw away the wreath prepared for his acceptance, but
would justly expose himself to the most serious reproach.

The undersigned, &c.,

(Signed)   D. TURNBULL.

The Right Hon. Viscount Palmerston,
    G.C.B., &c., &c., &c.

Since the foregoing letter was written several changes
have taken place in the aspect of the horizon which the
writer then contemplated ; but, in so far as the chief argument is concerned, the reasoning remains as cogent as ever.
The differences which then existed, on this very subject, with
Portugal have been happily set at rest ; and, instead of
throwing the protection of her flag over the odious traffic,
our most ancient ally joins us, heart and hand, in promoting
its suppression. Every packet brings us fresh evidence of
the progress which Portugal is making in the career of
freedom and civilisation ; and we ask no better proof of her
sincerity, for the last five or six years, than we find in the
fact of her having sent and maintained in Jamaica, to sit in
the Court of Mixed Commission, a judge like the Chevalier

Altavilla, whose sentiments in favour of the suppression of
the slave-trade are well known to this community, and who
is not encumbered, as Spanish and Brazilian officers have
been, *with double sets of instructions.*

Then, with regard to the United States of America, it is
true that the two great boundary questions have been happily
adjusted; but the insatiable spirit of aggrandisement which
pervades the people of that country has only taken a different
direction. Their career on the side of Maine and Oregon has
been restrained; Texas, New Mexico, and California have
added immensely to their territorial possessions; but Cuba
itself has long attracted their attention, and as the Wilmot pro-
viso will probably be applied to their new acquisitions on the
Pacific, the slaveholding interest requires a counterpoise' on
the Atlantic side of the republic, to maintain its equilibrium
in the Senate. The necessary acknowledgment of the independence of Liberia; the growing conviction that the institution of slavery is inconsistent with the principles of a
republican form of government; and the manifest impossibility
of transferring more than three millions of slaves to the other
side of the Atlantic, appear to have engendered the idea that,
by the well-tried process of annexation, the thinly-peopled
islands of this Archipelago might form a convenient outlet
for their African population.

The insular position of Cuba forms of itself some protection against the gradual form of operation which led to
the annexation of Texas; and there is every probability
that the force at the disposal of the Spanish Government
will be sufficient, for a time at least, to defeat the sympathising
system which is known to be now in agitation. It is true
that the present chief of the North American republi?
has declared himself strongly against any attempt, on the
part of his fellow-citizens, at open invasion. But it is
equally true, that more than one of his predecessors have

cherished the idea of establishing a footing in Cuba, and of laying the foundation for that sort of sympathy, which, although it failed on the St. Lawrence, might possibly be attended with better success, if the apparatus were directed from the Capes of Florida.

It is not many years since an officer, of the highest rank in the diplomatic service of the United States, was charged with repeated missions to Cuba, of a special, secret, and confidential character ; and when, after travelling about the island without any ostensible object, this gentleman was plied with questions, somewhat in the Yankee fashion, as to the nature of the business with which he was occupied, he discovered, by the assignment of a motive which could not be true, that his real object was not fit for disclosure. It was not very likely that a person, of the high rank and attainments of Mr. Alexander Everett, who had filled the office of Minister Plenipotentiary at the courts of Spain, Russia, and the Netherlands, should be sent to the Havanna to inquire into the conduct of a mere consul; and as Mr. Everett was observed to court the society of many of the leading creole proprietors, and to seek the intimacy of persons entertaining the most exalted and enthusiastic ideas upon the subject of Cuban independence, his long sojourn in the island, on more than one occasion, leads pretty clearly to the inference, that the true object of his mission was to feel the pulse of the people on the subject of annexation.

It may fairly be presumed, that the present policy of Spain, with regard to this question, is confined to the main-tenance of her dominion over her dependencies in these seas, and the perpetuation of the advantages arising from it. The policy of the United States embraces two points—the extension of territory, and a good riddance of the plague-spot of slavery from the continental possessions of the republic. The policy of Great Britain is also two-fold, combining the assertion of her right to extinguish the slave-trade, on the broad principles of humanity, of which she is the acknowledged champion, with the protection of her own emancipated colonies against a hopeless competition with rapine, murder, and piracy.

Unless, therefore, we are prepared to sanction a scheme so eminently calculated to rivet the fetters of slavery in this quarter of the world, to throw the Gulf of Mexico into the hands of the sympathisers, and to endanger our own dominion at this side of the Atlantic, it appears that the time is now arrived for the serious consideration of the hint thrown out under the fourth head of the collateral advantages suggested in the foregoing letter,—that her Majesty's Government would be justified, in the event of any serious difficulty presenting itself in the course of the proposed negotiation, either to threaten, on the one hand, to recognise and guarantee the independence of Cuba, in case of refusal, or to undertake, on the other, as the price of her consent to an effectual and *bonâ fide* suppression of the slave-trade, to secure the mother country in the possession of this valuable dependency, so long as it remained practically free from the stain of slave-trading.

The policy of the Spanish Government has been always of the same selfish character. When the people of Cuba were supposed to be meditating a serious attempt to throw off the yoke of the mother country, and assert their independence, in imitation of the continental states of Spanish America, it was regarded as a very clever manœuvre to glut them with bozal negroes, and to inspire the plantocracy with the salutary dread of a servile war. But when the wolf did come, or, in their dastard terror, was supposed to have come, a few years ago, it was found to suit the views of the Government to interrupt the course of importation; the result of which, by raising the price of slaves in the market, has been to induce the sugar planters to offer such a price for the commodity, as to make it the interest of the coffee proprietors, whose estates are no longer profitable, to abandon their cultivation, and dispose of their slaves to the best advantage.

This source of supply was of course of a limited nature; the absorption is already complete; the fear of insurrection begins to be forgotten; and the price of sugar in the markets of Europe being remunerative and profitable to the planter who pays no wages, the demand for fresh supplies of Africans is already brisk in the barracoons at the Havanna; and it is well known that sundry expeditions have been fitted out from thence for the coast of Africa, the return of which, if they succeed in running the blockade, may now be daily expected, and are doubtless anxiously looked for from every headland of the coast. Success, then, to the good ship " Helena," and to De Courcy, her gallant commander, in the cruise against the slave-trade, in which she is now engaged; and thanks to our worthy Commodore, and our noble and illustrious Admiral, for the orders which have given us the chance of striking a blow.

When the negotiation was opened with the Court of Madrid, for the extension of the powers of the Mixed Commission at the Havanna, in the manner already described, it was not, of course, to be expected that any great degree of alacrity would be shown in meeting the views of her Majesty's Government. Just in proportion, in fact, to the probable efficiency of the new measure of suppression would be the reluctance of the Spanish authorities to assent to it; and, accordingly, we find, in the course of the negotiation, that every imaginable obstacle was raised to impede its progress. The dilatory proceedings, anticipated in the foregoing letter, assumed every conceivable form; but the burden of the song was the recall of its author from the joint offices of Consul and Superintendent of liberated Africans, to which he had been appointed on the concurrent nomination of Lord John Russell, who then held the seals of the colonial department, and of Viscount Palmerston, the Foreign Secretary, for the known purpose of enabling him to watch over the execution of the treaty about to be negotiated. Avoiding, as much as possible, what is personal, here follows the correspondence which took place on the subject :—

Mr. Aston to Viscount Palmerston.

Madrid, June 13, 1840.
(Received, June 24.)

MY LORD,—I lost no time, upon the receipt of your lordship's despatch of the 25th ultimo, in submitting to M. Perez de Castro the draft of the convention, having for object to invest the Mixed Court of Justice, established at the Havanna, with authority to investigate the cases of negroes who are held in slavery in the island, and to declare whether such negroes have or have not been imported into that island since the 30th of October, 1820, and whether, therefore, they ought or ought not to be restored to freedom.

His excellency said he regretted he should not be able to inform me of the decision of the Spanish Government pre-vious to the departure of the Queen Regent, but he assured me that he would take the proposal into immediate con-sideration.

I have left a copy of the draft of the convention in his excellency's hands.

I have, &c.

(Signed)   ARTHUR ASTON.

Mr. Aston to Viscount Palmerston.

Madrid, December 30, 1840.
(Received, Jan. 8, 1841.)

MY LORD,—I have the honour to forward to your lord-ship a copy of a note which I have addressed to M. de

Ferrer, enclosing the draft of the convention which I received from your lordship, having for object to invest the Mixed Court of Justice, established at the Havanna, with authority to investigate the cases of negroes who are held in slavery in Cuba, and to declare whether such negroes have or have not been imported into that island since the 30th of October, 1820, and whether they ought or ought not to be restored to freedom. I had previously explained to M. de Ferrer the object of the proposed convention.

I have also the honour to enclose a copy and translation of his excellency's answer to my communication, in which he states, that the Spanish Government will take the subject into consideration; but that, before a decision can be taken, it will be necessary to obtain further information from the authorities of Cuba.

I have, &c.

(Signed)   Arthur Aston.

To the Right Hon. Viscount Palmerston,
    G.C.B., &c., &c., &c.

Mr. Aston to M. de Ferrer.

Madrid, December 17, 1840.

Sir,—Although the slave-trade under the Spanish flag has been, in a great measure, suppressed by means of the treaty of June, 1835, between Great Britain and Spain, yet slave traders have hoisted other flags to protect these vessels, and thus, the island of Cuba has continued to be supplied with fresh importations of negro slaves from Africa.

It has, however, been suggested that these abuses might be stopped by investing the Mixed Court of Justice, established at the Havanna, with authority to investigate the cases of negroes who are held in slavery in the island, and to declare whether such negroes have or have not been imported into that island since the 30th October, 1820, and whether, therefore, they ought or ought not to be restored to freedom.

With this view, her Majesty's Government have prepared

a draft of convention, and I have been instructed to propose it to the Spanish Government.

I submitted to M. Perez de Castro, some months ago, a copy of this convention, and his excellency promised to take the subject into immediate consideration.

I have now the honour of transmitting to your excellency another copy of the draft of this convention, the object of which I, sometime ago, explained to your excellency.

Her Catholic Majesty's Government have constantly professed as ardent a desire as the Government of Great Britain to concur in all the measures already proposed for the suppression of this abominable traffic; and yet the fact is undeniable that, in the place of being diminished or modified by any of the measures of restraint which have hitherto been resorted to, the evil is actually on the increase in the Spanish colonies; a position satisfactorily established by the progressive nature of the official returns of the amount of the slave population.

To remedy this great abuse and violation of existing treaties, it is proposed to confer on the Commission the power of enforcing the law of the country in which it is established, and to raise it to a degree of efficiency and vigour which will enable it to overthrow this grievance. It is by cutting off the demand for victims that the supply is to be suppressed. It is by making the purchaser and possessor of an imported African slave insecure in the enjoyment of his unlawful acquisition that he is to be deterred from paying the price. It is by demonstrating to the slave dealer that imported Africans will no longer be a marketable commodity, and by that process alone, that he will willingly abandon a trade which has ceased to be profitable. Those objects will be attained by the conclusion of the proposed convention.

It may, possibly, be argued that discontent and insurrection would arise amongst those slaves who will not be entitled to a declaration of freedom in their favour, in consequence of the place of their birth, or the date of their introduction; but, in regard to such an objection, if raised, I have to observe to your excellency, that it forms no part of the proposed plan to disturb the condition of the creole population, or of those slaves who have been imported from Africa before the 30th of October, 1820. It is, besides, by "*units*," and not by cargoes, that the process of liberation will take place; so that the proceedings under the proposed convention will be much less alarming in their general aspect, or in their individual amount, than those already sanctioned by existing treaties.

The Court of Mixed Commission has been established in the Havanna for upwards of twenty years; in the course of which, discussions have frequently arisen affecting the freedom of entire cargoes of Africans, without producing a single practical case to give the Captain-general or the Spanish Government any substantial cause of complaint, and this fact affords a strong presumption that the request for the enlargement of the powers of the Court may be granted without danger or inconvenience.

In submitting the foregoing observations to your excellency I have to add, that her Majesty's Government and the British nation take a deep interest in the question; and the Government of her Catholic Majesty will acquire great and lasting honour by agreeing to the proposed convention, and thus putting an end to a practice so revolting to humanity.

I have, &c.

(Signed)   ARTHUR ASTON.

His Excellency Don Joaquim Maria
     de Ferrer, &c., &c., &c.

SECOND ENCLOSURE.—(TRANSLATION.)

M. J. M. de Ferrer to Mr. Aston.

Madrid, December 26, 1840.

SIR,—I have received the note which you were pleased to address to me on the 17th instant, relative to the measures which her Britannic Majesty's Government propose for the purpose of preventing the continuation of the abuses which may be committed in the traffic of slaves in the island of Cuba.

The reasons which you adduce, in order to prove the expediency of her Majesty's Government's approving the project of convention which you have enclosed to me, are of the highest importance, and require that a matter which, from its grave nature, has always attracted the serious attention of the Spanish Cabinet, should be deeply meditated; and, acknowledging the honourable sentiments of the British Government and nation, I can assure you that the Provisional Regency of the kingdom are animated with the same philanthropic ideas, and that they are only restrained by having to combine them with local interests which they are bound to support and protect.

Nevertheless, as in order to take this matter into consideration, which of itself is of sufficient interest, and besides, it being proposed by the British Government, with which her Majesty's Government are united by such close ties of amity and good relationship, it becomes necessary to collect together all the data that can elucidate the matter. Information has been demanded from the superior authorities of the island of Cuba, in order to be enabled to judge of the effects which the adoption of the aforesaid project of convention might produce; and, flattering myself that her Britannic Majesty's Government will view the above resolution as indispensable, I shall take care to inform you of the result, and avail myself, &c.

(Signed)   JOAQUIM MARIA DE FERRER.

The British Minister,
   &c., &c., &c.

(EXTRACT.)

Viscount Palmerston to Mr. Aston.

Foreign Office, March 6, 1841.

It has long been notorious to all the world, that the treaty with Great Britain and the law of Spain against the slave-trade are a mere dead letter in Cuba; that the slave-trade is carried on by many persons established in that island, and is pursued by them openly and incessantly; and not only with impunity, but even with the sanction and under the positive protection of the Governor, and of all the subordinate authorities. It is well known that all the orders against the slave-trade which have been sent to Cuba from Madrid have been either set at defiance by the Governor, or have been considered by him to be merely matters of form, issued, for the sake of keeping up outward appearances, and such as he might safely disregard and disobey.

This state of things has long cast a deep stain upon the honour and good faith of the Spanish Crown, and nothing could justify the British Government in not pressing, even more strongly and more urgently than it has done, for a faithful and full execution of the engagements of the treaty of 1835, but a consideration for the internal embarrassments under which Spain has been labouring, by reason of the civil war.

But as the Government of Madrid has shown itself unable to cause the local government of Cuba to observe the treaty, her Majesty's Government has thought necessary to send to Cuba agents, whose zeal, courage and activity would enable them to make head against all the local obstructions which they would meet with; and who, in spite of difficulties, and in defiance of threats, would perform their duty to the British Crown, and watch, and denounce, and as far as possible impede the criminal proceedings of the Cuba slave-traders.

But no man could have energy enough to perform so arduous a task, who had not a strong feeling upon the subject to which his duties relate. For her Majesty's Government well knew that every impediment would be thrown in the way of the British agents; that every white man in the island, from the Governor downwards, would do his utmost to prevent them from successfully performing their duties; that frivolous and unfounded complaints would be got up against them; and that every effort would be made to drive them away by disgust, or to obtain their recall by misrepresentation. *   *   *   *   *   *   *

Her Majesty's Government, however, earnestly entreat the Government of Spain to reconsider the whole of this matter, and her Majesty's Government beg strongly to urge that the Spanish Government, instead of allowing itself to be led into the course which the slave traders of Cuba and the colonial authorities who protect them would wish to point out, should come to the honourable determination of compelling the Governor and people of Cuba to respect and execute the treaties which Spain has concluded on these matters with England.   M. Ferrer, indeed, sends the copy of a despatch addressed to the Governor of Cuba, and appeals to that despatch as a convincing proof of the resolution of the Spanish Government to carry the treaty of 1835 into execution; but her Majesty's Government are obliged to say, that they cannot consider that despatch in any degree satisfactory. Such general injunctions have, over and over again, been sent to Cuba ; and even if the Governor for the time being has given himself the trouble to read them, he has never paid the slightest attention to their contents.

The same fate will inevitably attend the despatch in question; but if the Spanish Government wishes to afford convincing proof of its good faith in this matter, let it send orders that all the negroes now in Cuba, who have been emancipated by sentence of the Mixed Commission, may at once be removed to a British colony, in order that they may be rescued from the real slavery under which they are suffering.

Let the Spanish Government take effectual measures for restoring all the colonial British subjects who have been kidnapped, and who are detained in slavery in Cuba, in violation of the law of nations.

Let the laws of Spain be rigidly enforced against the numerous slave traders in Cuba, whose occupation is as well and as publicly known as that of any man engaged in legitimate commerce.

And, finally, let the Spanish Government take steps for restoring to freedom all those negroes who have been introduced into Cuba as slaves, in violation of the laws of Spain, and who, therefore, not being the legal property of any man, are *ipso facto* free, by the law of the country itself.

If the Spanish Government will pursue such a course, which is recommended as much by a consideration for the well understood interests of Cuba, as by a regard of the obligations of treaties, there will at once be an end to those disagreeable discussions which have been so long carried on between the two Governments on this matter; and Spain will afford an honourable proof of its strict regard for its national engagements.

I am, &c.,

(Signed) PALMERSTON.

The next point for consideration, in the course of this inquiry, is the actual state and condition of our international relations, on the subject of the slave-trade, with the imperial Government of Brazil; and we shall have no difficulty in demonstrating, that our claims on that Government, for its entire and final suppression, are just as incontestable as those we have already shown to be so with reference to Spain.

The only substantial difference between these two peccant and faithless Governments is, that, in the case of Spain, the annual amount of their violation of their engagements appears to have been for some years on the decrease,—not in consequence of any desire to fulfil the obligations by which they are bound to us, but simply because it happens to suit their own convenience as a Government, and that of the buyers and sellers in the slave market, consisting of the proprietors of the soil, or the planters of Cuba, and the miscreants who resort to the coast of Africa for the purpose of tempting these planters and proprietors with their stolen merchandise.

In order to understand the true nature and extent of the obligations by which the Brazilian empire is bound to her Majesty's Government, it is necessary to look back to a period antecedent to the acknowledgment of Brazilian independence.

So long ago as the year 1810, a treaty of alliance was concluded at Rio de Janeiro, by which his Royal Highness the Prince Regent of Portugal declared his determination to co-operate with his Britannic Majesty, in the cause of humanity and justice, by adopting the most efficacious means for bringing about a gradual abolition of the slave-trade.

And by a treaty, negotiated by Lord Castlereagh, and signed at Vienna, on the 22nd of January, 1815, it was stipulated, that from and after its ratification it should not be lawful for any subject of the Crown of Portugal to purchase slaves, or to carry on the slave-trade on any part of the coast of Africa to the northward of the equator, upon any pretext, or in any manner whatever.

By the fourth article, the high contracting parties reserved to themselves, and engaged to determine, by a separate treaty, the period at which the trade in slaves should universally cease, and be prohibited throughout the entire dominions of Portugal; and the Prince Regent of Portugal thereby renewed his former declaration and engagement, that during the interval which was to elapse before such general and final abolition took effect, it should not be lawful for the subjects of Portugal to purchase or trade in slaves, except to the southward of the line; nor to engage in the same, or permit their flag to be used, except for the purpose of supplying the transatlantic possessions then belonging to the Crown of Portugal.

And, by the succeeding article, his Britannic Majesty agreed to remit, from the date of the promulgation of the ratification, such further payments as might then remain due upon the loan of £600,000, made in London, for the service of Portugal, in the year 1809, in consequence of a convention, signed on the 21st of April of that year, which convention was, in consequence, declared to be void.

Two years afterwards, an additional convention was negotiated by Lord Castlereagh, in London, with the Duke of Palmella, for the purpose of preventing the subjects of the two Crowns from engaging in the slave-trade ; by the pre- amble of which it is declared, that his Majesty the King of the United Kingdom of Great Britain and Ireland, and his Majesty the King of the United Kingdom of Portugal, Brazil, and Algarves, adhering to the principles they had manifested in the declaration of the Congress of Vienna, and being desirous to fulfil faithfully, and to their utmost extent, the engagements they had mutually contracted by the treaty of 1815, it was declared, by the first article, that the object of the convention, on the part of the two Govern- ments, was mutually to prevent their respective subjects from carrying on an illicit slave-trade ; and, by succeeding articles, specific arrangements were entered into for the toleration of the importation of slaves into the Brazilian dependencies of Portugal, from certain specified portions of the coast of Africa, beyond which the trade was prohibited absolutely ; and, in case of contravention, power was given to British cruisers to capture the vessels engaged in it; and Mixed Courts were established, to which were granted the power of declaring a vessel condemned for an unlawful voyage to be a lawful prize, as well as her cargo, of whatever description it might be, with the exception of the slaves who might be on board as objects of commerce ; and as to the slaves, they were to receive from the Mixed Commission a certificate of emancipation, and were to be delivered over to the Govern- ment on whose territory the Commission was established, to be employed as servants or free labourers.   And each of the two Governments bound itself to guarantee the liberty of such portion of those individuals as should be respectively consigned to it.

By a separate article, agreed to at London, by the same plenipotentiaries, on the 11th of September, 1817, which was to have the same force and validity as if it had been inserted, word for word, in the previous additional convention, it was declared, that as soon as the total abolition of the slave-trade, for the subjects of the Crown of Portugal, should have taken place, the two high contracting parties agreed, by common consent, to adapt, to that state of circumstances, the stipulations of the additional convention of the 28th of July ; but, in default of such alterations, the additional convention of that date was to remain in force until the expiration of fifteen years from the day on which the general abolition of the slave-trade should so take place on the part of the Portuguese Government.

And, by additional articles, negotiated at Lisbon by Mr. Ward, in 1823, it was stipulated, that Portuguese vessels might be captured by British cruisers, and condemned by the Mixed Courts, although no slaves were found on board at the time of the capture, provided there were clear and undeniable proof that a slave or slaves, of either sex, had been put on board for the purpose of illegal traffic, in the particular voyage on which the vessel was captured.

Soon after the recognition of Brazilian independence, on the 22nd of November, 1826, a convention was entered into, between his Britannic Majesty and the Emperor of Brazil, for the abolition of the slave-trade, which proceeds on the following preamble :—

Whereas, upon the separation of the Empire of Brazil from the Kingdom of Portugal, his Majesty the King of the United Kingdom of Great Britain and Ireland, and his Majesty the Emperor of Brazil, respectively, acknowledged the obligation which devolved upon them to renew, confirm, and give full effect to the stipulations of the treaties subsisting between the Crowns of Great Britain and Portugal, for the regulation and final abolition of the African slave-trade, in so far as their stipulations were binding on Brazil :

And whereas, in furtherance of that important object, their Majesties are animated with a sincere desire to fix and define the period at which the total abolition of the said trade, so far as relates to the dominions and subjects of the Brazilian empire, should take place, their said Majesties appointed plenipotentiaries, who agreed upon, and concluded the following articles :—

I. At the expiration of three years, to be reckoned from the exchange of the ratifications of the present treaty, it shall not be lawful for the subjects of the Emperor of Brazil to be concerned in the carrying on of the African slave-trade, under any pretext, or in any manner whatever ; and the carrying on of such trade, after that period, by any person, subject of his imperial Majesty, shall be deemed and treated as PIRACY.

II. His Majesty the King of the United Kingdom of Great Britain and Ireland, and his Majesty the Emperor of Brazil, deeming it necessary to declare the engagements by which they hold themselves bound to provide for the regulation of the said trade, till the time of its final abolition, they hereby mutually agree to adopt and renew, as effectually as if the same were inserted, word for word, in this convention, the several articles and provisions of the treaties concluded between his Britannic Majesty and the King of Portugal, on this subject, on the 22nd of January, 1815, and on the 28th of July, 1817, and the several explanatory articles which have been added thereto.

III. The high contracting parties further agree, that all the matters and things contained in those treaties, together with the instructions and regulations, and forms of instruments annexed to the treaty of 1817, shall be applied, *mutatis mutandis*, to the said high contracting parties, and their subjects, as effectually as if they were recited word for word herein; confirming and approving hereby all matters and things done by their respective subjects under the said treaties, and in execution thereof.

IV. For the execution of the purposes of this convention, the high contracting parties further agree to appoint,

forthwith, Mixed Commissions, after the form of those
already established, on the part of his Britannic Majesty
and the King of Portugal, under the convention of the
28th of July, 1817.

The ratifications of this convention were duly exchanged
in London, on the 13th of March, 1827, which established
the illegality of all Brazilian slave-trade, from and after the
13th day of March, 1830.

It is in right of the treaties and conventions thus briefly
recited, that the proprietors of plantations in the British
emancipated colonies, the emancipated negroes themselves,
and the friends of humanity of every class and colour, think
themselves entitled to claim the assistance of her Majesty's
Government, in requiring and enforcing the exact fulfilment
of these solemn obligations.

It is in consequence of the infraction of these treaties that
a state of the most savage internecine warfare is maintained
throughout the interior of Africa, as the normal condition of
its inhabitants; counteracting the pious labours of the
Christian missionary ; retarding the slow progress of social
improvement; imposing an absolute prohibition on the
cultivation of the soil, and making the exportation of the
natural products of the country a mere subsidiary to the
traffic which forms the only staple of this hideous waste ;
compelling the victim of the open foray, the clandestine
theft, or the more unnatural domestic crimes which the trade
engenders, to carry, like a beast of burden, from the interior
to the coast, the ivory, the gum copal, and the gold dust,
which are to serve as a make-weight, with his own bones
and sinews, in chaffering with the wretches of the barracoons, natives or foreigners, against as large a share as
possible of the coast goods of Manchester and Glasgow,
the fire-arms and cutlasses of Birmingham and Sheffield,

the gunpowder of Dartford and Hounslow, or the liquid fire, called aguardiente, from the Havanna and Rio de Janeiro.

But suppose for a moment that the barracoons are full of negroes of the most marketable class, in the usual proportion of three or four males to every female; that the speculators are fortunate; that the cruiser on duty has left the place for a time unguarded, to seek the needful supplies of water or provisions; or that the decoy consort of the slaver has succeeded in wiling her away for the nonce, in pursuit of a promising prize: suppose that the Baltimore clipper, or the steam vessel from New Orleans, has arrived opportunely, with her double set of papers, her American captain, and American crew, in actual possession; but with a practised navigator on board, of Spanish or Brazilian birth, in the guise of A PASSENGER, prepared, at the suitable moment, to pay the stipulated price, to receive the bill of sale, and the other legal documents with which the American captain has come provided, and at once to assume the command of the vessel, assisted by the gang of ruffians, whom he either brought with him as fellow-passengers, or whom, perhaps, he has found on the spot,—the remnant of the crew of some less fortunate adventure, who, after the capture of their vessel, had been landed, according to the present unwise practice, on the coast, at liberty to follow out their criminal career.

The Americans, if they are not more than usually foolhardy, retire into the shade at this stage of the transaction, seeking shelter and hospitality from the owners of the barracoon, until a less hazardous opportunity presents itself for returning to their own country. But there have been cases in which, after this exchange of papers and shuffling of the cards, the American parties to the odious piece of legerdemain are content, for the sake of "going a-head," to set the laws of their country at defiance; and, simply changing places with their Spanish or Brazilian confederates, proceed, as passengers in the vessel, to Cuba, or Rio de Janeiro, to pursue a trade so exciting, so profitable, and, if they are not too eager, so safe.

In the case we have imagined, the barracoons supply their contingent of slaves at a moment's notice. Every boat is in requisition; and at the startling sound of a cart-whip, such as was never heard within the pale of civilisation, the involuntary travellers are hurried forward, at some risk of loss to the shippers of the cargo, in a frame of mind for which it would be idle to seek a parallel in any European community. Torn from those who are dearest to them, pushed through the raging surf, and thrust into the shallow 'tween-decks of the slaver, they are hurried away under a fresh salute from that horrible cart-whip, every cut of which, when vigorously applied, lays open the very muscles of the sufferer, while the mere report, compared with which the unearthly shriek of the railway-whistle is melody itself, cannot be very soothing to the nerves of the hearers in the first agony of their expatriation.

Outside the bar, the sea is smooth, the breeze is fair, or the steam is up; the unhappy wretches have been jammed into their places, and everything denotes a prosperous voyage for the craft, which might well bear on its ensign the celebrated inscription over the gate of Pandemonium:—

> " Per me si va nella citta dolente ;
> Per me si va nell' eterno dolore ;
> Per me si va tra la perduta gente.—
> Lasciate ogni speranza, voi ch'entrate."

The combings of the hatchway have been stowed away until it should come on to blow, and have been replaced by open gratings. But the thirst of gain, the *auri sacra fames*, more furious than that which it provokes in its victims, has induced the reckless traffickers to embark a much larger number of persons than can be supplied with a sufficiency of vital air, more constantly necessary than even bread or water to sustain the breath of life. Then begins the mortal struggle to approach the gratings, and take in one mouthful of that without which they die.

But there is no remedy. If the cargo be composed of men of a warlike or dangerous tribe, the fear of mutiny overcomes the lust of gain; and the dastard ruffians are ready to assert their supremacy, by the free use of the boarding pike, or the cutlass, the capstan bar, or the handspike. But the aspect of death which presents itself from above, is not so terrible as the horrors of that infernal abyss; of which no man can form the most distant conception who has not stood, as the writer of these pages has stood, by the hatchway of a slaver full of negroes, at the end of a voyage, before the gratings have been removed. On this point we are entitled to speak with some authority, having, in the execution of a public duty, been the first to board that wretched schooner the "Jesus Maria"—what a profanation of holy names!—when, with an admeasurement of five and thirty tons, she brought into the Havanna, some eight years ago, no less than three hundred and twenty human beings, the miserable remnant of a much larger number, and forming, with its varied and appalling catalogue of crime, one of the most atrocious cases to be found on the records of our Mixed Courts of Justice.

In the adventure we have been imagining, the middle-passage has been accomplished with less than the ordinary number of casualties. The land heaves in sight—a sharp look-out is kept up from the shore—signals are exchanged; and, if need be, a steamer is sent out to secure the prize, and hasten the process of landing. Those who are able to stand upright are marched to the appointed barracoon, which is also to be the market place, *in puris naturalibus.*

The rest are provided with quitrins and volantes from the nearest stand, to carry them to the same destination.

From that moment, until they are fit to appear in open market, they are treated with the greatest attention, such as a careful groom, with the aid of a veterinary surgeon, would take of a sick horse, in order to qualify him to appear at Hyde Park Corner, and be submitted to the ordeal of Tatter-sall's hammer.

But the comparison is tame and feeble, and does great injustice to the superior attainments of the crafty man-jockey; who, for the purposes of his trade, is an adept in moral treatment, as well as in the more ordinary qualifications of the nurse and the physician. It is no longer his interest to poison his victims with foul air, or to decimate them with lance or spear. He has discovered, by costly experience, that the bozal negro, the name which is given to unseasoned Africans, is extremely liable, during the first months of his captivity, to a disease analogous to the home sickness of the Scottish mountaineer, or the *maladie du pays* of the emigrants from Switzerland and Savoy; and he takes care to guard against it, by means which perhaps have never been thought of in the Canadian back-woods, or beyond the Rocky Mountains.

A home-sick Foulah or Mandingo is of more value to his owner than a farcied coach-horse, or a broken-down racer, and requires more delicacy and tact in the treatment of his case, on account of the peculiar maladies to which he is subject, by reason of the *mens divinior* with which the Almighty has inspired him—the intellectual and sentient condition which distinguishes him from the brute.

There is no chair that we know of, in any of our Universities, which professes to deal, in a practical manner, with this peculiar branch of pathological inquiry. And yet it is one of the indispensable accomplishments of the keeper of a respectable barracoon, that he should be able to furnish his subordinates with a course of clinical instruction on the subject of this *opprobrium medicorum*, and provide a new pharmacopœia for the relief of the unhappy patients.

In this class of cases the most learned of the faculty would be at fault. The sufferer knows how to endure the pains of hunger, and the agonies of thirst—the sense of nakedness, and the scantiest allowance of vital air; but he has not yet been taught how to bear up against a hopeless separation from home and country, from family and kindred, from the " *domus et placens uxor;*" and may be heard to exclaim, in language less classical, but not less true :

> " Pone sub curru nimium propinqui
> Solis, in terra domibus negata :
> Dulce ridentem Lalagen amabo,
> Dulce loquentem."

To the home-sick exile the most enticing food has become distasteful. The pickled mackerel and the jerked beef have lost their wonted attraction. He will reject even the drops of aguardiente and the cherished cigar, which form leading ingredients in the *materia medica* of the barracoon. Air and exercise, music and the dance, nay, the imported banjo itself, with all its home associations, has lost its pristine charm, or perhaps even aggravates the malady. The more cheerful society of the *ladino coartado* is provided; that is, of the seasoned negro, who, under the influence of a merciful code, most faithlessly administered, becomes legally entitled, after payment of the first fifty dollars on account of his value, to have himself judicially appraised, and to withdraw himself from the immediate service of his owner, on the condition of bringing home a daily stipend of twelve and a half cents, for every one hundred dollars of the unredeemed portion of his estimated value.

But in the great majority of cases the evil is beyond all

human remedy, and society becomes as abhorrent to the moody monomaniac as the rest of the leech's remedies. He retires into the darkest corner of the barracoon, and takes to the eating of "dirt,"—the most intractable of all the symptoms which mark the fatal progress of the disorder known to science by the name of the Cachexia Africana. In the sick-bay of a Cuban or Brazilian barracoon the attendant physician must often be beset with the difficulty which the profoundest of all inquirers into the mysteries of the human heart has expressed, in language so thrilling and so true, and has put into the lips of one of the greatest of the creatures of his imagination, in addressing another of the craft:—

> " But canst thou minister to a mind diseased,
> Pluck from the memory a rooted sorrow,
> And, with some sweet, oblivious antidote,
> Cleanse the full bosom of the perilous stuff
> That weighs upon the heart ?"

It is not a little curious, however, and it throws a striking light on the view we are taking of this point of our subject, that, unless it be historically or theoretically, the disease is no longer known in Jamaica, having disappeared with the trade which gave rise to it, as if to prove that its origin was less physical than moral in its nature, and to show the distinctional degrees of susceptibility between the various races of mankind. The nations of the most barren and mountainous regions are supposed to suffer more than others from this exile's malady ; and it is believed to be generated among the tribes of Celtic or Scandinavian origin, without any reference to the cause of the expatriation, whether voluntary or otherwise ; while with the African we find that it came with the slave-trade, and with it has vanished,—just as the marsh fever ceases, where, by a proper course of drainage, the malaria is no longer produced. The circumstance of the eating of dirt is of course peculiar to the African class of sufferers, and, in any rational course of treatment, like that of our Esculapius of the barracoon, it should no doubt be regarded as simply symptomatic. Was it with any hidden allusion to the secret horrors which this diseased appetite indicates, that the great poet of Germany makes his hero threaten the object of his malice, that like his renowned cousin the Serpent—

"Staub soll er fressen, und mit lust?"

Before taking leave of our worthy medical practitioner, whose dovelike gentleness can only be surpassed by the peculiar wisdom of the cousin of Mephistophiles, let us not forget the new interest which has arisen in favour of certain functionaries, high and mighty, whose blood-hounds have already taken up the scent of the new importation; and who, if they be not prompt in their proceedings, may possibly lose a certain number of ounces of gold, by the progress of the ship fever, which the bozals may have brought on shore with them.

There they are, in breathless haste, on the nearest road from the seat of Government to the barracoon, which may possibly be situated, for the sake of more constant surveillance, under the windows of the suburban retreat of the chief of the Government,—as was literally the case with the first within whose precincts we succeeded in obtaining an entrance, under the guise of a purchaser, now a good many years ago. The numbers are soon told over; the spoil, being a ready money transaction, is reckoned by the simplest of arithmetical rules, and is forthwith distributed among the official recipients according to their degree, unless the chief may be safely cheated by a transaction with some greedy subordinate, who will be delighted to take more than his quota, but less than the whole tribute, in the shape of hush-money.

And then the thriving speculators begin to cast up their

account of profit and loss.   Upon the whole, the adventure
has been exceedingly prosperous.   They have risked a sum
of twenty thousand dollars, to bring back a return of a
hundred thousand.   But perhaps they have not had the
courage to expose their little capital to hazard; in which
case there are public officers at hand, and private underwriters without number, who are ready to assure them
against the loss of a single dollar, for a reasonable premium,
which may vary, according to the strength of the blockade or
the activity of the cruisers, the sailing qualities of the clipper,
or the skill of her captain, to some forty or fifty per cent. on
the whole of the risk, except that portion of it which arises
from the dishonesty of the parties, among whom, nevertheless,
—to do no injustice even to the man-stealer—it must be confessed that we do occasionally hear of the prickings of that
bastard sense of honour which is said to be found among
other sections of the fraternity to which they belong.

But sure we are that we have heard from the lips of one of
the least disreputable of those brokers who undertake to provide a regular policy of insurance against the loss which the
buccaneer may sustain, through the recovery of his piratical
acquisition by due course of law, that, in order to avoid the
imputations to which they might themselves be exposed, if
they discovered any hesitation on the subject, they had actually
paid largely for losses which, according to their sincere belief
and conviction, had never been incurred.

The case we have just supposed, has been of a successful
adventure, when the parties had only to regret the loss of ten
thousand dollars thrown away on the underwriters.   It is
true that they had been obliged, in self-defence, and in order
to inspire the survivors with a salutary idea of the danger of
impatience under restraint, to part with a portion of what was
already their property, at the point of the bayonet or the
boarding pike,—just as, under other circumstances, an honest

trader might cut away his spars and lighten his cargo, in order to save his ship from foundering. It is true, also, that a certain per centage of the shipment had been suffocated, and another portion had been trodden to death in the unsuccessful struggle to avoid suffocation. But these were not so much to be regretted as the more daring malcontents would have been; because, from their feebler constitutions, they probably occupied more space than they were worth; and, besides improving the chances of those who had proved, by the fact of their survivorship, the superiority of their powers of physical resistance, it was a matter, after all, which had been well considered beforehand.

The loss, moreover, had been decidedly within the average. The captain had done his duty by his employers; and, over and above the double pay agreed upon, deserved a handsome bounty, *pour encourager les autres*. And of what could the grumbling members of the firm complain, if they only called to mind that the little accidents of the voyage were all of a sort just as inseparably incident to the nature of their business, and of much less frequent occurrence than the rot or the murrain among the flocks and herds of the grazier; the hail-storm or the blight in the corn-fields of the husbandman; a hurricane or a drought to the grower of coffee or the cultivator of the sugar-cane?

> " —— Our life is turned
> Out of her course, wherever man is made
> An offering, or a sacrifice, a tool
> Or implement, a passive thing employed
> As a brute mean, without acknowledgment
> Of common right or interest in the end;
> Tried or abused as selfishness may prompt.
> What can follow but weakness in all good,
> And strength in evil? Hence an after-call
> For chastisement, and custody, and bonds,
> And oft times death, avenger of the past,
> Sole guardian of the future."
>
> *"The Excursion," Book IV.*

As soon as the requisition for the first great public meeting
in Spanish Town had appeared in the newspapers, the subject
was taken up with great cordiality by the public press. At
that period there existed only two daily papers in the island,
both published in Kingston; the " Morning Journal," representing the views of the King's House, or Government party,
which has not, for some time, been able to command a
majority in the House of Assembly, and the " Jamaica
Dispatch," which at that time represented the planting and
mercantile interest, opposed to the Government, and calling
itself the Country party. But although public opinion has
been excited to a higher pitch than ordinary, on the political
questions which are constantly presenting themselves, it is no
small satisfaction, to the friends of freedom and humanity,
that those differences have been laid aside, as if by common
consent, that debateable topics have, in general, been carefully
avoided, and that the whole subject has commanded the most
perfect unanimity.

The following notice appeared as a leader in the " Dispatch,"
of Wednesday, the 16th of May :—

We feel no ordinary satisfaction in directing public attention to the requisition which appears in another column, by
which the inhabitants of Jamaica are invited to meet, for the
purpose of considering the effect produced on this country by
the non-observance of the treaties for the suppression of the
slave-trade, by which Spain and Brazil are bound to her
Majesty, and of devising such a measure as may tend to promote at once the great interests of humanity, and the relief of
the tropical possessions of the Crown from the deep distress
in which they are involved. The subject is so important as
to recommend itself, without the aid of influential names, to
the general interests of the public ; but it becomes doubly
interesting when supported by character and influence, such
as we find associated with the present movement.

We are authorised to state that the proposed meeting

will take place in Spanish Town, on the 24th instant, (her Majesty's birthday,) at one o'clock, and that the Lord Bishop will take the chair. We have no doubt that the meeting will be such as to do honour to the occasion.

Next day, the 17th, the following article appeared in the " Morning Journal:"—

The importance of the public meeting to be held in Spanish Town, on the 24th instant, can scarcely be overrated. Great as are the material interests involved in the competition of free with slave labour, it cannot be concealed, that there are moral considerations which render the subject of far more general interest. Utilitarian politicians may disregard the sacrifice of private rights in the pursuit of seductive theories; but even these will pause, when they find that their object can only be attained at the expense of humanity. We have always treated the Sugar Duties of 1846 as apart and totally distinct from the question of free trade, however Ministers may have chosen to identify them. What freedom of trade can there be in a policy which admits to equal privilege in the home markets the produce obtained from the compulsory labour of the slave, and that which springs from the independent industry of the free man in the British colonies? Let Cuba, Porto Rico, and Brazil be placed on an equal footing with Jamaica, in point of labour, and we shall be among the last to ask protection as a stimulus to exertion.

For many reasons, the meeting of Thursday next will, no doubt, be as neutral in respect to politics as the important question to be discussed will admit of. On every account it is desirable that it should be so, and perhaps there is no ground on which all parties may meet with such little difference of opinion as on this. It is hardly possible, however, to avoid in some degree a general reference to the great political question which has undoubtedly given rise to the meeting. The terms of the requisition itself suggest a powerful condemnation of a great public policy, which, whilst it has effected grievous injury to every one who has been engaged in the cultivation of sugar by free labour, has undoubtedly given vast impetus to the slave-trade, in defiance of treaties which England herself is bound by every honourable principle to enforce.

It is impossible for any one to disunite "the deep distress," in which the intertropical possessions of the Crown are now involved, from "the effect produced on this country by the non-observance of the treaties for the suppression of the slave-trade, by which Spain and Brazil are bound to her Majesty." In other words, conceal the sense as you may, the truth is—and the truth ought to be told—the Queen's possessions, inhabited and cultivated by free men, are sunk in the deepest distress, by being exposed to an unequal competition with foreign proprietors, who produce their crops by means of a systematic defiance of national treaties, with which the honour and dignity of the Crown of England are intimately associated.

And the best and the most humane have not shrunk from this political view of the question. One, who bears a name that history will hand down to all future generations, as the devoted friend of the slave throughout the world, has registered his solemn denunciation of the measure of 1846. Sir E. N. Buxton, as a member of Lord George Bentinck's Committee, submitted the following resolutions, as embodying his sentiments upon this important question :—

1. "That the British sugar-growing colonies are suffering under great depression and distress.

2. "That this depression and distress arises from the inadequacy of the price of sugar, which at present prevails, to cover the cost of production and mercantile charges.

3. "That the lowness of price results in great measure from the supply of sugar consequent upon the opening afforded by the Act, 7th and 8th Victoria, chapter 22, for the introduction, for home consumption, of foreign sugar.

4. "That under present circumstances the British sugar growers are unable to compete with foreigners, who raise their produce by slaves, whose numbers are kept up and augmented, if required, by the slave-trade.

5. "That in consequence of the introduction of foreign sugar, nearly the whole of which has been slave produce, the foreign African slave-trade has been greatly increased, and slavery in Brazil and the Spanish colonies strengthened and extended.

6. "That unless the British growers are immediately and effectually relieved, a still greater extension will be given to the growth of sugar in slave countries, and consequently a still greater impetus imparted to the slave-trade and slavery.

" That your Committee therefore recommend,

1. "The entire exclusion of slave-grown sugars from the British market, and the admission only of those which are free grown to competition with those from the British plantations and possessions abroad.

2. "The removal of all restrictions on the trade and commerce of the colonies which fetter its development and otherwise impede its extension.

3. "The reduction of the duties on free-grown sugars, whether from British possessions or foreign countries, as soon as the Imperial Treasury will permit the experiment, with a view of increasing their consumption.

4. "The thorough revision of the whole system of colonial taxation, having for its object as large a reduction in its amount as is compatible with the efficient working of the local government."

It is in vain to deny the truisms embodied in these resolutions. The act of 1846 has, beyond a doubt, greatly increased the African slave-trade, and has imparted a still greater impetus to slavery in Cuba and Brazil. The facts admitted, nothing remains to us but to protest against so unholy a policy ; and when we find that these nations are bound by solemn treaties with the Crown of England to put down that very trade, which, illicitly conducted, enables them to compete on most unequal terms with the hired labour of the free British colonies, it is time, indeed, that Ministers were urged to enforce those national treaties which are so openly infringed. It ought never to be lost sight of that, so late as last year, Lord Palmerston deposed, before a Committee of the House of Commons, that so far as his means of information went, TWO-THIRDS of the present slave population of Cuba were entitled to their freedom under the treaties with Great Britain, and the laws of Spain enacted for the purpose of carrying out those treaties. If this be so, and it is impossible to doubt the authority on which the fact is stated—why are these people slaves? England has known how to enforce her treaties, when interests inferior to those of humanity have been concerned. Why are her treaties useless parchments, when the liberty of two-thirds of eight hundred thousand slaves is the penalty to be enforced? This is the question to be considered at the meeting of the 24th. That it will be treated in such a way as to place the subject in its most tangible form before the Government and the public, the names which are subscribed to the requisition are an abundant guarantee. We hope, therefore, that the meeting will be fully attended. It is the meeting, not of a parish section, but of the whole island; and gentlemen residing within a reasonable distance of town cannot devote a little exertion to so valuable a purpose at the present moment as to attend it. If we ARE to have FREE TRADE, we must have FREEDOM, or the colonies must cease to exist.

The immediate locality which was chosen as the place in which the first of these great meetings was to be held, is not without its historical associations. It is now the library of the House of Assembly, flanked by a suite of waiting-rooms, and separated from what is now the House itself by its spacious lobby, the whole of which became available for the purposes of a great public meeting, from the existing means of ventilation required in a tropical climate. What is now the library was occupied, until within the last few years, as the House of Assembly; and it was, therefore, in the very room where this first meeting was held, that the discussions took place, and the bill was passed by the legislature of the island, which conferred the boon of freedom on its labouring population.

Long before the hour appointed for the commencement of the proceedings, the whole range of buildings set apart for the purpose were crowded to overflowing, insomuch that many were shut out, who had relied on finding places, after the arrival of the last of the railway trains from Kingston.

On the motion of the Hon. Samuel Jackson Dallas, Speaker of the House of Assembly, seconded by the Hon. Edward Thompson, Custos of Clarendon, the Lord Bishop of the diocese was respectfully requested to take the chair, which he did amidst the cheers and acclamations of the meeting.

The Right Reverend Chairman said,—Gentlemen, I should be insensible if I did not perceive, and ungrateful if I did not acknowledge, the high and distinguished honour which you have conferred on me, by calling me to preside over this meeting. In the responsible position which, in compliance with your wishes, I have ventured to occupy, I am greatly sustained and encouraged by seeing around me so many of the most enlightened and influential members of the community — judges, legislators, magistrates, clergymen, commingled with the representatives of your planting and commercial interests — all assembled and associating without political or religious distinction, for the furtherance of an object well worthy of such a coalition, and which, if pursued with unanimity and moderation, can scarcely fail to be accomplished. Gentlemen, it is for no party, no trivial or idle purpose, that this great meeting has been called. It has been called, too, on a day which may be considered as eminently auspicious, commemorative as it is of the birth of our gracious and beloved Sovereign; and it has been called on a strength and respectability of requisition that has, perhaps, no parallel in the annals of this island. The object which it contemplates is one of the highest and holiest that could engage the affections, or stimulate the energies of Christian and reflecting men. It is an object which stands out in lofty prominence above the narrow sphere of local politics; and, in soliciting for it the consideration of her gracious Majesty and the Imperial Parliament, I have no fear that we shall give umbrage or embarrassment to a liberal

Ministry, one of whose members did, in fact, devise the very measure to which we recall their attention, and which, if faithfully carried out, would imply all the relief which we ask or desire. Gentlemen, it must, I think, be readily admitted, that the great and predominant evil under which Jamaica, in common with the other West Indian islands, is at present suffering, arises from the projected admission of the produce of slave labour into the markets of Great Britain and her dependencies, without the discriminating and protective duty which had heretofore been allowed to operate in favour of the free-born, or free-made cultivator of the soil. It must, however, at the same time be confessed, that this extinction of the principle of protection is now so entirely essential to the sustainment of the free-trade system which has been adopted by the mother country, as to render any restoration of the former system, be it good or evil, just or unjust, in its intrinsic character, utterly and for ever hopeless. It comes not, then, within the province of the present meeting (and to this point I would especially direct your attention) to confederate for the purpose of impugning a policy, which, whatever may be our individual opinions of its nature, seems now to have assumed the shape of the settled policy of the empire; and although our legislation, in these days of continued change and reform, can hardly be compared to the celebrated "law of the Medes and Persians which altereth not," I see little reason to expect any alteration in this particular. But our plain and single object is to press upon our rulers, by all the constitutional means within our reach—by petition heaped upon petition—by proclamation, loud and continuous, of what we know to be the truth—by such advocacy as we can procure within and without the walls of Parliament— the justice and the necessity of compelling the States of Spain and Brazil to a fair and full compliance with those treaties by which they are solemnly bound to her Britannic Majesty; treaties which had, and have, for their express object, the extinction of the heaviest curse that ever fell upon mankind—the suppression of the inhuman traffic in slaves, with all its hideous and murderous incidents, and the gradual abolition of slavery throughout every portion of the civilised world. In the series of resolutions which will be presently submitted to you, and in the able manner in which, I doubt not, they will be advocated, you will have this purpose, and the means by which we propose to effect it, clearly and completely developed. You will perceive that our object is pure, our instrumentality unexceptionable, our expectation reasonable, and our cause such as to induce the belief that the Divine blessing will be largely in our work. Averse as I have always been from entering on the stormy arena of political agitation and party politics, cautious as the ministers of God's altar should ever be to exercise their ministry without offence—I cannot think that we shall so offend in the present instance, even should we become the most prominent and uncompromising advocates of a cause which is based on a great and godlike charity. I cannot think that it would derogate from the dignity of the judicial ermine, I know that it will not sully the purity of the episcopal lawn, to be associated with the humblest member of society in a cause which claims the affection and support alike of the high and low, of the statesman and the divine, of the common friends of humanity. It is a cause, gentlemen, which, whether in success or failure, will, by its inherent excellence, hallow every legitimate instrument that may be used for its advancement; and it is a cause which, if successful, as I trust in God's mercy it will succeed, will regenerate the life and energies of this country, bring back to us no inconsiderable share of the prosperity we have lost, and communicate the inestimable boon of liberty to untold thousands of our fellow-men. Gentlemen, with so many able speakers to follow me on this subject, I shall not detain you by dwelling on the nature and extent of the intolerable wrong committed by our faithless allies, for which we seek redress—I shall not endeavour to excite your imagination, or harrow up your feelings by any detailed account of the progress of the detested slave-trade, of the barbarous wars of Africa, of the horrors of the middle passage, and of the scarcely less unhappy fate of the victims of avarice that survive that miserable transit,—but I will tell you that the demonstration which we shall this day make against these atrocities will not be solitary. It will be accompanied, like Banquo's progeny, " by another, and another, and another," from every town and port in the Antilles. It will be followed, if I read the signs of the times aright, by many a similar movement in Great Britain ; and it will, at least, have the effect of bringing, with unmistakeable emphasis, before the British Government, the British Parliament, and the British public, a fair exposition of our grievances, together with the means by which we believe that they may at once be mitigated and ultimately removed. Gentlemen, am I too sanguine in attributing such results to the proceedings of to-day? I think not. I am happy to believe that the great nation, to which we all claim affinity, " is a wise and understanding people," and I am still happier in believing that their wisdom and understanding is the wisdom and understanding which are derived from Christianity. Let England, Christian England, then, only retain the place among nations which she has assumed—let her continue to tread the path which, at the cost of so much blood and treasure, she has opened out—let her, as far as her ability extends, procure freedom for the slave, and religious instruction for the emancipated—and she will let in a flood of light and glory on mankind, which will go further to embellish and emblazon her immortal history, than the thousand victories by which her wondrous dominion has been achieved, or than her naval supremacy, by which the standards of her power have been unfolded from Indus to the Pole.

The Hon. Dowell O'Reilly, her Majesty's Attorney-general, a gentleman of the Roman Catholic persuasion, having been called on by the Right Rev. Chairman to propose the first resolution, addressed the meeting as follows :—

My Lord and Gentlemen,—I feel it strange that at a great public meeting like this you should call on me to propose the first resolution ; but, though I know there are here many fitter men for such duty, I confess I cannot refuse to aid you in the great object of your assembling. Of infinite consequence, indeed, to this colony is the gathering together this day of the gentlemen of Jamaica. In their assertion of the rights of their fellow-men to liberty, their own strength, their prosperity, and their own hopes of future tranquillity and happiness are deeply involved. It is now, gentlemen, sixteen years since I first came amongst you, called then to the councils of my Sovereign here, even whilst this was a slave country. I was witness to the generous exertions made by the leading spirits of this land in the cause of humanity's dearest privileges. First in the glorious movement then taking place, you, making the greatest sacrifices, led your sister colonies in the enfranchisement of your slaves. Well, gentlemen, do I remember our admiration of your devotion to generous principles. Right well do I recollect how your Governors, the representatives of your Sovereign, cheered you on with their congratulations ; how they promised, how they pledged themselves that your excellent exertions should be steadily maintained by all the power of the Crown ; that your acts never should be forgotten, whilst, on the other side, your own rights should have the most ample development. I cannot, gentlemen, forget that they said the empire thanked you, and, through them, gave you the most solemn assurances of enduring support. My lord and gentlemen, during these sixteen years many Governors have passed away. I still am here ; and when I reflect on all this, I begin to understand why you call on me, the witness of these pledges, almost myself directly concerned in these assurances, to stand by you in your demand that the Government of Great Britain remain firm to its ancient faith, and that it redeem the honour of those Governors, and that Sovereign, whose counsels you followed in the achievement of that which was to the human race a great good, and to the other nations a most glorious example ; but which, all-admirable as it was, has since proved the cause of your most cruel injury. In my hand, my lord, I hold the treaty of

1817; here, in its very commencement, the Spanish King adjures the Holy Trinity of God to protect and govern it. He states that all the best feelings of his own nature appeal, in terms of resistless force, to his heart, in maintenance of the demands made by the Sovereign of Great Britain for the liberation of the enslaved. On the other side, stand forth the statements of proud England; solemn, too, are the engagements she makes to the King of Spain, and most faithful has been the performance of her holy covenants. My lord, certain steps were to be taken and acts done prior to 1820; thence, and for ever, the importation of slaves was to cease. According to the stipulations of this treaty, Great Britain was to give to Spain £400,000; she did so. This great disbursement she made, not for her own benefit, but on account of the noble principles she advocated, as the great protectress of mankind's rights. In addition to the immense outlay she has made on her own part, she has supplied Spain's treasury, that Spain's King might, as he said, give way to the pleadings of his own honourable nature, and do that which he said God himself commanded. Could we, my lord, after all this, have pictured to ourselves such conduct as that which since has brought dishonour on the name of Spain? But, alas! Spain stands not out alone to the repro-bation of man; Brazil is by her side—Brazil, with whom, shortly after, England entered into similar treaties of high regard. Here, from this island, we have seen pass our very ports, ship after ship, of Spain, heavily laden with horrid cargoes of human misery, in open, daring violation of every sacred contract of that nation. Need I, my lord, call over the tens, the hundreds of thousands of innocent men, torn from their families, and in manacles hurried on to that vast depôt of sin and shame, which, boasting in its iniquity, lies next our shores, in its luxurious length, a monument of violated engagements—a blot on humanity itself? Have we not, my lord, heard of the mockery most heartless, of men's most solemn assurances flaunted on the world by the empire of Brazil, whilst its fast-sailing ships swept along the deep, almost borne down by the weight of innumerable men in chains, doomed to slavery only to end with their existence? But why should I trouble you more with these hateful details? I will now simply say that amidst the nations, where kings were pledged and heaven invoked, in the protection of man's most sacred rights, England, in a short while, stood alone; whilst she, with rare truth, observed her engagements, the others either falsely evaded or auda-. ciously spurned them. Nor did this suffice; they mocked and taunted you; they cried you down in your own markets; displaced your products with the fruits of slavery even in your own homes, and made the very nobleness of your nature the cause of your destruction—this in the face of the world at large. My lord, this was not well. Gentlemen, you meet this day to put an end to this; you call on your dearly loved and greatly honoured Queen, full of affection for her subjects, her heart beats warmly for everything that interests their happiness. You call on the empire of Great Britain to redeem its pledge—to look to the fulfilment of solemn treaties, and to compel their enforcement. In the impressive words of my lord, I feel assured that your demand will give such spirit and life to the love of freedom, bounding in every British heart, as will, must render it impossible, a thousand times impossible, that the violation of all your rights should dare to continue its existence. Gentlemen, your industry, your prosperity, and your happiness, can no longer be chained down. My lord, the words and pledges of kings and queens shall be no longer held up to the world's scorn and contempt. Gentlemen, your union must be complete; no man now should stand aloof; let every voice within the land be raised; loud will be the approving shout borne, in unison with yours, from every colony in the West; from the Frenchman, from the Swede, and from the Dane; from India, too, the reverberation with heavy swell will come; from the isles of India's Seas, before the throne of our Sovereign, your rights will confront the prejudices of other lands; then, high in her excelling power, but full of kindness in her every act, your Queen, through her Government, will say,—Sovereigns of Spain and Brazil, the kings who preceded me, and I, too, felt the difficulties you were surrounded with,—your thrones attacked, the existence of your kingdoms menaced,—we saw, too, our people's great injury, caused by your infraction of the solemn treaties you made with us. In the situation in which you were a long time, we forebore to urge you; but now the wrongs of our people are grown too great. We cannot shut our heart to their cry; it is impossible to resist their appeal; an end must be put to this most unholy violation of all that is right; our sacred treaties must be fulfilled, and the guaranteed honour of kings and queens maintained.

The honourable and learned gentleman concluded by moving the following resolution:—

" 1st. That so long as the sugar planters of Cuba, Porto Rico, and Brazil, in defiance of the laws of their respective countries, and of the treaties by which the Spanish and Brazilian Governments stand bound to her Majesty, are permitted to reinforce, by fresh drains from slavery, the means of increasing their profits, it is hopeless, in countries so thinly peopled as Jamaica, Guiana, and Trinidad, for the proprietors of the soil to persevere in its cultivation."

The Rev. Dr. King, of Glasgow, in rising to second the resolution, said—It is with much diffidence as well as respect that I rise to address this great meeting. If the observations I am about to make shall betray some unacquaintance with your position and its claims, the kindness which many of you have already shown to a stranger convinces me that I shall not appeal in vain to your candour and forbearance. Allusion has been made to the distressed condition of Jamaica, and I am sure that its distress has not been exaggerated. You inhabit a beautiful island. Its climate is so good, that when its advantages for health shall be better known, I think your colony must come to replace Madeira, in British estimation, as a desirable retreat for consumptively-disposed patients. Your soil is confessed to be, generally, excellent. The weeds of your public roads are the ornamental plants of our greenhouses and hot-houses. Your very wilds are orchards. The grandeur of your mountains is qualified only by the soft charms of their vegetation, and the bounty of nature has transformed your rocky cliffs into hanging gardens. Your isle has a central position in the ocean, as if to receive and to dispense the riches of the earth. You speak one language, and the composition of this meeting shows that a happy harmony subsists among the sections of your community. Such facts as these would lead us to expect prosperity. But, instead of prosperity, we witness prostration. You have peace, fertility, health—all the usual guarantees of national well-being—and yet, your leading families are disappearing; your stately mansions are falling into decay; your lovely estates are thrown up; men's hearts are everywhere failing them for fear, as if war, or famine, or pestilence, desolated your borders. The existence of such distress is matter of notoriety; but I think it has not been sufficiently pressed on public attention, and especially on British attention, that religion and education are largely sharing the general calamity. But it is too certain that these highest of all interests are suffering. On the north side of the island, and on the south side of the island, numerously attended meetings of missionaries, belonging to different denominations, have been recently held to deliberate on matters of common interest to them, and all the brethren assembling on these occasions were agreed in the conviction that the secular and spiritual instruction of the island are, for the most part, in a low and declining state. They were not less united in assigning the temporal distress of the colony as a principal cause of their peculiar difficulties and discouragements. While churches and societies at home are diminishing the amount of their assistance to missionary institutions here, the inhabitants are disabled, by their sad reverses, from supporting their own ministers and teachers, as they otherwise might; and persons, who have still some means at their disposal, are tempted to plead the badness of the times as a sufficient apology for restricting their exertions. The consequence is, that ministers are returning home; schoolmasters are returning home; and the places of those competent and devoted benefactors are left vacant, or filled by others poorly qualified to succeed them. To what will these things grow? To what

condition is this lovely island retrograding? Ye friends of
humanity, who have done so much, awake and bestir yourselves, lest all that you have done be undone—lest your work
be ruined and your reward lost! From the scene of the facts,
amid a great assembly perfectly qualified to judge the accuracy of my statements, I tell you that the objects on which
you have expended so much money, so much labour, so much
time, so much life, are in jeopardy; and ignorance, irreligion,
superstition, intoxication, profligacy, are hovering, like birds
of prey, over your schools and chapels, and threatening them
with destruction. But how are these evils to be arrested? I
reply, that, to all the extent that temporal adversity is a cause
of them, a revival in trade would be a cure for them. If profits and wages were to rise, persons would have more to give
for moral purposes, and more heart to give it, and new life
and energy would be infused into all benevolent enterprises.
But the resolution to which I am speaking declares that commerce cannot revive here, while the slave-trade pours its victims into those countries with which Jamaica is now brought
into competition? This may appear to some a startling
proposition; it may seem to them a libel on the Divine
government to allow that free labour is unable to contend
with slave labour. If that admission be made, where, it may
be asked, is the noble adage that "honesty is the best policy?"
I am anxious to present this subject in a just light; and I
begin by granting to these objectors, that the largest confidence may be reposed in equity. If it be confessed to me
that a system is wrong in principle, and I be at the same time
counselled to let it alone because it is old and respected, and
upheld by adventitious circumstances, I reply, "Down with
it!"—*Fiat justitia, ruat cœlum*—Let justice take its course,
though the heavens perish. But, in proving a great principle,
you must test it fairly. Partial justice is often the grossest
injustice; and a partial freedom may be tantamount to oppression. You think it strange and sad that slave labour
should be more productive than free labour. But of what is
it more productive? Of morals? health? happiness? No—
only of money. And what is there discreditable to liberty, in

the idea that violence may have an unrighteous advantage over it in the single article of pecuniary profit? If unprincipled force were never successful in its extortions, much of the language of Scripture would be unmeaning or fallacious. There would then be no room for the wages of iniquity, and no place for the trials, and, I may say, for the triumphs of nature. If one man employ his workman for ten hours a day, and another his bondsman for eighteen hours daily, and the latter is allowed to repair his cruel waste of life by grafting on the slave-owner the functions of the man-stealer, then I know of nothing but a miracle that can give the humane master and the inhuman monster the same amount of mercantile return. The slave trader adds to his revenue, but the great principle is not disproved or compromised by his success; that success is limited and short-lived, even to the individual; guilty gains are infinitely worse than guiltless losses; and if we view the world generally, what sordid acquisition of Spain or Brazil can compensate for the unfathomable wrongs and sufferings of Africa? I hold myself entitled, then, to advocate the general advantageousness of virtue, and yet contend, in the words of this resolution, " that so long as the sugar planters of Cuba, Porto Rico, and Brazil, in defiance of the laws of their respective countries, and of the treaties by which the Spanish and Brazilian Governments stand bound to her Majesty, are permitted to reinforce, by fresh drafts from slavery, the means of increasing their profits, it is hopeless, in countries so thinly peopled as Jamaica, for the proprietors of the soil to persevere in its cultivation." Jamaica cannot prosper while slavery is dominant in other sugar-growing and coffee-growing countries. But slavery may be, must be abolished. The mode of its abolition will be discussed by others, to whom the discussion of it is assigned in the order of the resolutions. I only remark, in passing, how deeply we are indebted to Mr. Turnbull for drawing attention to those treaties with Spain and Brazil, by which the discontinuance of the slave-trade is provided for, and the extinction of slavery itself indirectly secured; and more especially for taking up the ground, characteristically his own, that when

a man's right to liberty is invaded, it should not lie with
him to show that he is free, but with others to prove that
he is a slave.   His views still opposed and thwarted, he has
still maintained and urged.   In defiance of all obstructions
and delays, and repulses, he has held on his course.   I trust
this meeting will be premonitory of the fulfilment of his
aspirations, and there are few satisfactions of a purer nature
than to see the benefactors of the human race attaining the
ends to which their lives and labours have been devoted.
Let it not be said that the Government has not power to
enforce the execution of treaties.   If they could not be
enforced, they should never have been formed.   Better not
stipulate, than enter into stipulations only to have them
trampled under foot.   But the power of the Government
will be considerably affected by the power of this movement.
And will not this movement be powerful?   Is it not strong
in its simplicity, its justice, its mercy?   Observe on what
day we meet—in what seat of rule we are congregated—
by whom we are presided over—of what nature also this
great meeting is constituted.   Surely, this first of public
meetings is auspicious.   And will not Kingston, Montego
Bay, and Falmouth, and all other towns participate
in the movement?   I dare not speak for British society;
such presumption would be fitted to defeat its object;
but I may be allowed, from a personal knowledge of the
facts, to controvert the representations of parties who allege
that the anti-slavery feeling is extinct in Great Britain.
The manifestation of that feeling has been latterly qualified
by questions of principle, and by the want of a specific
object.   But in this movement there is no debateable
question, and the remedy which it proposes is perfectly
explicit.   In these circumstances I have a strong confidence
that British humanity will not fail you at this juncture.   I
trust that missionary societies, and Christian churches, and
municipal corporations, will join in your demand, till even
the loud calls of this meeting shall seem to be lost in the
thunders which it has evoked.   When it shall be so,
the treaties must be fulfilled, and then will slavery fall
down in the Spanish and Brazilian territories; and when

these buttresses are removed, the whole bastile of bondage
will tumble into ruins.   Already, America—alas, that such
a name should be allied with slavery as its principal hope !—
inclines to emancipation.   In Virginia, a slave State, four
newspapers advocate the liberation of the slaves, which is
a preliminary to their disenthralment. — The district of
Columbia is allowed by the general government to decide
for itself, and of course it will declare for freedom.   Then
France, Denmark, Portugal, Mexico, are already on the
side of free labour ; and they are equally interested as we
are to hasten its triumph.   If I were asked for some
encouragement greater than all these, I might point to
that expectation of the result which precedes and insures
victory.   The apologists of the slave-trade show a consciousness, in their very mode of expressing themselves, that they
are speaking against fate, or shall I say against God.
Slavery is doomed, its defenders know it is.   Its end
is a question not of fact, but of time ; and it lies with us to
decide the latter question, by insisting that it should cease
now, or at all events that the blow shall now be given
which shall shake the Colossus on its pedestal, and ere long
bring it to the dust.   As I have passed through Jamaica, I
have marvelled at the dispensations of Providence, and
have wondered what all this distress could mean.   I trust
that its meaning is becoming apparent now.   Slavery has
been abolished here, but not elsewhere.   Our work is not
finished, and therefore our recompence is not communicated.
To all the extent of our influences we must eradicate the
curse of bondage, and then the blessing from on high will
descend on us till there be not room enough to receive it.
You have suffered much—you are still suffering—but you
will bear these adversities with patience, and may yet review
them with pleasure, when you are made to perceive that
their end is merciful, and that God has involved you in a
limited distress to make you the honoured instruments of
working out an unlimited deliverance.

The Honourable the Vice-Chancellor said — In giving
their unanimous approbation to the resolution which had

been moved with so much eloquence by the Attorney-
general, and seconded so forcibly and with so much feeling
by the Rev. Dr. King, the meeting had affirmed one great
proposition; namely, that this island, Guiana and Trinidad
cannot continue the cultivation and manufacture of sugar, so
long as other countries, which are bound by solemn engagements, are permitted with impunity to violate those engagements; but that declaration was not sufficient—he did not
understand by that resolution that they were to be satisfied
with the language of despondency and despair. It was
not simply by declaring to the world that the impropriety
and injustice stated in that resolution exists, that they would
achieve the object they had in view. It would be his duty,
before he sat down, to point out a remedy for the evil complained of, and he hoped to be able to do that duty
fully and satisfactorily. He hoped to point out a remedy
which was within our own beck—a constitutional remedy,
founded on the highest principles of humanity and justice.
He was at a loss to understand how any man could object,
upon moral grounds, to the course he would propose—how
any one could advise them—men of the Anglo-Saxon race—
men who proverbially regard the strict adherence to treaties, to
hesitate in enforcing the performance of treaties by others,
upon whom they were equally binding. The remedy which
he would point out was that which is sanctioned by the law
which governed foreign nations; namely, when it is found
that a nation will not do that which they are pledged to
another nation to do, then it shall be done for them. That
was the footing upon which Spain and Brazil, two countries
which now carry on the detestable traffic in slaves, should
stand in relation to Great Britain. If he pointed out to
them, as he would, that these countries had entered into
solemn treaties to abolish that traffic, they would then have
nothing to do but to call upon the mother country, and our
rulers at home, to compel the observance of those treaties.
In 1840, it having been pointed out that Spain and Brazil
were shamefully evading their treaty obligations, a convention was proposed between Great Britain and Spain, by

which it was declared that the Mixed Commission should have the power to declare all slaves brought from the coast of Africa free; and that the burden of proof that they were not illegally imported should lie on the party claiming, or attempting to hold his fellow-man in bondage. If that convention had been carried out fairly and fully, he had no hesitation in saying that two-thirds of the slaves now in Cuba would be free. Did they wish for proof of this assertion? He would give it from the best authority—from the evidence of Lord Palmerston, who, in his evidence before a Committee of the House of Commons, thus states—" I believe there was a fixed sum paid to the Government of Cuba for each negro imported, and that, besides that, bribes were given to the whole of the officers of customs and police, in order to induce them to wink at what was doing. The illegality stands on more than one ground; there is a treaty which binds the Spanish Crown to prevent the importation of negroes; and there is a law of Ferdinand VII., by which it is illegal to import slaves into any Spanish colony, and by which, moreover, any slave, imported in violation of that law, is, *ipso facto*, entitled to his freedom; so that, in truth, if the thing was minutely investigated, I doubt whether one might not say that at least two-thirds of the negroes in Cuba are, by the Spanish law, freemen; it is only those who were born in the country who would ever be liable to servitude." That was the evidence of Lord Palmerston, and it was the result of great experience and sagacity—of Lord Palmerston, from whom emanated the very convention which he hoped they would join him in bringing to the notice of Parliament and of the British nation. And could they suppose that in so doing they were impeding the Government? Could any one doubt that in so doing they were carrying out the wishes and desires of Ministers themselves; or could any one anticipate any objection to such a course? It were in vain to argue with any man who maintained such a proposition as that. He would not, however, rest alone on the evidence of Lord Palmerston; but he would refer to the evidence of a gentleman connected with this country, of whom he hoped they

would allow him to speak ; he alluded to the evidence of Mr.
Geddes, formerly a member in the Assembly for the parish of
St. Ann.   In his evidence before the Committee, he says, "At
Havanna I was carried to see some fine vessels, the swiftest
sailing vessels that were ever built, as being those that were
engaged in the slave-trade, and which defied British cruisers
to overtake them ; they were called ' Baltimore clippers.'   I
heard a merchant of eminence say, who, I have no doubt at
all, was engaged in the slavé-trade, that the Governor of that
day would receive no more representations at all from Mr.
Turnbull, the Consul, 'that he dreamed dreams overnight,
and sent them to him in the morning.'   My own conviction
is, that one-half of the persons held, at this moment, in slavery
in Cuba are held in that state in violation of the existing treaties
between this country and Spain."   And then, this is added,
with all that acuteness of intellect which Mr. Geddes so fully
possesses ; "and I say so, seeing the ages of those people,
knowing how soon the slaves are worked out and killed
in that country, for there is no reproduction there."   That
was the testimony of an individual who was known and
respected among themselves.   Let him now call their attention to the treaties.   The Attorney-general had told them
that the first was in 1817.   He would not occupy their time
in reading long extracts from books—these treaties were
drawn up so clearly, and their object was so defined, that
it would not require any length of time to understand them.
In the first of these treaties it is stated, " His Catholic Majesty
concurs in the fullest manner in the sentiments of his Britannic Majesty, with respect to the injustice and inhumanity
of the traffic in slaves, and promises to take into consideration,
with the deliberation which the state of his possessions in
America demands, the means of acting in conformity with
those sentiments."   "And his Catholic Majesty, conformably
to the spirit of this article, and to the principles of humanity
with which he is animated, having never lost sight of an
object so interesting to him, and being desirous of hastening
the moment of its attainment, has resolved to co-operate with
his Britannic Majesty in the cause of humanity, by adopting,

ın concert with his said Majesty, efficacious means for bringing about the abolition of the slave-trade. His Catholic Majesty engages that the slave-trade shall be abolished throughout the entire dominions of Spain on the 30th day of May, 1820, and that from and after that period it shall not be lawful for any of the subjects of the Crown of Spain to purchase slaves, or to carry on the slave-trade on any part of the coast of Africa, upon any pretext or in any manner whatever. And for this his Britannic Majesty engages to pay, on the 26th February, 1818, the sum of £400,000 to such person as his Catholic Majesty shall appoint to receive the same." Could any language be more plain, explicit, and decisive than that? That was the first treaty in 1817, between King Ferdinand and the King of Great Britain. Let them now see in what way King Ferdinand expresses himself in a Royal cedula, published in 1817. After admitting the illegality of the slave-trade, " and meditating incessantly on the measures which might be most proper for restoring good order to those remote countries" (the Spanish American possessions), " and affording them all the protection of which they are capable, I quickly discovered that an entire change had taken place in the circumstances which induced my august prede-cessors to permit the traffic in slaves on the African coast. And being aware that the moment for the abolition is arrived, in consequence of the interests of my American States being in accordance with the sentiments of my royal mind, as well as with the desires of all the Sovereigns, my friends and allies, I have resolved as follows :—First. From this day forward I prohibit for ever, to all my subjects, both in the Peninsula and in America, to resort to the coast of Africa north of the equator for the purchase of negroes ; all the blacks bought on those coasts shall be declared free in the first seaport of my dominions, at which the vessel containing them shall arrive ; the vessel, together with her remaining cargo, shall be confis-cated for my royal treasury, and the purchaser, the captain, the master, and the pilot, shall, without fail, be sentenced to ten years' confinement in some fortress in the Philippine Islands." The Vice-chancellor feared that if the terms of this cedula

had been strictly carried into effect, the fortresses in the
Philippine Islands would not be sufficiently large to hold all
those that would rightly be immured there. The cedula
then goes on to declare, "From the 30th of May, 1820, I
forbid likewise all my subjects in the Peninsula, as well as in
America, to proceed to the coast of Africa, south of the
equator, for the purchase of negroes, under the same penalties
as are denounced in the first article of this my royal cedula;
granting also the term of five months from the date before-
mentioned, for the completion of their voyages, to those
vessels that shall have duly obtained permission, prior to the
said date of the 30th of May, 1820, at which time the slave-
trade shall cease entirely in all my dominions in Spain, as
well as in America." And, as if that was not enough,
another treaty was entered into, in 1835, between the late
King of England and the mother of the present Queen of
Spain, in which it is declared, "The slave-trade is hereby
again declared, on the part of Spain, to be henceforward totally
and finally abolished in all parts of the world." The Vice-
chancellor had heard with surprise that it had been objected
that this treaty was extracted from the fears of Spain, and,
therefore, was not binding. If that language could be used,
then no treaty would be binding. He wanted to know how
it could be said to have been extracted from the fears of
Spain, when it was entered into with the power whose exertions
had kept the present reigning family dominant on the throne
of Spain? That this treaty, like all the rest, had been most
scandalously violated, there could be no doubt. Let him call
their attention to the evidence of Dr. Cliffe, a naturalised
subject of Brazil, an American by birth; he stated, in his
evidence before the Committee of the House of Commons,
appointed to report on the slave-trade, that between November, 1846, and November, 1847, not less than from sixty to
sixty-five thousand Africans were imported into Brazil; and
then he is called upon to say, in order to produce this number
landed in Brazil, how many persons must have been captured
in Africa; he enters into the calculation, and allows so many
for captures by the cruisers, so many for deaths, and he

shows that there must have been exported one hundred
thousand Africans to have produced that number, and those
in one year. This evidence was unblushingly given to the
Committee of the House of Commons, and could it be
doubted, for one moment, that this traffic was carried on with
redoubled vigour? But, it might be asked, what has Great
Britain to do with it? Why should she go to war on account
of the traffic in slaves by other countries? If that were the
case, no treaty could be enforced; but he did not apprehend
any such results. He had already alluded to Lord Palmerston. The meeting would allow him once more to allude to
him. They all knew that last year—the most eventful year
that has passed—when revolutions raged on the Continent, and
England herself was threatened with an outbreak, differences arose between the Government of Spain and the
British Minister, and it was thrown in the teeth of Lord
Palmerston that he had no right to interfere with the
Government of Spain,—what then was Lord Palmerston's
answer? The Duke de Sotomayor asked what would Lord
Palmerston say if M. Isturitz should, at his instructions, give
her Majesty's Minister for Foreign Affairs advice as to his
policy in the United Kingdom, or suggest the formation of
another Cabinet in lieu of that presided over by Lord John
Russell? Lord Palmerston replied, "If the right of her
Britannic Majesty to the throne of the United Kingdom had
been disputed by a pretending rival; if civil war had arisen
out of such a conflict of claims; if the British Government
had only a few years ago sent a special Envoy to Madrid to
solicit the assistance of Spain, in order to place her Majesty
on her throne; if that assistance had been given, both morally
by treaty engagements, and physically by military and naval
force; if the aid thus afforded by Spain had contributed
in so essential a degree to secure the Crown to her Majesty
that it might, with truth, be said that without such aid her
Majesty would not now have been Queen of England; if,
moreover, there still remained a pretender who asserted his
right, and whose pretensions were backed by a large party
in the United Kingdom; and if, upon every symptom of

danger from that pretender and that party, the British Government was in the habit of reminding Spain of the treaty engagements which she entered into, was also in the habit of asserting that those engagements were still in force, and was continually claiming the benefit of the alleged existence of those engagements; if all those things existed, and if the Government of Spain had, in a moment of general disturbance in Europe, warned the British Government of dangers by which, in their opinion, the security of her Majesty's throne was menaced, I think I may confidently affirm, that, under such circumstances, any statesman who might be Minister of the British Crown, instead of sending back the note in which such representations were conveyed, and instead of replying to it in discourteous terms, would have accepted the communication in the same spirit of friendship in which it was made." Now, that which is thus put hypothetically with respect to the relations between Great Britain and Spain, is known to be historically true as between Spain and Great Britain. They knew that Spain was in the habit of reminding Great Britain of the treaty engagements she had entered into; then why not require Spain to observe her treaties also? Why should those treaties be invoked for the benefit of Spain, and not for the benefit of Great Britain? They knew that Spain leans upon Great Britain, and they had a right, at least, to call upon her to perform her engagements. Exactly the same argument would apply to Brazil; the Government of that country was bound both by treaty and by law, and Great Britain had the right to call upon Brazil to observe her treaties. If the meeting was satisfied that it was hopeless to expect that Spain and Brazil would observe these treaties, and enforce their laws against the slave-trade, then he asked them to call upon the Government with their united voice, which would be echoed and responded to, he hoped, by all the Antilles, to enforce that which they were entitled to; he asked the meeting now to commence a work which would send forth a voice which would yet be thundered throughout the mother country—let them call upon the Government to demand of

Spain and Brazil to carry out the contracts into which they had entered with Great Britain. The convention to which he had alluded had been abandoned altogether, though it had been suggested and urged upon the Government by Mr. Turnbull, who, through good report and evil report, had been the continued and unflinching advocate of the emancipation of the slaves. Had the terms of the convention of 1840 been carried out, it was more than probable that there would not be one person in Cuba now a slave, who is illegally kept in bondage. It behoved them to call upon Great Britain to insist upon the abolition of the traffic, and, that done, he cared not what else was done; for once abolish that accursed traffic, and slavery would speedily cease to exist, and then might the British colonies enter into competition with Cuba and Brazil, for then they need not fear competition with any nation in the world.

The resolution was then read.

2. "That in the opinion of this meeting the plan which was embodied by her Majesty's principal Secretary of State for Foreign Affairs, in the draft of a convention with Spain, and transmitted to her Majesty's Minister at Madrid, on the 25th of May, 1840, as appears from the papers on slave-trade, presented in that year to Parliament by her Majesty's command, is practical and feasible; and if now urged on the Spanish and Brazilian Governments with suitable energy, would prove beneficial and effective, in enabling the emancipated colonies of Great Britain to meet and overcome the competition in the home markets and other countries of Europe, on the equal terms to which they are about to be exposed by the Sugar Duties Act of 1846."

Mr. W. T. March, member of Assembly for Spanish Town—My lord, after the able and eloquent address of the hon. the Vice-chancellor, in moving this resolution, I ought possibly to be content with merely seconding it; but, having taken a prominent part in forwarding a memorial on the same subject from the Assembly to the Crown, I cannot give my support to the object of this meeting without one or two remarks on the subject. On referring to the original treaty with Spain, one is at a loss to account for the necessity of any further provision on the subject. It is, therefore, necessary to explain the object of the proposed convention to which this resolution refers. By the original treaties Spain and Portugal agreed to abolish the slave-trade carried on by the subjects of these two countries—Spain, in consideration of £400,000, and Portugal, in consideration of the remission of a debt of £600,000; and, subsequently, Brazil, in consideration of the acknowledgment of her by Great Britain as an independent State, was induced to adopt the treaties previously executed by Portugal. The machinery arranged for carrying out these treaties was subsequently found insufficient and defective, as the Mixed Commission Courts were only authorised to adjudicate on captures made in the transition, before the slave cargoes were landed. To remedy this defect and insufficiency, Lord Palmerston, then Secretary of State for Foreign Affairs, prepared the draft of a convention which he desired should be entered into with Spain, enabling the Mixed Commission Courts to entertain and adjudicate cases of Africans illegally introduced into Cuba, in contravention of pre-existing treaties, and to declare them entitled to their liberty—leaving the onus of proof on the claimant, as is, in fact, the law of Spain in that respect. This is the convention to which the resolution refers, and which we hope not only Spain but the Brazils will ultimately be induced or compelled to adopt. From what took place, as detailed in the correspondence on the subject at the time, there is very little doubt that the convention would have been adopted by the Spanish Government had Lord Palmerston remained in office; at all events, it would have been adopted in a modified form; but, unfortunately for the cause of humanity, that distinguished nobleman retired from office, and was succeeded by Lord Aberdeen, who almost immediately abandoned the policy of his predecessor, and instead of pursuing the matter with the zeal evinced by his predecessor, contented himself, for what object is unexplained, with bandying compliments with the Spanish Minister; for I find a letter from Lord Aberdeen, immediately after his accession to office, complimenting the Spanish authorities on the faithful manner in which the previous treaties had been kept, and this at the very time at which he had a letter from the Commissioner at the Havanna, detailing facts which showed that the slave-trade was then carried on in all its horrors and with unabated energy. With all Lord Palmerston's zeal in the cause, we have nothing to hope from the justice of Ministers, trammelled as they are by popular clamour. I regret to be compelled to arrive at this conclusion; but previous events confirm me in this opinion. We have nothing, in fact, to hope from the mere justice of our case, opposed to interest; our only hope is to enlist the feelings of the British people in the cause—to awaken their sympathy and dormant humanity on behalf of the poor African, and then, and not till then, may we hope for success. There is, even now, a powerful party organised and increasing in the mother country, for taking away the only restraint now in force against the unholy traffic—the blockading squadron on the coast of Africa and Brazil. I have in vain endeavoured to find a reasonable argument in favour of this movement, but have hitherto been unsuccessful. I have read most of the examinations of persons recommending the withdrawal of the squadron, and all the reasons they give for their recommendation appear to amount to this: Because the laws existing against a criminal act render the sufferers by it liable to harsh treatment at the hands of the criminal, that therefore it would be better to legalise the crime under certain restrictions. As well might it be argued, that because burglars and robbers frequently murder their victims to prevent detection, that therefore robbery and burglary ought to be legalised. The time chosen for this demonstration is propitious. Lord Palmerston is now in the Ministry, and still zealous in the cause. The people of Cuba, since the last revolt of their slaves, dread the increase of their slave population by fresh drafts from Africa. The late revolts of slaves in Brazil must also make the Brazilians anxious for some measure tending to secure them in the possession of those they already possess; and although we may hope for nothing from their honesty and good faith, we may obtain what we require through their fears and from their feelings of interest. There is one policy of the British Government on this subject, which I have never been able to understand, and that is, why there should be any difference between the infraction of treaties relating to traffic in merchandise, and those relating to the traffic in human beings. The one is considered a *casus belli*—the other is made the subject of useless, unsatisfactory, and prolonged diplomacy. I have never been able to comprehend why piracy and robbery of a bale of merchandise should be visited with the penalty of death, whilst piracy and robbery of human flesh and blood are considered sufficiently punished by confiscation of property; but so it is—according to British policy. Lord Palmerston, in his evidence before the Committee on the Slave-trade, admits that distinction, but gives very unsatisfactory reasons to my mind for the distinction. The British Government has in its own hands the remedy for the evils of which we complain; and although I do not hope to obtain that remedy from the justice of the cause, I trust we shall owe it to those feelings of humanity for which the British people claim pre-eminence, and which, when put in motion, is only satisfied by the attainment of its object. We have the right to demand, as an act of justice to ourselves, to the African race, and to the British people, for the sacrifices made at our expense, that the products of the Brazils and Spanish colonies shall be excluded from the British markets until the Governments of those countries are compelled to act in good faith, and desist from breaking through solemn engagements entered into by them for consideration paid and given by Great Britain. We have a right to require that the products of free labour shall not be put in competition with the products of countries cultivated by labour procured in contravention of solemn treaties. I now, my lord, second this resolution, which I feel confident, when I look around me, will be unanimously adopted.

The resolution was then put and carried.

The Honourable Hector Mitchell, Mayor of Kingston, being called upon to propose the next resolution, said—My lord and gentlemen, I have considerable pleasure in giving my trifling support to the exertions of this meeting. After the eloquence of the gentlemen who have preceded me, I feel that the resolution which I am about to propose requires but few observations on my part, and that these need only be such as have arisen from a memory of things gone by, and which this day's proceedings bring forcibly to my recollection. They bring to my recollection my acquaintance with Mr. Zachary Macaulay, the celebrated advocate of those measures which have led to the present deplorable condition of this island. He was horrified at the mere idea of slavery. He went to England and associated himself with the African Society, and became an agent for the dissemination of those doctrines which filled the halls of Parliament with eloquence on behalf of suffering humanity. But that Society went to sleep, after it had succeeded in respect to the West Indies. The African Society failed to exert itself when those sufferings of the Africans had increased ten thousand fold, and not one voice of commiseration was heard in their behalf. Mr. Macaulay educated a son, and that son is the celebrated statesman—the elegant, the eloquent modern historian. Had those brilliant powers of reasoning been used to convince his colleagues, the Ministry, of the injury which their conduct would inflict on the best interests of humanity, there is no saying to what an extent the evils under which we now suffer might have been mitigated, and we should not have experienced the bill of 1846, which has reduced the island to ruin; but the occasion was suffered to pass, and from that time the greatest ruin and misery have fallen on these islands. My lord, another circumstance has been brought to my recollection. I remember twenty-two years ago, in this room, as a member of the House of Assembly, in the session of 1827, the end of the year, being in committee, with Mr. Hugo James, afterwards Chief-Justice of this island, in the chair, on the subject of the extension of privileges to persons of free condition—I took a retrospective view of the various acts and proceedings of the African Society, and other exertions in furtherance of their purposes,

down to that period, through the exertions of the sectarians
and other agents; and, considering all their acts and movements, I prophesied that it was impossible for slavery to
survive longer than five years. I found afterwards that I
had made my deduction on sure grounds. From that
session of 1827 to the close of the year 1833, completed five
years, and at the beginning of the year 1834 slavery was
abolished in the British dominions. I confess, my lord, that
I, as a member, felt aggrieved that Great Britain should have
forced such a measure upon us, in the manner in which it
was done. But we could not resist. I endeavoured, by
advocating the resolutions which were carried at that period,
to make the measure as passable as possible. This was
done under the solemn protest and fullest assurances by the
Marquis of Normanby, then Lord Mulgrave, that every
encouragement and protection should be given to these
islands. With this belief we did not hesitate to yield all
that was sought at our hands. But free trade has utterly
ruined our exertions and prostrated our strength. We do
not hesitate, my lord, while we give expression to our complaints, also to state our conviction that there are severe
trials at home. But we have deeply suffered—we are
brought, my lord, to a fearful state of ruin. If, however,
my lord, I presumed, at the period to which I have already
alluded, to be prophetical, I will again be bold enough to
say, and to say with confidence, that Great Britain cannot
any longer refuse to listen to our just demands. I will go
so far, my lord, as to prophesy that the ruin which free
trade has occasioned to the manufacturing and other interests
at home, the suffering agriculturists, united with the grievances of the West Indies, will make so powerful an appeal
upon Parliament as to be irresistible; and, ere this session of
Parliament shall have passed over, relief to this island will,
nay, must and shall be afforded. Such is the condition of
things that they may be compared to an undue mixture in
physics, which, as well as in morals, work their own remedy.
Perhaps, my lord, as usual with me, I am too positive in my
manner, but I feel sincere pleasure in giving expression

to these sentiments, because I am satisfied that they are quite true.

The Mayor then proposed the following resolution :—

3. "That the memorial to her Majesty, and the petitions to the two Houses of the Imperial Parliament, now read, be adopted, and that the chairman be requested to sign the memorial to her Majesty on behalf of this meeting."

The memorial to her Majesty the Queen, and the petitions to the two Houses of the Imperial Parliament, at the request of the Right Reverend Chairman, were then read by M. Mackeson, Esq., who had consented to act as Secretary :—

To the Queen's most excellent Majesty.

The humble Memorial of the inhabitants of Jamaica, in public meeting assembled.

May it please your Majesty,

We, your Majesty's devoted and loyal subjects, beg leave, once more, to approach the throne, and to beseech the interposition of your Majesty's Government in requiring from the Governments of her Catholic Majesty, and of the Emperor of Brazil, the faithful and exact observance of the treaties by which these Governments are bound to your Majesty for the suppression of the slave-trade.

To this end, believing the plan to be practical and feasible which was embodied, by your Majesty's principal Secretary of State for Foreign Affairs, in the draft of a convention transmitted by his lordship to your Majesty's Minister at Madrid, on the 25th day of May, 1840; and that, if now urged on the Spanish and Brazilian Governments with suitable energy, it would prove beneficial and effective in enabling the emancipated colonies of Great Britain to withstand and outlive the competition with the slave-grown produce of Cuba, Porto Rico, and Brazil, in the home and other markets of Europe, on the equal terms to which they are about to be exposed by the operation of the Act of 1846, we earnestly implore your Majesty to direct that the necessary measures be taken for bringing the negotiation thus opened by your Majesty's Government to a satisfactory and successful issue.

And we beg to be permitted to lay at your Majesty's feet the renewed assurances of the devoted loyalty and unalterable affection of your Majesty's ever faithful subjects, the inhabitants of Jamaica.

Signed in our name and behalf by our Chairman, this 24th day of May, 1849.

AUBREY G. JAMAICA.

To the Honourable the Commons of the United Kingdom, in Parliament assembled.

The humble Petition of the inhabitants of Jamaica, without distinction of class or colour, political opinion or religious creed, at a meeting convened by the Chief Magistrate, at the seat of Government, in the Cathedral City of Spanish Town, and held on the 24th day of May, 1849.

We, her Majesty's devoted and loyal subjects, the inhabitants of Jamaica, relying on the sympathy of our countrymen at home, appeal with confidence to your honourable House, and beseech of you to concur in any measure which her Majesty's advisers may deem expedient, for the purpose of procuring from the Governments of her Catholic Majesty and of the Emperor of Brazil, the faithful and exact observance of the treaties for the suppression of the slave-trade, by which these Governments are solemnly bound to our most gracious Sovereign.

It is matter of notoriety, that the more thinly peopled portions of the intertropical possessions of the Crown, such as Jamaica, Guiana, and Trinidad, are utterly unable to sustain a competition, on equal terms, in the home market and the other markets of the world, with the produce of Cuba, Porto Rico, and Brazil, so long as the inhabitants of these countries, in defiance of their own municipal laws, and of the treaties by which their Governments are bound to us, are permitted to reinforce their gangs of labourers by fresh importations of African slaves.

We have the admission also of the highest authority, that the deep distress in which we are now involved is the result of the concurrent operation of two measures of the Imperial Parliament, passed, the one in 1833, the other in 1846, by the former of which it was made more expensive to procure labour in these colonies, and by the latter the price of the produce of that labour was diminished.

It is our sincere belief that this distress would be remedied, and these important colonies restored to their former prosperity, if they could be relieved from that contraband in labour which their Spanish and Brazilian rivals are still suffered to maintain on the coast of Africa.

A measure to this effect, which appears to your petitioners to have been eminently practical and feasible in its nature, was prepared by her Majesty's principal Secretary of State for Foreign Affairs, in the year 1840, and after having been formally submitted to the Government of her Catholic Majesty by the Queen's Minister at Madrid, was communicated, by her Majesty's command, to both Houses of Parliament; but it does not appear that either the Spanish Government or that of Brazil has yet been persuaded to accede to the convention thus proposed, by which existing treaties would be carried into effect.

From the progress which was formerly made in this negotiation with Spain, from the sensible diminution which has since taken place in the illicit intercourse of Cuba and Porto Rico with the coast of Africa, and from the efforts which are now making in these dependencies of Spain, by the introduction of free labour, to supply the deficiencies which the laws of mortality are constantly producing among a slave population, destructively overwrought and consisting for the most part of one sex only, it is to be presumed that the negotiation so long suspended might now conveniently be revived, and brought to a speedy and prosperous issue.

Brazil is now the only other State which perseveres in deriving a disgraceful profit from this piratical contraband in human beings; and unhappily, from the great extent of the coasts of that empire, and their comparative proximity to the African continent, it has not yet been possible, with all the naval force at her Majesty's command, with all the zeal and devotion embarked in the cause, and with all the assistance afforded by the cruisers of other nations, to make any sensible impression on the amount of the traffic; and it is a melancholy fact that the Brazilian share in it continues to increase, leaving it, to this day, the opprobrium of our common nature, and the means of working the irretrievable ruin of her Majesty's emancipated colonies. But the negotiation already opened with Spain is equally applicable to Brazil, and has only to be urged, as your petitioners believe, with suitable energy, to lead to a similar result.

Such a result is now the more easily attainable, inasmuch as the Governments of France, Denmark, and Sweden have recently followed the beneficent example of England in the emancipation of their slaves, so that the inhabitants of Martinique and Guadaloupe, Bourbon and Cayenne, Santa Cruz, St. Thomas, St. John, and St. Bartholomew are all now suffering in the same way that Jamaica, Guiana, and Trinidad are suffering from the piratical proceedings of which your petitioners now justly and earnestly complain.

The system of slave-trade suppression, which it is the object of the present petition to recommend to the notice of your honourable House, possesses the advantage of not being incompatible with any known policy of her Majesty's Government; of accomplishing its object with the aid of the machinery of the Mixed Courts, which has already been long in operation, and by means which are not only moral and peaceful, but comparatively inexpensive in their nature. Your petitioners cannot doubt, therefore, that while they invoke the sympathy of their more prosperous fellow-subjects, they will not be denied the countenance of your honourable House in obtaining such a measure of justice as is required at once by the laws of Spain and Brazil, by the first principles of humanity, and by the stringent obligations of solemn treaties.

And your petitioners, as in duty bound, shall ever pray.

The petition to the Upper House of Parliament, with the mere difference of style and title, being in substance the same with that to the Commons, it is not necessary to repeat it in this place. After these addresses had been read by William Wyllys Mackeson, Esq., Barrister-at-law, who, at the request of the Chairman, had kindly undertaken to act as Secretary :—

Mr. Robert Osborn, from Kingston, one of the editors of the "Morning Journal" newspaper, on being called upon to second the resolution, appeared at the farther end of the room and said—I dare say you all see the position I occupy : I did not come here to take part in the proceedings of the meeting ; but, being selected to second the resolution proposed by the venerable Mayor of Kingston, your object is, I imagine, to show that we are perfectly unanimous on this subject ; that there is a oneness of feeling characterising this meeting, which is desirable to the attainment of our object. And, if for no other reason, I would second the resolution proposed by the worthy Mayor, because it is generally said that he and I do not "set horses." The resolution just proposed is one of those, my lord, that will scarcely admit of a speech at all, or else a speech without end. It is, that the memorial to her Majesty, and the petitions to the two houses of Parliament, now read, be adopted, and that the chairman be requested to sign the memorial to her Majesty on behalf of this meeting. On the first blush it will be asked, "what can a person have to say on this subject?" Dr. King, who has addressed the meeting, and certainly very eloquently, has dealt with the moral part of the subject, and Mr. Panton (the Vice-chancellor), and Mr. March have treated it politically ; therefore, nothing was, at present, left for the Mayor to do but to give us a little of his personal experience. I did not hear much of his Honour's speech, but, no doubt, it was very interesting. I wish, however, my lord, to say a few words on the subject. I do not intend to allude to the political part of it, because I fancy it would not be very interesting to the ladies to read them long speeches made in Parliament by Lord Palmerston and others, but I wish to address myself to this point—to show the inconsistency of the people of England, and, with all respect for the ladies, to show likewise that they have no small share in it. I, and, no doubt, my lord, most of us witnessed the exertions of the ladies of England at Clapham, and Clayton, and places about there, to put an end to the abominable slave-trade; and we have also witnessed the success which attended those efforts, which shows that when- ever the ladies have interested themselves in a cause the ladies have ruled. It consists with my own knowledge, that, in the year 1831, highly respectable ladies at home positively refused to have sugar which was then made by our slaves introduced into their families. They positively refused to take our sugars if slavery was not abolished. This was the feeling that actuated them in 1831, when they held slave-grown sugar in abhorrence; but, now twenty millions have been subscribed by the English people for the abolition of British slavery, the ladies of England think it hard to pay fivepence a pound for their sugar, to preserve their fruits, if they can get it elsewhere for fourpence. From the year 1830, my lord, I had myself something to do with the abolition of slavery; for the sublime principles of Buxton, Clarkson, Macaulay, and Lushington, which were wafted across the ocean from shore to shore, convinced me that man was never created to be the slave of man. These were my feelings, and the feelings which must have governed the distinguished men I have named, and a Canning, and a Huskisson. They carried out the doctrine of their God in Heaven, that man was never intended to be the slave of man. But the twenty millions subscribed have thrown entirely a new light on the British people. If slavery was incompatible with religion in 1831—if, then, slavery was not allowed to exist on British land, on what principle does Britain support it elsewhere? If it is not righteous for Christian England to tolerate slavery in her own dependencies, on what principles, I would ask, does Christian England promote slavery among her foreign neighbours, with all its horrors? They are not justified on the score of obtaining cheap sugar. Is it the new doctrine of English ladies—do they think, that having subscribed twenty millions towards the abolition of British slavery, they may now preserve their fruits as cheap as they can? Free trade is well known now—it has been well tested by the calico manufacturers, and by the calico merchants; but I deny, my lord, that we have free trade here. There can be no free trade on principles utterly dissimilar. It seems that it is sought to gain a market over the world for the manufactures of England. We are not singular in our distress—it is felt at home, in England; the farmers there themselves are feeling it; but if it be really the case, that, for the sake of the manufactured goods of England, all other interests are to be destroyed, it is, at least, but fair that England should declare it. I am quite unwilling, ladies and gentlemen, to detain you with any remarks on cheap sugar; I dare say you know it is cheap enough. I am told that in our markets it may now be bought at threepence per quart. But the ladies, no doubt, know something of free trade in their houses—they have to see how the moneys are expended, and cannot misunderstand it. They feel it operating, perhaps, somehow in the shape of half-diet—I am glad to see the meeting in a good humour, ladies, of course, included. Having been called upon, my lord, to second this resolution, I do so; but I would first state that I have some objection to this being considered a meeting of the inhabitants of Jamaica; I should like it to be altered to something like a county meeting. It might then be followed up, as no doubt it will be, in Kingston and elsewhere. And, in Kingston, I may be able to express myself a little more freely than here, among new faces. I think, my lord, that would be better than calling it a meeting of the inhabitants of Jamaica. Of course, this may be followed up in Kingston, where we can speak a little more at our ease, and say something more pungent.

The Chairman—I think, Mr. Osborn, the requisition will

determine that. The requisition, if I recollect, invites the inhabitants of Jamaica. Besides, we could hardly confine this to a meeting of Kingston and Spanish Town, because I recognise gentlemen here from far more distant parts of the island. I think it would weaken the meeting. It need not prevent this measure from being followed up, as I hope it will be, elsewhere. Let it be considered a meeting of the inhabitants of this island, composed of as many as could attend.

Mr. Osborn—Very well, my lord, let it be so, and I hope it will be carried out. There is no doubt that things cannot go on much longer as they are. A man, in these days, is obliged to search in order to find out the door of his former habitation. I will better explain what I mean; perhaps the ladies do not understand me. I mean that a man's property now is so overgrown with bush that it is difficult to find out his own door, and something must be done to clear away the bush, that a man may get into his field again. Now, my lord, I second the resolution submitted by the venerable Mayor, and hope my being called upon to do so, will be accepted as an earnest that when we meet on our own ground, in Kingston, we shall coalesce together.

Mr. Barclay, Receiver-general, in rising to propose the fourth resolution, said—My lord, it is extremely gratifying to me, on being called upon to take an active part in the proceedings of this day, to find, by the ample attendance of all classes, and especially of the first men in the country, the interest which is felt on this important subject. The meeting has been already addressed in a most able and eloquent manner by several gentlemen, and if I might be allowed to make any distinct allusion, I would beg to instance the gratifying address of the Rev. Dr. King. That gentleman is a stranger among us, and I am satisfied that the language he has this day made use of will make itself heard far beyond the limits of the island of Jamaica. Our object, gentlemen, is a simple one. We desire only to call upon the Government to finish that which it has begun—to complete that which it stands pledged to do. Half measures, gentlemen, are always bad; and they have proved very bad in this case. If the engagements which have been entered into had been properly carried out at the proper time, what blessings would have followed! —what happy results would have been obtained! But those engagements have not been carried out; and what do we find to be the consequence? The slave-trade continues, with all its dreadful horrors aggravated. The march of progression and civilisation has been obstructed, and the friend of freedom sinks in the struggle with the man-stealer. But, gentlemen, I think it impossible that England and France especially can any longer submit that the property of their own subjects—of their freed slaves — should be ground down through the infringement of solemn treaties made with them. Gentlemen, in the several speeches which have been addressed to you there has been much to recall an incident in my own life. Some seven or eight years ago I went to Africa. Never shall I forget the beautiful morning when I found the coast spread out before me; and, as I gazed, I remembered the misery to which the natives of that land had for so many years been subjected—how they had been treated as beasts of burden—huddled into ships and transported to toil in different countries, under the orders of a foreign driver. I went on board a vessel in Sierra Leone, gentlemen, and my eye has seen the misery to which these unfortunate beings are often subjected. I measured with my own hand the height between decks, and found it to be only thirty inches. Could any one conceive the misery of such a situation as that? Who would believe that such a state of things could exist? And if an end be put to this detestable traffic, gentlemen, what will follow? Why, it will be the end of slavery itself, and the result will be that great changes will take place. There will be free inter-course between Africa and the West Indies. Many who are here will go and visit their fatherland, and the blessings of religion and civilisation will go with them. Perhaps the inscrutable ways of Providence have directed that the suffer-ings of Africa should be made the means of her civilisation—for I have always believed that Africa will never be civilised until the work is undertaken by her own sons. The object of this meeting, then, is to raise our voice in behalf of suffering humanity.   It is impossible, gentlemen, that this voice can be disregarded.   I need not say much more, gentlemen, on the subject of the resolution which has been entrusted to me.   I will, therefore, beg leave to read it at once :—

4. " That the British members of the Mixed Court for the sup- pression of the slave-trade, established in Jamaica, but about to be abolished, be requested to take charge of these addresses to the three branches of the British Legislature, and to lend their aid on their return to Europe in giving them effect."

It only remains for me to say, gentlemen, that the ample attendance this day of all classes is a sufficient earnest of the interest which is felt in the cause.   And we are, indeed, indebted to the gentleman on my right, Mr. Turnbull, for the energy and zeal which he has manifested in this matter.   Our advocate is not idle, and we should, therefore, to the utmost of our power, assist in carrying out the object which has been so ably begun.

The Rev. S. Oughton then rose.   He observed, that when invited to attend this meeting he had not the least idea that he should have been called upon to take part in its proceed- ings.   He had come for the simple purpose of expressing his sympathy with the inhabitants of Spanish Town in what he considered a common calamity, and of contributing any influ- ence he might possess in their endeavours to work out a common good.   It was, therefore, with some surprise that he received information that he would be expected to second this resolution ; he felt at a loss to imagine why, in a town so distinguished as the residence of many gentlemen of extensive information and ability, and in which so large an amount of forensic talent was concentrated, he should have been called upon, and experienced something akin to trepidation at the thought of appearing before such an audience.   But when he looked around the room his fears were assuaged, for he beheld the well-known faces of many of the most influential and respected of his fellow-citizens amongst them.   And at length his wonder was removed also, for he had learned from the memorial read that this was not a meeting of the inhabitants of St. Catherine's parish merely, nor even of the county of Surrey, but that it was a general meeting, intended to represent the united sentiments of the entire body of the inhabitants of Jamaica. He thus felt that he was no intruder—that he had a right to be present, and that it was his duty, by every means in his power, to assist the object of the meeting. He was an inhabitant of Jamaica, bound to her by the closest and the dearest ties, and no object was dearer to his heart than to promote her interests and to advance the happiness of her people. He considered that the present might, with the utmost propriety, be called a meeting of the inhabitants of Jamaica; for, as he looked around, it seemed as though in this hall of representatives every class of her population was fairly represented : the patrician and the plebeian were represented; he saw representatives of the white, the black, and the coloured inhabitants of the island; here we have representatives of the Established Church of England, of the Presbyterian Kirk of Scotland, and of the various bodies of religious dissenters, all suffering under one common calamity, all complaining of one act of common injustice, and all forgetting the distinctions of class, colour, or sect, and uniting together to advance and secure one common interest. The enforcement of the treaties between Great Britain and the Governments of Spain and Brazil was a subject of the utmost importance to the prosperity of the British colonies, and could not be too earnestly advocated; it had occupied his attention for nearly twelve months past, and on one occasion he had intended to have brought it before the attention of the public; but circumstances prevented the carrying out of his design. It appeared to him that it was only by the rigid and faithful observance of those treaties being insisted upon that this island could hope to exist as an exporting colony. To talk of protection was, in his opinion, worse than useless : the fever of free trade seemed to have so entirely incorporated itself with the English constitution, that it would be vain to attempt to check the malady by introducing protection as a specific ! No; our hope must not rest on being protected from the innovations of slavery, but in the destruction of slavery itself. Jamaica has occupied, during the last few years, a most conspicuous position in the political movements of England; and this is not the only time that it has been called to bow to its will, and to suffer, in compliance with its wishes. In 1834 the fever of philanthropy raged through the British dominions, and the commercial interests of this island were, to a considerable extent, sacrificed to appease it; now, the fever of free trade is raging throughout its veins, and we must wait until its malignity is assuaged, ere we can hope for the restoration of reason and justice, or that these islands may be treated with their wonted liberality. I do not disapprove of the act by which slavery was abolished throughout the British dominions. I bless God for the noble deed by which the greatest curse and the foulest stain was removed from our colonies; but that Jamaica has suffered greatly, both in its agricultural and commercial interests, is a fact so plain and obvious that it cannot be denied; it was unavoidable that it should be so; slavery in Jamaica stood between England and England's conscience, and to appease the clamours of that conscience, and enable England to be just, it was necessary that Jamaica should suffer, and suffered she has! But, now that the claims of justice would once more raise her to prosperity, ought not justice to be awarded to her? He had no notion of one-sided justice; if justice in 1834 required the abolition of slavery in the British dominions, justice in 1849 demands the enforcement of these treaties with Brazil and Cuba, which will go far to secure the extinction of slavery throughout the world. Justice ought to be impartial in its decisions, whether they affect the king or his subject, the high or the low, the weak or the strong. There was not an argument employed, from 1832 to 1834, in favour of the abolition of slavery in this colony, but may be applied with equal propriety to the destruction of slavery and the slave-trade in Spain and Brazil; but England has ceased to be just—England has not been faithful either to her conscience or her God. But the object of the meeting was not only to secure the claims of justice, but also those of a higher character—the exalted, the benign, the godlike attribute of mercy! The woes of thousands of poor helpless slaves, pining in hopeless bondage, demand the enforcement of these treaties, and the miseries of tens of thousands more, torn from their homes and country to be sacrificed to the demon slavery, plead for it; and if England were consistent, and true to her own acknowledged principles, they would not plead in vain : she would have done in Cuba what she did in Jamaica. It were folly to say that she could not have done so ; she had the power, if she had chosen to wield it. Treaties with the Spanish Government had been entered into, solemnly ratified and confirmed by the payment of £400,000, to compensate Spain for her loss ; but those treaties had been disregarded, trampled under foot, and England mocked and laughed at. Why, then, does not England now insist upon the faithful observance of those treaties? A single word from the throne of Britain could awe the Spaniards into obedience. It needs only that, as the genius of liberty, she should cast one lightning glance on the fetters of the slave to cause them to fall from his limbs, and render Cuba as free as is Jamaica. No, it is not because England lacks the power to do this—it is because she lacks the will—it is because a false policy, or some still meaner motive, has chilled her benevolence, and paralysed her activities. Perhaps such a step would disturb her friendly relations with that faithless nation. Perhaps it might interfere with some family relations, or, what is more likely, it might mar her interests; and thus worthless motives are allowed to operate, that England may profit by that which secures the destruction of her faithful colonies. But (continued the Rev. Gentleman) they will find, in the end, that their policy is as foolish as it is wicked—they may, as Mr. Osborn said, be able, by encouraging slavery, to obtain sugar cheaper, to preserve their fruits and manufacture their luxuries; but, by doing so, they will bring destruction on their noble colonies. Already this has been to a considerable extent accomplished ; and, unless some remedy be speedily applied, soon will their ruin be complete. They will cease to be exporting countries—and then, having ruined us, the people of Great Britain will, in return, be left to the mercy of Spain and Brazil for their supplies. Our ruin will put into the hands of the slaveholding Spaniards the monopoly of the markets of the world — then will the wickedness of England come down upon its own head, and its iniquities on its own pate, and, instead of sixpence, they will have to pay ninepence a pound for their sugars, whilst, in bitter disappointment and shame, they will learn, when it is too late, the truth of the old adage—" That honesty is the best policy;"—then will England know, by dear-bought experience, that, by protecting the interests of her colonies, she would most certainly have secured her own. It was to stimulate England to this (continued the Reverend Gentleman) that the present meeting was convened, and he could not but think that there were several circumstances connected with it that might be augured as omens of good. There was the place in which they were assembled, that was not without its inspirations—that spacious hall was once the place where the Assembly held its sessions—in that very hall the British act of emancipation of the slaves of Jamaica received the sanction of the colonial legislature ; and may we not hope that the meeting then assembled in the very same place would render it still more distinguished and honourable, by advancing those measures which shall result in the emancipation of the world? There was another feature in the meeting, as interesting as it was novel in this island—that was, the presence of so many ladies. He had heard some intimation that ladies intended to grace the meeting with their presence, and had brought over his wife and daughter to be present at the meeting, but must confess, that as he drew near the town his faith failed. He well knew that it was no uncommon thing for the ladies of England to lend their countenance and valuable aid in every good and benevolent undertaking, but feared the thing was too good to be hoped for in Jamaica, and therefore left them at the house of a friend, lest they should appear singular and alone. He regretted that he had done so ; whilst he rejoiced that the event had not justified his fears. Yes, my lord, (said Mr. O.) we have the ladies

with us—the ladies on our side, and interested in our enterprise; and, with such lovely and invaluable auxiliaries,
defeat is impossible, and victory is certain. When did the
ladies ever undertake a good cause and that cause fail?
Never. They have the clearest heads, the warmest hearts,
and the most ready hands for every enterprise of benevolence;
and I consider the fact of there being here a certain augury
of success. They have felt the justice of our cause—they
have mourned over their ruined and suffering country—and,
casting aside the reserve of their sex, have nobly united with
us in our efforts to obtain universal freedom. There was
another subject (said Mr. O.) connected with his resolution to
which he would refer. It appeared that England and
Portugal had now agreed to abolish the Mixed Commission
Court in Jamaica—he supposed the next step would be to
abolish the British squadron on the coast of Africa, and
allow the Spaniards and Brazilians to have free trade in slaves,
for it appeared to him that they had abolished the Court of
Conscience long ago. What was the consequence? Why,
that the gentlemen composing the Mixed Commission Court
were expected to return to their countries. He had the
honour of being acquainted with both of those gentlemen.
One of them had been known as the firm, intrepid, and consistent friend and defender of the slave for many years; the
name of Turnbull was too intimately connected with anti-
slavery movements not to be known; for them he had
suffered opprobrium, and persecution, and danger, whilst he
stood a living martyr in Cuba for the cause; the other, Signor
Altavilla, he believed, was a gentleman possessing the same
noble spirit; and is it not (said Mr. O.) a token for good
that to the care of such gentlemen as these our memorials
are to be entrusted? He doubted not the zeal and perseverance with which they would fulfil their mission, and
looked with confidence to their advocacy and influence being
successfully employed to secure a favourable result. The
Reverend Gentleman observed, that he felt somewhat jealous
that Spanish Town had taken the lead in the movement—it
had gathered the first sheaf, but he trusted others would

follow and complete the harvest. Spanish Town had certainly stolen a march on Kingston, but they might depend on it Kingston would soon be on their heels. Yes, and he hoped that every other county and parish in the island would speedily follow in the train; that St. James, Trelawny, St. Ann's, and every other parish would unite with heart and hand in the accomplishment of the great object in which all were alike interested. Let us adopt the tactics of our opponents. Let us inundate the House of Commons with statements of our wrongs. Let us make the walls of St. Stephen's echo with our demands for justice. Let us petition! *petition!!* PETITION!!! and give Ministers no sleep to their eyes, nor slumber to their eyelids, until justice be done to the British colonies. We have (said Mr. O.) the means of doing this; even this single meeting possesses a strength and power that it will be hard to resist. We are strong in the individuals who compose it, representing as it does all classes of society in the island. We are strong in intelligence, for we speak from observation and dear-bought experience. We are strong in our union, for every minor distinction is here swallowed up in our one common cause. And, more than all, we are strong in the justice and righteousness of our object, and these make us invincible; for

> " Thrice is he armed who hath his quarrel just;
> And he but naked, though locked up in steel,
> Whose conscience with injustice is corrupted."

Only let us, with these weapons, go forth to the battle, firm, united, and undaunted by fear, and slavery must fall before us; whilst we, who now have met to arrange for the conflict, will soon again have to assemble, that we may join in the shout of victory.

The Baron Von Ketelhoot proposed the fifth resolution, and said, — My lord and gentlemen, after the many excellent speeches which we have had the pleasure to listen to, it would indeed be hard for me to attempt to arrest the attention of this large meeting. But, my lord, there is one observation, suggested by the resolution it has fallen to my lot to support, and which I beg leave to bring to your notice. It is, that there is no cause for depression or despondency. What we now seek, we shall have very soon. When we see what other nations are doing in regard to this great question,—when we observe what progress it has made, within a comparatively short period, in the mind of Europe, and even of America, and how this tendency of the age has betokened itself in the measures taken for the abolition of slavery, by Sweden, Denmark, Portugal, Mexico, and last, not least, by France, we should be wrong to regard the ultimate abolition of slavery,—admitted by all, as it is, to be a question of time,—as being distant from us. My lord, among the Governments of which I have made mention, as having been foremost in following the glorious impulse given by the people of England in the abolition of slavery, I think myself particularly called upon, under the present circumstances, to distinguish the Government of Mexico. The resolution which I shall have the honour to submit for adoption, was intended to be proposed by the illustrious General, whose first act at the head of that Government, after having shaken off the foreign yoke of the Spaniard, was, unlike to his northern neighbour, to proclaim the liberty of the slave. I know that I express the sentiments of General Santa Anna, when I say that it would have afforded him a genuine pleasure could he have added, to-day, the weight of his opinion to your exertions, and could he more particularly have given utterance to his abhorrence of the inconsistency of a nation, which, while it founds its own title of independence on the absolute rights of man, yet withholds those rights from a vast multitude of fellow-men, whom, in defiance of the public opinion of the world, it continues to keep in the most abject state of slavery. A domestic occurrence has unfortunately rendered it impossible for my distinguished friend, the General, to be present, and I beg on his behalf to apologise to the meeting for his absence. I will only make one remark more, in justification of the resolution I hold in my hand. The abolition of the slave-trade and of slavery is certainly a West India question ; but, my lord, it is more,—

it is a European question, which concerns the civilisation of
the world, and the honour of the nineteenth century. We
are, therefore, justified in calling on the other communities
in these seas, to urge their respective Governments to co-
operate with us in this matter. The moment is favourable.
Let us hope, whatever may be the final results of the great
commotion which ushers in the middle of our century, as to
political forms of government, that the practical recognition
of the right of man to his liberty will be, at all events, one of
them ; and that the foul blot of slavery, which past centuries
have transmitted to us, will be wiped out of the European
escutcheon before the nineteenth has much further advanced.
I will now read the resolution :—

5. " That it is desirable and expedient to bring the views of this
meeting under the notice of the inhabitants of the recently emancipated foreign colonies, and more especially of the French, Danish,
and Swedish possessions in these seas, suggesting to them the
advantage of engaging their respective Governments to co-operate
with that of her Majesty in the negotiations with Spain and
Brazil which this meeting recommends ; and that the chairman be
requested to take such measures as his lordship may think convenient for carrying this resolution into effect."

Mr. Charles Farquharson, barrister-at-law, said — My
lord, after the very able addresses which have been made to
this meeting, by gentlemen who have shown themselves so
very competent to deal with the subject, I feel that I would
not be justified in detaining this meeting beyond a very few
moments ; but there is one point which it appears to me has
escaped the attention of those gentlemen who have addressed
you. If we look back into history, to ascertain the motives
which led to the first attempt to abolish the slave-trade, we
will find that it was the civilisation of Africa. If we look at
the treaties, of which so much has been said, we will find
that in entering into those treaties the great object in view
was the civilisation of Africa, of the country whence the
slave-trade has its origin ; we will find that all efforts which
have been made to accomplish this object had the same end
in view. In the despatch of 1830, relative to the expedition

to the Niger, Lord John Russell stated that to be his object, because it was only by the abolition of the slave-trade that any hope of the civilisation of Africa could reasonably be entertained. With this view vessels were fitted out, and negotiations were to be entered into with several chiefs. Need I point out the melancholy failure of that expedition? It went up the Niger, and returned without accomplishing the object, and the only result was the loss of men, and the sacrifice of some of the most distinguished and gallant blood of the nation. All the attempts hitherto tried having failed, others must be made, and I think we are now upon the right track. Upwards of thirty years ago treaties were entered into, by which it was agreed that the traffic in slaves should be entirely abolished by Spain and Brazil, and municipal laws were passed, which rendered it highly penal for any of the subjects of those countries to be engaged in the slave-trade. If those laws had been fully carried out by the respective States, slavery would have long since ceased ; and if those laws and treaties were now strictly enforced, I venture to say that in six months there would be an end to the slave-trade; for no one, except perhaps some very reckless individual, would be found willing to brave the penalty of those laws. But they were not carried out. Great Britain quietly witnessed the infraction of those laws, and of the great treaty of Vienna, and not one act was done to vindicate the rights of Britain, except the issuing of a few useless protocols. It is true, that within the last few years she has entered into negotiations with France to aid in her attempts to suppress the slave-trade ; and it is true that France has sent vessels to cruise on the coast of Africa for that purpose, and that our own officers are exerting themselves in that service ; but to such a pitch of audacity have the slave-traders gone, that steamers are fitted out to assist them in evading the cruisers, and it was only a few months ago that one of the slaving steamers led one of our most active cruisers to leeward, left her there, and took in a large cargo of slaves, which she landed at Brazil; therefore, in such a state of things, it were needless to expect that the slave-trade will be suppressed, unless other means are used better adapted to that end. Now, my lord, in calling upon other nations to comply with the terms of their treaties, we are only carrying out the same principle that was adopted towards Jamaica, when the abolition of slavery in these colonies was desired. Can any one, who remembers the occurrences of 1831 and 1832, deny that agitation was the immediate cause of the emancipation? Had that agitation not taken place, slavery would not have ceased; at all events, for some years. It was agitation and the fever of philanthropy which caused emancipation, and agitation will cause the abolition of the slave-trade. France, we know, will aid us, for her colonies are ruined, and she will no longer submit to that ruin of her colonies, through an unequal competition with slaveholding countries. Sweden and Denmark, when placed under the same unequal competition as ourselves, will soon see the impossibility of carrying on that competition, and that their only chance of succeeding as sugar-cultivating countries will be the suppression of the slave-trade, and ultimately the total abolition of slavery. Let us, then, my lord, call upon other nations to aid us in our efforts—let not our proceedings be confined to this room; let us remember that the largest rivers spring from small sources. We have friends here who are going home: I will mention one of great influence—the Rev. Dr. King; he and others will carry on what we have but begun, and, like the snow-ball, our agitation will increase and our cause will gather strength as it goes, until it will be too strong for resistance. Then the slave-trade will be abolished, and the death-blow of slavery will be struck. Cuba and Brazil will then soon be free, for it is but by the slave-trade that their slaves are kept up. With this view, my lord, I second the resolution, and I am satisfied that if our case is properly placed before the British Government and the British people, their sense of justice will be aroused, and they will see the necessity as well as the justice of enforcing the treaties, for it is only by those means that Great Britain can hope to resuscitate her colonies.

The resolution was then put and carried.

The Rev. Dr. S. H. Stewart, rector of Clarendon, proposed the sixth resolution. He said,—My lord, were I inclined to shrink from the task imposed on me, I might shield myself behind the excuse that I am wholly unprepared to address this meeting, not having been aware I should have been called upon to do so ; but I seek for no excuse. So long as I shall be able to speak, I shall never omit an opportunity of raising my voice, and of exerting any power I may possess, to aid in furthering a cause which, by its success, must benefit the country as well as advance the happiness of the human race. I am satisfied the great and noble object which this meeting aims at must, ere long, be attained. Slavery must be abolished, and those who now remain tied and bound by its fetters must be permitted to go abroad in the enjoyment of unrestrained freedom. My lord, as a churchman, I rejoice most heartily to see your lordship occupying the place you now fill,—presiding over a meeting composed of all the varied classes of this community, united together, without one jarring feeling, to promote so good, so holy a purpose. Amongst the many duties incident to your lordship's exalted station, the one you are now engaged in yields to few in value and importance ; and the readiness and zeal you have brought into the work furnish an additional proof of your lordship's anxiety for their full and faithful discharge. My lord, most of those who have already addressed the meeting have attributed to the continuance of the slave-trade the prostrate condition of this and the other western colonies. There can be no doubt much of the evil we endure may be traced to the impossibility of competing with countries that still employ slave labour ; and, unless the slave-trade be speedily put an end to, our state must become still more disastrous. I come from a part of the island which has suffered much. Estates have been abandoned, and on others cultivation has been narrowed. A large district, which was recently covered with coffee cultivation, has become a waste, and the middle classes of society, who lived in comfort, and many in affluence, are reduced to the verge of want. All descriptions of men, from the proprietor down to the humblest individual, are surrounded with crushing difficulties. Were the abolition of slavery in our own colonies the sole cause, the approval of Almighty God, and the benefits conferred on a large section of our fellow-men, would afford cheering reflections in all the trials we have to undergo. But we cannot patiently endure that our hopes of revival, nay, our prospects of existence, should be blighted by the toleration of this accursed traffic in foreign countries. But, my lord, this need not be; for if justice were done to the British colonies, if Great Britain did justice to herself in this behalf, prosperity would again return to our land. The rendering of that long-due meed of mercy and justice to the African race would mainly help in bringing back again prosperity. I have heard it said that we are hasty in our present proceedings, that we are likely to give offence to those on whom we are about to urge the necessity of enforcing those treaties, the observance of which would ensure to us so many blessings. I do not believe our doing so will give offence. Be that, however, as it may, necessity is laid upon us. When I look around and see the results of the present system—when I see men destitute, their families in the depths of poverty, their children, the rising generation of the country, deprived of the means of obtaining the merest elementary education — schools abandoned, instead of being increased in number and rendered more useful and efficient — when I daily see that those who have, at immense national, and far greater individual sacrifice, been made free, cannot, however they grasp after them, obtain the natural advantages and benefits of freedom— I think we cannot too speedily press this great question on the consideration of those who have the power, and, I firmly believe, have the will, to do what we require. Political State reasons, and complicated questions of international relationships, will yield—nay, must yield—to a simultaneous demand, respectful but still urgent; and thus we shall find, that what might, in the accumulation of great and important interests, be overlooked, shall be deemed worthy of merited consideration and undelayed settlement, in consequence of our importunity. Cultivation that is remunerative, industry that is responded to, and enterprise that is rewarded, are the surest bases upon which a healthful state of society can rest. Let us have these advantages, as far as the fluctuating state of earthly things will permit. Let us have the benefits of England's measures of humane amelioration and commercial freedom, and then we shall be able to defy the temporary embarrassments arising out of our recent social and civil change, as well as the gloomy anticipations of the enemies of Britain's present liberal policy, and the competition of those who, in the enjoyment of denounced and unhallowed advantages, threaten cur ruin. My lord, if this atrocious system be not crushed, our situation must daily become more fearful. The means of social, moral, and religious improvement must gradually be withdrawn; schools and places of religious worship be broken up; industrial habits from desuetude wear out; cultivation be abandoned; the unengaged and unrewarded labourer will quickly descend in the scale of society, dragging down with him all those who depend upon him. This will be the first step; then will come his retirement from the districts where habits calculated to advance, and restraints tending to prevent him, prevail; and thus, the instructions which admonish, the knowledge which enlightens, the influences which regulate, and the righteousness which exalts, being withdrawn, he will sink into worse than his original barbarism, and freedom, which God designed, and man conceded, as a blessing, will become a dire and blighting curse. My lord, having said so much on the general subject of our meeting, I come now to the bearing of the resolution I have undertaken to move.

6. " That the Chevalier Altavilla, Commissary Judge of the Mixed Court, be furnished with a copy of these resolutions, and be requested to transmit the same, with his recommendation, to the Government of her most faithful Majesty."

This brings me, my lord, to another element of this great subject. It is no longer a question entertained by the

English nation alone. Almost all others on the earth have entertained and ruled it as we desire it to be, and I am confident my worthy friend—I am happy to call him so—will not be wanting in his representations to his Queen and Government, and that we shall find in him a faithful and zealous ally. I cannot conclude without ardently praying that the great God, whose service is perfect freedom, may sanction our purpose and bless our exertions, for that alone can ensure success.

The Reverend W. West, Wesleyan minister, from Kingston, having briefly seconded this resolution—

The Chevalier Altavilla, on its being put from the chair, said—My lord, I beg to state to your lordship and this meeting that it will afford me much pleasure to accede to the request contained in the resolution which has just been adopted. I am delighted to see such a large and influential assembly engaged in the promotion of an object so sacred; and knowing how sincerely the Government I have the honour to serve desires the complete abolition of the slave-trade, I am quite sure that the Ministers of her most faithful Majesty will be gratified in the highest degree with the report which I shall have the honour to make to them of your proceedings here this day.

Mr. William Wemyss Anderson, solicitor, from Kingston, and member of Assembly for Portland, proposed the seventh resolution, and said—I should only be happy, my lord, if it were possible that I could make the friends of humanity in England and America hear my voice; and it is only in the hope that what has been said to-day will come before those friends, whom it was my pride and my pleasure to associate with in my boyhood, that I would now add a few words to what has already been said on this occasion. I would make it known to those friends of humanity, that in consequence of those great measures of emancipation and philanthropy, to which many good men have devoted their lives, not having been fully carried out, and faithfully supported, there have resulted consequences fearful to contemplate. Not only, as the Rev. Dr. King has stated, is ignorance, superstition, and vice, stalking through the land, but an amount of misery and wretchedness is pervading the whole country, and is visiting families on all hands. I could, my lord, point to this man who has died of a broken heart from the ruin which this neglect of carrying out the principles of emancipation had entailed on him. I could refer to this man, who has become the inmate of a lunatic asylum from the same cause; to widows and orphans unable to work, and who are driven in the utmost distress and wretchedness to seek the pity of a heartless world. And all this has been the result of the policy pursued towards this country for several years past. I trust, my lord, that these truths will be heard and believed, and that, being heard and believed, we shall speedily obtain redress of our grievances at the hands of the British Government. I believe that, though our rights have been delayed, our cause being just, we must ultimately succeed, for there is a settled principle of justice in England which never can be appealed to in vain; and I feel that in submitting to the people of England the consideration of these great truths, we will again receive their support and co-operation. Before I sit down, my lord, allow me to correct a mistake which has occurred in the "Anti-Slavery Reporter"—a mistake which can only be corrected here, and which, were it not for the importance of the thing, I would not obtrude on the notice of this meeting. There are three lines in the "Anti-Slavery Reporter" of the 1st April, in which it is stated that the West India colonies seek a protective duty of ten shillings per ton over sugars produced in all other countries in the world. This is a mistake, which, I am sure, the respectable editor of that paper, with whom I am acquainted, would not willingly be guilty of. The West India colonies do not claim protection against the sugar of all other countries in the world. What we demand is protection against slave-grown sugar. The resolution I hold in my hand is as follows:—

7. "The friends of humanity in England and America are hereby invited to co-operate with this meeting in attaining the object it has in view."

Mr. George William Gordon, a gentleman of colour, merchant of Kingston, and member of Assembly for St. Thomas in the Vale, in seconding this resolution, expressed his surprise that none of the speakers had urged the measure on the ground of humanity, but that all their arguments were confined to the effect that slavery had upon our own interests ; he declared, that though deeply involved, and connected as he was with sugar estates, that would not be the inducing cause for him to advocate this measure, but he did so on the principles of humanity.

The resolution was then put and carried.

Mr. A. R. Scott proposed the eighth resolution. He said—My lord, after the very able speeches which we have heard delivered, and the unanimous manner in which the resolutions proposed have been passed, it is not necessary for me to do more than to read the one entrusted to me, and to propose it to the meeting.

8. " That these resolutions be inserted in the daily newspapers of the island, and in publications elsewhere at the discretion of the chairman."

Commissary-general Yeoland seconded this resolution. He said—My lord, I rise with peculiar pleasure to second that resolution. After the able manner in which we have been addressed, I assure you, my lord, I feel my heart warm in the great cause. It would indeed be a pity if, after so many years of misery which have been endured by the people of these islands, a ray of hope should not at length enter their breasts that their sufferings were about to end. I trust that the proceedings of this day will produce the happiest results, not only to Jamaica but to all the other islands. I sincerely hope that your beautiful estates will be resumed, that your houses will be again built up, and that you will speedily be freed from the ruinous competition with the slaveholders which now depresses your interests. At this advanced hour it would be indecorous in me to take up the time of the meeting with any lengthened remarks, but I must be allowed, before I sit down, to congratulate you, my lord, on your position at the head of this meeting.

The business of the day having been brought to a close, the Bishop vacated the chair, and the honourable the Attorney-general having been called to it, it was proposed by Mr. George Estridge, manager of the Colonial Bank, seconded by the Rev. J. Phillippo, Baptist minister of Spanish Town—

9. "That the thanks of this meeting be respectfully offered to our Right Reverend Chairman, for the able and impartial manner in which his lordship has presided on this occasion."

The Attorney-general, in moving the thanks of the meeting to the Lord Bishop, said,—My lord, it affords me singular satisfaction to propose to the meeting the resolution of their thanks, the expression of their sincerest regard, and the testimony of their unbounded respect for your lordship. My lord, not alone of the gentlemen of Jamaica is this a meeting—it is, my lord, one in which every church, of every denomination of religion, formed for the worship of the great God of nature, is represented. I cannot, indeed, express to you what pleasure I feel in seeing you, accompanied not alone by your own respectable clergy, but surrounded, too, by those of every other denomination of dissenting faith. That the Bishop of the Established Church should be the object of the universal people's esteem, and most true regard, is a matter, not of greater congratulation for those of that Church, than of high satisfaction to every person connected with the Government of the State.

The resolution having been carried unanimously,

The Bishop said—Allow me, gentlemen, to acknowledge the compliment you have been pleased to pay me for my poor services in the chair. In dismissing this meeting, which is all that is now left for me to do, allow me to assure you, by the pledge of an honest man, that I will do all in my power to carry out our object; all that my tongue can speak—all that my pen can write, shall be done for the accomplishment of the great end which we have in view.

OPINIONS OF THE PUBLIC PRESS.

Thus happily terminated the first of those great meetings, through which the public mind of Jamaica has been so earnestly and harmoniously expressed on the subject of the enforcement of the existing treaties with Spain and Brazil for the suppression of the slave-trade. It is a great mistake, on the part of one or two of the London newspapers, to imagine that this movement had its origin with the planting or mercantile interest of Jamaica. When the first step was taken, and the machinery once set in motion, it was not of course to be supposed that because this measure of justice and humanity, thus earnestly demanded, was destined to produce substantial benefit to the material interests of the country, those who might expect to share in that benefit should either throw cold water on the proceedings, or stand wholly aloof from them. In point of fact, however, the religious and moral interests involved in the question, as represented by the bishop and his clergy of the established church, the dissenting ministers of every denomination, the judges of the land, and other public functionaries, have been much more zealously and efficiently supported, than those views of the subject which are calculated to promote the material prosperity of the island. Those over-clever persons who have undertaken to recommend the direct encouragement of the Brazilian slave-trade, by means of the repeal of the British statute which imposes certain obstacles in its way—in the face of the fact, that a similar statute, affecting the slave-trade of Portugal, has been entirely successful, in accomplishing its suppression—have been somewhat too eager in ferreting out a few hasty sentences from the speeches of one or two of the gentlemen who addressed these meetings, for the purpose of making it appear that the whole movement was an anti-free-trade movement, and that protection and discriminating duties were all that was sought for. As far as we have yet come in our history, it is manifest that nothing has transpired to justify such an assumption ; and it will be found in the sequel that the speakers who were provoked to speak somewhat irreverently of the ultra-free-trade measure of the right hon. member for Manchester, on the subject of the slave-trade, were neither planters nor merchants, but ministers of religion,—the one being a Jewish rabbi, the other a Presbyterian parson. In a country like Jamaica, where every topic of any public interest is so apt to assume a controversial aspect, the unanimity which has prevailed throughout this discussion is undoubtedly its most remarkable feature. Even the habitual hostility of rival newspapers has been appeased ; and writers who were never known to agree on any one subject, are now seen fraternising, and forgiving each other their political offences, because their effusions on this subject have been so honest, so agree. able, and so true.

In corroboration of this statement we refer to the following articles from the daily newspapers :—

(*From the " Dispatch."*)

The meeting, of which we record the particulars in our paper of to-day, will long be remembered in the annals of Jamaica. Its internal aspect was as gratifying to the eye, as the purpose for which it was summoned was hallowed and exalted. The hall was filled with an audience so respectable that the utmost decorum prevailed amongst its least distinguished members, whilst around the Right Rev. Chairman sat the leading personages of the island, and amongst them many of the sex whose sensibility ever recognises distress, and whose hand is ever open to charity. Altogether, Jamaica has never witnessed such an assemblage, so conspicuous for its eloquence, its harmony, and its beauty. Many of the speeches were excellent, and, in truth, we shall be deemed

guilty of no injustice in venturing to select for particular
commendation those of our Bishop, of Dr. King, and Mr.
Oughton, whose eloquence was either chaste, classical, and
elegant, or distinguished for its fluency, declamation, and
vigour. The Vice-chancellor's, too, was most valuable for
its information; and Mr. Osborn made a speech of such
sound sense, embellished with humour, as demonstrates our
contemporary to be one of us at heart, in spite of his occa-
sional aberrations. We forgive him all his political sins for
this one effusion, as it was so honest, so agreeable, and so
true. But, indeed, all performed their parts with credit
and discretion, and this is the more to be applauded as we
believe the mover and seconder of the resolutions were, in
general, called upon on the sudden, which must be very
trying to all but practised speakers, and even they will be
gainers by a little previous meditation.

But, as we have mentioned the principal speakers, we cannot
refrain from alluding to one gentleman, whose exertions,
we believe, gave symmetry to the meeting, though he made
no display himself. He will forgive us for particularly re-
cording the name of Turnbull amongst those present, though
his friends, who know his energy of character, his singleness
of purpose, and his uncompromising hatred to oppression,
would only be surprised at anything short of a death-bed
withdrawing him from the spot on which men assemble for
an object of benevolence.

The speeches themselves require no elucidation at our
hands. Perhaps as, since the emancipation, two periods,
comprising the years 1845 and 1848-9, have been remarkable, as testing the great experiments of the admission of
foreign free and foreign slave labour sugar into England,
something might have been said respecting them by way of
contrast, as they exemplify the operation of two principles
that are antagonistic in their nature. An allusion, indeed,
bordering on them, was made by Mr. Anderson, for the
purpose of correcting a very material error into which the
"Anti-Slavery Reporter" had fallen, in one of its recent
numbers; for it there asserts that West Indians injudiciously

required a protection of 10s. against all foreign sugar, whether slave or free. Nothing can be more incorrect. We believe some Mauritius planters asked for it, in their examination before the late Committee of the House of Commons; but they were not well-informed men, and certainly their doctrine has ever been repudiated by the great body of West Indians. All that we have asked, or ask for, is protection against SLAVERY.

It may not be unprofitable to compare the two periods of 1845 and 1849. In the former, the imperial act had not long been passed admitting foreign free-labour sugar into England, with a reduction on our duty, and then agriculture was extending itself, commerce was flourishing, and hope beamed upon the country. But now, by the act of 1846, the simoom of the desert—the hot breath of slavery—has been let loose, and is passing over us, withering the fruits of the earth, and palsying the hand of industry. But in the midst of our deepest distress we have never despaired, through feeling that the time must come when the justice, the humanity, the power of the mother country, would exert themselves to destroy the monstrous evil. To quicken its sense of justice—to kindle its feelings of humanity—and to rouse its slumbering power, the meeting was held on Thursday; and a voice will go forth from it, appalling as the hand-writing on the wall, to announce to slavery that its days are numbered, and, like the doom of the eastern tyrant, as described in the awful chapters, that that " which opened not its house to the prisoners," and " made the earth to tremble," " shall be brought down to the grave, whilst the whole earth is at rest."

High and holy as are the objects of the meeting, they are still further consecrated, and have a greater warranty of success in its having been presided over and enlightened by that church which has ever led the van in the great movements of the human mind. Nor had Wickliff a deeper satisfaction, nor Luther a prouder triumph, in combating and dispelling the medieval darkness, than Spencer must enjoy in seeing his name enrolled amongst the benefactors of our

race, for breaking chains more galling than those of superstition, because riveted by more sordid and oppressive hands.
His example must operate through this Archipelago of
islands; and "JAMAICA EXPECTS EVERY BISHOP TO DO HIS
DUTY," should echo from one sea to another, and be rever-
berated to England, as the memorable signal that filled our
men with confidence, and carried death to our enemies, was
borne, on a shout, from ship to ship, at Trafalgar. The
subject has led us into more elevated expressions than we
have been in the habit of using; but we cannot altogether
repress the exultation we feel at seeing that which too long
has been regarded as a mere visionary longing, assume
shape, consistency, and firmness, and be put in motion by an
energy and intelligence that cannot fail to attain its end.
SLAVERY MUST FALL, and, when it falls, JAMAICA WILL
FLOURISH.

From the " Morning Journal."

We mentioned, in our mail edition of the 23rd of May,
that a public meeting was announced to take place in Spanish
Town, to consider the effect produced on this country by
the non-observance of the treaties for the suppression of
the slave-trade, and to devise such a measure as may tend
to promote at once the great interests of humanity, and the
relief of the intertropical possessions of the Crown from
the deep distress in which they are now involved. That
meeting took place on the 24th of May, and was the most
numerously and respectably attended of any that has ever
been held in the capital. It was presided over by the Lord
Bishop of this diocese. A report of the proceedings which
took place at it will be found in our impression of the 28th
ultimo. The resolutions which were agreed to by it will be
found in that of the 26th. We give the following as the
most important of the series :—

" 1. That so long as the sugar planters of Cuba, Porto Rico,
and Brazil, in defiance of the laws of their respective countries,
and of the treaties by which the Spanish and Brazilian Governments stand bound to her Majesty, are permitted to reinforce, by
fresh drains from slavery, the means of increasing their profits, it

is hopeless, in countries so thinly peopled as Jamaica, Guiana,
and Trinidad, for the proprietors of the soil to persevere in its
cultivation.

" 2. That, in the opinion of this meeting, the plan which was
embodied by her Majesty's principal Secretary of State for Foreign
Affairs, in the draft of a convention with Spain, and transmitted
to her Majesty's Minister at Madrid, on the 25th of May, 1840,
as appears from the papers on the slave-trade, presented in that
year to Parliament, by her Majesty's command, is practical and
feasible; and if now urged on the Spanish and Brazilian Governments with suitable energy, would prove beneficial and effective, in
enabling the emancipated colonies of Great Britain to meet and
overcome the competition in the home markets, and other countries
of Europe, on the equal terms to which they are about to be
exposed by the Sugar Duties Act of 1846."

Our fellow-colonists to windward, and the philanthropists
of Great Britain, will perceive that Jamaica is moving in
earnest on the subject of the enforcement of the treaties for
the suppression of the slave-trade. And it is no party
movement—no effort made by planters and persons interested
in estates for their own benefit. There were very few such
present at the great meeting in Spanish Town, and only two
at the meeting in St. Andrew's. Clergymen of the Established
Church, with the Bishop at their head—Baptist, Wesleyan,
London Missionary, Presbyterian, Independent, Congrega-
tional, and Wesleyan Association Ministers, with laymen of
every class and creed, and all shades of political opinions—
from High Tory to Radical—Protectionist to ultra Free-
trader—are banding themselves together in this attempt to
vindicate the rights of humanity, and to obtain justice for
the colonies. The other parishes will respond to the call
which has been made, and by public meetings show their
approval of the step that has been taken, and willing-
ness to co-operate in the attempt to induce her Majesty's
Government to adopt some efficient measure for enforcing
the treaties in question. And we have no doubt Guiana,
Trinidad, and, indeed, all the British sugar colonies, will do
likewise. Hitherto, the Government has manifested the
most unaccountable indifference in this matter, if it has not

actually connived at the treachery and bad faith of the Spanish and Brazilian Governments. Its attention has been repeatedly called to the subject, but without effect, and nothing short of the most urgent importunity will induce it to move with energy in reference to it. Let the question be brought to an issue as quickly as possible. It cannot too soon be known what the result is to be. The intelligence of the Protectionist meeting in London, to back up the Lords in their intention to reject the bill to amend the Navigation Laws, has been received, by all who look forward to the return of that party to power, and the restoration of the sugar monopoly as a necessary consequence, with delight. Those who put no faith in parties, and doubt the restoration of the monopoly in question, even though the Protectionists should succeed in wresting power from the Whigs, look upon the entire proceeding as one intended, by certain leading men of the former, to serve themselves and their friends. Reliance upon Government—upon the Minister of the day—is the rock upon which the West Indians have split; and, although parties in England may retain their predilections for Ministerial favour, the colonists—that is, the men residing in the dependencies of the empire—will perceive the necessity for resting upon something more enduring and effectual. The condition of Ireland, and of the West India colonies, at the present moment, is proof of the folly of that course. It is time that the latter let go the leading-strings, and insist upon being placed in their proper position. Of course, all will be anxious to learn how Lord Stanley gets on with his attempt at restoring protection. His lordship, doubtless, has perceived the ground slipping from under his feet—the tenant farmers becoming restive, and throwing themselves into the arms of the free traders and financial reformers—and has determined upon making a desperate effort to recover lost ground. Now or never, is his lordship's watchword—now or never will be responded by the free traders. The struggle will be a fierce one. We wish the mother country safely through it. In the meantime, everything else will be neglected, and trade will be injured.

In compliance with the request contained in the resolution to that effect, her Majesty's Commissioners for the suppression of the slave-trade took an early opportunity of waiting on his excellency the Governor, Sir Charles Grey, with the memorial to the Queen, which was duly presented by the Secretary of State for the Colonies, and was most graciously received by her Majesty, as will be seen by the following correspondence :—

Sir Charles Grey to the Lord Bishop.

King's House, August 17, 1849.

MY LORD,—With reference to the address to her Majesty, passed at a meeting, in May last, at which your lordship presided, praying that a due observance may be enforced of the treaties for the suppression of the slave-trade by which the Crowns of Brazil and Spain are bound, and which, at your lordship's request, I transmitted, on the 8th of June last, I have now the honour to put into your lordship's hands a copy of a despatch from her Majesty's principal Secretary of State for the Colonies, intimating, that the address has been very graciously received by the Queen. Enclosed, also, is a copy of an answer, which has been returned to certain inhabitants of Barbadoes, who had presented a somewhat similar petition, and which expresses the sentiments of her Majesty's Ministers in relation to this object.

I have the honour to be, my lord,

Your lordship's faithful, humble Servant,

CHARLES EDWARD GREY, Governor.

The Honourable and Right Reverend
    the Lord Bishop of Jamaica.

(COPY.)

Downing Street, 9th July, 1849.

SIR,—I have to acknowledge the receipt of your despatch of the 8th ultimo, No. 58, transmitting an address to her Majesty, passed at a meeting of inhabitants of Jamaica, presided over by the Lord Bishop, praying that a due observance may be enforced of the treaties for the suppression of the slave-trade by which the Crowns of Brazil and Spain are bound.

I request that you will inform his lordship that I have laid this address before the Queen, and that her Majesty was pleased to receive it very graciously.

You will further acquaint his lordship that the matter will receive the serious consideration of her Majesty's Government, and I transmit to you a copy of an answer returned to certain inhabitants of Barbadoes, who had presented a somewhat similar petition, which may be communicated to his lordship.

I have the honour to be, &c., &c.,

(Signed)   GREY.

The Right Honourable Sir Charles Grey.

(TRANSCRIPT COPY.)

Downing Street, 1st May, 1849.

SIR,—Having referred for the consideration of Viscount Palmerston a copy of the memorial from Barbadoes, relative to an enforcement of the treaties for the suppression of the slave-trade, transmitted to me in your despatch, No. 12, of the 20th of February, I have to request that, in addition to the communication which you were instructed, by my despatch, No. 30, of the 9th instant, to make to the petitioners in reply, you will convey to them an assurance that her Majesty's Government fully share the sentiments of detestation expressed by the petitioners of the criminal practice of man-stealing, commonly called the slave-trade, and that her Majesty's Government have not relaxed in their efforts to put a stop to the perpetration of this crime; that the slave-trade of several nations of Europe has already entirely ceased; that Holland has abandoned this practice, and that France and Denmark have not only left off slave trading, but have emancipated their slaves; that Sweden also has not only abandoned slave trading, but so long ago as 1847 had nearly completed the emancipation of her slaves; that the Portuguese flag has almost ceased to be used to cover slave-trade undertakings, and that the importation of slaves into Cuba has, of late years, been extremely small; that the chief remaining offender in this matter is Brazil, and that her Majesty's Government are in communication with the Brazilian Government, with a view of obtaining from that Government a more faithful performance of the treaty engagements by which the Brazilian Government is bound to prevent Brazilian subjects from being engaged, directly or indirectly, in slave-trade.

You will further acquaint the petitioners that her Majesty's Government do not confine themselves to exercising on the coast of Africa those measures of naval police which are warranted by treaties between Great Britain and other maritime States, but they are actively engaged in negotiating with the native chiefs on the western coast of Africa, treaties binding those chiefs to prevent slaves being exported from the territories under their respective control. The number of such treaties already concluded is considerable; and there is reason to believe that the engagements so contracted have, in general, been well fulfilled. Her Majesty's Government have also recently acknowledged and made a treaty with the Republic of Liberia, and that State has entirely driven out slave-trade from a considerable extent of coast from which formerly it was much carried on.

The people of Barbadoes will thus see that her Majesty's Government are strenuously directing their attention to the attainment of the object which the petitioners have at heart, and the progress which has been made towards its accomplishment encourages the hope that further and greater success will be arrived at.

I have, &c., &c.,

(Signed)   GREY.

Sir William Colebrooke, &c., &c.

The petitions to the two Houses of Parliament were transmitted in due course to Viscount Palmerston, who, on the 9th of July, transferred the petition to the Lords to the Bishop of Oxford, with an intimation that it was the desire of the petitioners that their petition should be presented by him to the House; and, on the 27th of the same month, Lord Palmerston presented the petition to the House of Commons in person. In furtherance of the same object, we understand that the Right Reverend Chairman, having addressed a letter to the Bishop of Oxford on the subject, has recently received a very satisfactory answer, to the effect that the petition will be presented to the Upper House at the commencement of the next session of Parliament, and that its prayer will receive the cordial support of the Right Reverend Prelate.

The following is the public correspondence which has passed on this subject:—

Her Majesty's Commissioners to Viscount Palmerston, G.C.B.,
&c., &c.

Jamaica, 6th June, 1849.

MY LORD,—We have the honour to report that a public meeting was held in our colonial capital of Spanish Town, on the Queen's birth-day, on the requisition of a number of persons of the highest respectability, " for the purpose of inviting the inhabitants of Jamaica to consider the effect produced on this country by the non-observance of the treaties for the suppression of the slave-trade by which Spain and Brazil are bound to her Majesty; and of devising such a measure as may tend to promote at once the great interests of humanity, and the relief of the intertropical possessions of the Crown from the deep distress in which they are now involved." The terms of this requisition, together with the names of the requisitionists, your lordship will find in a copy of the " Jamaica Dispatch " newspaper of the 24th of May last, addressed to your lordship under a separate envelope, and marked No. 1.

The " Morning Journal " newspaper of the 26th of May, also addressed separately, and marked No. 2, contains a copy of the resolutions adopted at that meeting, by the fourth of which your lordship will find that "the British members of the Mixed Court for the suppression of the slave-trade established in Jamaica, but about to be abolished, were requested to take charge of the addresses to the three branches of the British Legislature previously adopted, and to lend their aid, on their return to Europe, in giving them effect."

The "Dispatch" of the 26th of May, and the "Journal" of the 28th, marked Nos. 3 and 4, contain reports of the proceedings of this meeting, to which we take the liberty of entreating your lordship's attention; and, although we did not take any personal share in the discussion, we trust that your lordship will not disapprove of the fact of our presence on an occasion so deeply interesting to us.

Since the date of the meeting, we have received from the Lord Bishop, who acted as chairman on the occasion, the memorial to her Majesty the Queen, and the petitions to the Houses of Lords and Commons, with a repetition of the request contained in the fourth resolution; and having waited on Governor Sir Charles Grey with the memorial to her Majesty, his excellency was good enough to assure us that it should be transmitted in due course to the Secretary of State for the colonial department. A copy of that memorial forms the enclosure No. 5.

The petition to the Commons, with its respectable array of signatures, we take the liberty of transmitting to your lordship's address, under a separate envelope, marked No. 6, in the hope that your lordship will have no objection to present it in person to the honourable House.

And the petition to the Lords, which is conceived in similar terms, and which our Right Reverend Chairman was desirous of having transmitted for presentation to the Lord Bishop of Oxford, we take the liberty of recommending to your lordship's attention and care, and which will be found addressed to your lordship, under a separate envelope, marked No. 7.

We have, &c.,

(Signed)   D. TURNBULL,
A. R. HAMILTON.

Viscount Palmerston to her Majesty's Commissioners.

Foreign Office, August 1st, 1849.

GENTLEMEN,—I have received your despatch, No. 13, of the 6th of June, and the petitions therein enclosed, from the inhabitants of Jamaica, to the Houses of Lords and Commons, praying for the suppression of the slave-trade of Cuba and Brazil.

I have, in reply, to acquaint you that I transmitted to the Bishop of Oxford, on the 9th ultimo, the petition addressed to the House of Lords, and I, at the same time, acquainted him that it was the desire of the petitioners that their petition should be submitted by him to the House.

The petition to the House of Commons I had the honour of presenting to that House on the 27th ultimo.

I am, with great truth, &c.,

(Signed)   PALMERSTON.

Her Majesty's Commissioners to the Bishop of Jamaica.

Spring Garden, St. Andrew's,
Sept. 1st, 1849.

MY LORD,—Having received, by the packet which has just arrived, two very interesting despatches from Viscount Palmerston, on the subject of the proceedings which have been taking place in Jamaica for promoting the enforcement of existing treaties for the suppression of the slave-trade, we have the honour to transmit, for the information of your lordship, and of all who may feel any interest in the subject, a copy of one of these despatches, acquainting us that his lordship had transmitted to the Bishop of Oxford, on the 9th of July, the petition to the House of Lords from the great public meeting held in Spanish Town on the 24th of May last, over which your lordship was good enough to preside, and stating that the noble Secretary had at the same time informed the Right Reverend Prelate that it was the desire of the petitioners that their petition should be submitted by him to the House.

Lord Palmerston informs us, also, that he had himself the honour of presenting the petition, from the same meeting, to the House of Commons, on the 27th of July.

We have, &c.,

(Signed)   D. TURNBULL,
A. R. HAMILTON.

The Hon. and Right Rev. the
   Lord Bishop of Jamaica.

The Bishop of Jamaica to Her Majesty's Commissioners.

Charlottenberg, 4th September.

GENTLEMEN,—I have had the pleasure of receiving your letter under date of the 1st inst., and the accompanying copy of a despatch addressed to you by the Secretary of State for Foreign Affairs, dated on the 1st ultimo, by which I am happy to learn that the two petitions, agreed on at the meeting of the inhabitants of Jamaica, over which I had the honour to preside in Spanish Town, have been presented respectively to the House of Lords and to the House of Commons, by the parties to whom they were entrusted.

I am also much gratified to collect from your letter that the proceedings of that meeting, convened for the purpose of considering the best means of obtaining the enforcement of the treaties regarding the suppression of the slave-trade, have been honoured with the approbation of the noble Secretary; and I have good hope that the measures contemplated by her Majesty's Government will result in the final extinction of a traffic which must be viewed with detestation and abhorrence by every considerate friend of humanity.

I have, &c.,

(Signed)   AUBREY G. JAMAICA.

THE CASE OF THE EMANCIPADOS.

We have seen that in the original conventions negotiated with Portugal, as well as with Spain, the British plenipotentiaries fell into the mistake of committing the guardianship of the emancipated negroes to the foreign Governments with whom they were in treaty; and that, until these conditions were altered, in the case of Spain, by the clauses of the Clarendon convention, which transferred the guardianship of the Africans found in slavers, captured at a later period, and condemned by the Mixed Courts, to the Government whose cruiser had made the capture, the trust had, in every case, been most grievously abused; insomuch, that the condition of the class became infinitely worse than if they had never received the supposed benefits of emancipation.

The reason of this will be obvious, on a moment's reflection. In the case of a slave, just as in that of a horse, or any other beast of draught or burden, it becomes, in general, the interest of the owner to maintain his living chattel in good working condition, and to preserve its life as long as the animal will command any price in the market. To this rule there are exceptions, even in England, in spite of the Acts of Parliament against cruelty to the brute creation; as in the case of postmasters, who, to gratify the prevailing taste for rapid motion, will knowingly shorten the average term of the lives of their coach-horses, in order to secure an increased rate of speed.

The same is the case with the human beings who are set to work in the sugar fields of Cuba and Brazil. With these hard-hearted owners, as with the postmaster at home, it is a mere question of calculation, whether it is cheaper to work his slave to death, in a given number of years, by hard work, short commons, and the privation of needful repose; or, by a more moderate system, give the man or the beast a chance of preserving his health, and prolonging his existence to the average assigned by the Creator to the species.

But, in the one case as in the other, the chances of the thinking animal, as of the brute, will be materially altered, if it should turn out that the task-master has not acquired *a life interest* in his chattel, but has paid for his services by the year, or for any limited term. This, then, is the sad condition of the so-called emancipados. With them, the system is to sell their services for a term of five years, to any one who is willing to pay, in advance, the established and invariable price of 153 dollars for the assignment. On the expiry of the term, the emancipado is returned to the seat of Government, under a heavy penalty; or evidence of his death is produced, to the satisfaction of the authorities, who, having a direct interest in his return, take all possible care that no fraud is perpetrated, by the substitution of a dead slave for a living emancipado.

Now, as five years in the life of a man is not more than one in that of a horse, it may be conceived what care would be taken of a post-horse, if the jobber to whom he was hired had no interest in his existence beyond the year. And if, in the same stable, a certain number of the horses were the property of the postmaster, while the remainder were thus hired by the year, is it to be doubted on which class the weight of the labour would fail, when fast and killing work was to be done? Now, this is precisely the case with the unhappy emancipados, who are handed over to the first applicant, ready with his nine doubloons to pay for the assignment, without much regard to his character for tender mercy, because there is not the least probability that the individual who makes the assignment will still be in office when, at the end of five years, it comes to be renewed.

If, therefore, it should so happen that the assignee of the emancipado is also an owner of slaves, it may safely be assumed as a fact, that the hard work in the establishment will be thrown upon those in whose permanent welfare and longevity the master has no personal interest. The natural consequence is, that in slaveholding countries, among men and women of servile condition, there are degrees of degradation below that of the ordinary domestic, or even the field slaves, among whom the very term "*Emancipado Ingles*" has become a term of reproach, and a bye-word.

For a period of fifteen years, between 1820, when Lord Cowley's convention came into operation, and 1835, the date of the Clarendon treaty, some 12,000 Africans became entitled to their personal freedom, in virtue of the fact of their capture by British cruisers, and the solemn adjudication of their right by British judges, in the Court of Mixed Commission. Of this number, according to the customary average, the proportion of females was, probably, about 3,500; and as the condition of the children follows that of the mother, it is manifest that the Government of her Catholic Majesty are bound to render an exact account, not only of the original 12,000, of both sexes, but of the direct descendants of the female portion of them.

Now, it has been shown that an exact account of this unfortunate class of persons has really been kept in the office of the Captain-general at the Havanna; not for the purpose of watching over their interests, and securing them in the possession of their freedom, as the treaties had stipulated, but for the very opposite purpose of maintaining a constant surveillance over the parties to whom the assignment had been made; not in the interest of the victim, but in that of the Captain-general and his subordinates, who claimed and exercised a right of reversion, in the event of the emancipado surviving the current term of assignment.

The declared object of the register required by the treaty was, that it might serve as a general return, which the Captain-general was bound to deliver every six months to the Mixed Commission, in order to show the existence of the emancipated negroes, the decease of such as had died, the improvement of their condition, and the progress made in their instruction, both religious and moral, as also in the arts of life.

And as the principal object of the treaty was no other than that of improving the condition of these unhappy victims of avarice, the high contracting parties, animated with the same sentiments of humanity, agreed, that if in future it should appear necessary to adopt new measures for obtaining the same benevolent end, in consequence of those laid down turning out inefficacious, the said high contracting parties engaged to consult together, and agree upon other means, better adapted for the complete attainment of the object proposed.

It was not until the close of the year 1840, when a Consul, not in any manner concerned in mercantile pursuits, arrived at the Havanna, for the express purpose of watching over the execution of the slave-trade treaties, already concluded, or in the course of negotiation between Spain and Great Britain, that any serious attempt was made on the spot to carry their stipulations into effect.

At that period the office of Captain-general of Cuba was held by the Prince of Anglona, a poor Spanish grandee, with an Italian title, whose known object in accepting the appointment was to make a rapid fortune, partly by the perquisites exacted from the slave dealers, in the form of a capitation tax on the victims they had succeeded in landing, and partly from the established fee of nine doubloons on the re-assignment of each emancipado. In that particular year the fresh importations were considerable, and the sum arising from re-assignments chanced to be greater than usual,—a fact which was probably well known at Madrid before the Prince's appointment. The fixed salary of the Captain-general is just $25,000 a-year; but, although the Prince of Anglona was only one year in office, he is believed to have carried off with him not less than half a million of dollars, the fruit of his illegal exactions, under these two branches of income, in direct violation of the treaties by which the Government, of which he was the servant, were bound to that of Great Britain.

The new Consul was not many days in the Havanna when he received a visit from a Spanish gentleman, whose acquaintance he had formed two years before, at the table of a British officer, Dr. Madden, than whom a more determined hater of oppression has never held office under the Crown. In the course of this visit, the Spanish gentleman, whose name it is not convenient to record in these pages, recalled to the Consul's attention the purport of a former conversation which had occurred between them, on the subject of the iniquitous system pursued by the authorities with reference to the emancipados. His own cause of quarrel was, that, some seven years before, he had obtained an assignment of three or four of this class of persons, at the established rate of nine doubloons each, for five years' service. At the end of the term, he had been compelled to restore them to the Captain-general, very much against his will; because his wish was, having conceived an affection for them, not to retain them in his own service, but to prevent them from falling into the hands of hard task-masters, and, in fact, to secure them in the possession of the freedom to which he knew they were justly entitled. Finding this to be impracticable, he had consented, before the new Consul's arrival, to make the Captain-general a second payment of nine doubloons each, for a second term of service; and having parted with his money reluctantly, from a kind motive toward his people, he felt a high degree of irritation against the authorities, whom he charged with all sorts of atrocities with reference to this class of persons, furnishing, at the same time, the clearest evidence that considerable numbers of them had been hired, or sold out in this way, for terms of five years each, not once or twice only, but three, and even four times; thus levying a sum for the same individual, in the name of hire, much greater than the highest price demanded in the market for a life interest, or, in the case of a female, for the fee simple of herself and her descendants in perpetuity.

This was just such a case as was needed, to place the iniquity of the whole system in a clear and striking light before the world ; and there was, therefore, no hesitation on the part of the Consul to avail himself of the information and the evidence thus afforded, from a quarter which was, fortunately, above suspicion. Having selected, therefore, the strongest instance he could find from among those brought under his notice, he lost no time in stating it to the Captain-general, and in demanding not only future freedom, but, for his past sufferings, pecuniary redress, for the much wronged individual, including, of course, repayment of the money, thirty-six doubloons, which had actually been received by the Captain-general, or his predecessors, as the price of four successive assignments.

The individual case taken up was that of Gavino, an African, of the Lecumi nation, who had been nominally emancipated sixteen years before, and for whose services successive Captains-general had received, from the party to whom he had been assigned, not less than $612. In this instance the assigner was a lady, who, instead of having her charge instructed in the principles of the Christian religion, or in the arts of life, had employed him, from the first, in the laborious occupation of a water-carrier, which, of course, required no long apprenticeship ; and, with regard to his religious belief, he was, to all intents and purposes, just as much a pagan as on the day of his being landed from the slave ship.

But Gavino was still in the prime of life, of a robust constitution, and endowed with herculean strength, so that he was able to sell more water than most of his fellows, the *aguadores*, whose occupation would be gone as soon as the

Havanna should be supplied with water more economically, by a proper ramification of hydraulic apparatus. The exaction from Gavino, besides maintaining himself from his surplus earnings, was at the rate of a dollar a day for every day in the week—for Sunday shone no Sabbath on him. During the whole of his career he had never once been disabled by sickness, and he had already brought home to his mistress not less than $5,840 in hard cash, leaving a clear balance in her favour of $5,228, after paying the stipulated hire ; and had Gavino remained in captivity to the end of his allotted term, her clear profit, from this single emancipado, would have reached the respectable sum of £1,337 12s.

It was not to be expected that a practitioner so sharp as the Prince of Anglona would receive a demand like this, which struck at the very root of an important branch of his personal income, with marked favour or complacency. In his answer to the application, in the form of a written despatch, his excellency's feelings were suffered to transpire in a tone and manner which scarcely became a personage of his hereditary rank and present vice-regal dignity ; and he concluded his communication by intimating to the Consul, that if he presumed to interfere in such matters any further, it would be his excellency's painful duty to expel him from the island, under the convenient diplomatic periphrasis of sending him his passport. Nothing daunted by a threat which the Prince had not the courage to execute, the Consul pursued the even tenor of his way, and had the satisfaction to be firmly supported in his proceedings by the enlightened chief under whose orders he had the honour to serve, as will appear by the following correspondence :—

Viscount Palmerston to Mr. Aston.
Foreign Office, March 4th, 1841.
It appears that in the year 1824 Gavino was emancipated from slavery by sentence of the Mixed British and Spanish

Court of Commission at the Havanna; but that, nevertheless, he has been held in a state of bondage ever since, contrary to the engagements contracted by her Catholic Majesty with the Crown of Great Britain, by the treaty of the 23rd of September, 1817.

For the 7th article of the regulations for the Mixed Commissions attached to that treaty states, that the slaves emancipated by the Commission should be delivered over to the Government on whose territory the Commission which adjudged them is established, to be employed as servants or free labourers; and each Government bound itself to guarantee the liberty of such portion of those individuals as should be consigned to its care. But, in Gavino's case, and, as her Majesty's Government firmly believe, in almost every other case, the provisions of the treaty, in this respect, have been unfulfilled.

Gavino has been assigned over to a master four several times, for a period of five years at each assignment; the wages which Gavino has earned have not been given to him, but to his master; and Gavino is now in the course of his fourth assignment, and employed as a slave in the laborious occupation of a water-carrier at the Havanna.

You will by note communicate to the Spanish Government the accompanying papers, and, after stating the principal facts of the case, you will express the extreme regret of her Majesty's Government at the tone and contents of the letter which the Governor of Cuba addressed to her Majesty's Consul upon the subject, on the 22d December, 1840, and which her Majesty's Government cannot doubt will be marked by the disapprobation of the Spanish Government; for her Majesty's Government cannot believe that the Government of Spain will permit the Governor of Cuba to attempt to deter Mr. Turnbull from performing his duty, by threatening him with expulsion from Cuba. Her Majesty's Government must also observe, that Mr. Turnbull had a full right to receive Gavino, and to hear his complaint; and they are much surprised that the Government of Cuba should question that right.

You will, in conclusion, state, that the British Government

demands, as a right, from the Spanish Government, the immediate freedom of all the negroes who have been emancipated in Cuba, by sentence of the Mixed Commission, since the treaty of 1817, but who appear hitherto to have been retained in practical slavery by the authorities of Cuba, in direct violation of the solemn engagements of the Spanish Crown.

Her Majesty's Government cannot allow themselves to believe that, when the Cabinet of Madrid shall see, as is proved by this correspondence, that the treaty with Great Britain has, in this matter, been set at nought; that the faith of the Spanish Crown has been broken; that its engagements have been deliberately and systematically, and during a long course of time, violated; and that this has been done for the illegal profit of those public officers whose duty it was to have carried the treaty into execution; her Majesty's Government cannot doubt that when the Cabinet of Madrid shall see all this, it will hasten to redeem the honour of the Spanish Crown, by immediately putting an end to these monstrous abuses.

But it is evident that these emancipated negroes cannot hope for security from oppression as long as they remain in Cuba. Her Majesty's Government, therefore, demand that they shall all be brought before the Mixed Commission, according to the lists deposited in the archives of the Commission, and that they shall then, if they wish it, be handed over to the Superintendent of liberated Africans, to be by him sent to a British colony, where they would, by law, as well as by treaty, be free.

Her Majesty's Government hope and trust that immediate orders to this effect will be sent to the Governor of Cuba; and, in the meanwhile, directions will be sent to her Majesty's Commissioners, and to the Superintendent of liberated Africans, to place themselves in communication with the authorities of Cuba in this matter, and to make with them the preliminary arrangements for carrying into effect the orders of the Spanish Government, as soon as those orders shall have been received at the Havanna. I am, &c.,

(Signed)   PALMERSTON.

It was not until the 28th of August, 1841, although repeatedly stimulated by her Majesty's Minister at Madrid, that that officer received any answer to this communication, when it appeared in the following form :—

The Secretary of State to Mr. Aston.

Madrid, 28th August, 1841.

I have the honour to acknowledge the receipt of the note which you were pleased to address to me on the 10th inst., requiring, in the name of the Government of her Britannic Majesty, that the negroes emancipated by sentence of the Mixed Court of Justice, established at the Havanna, under the treaty of 1817, be brought before the Mixed Commission now existing in that city, and have the alternative allowed them of remaining in Cuba, or being sent to a British colony, at their option; and in case of their preferring the latter they should be delivered over to the Superintendent of liberated Africans, who would make the necessary arrangements for that purpose. Her Majesty's Government has not the least doubt that, as you state, in the British colonies these individuals would be free by law as well as by treaty; but, in this respect, their condition would not be improved, because, in the island of Cuba, they are in the enjoyment of the same benefits, and of the same rights, as all free men residing there. In order that the British Government may be convinced of this fact, I must inform you that the negroes emancipated under the treaty of 1817, are handed over to persons well known for their respectability, and who have rendered some service, or contributed, by voluntary donations, to the support of public establishments and charities, and which acts of charity they must prove by the receipts of the individuals belonging to these establishments; this is all which is required by the Captain-general, upon entrusting to them the education and bringing up of the emancipated negroes. After a certain time has elapsed, which has been fixed at five years, the negroes who are capable of maintaining themselves receive their letter of emancipation ; but those who, on account of their vices, stupidity, or bad state of health, are not in a condition to provide for themselves, remain in the power of the same individuals to whom they were entrusted, or of some other of known probity, because the whole community is interested that these unfortunate beings should not perish or plunge headlong into a career of crime, which measure is equally beneficial to the emancipados.   Their condition, you will allow me to observe, is very different from that which, upon various occasions, has been falsely and erroneously represented to the Government of her Britannic Majesty ; and this is proved even by the parties interested themselves, who very rarely indeed complain of their respective masters to the authorities, and even those few who do so are almost always urged on by persons who are secretly working to disturb the peace and tranquillity of Cuba.

The practice observed hitherto with the emancipated negroes is in conformity with the spirit of the treaty of 1817, and that concluded in 1835 is not in opposition to it.   The making so notable an alteration as that one proposed by you, presents difficulties of the highest importance, which her Majesty's Government cannot pass over.   Many of the emancipated negroes are married and have children, and the enabling them, in this manner, at their option to leave the country, would be productive of disturbance and ruptures among the families of those individuals whom it is erroneously intended to protect ; it would be affording to the vicious the means of abandoning their wives and children, and giving rise to a thousand just complaints on the part of those proprietors whose negresses, or negroes, might happen to be married to those who were requesting permission to proceed to the British colonies ; finally, it would be a project which, besides being considered as immoral by the Spanish Government, would tend to diminish in Cuba the coloured population already civilised ; it would deprive industry and agriculture of hands, and would notably injure the prosperity and wealth of the island, in order to augment that of those colonies where the Superintendent of liberated Africans would send them to.

Another inconvenience, no less serious, has occurred to her
Majesty's Government, in itself sufficient to counteract the
project; and it is, that to accede to it would be to invest the
Mixed Commission with powers to establish a minute research
of emancipated negroes, with the object of offering them the
option of becoming British subjects, in the event of their being
discontented to be Spaniards, or weary of the country in
which they live under the immediate protection of her
Catholic Majesty; such a concession would be indecorous, and,
as you will also easily conceive, it would also be to authorise
in the island of Cuba a foreign authority, which, investigating
by itself the condition of liberated negroes, might take
measures for their removal in the same way as a Spanish
tribunal could do.

Laying aside, if it were possible, the abuses to which these
official investigations might give rise, the said Commission
would appear to possess, in the Havanna, a power superior
to that of the authorities established in that island by the
Government of the mother country; they would lose the
prestige; and two members of the Mixed Commission would
exercise, even without wishing it, a pernicious influence over
the coloured population, which would become extremely prejudicial and dangerous to the welfare of the inhabitants of
Cuba. In consideration of the reasons which I have just had
the honour of stating to you, the Government of her Catholic
Majesty regrets to be unable to agree to the project proposed
by that of her Britannic Majesty, for the removal to the
British colonies of the negroes emancipated in virtue of the
treaty concluded between both nations in 1817.

I avail, &c.,

(Signed) ANTONIO GONZALES.

(EXTRACT.)

The Secretary of State to Mr. Aston.

Madrid, 31st of August, 1841.

With respect to the second part of your note above-men-
tioned, I think it right again to call your attention, notwithstanding my having already done so on the 28th of

this month, to the treatment and real condition of the liberated negroes in Cuba, in order that her Britannic Majesty's Government may become convinced that the reports on this subject, which are transmitted to it by its agents, are, more properly speaking, those of the Abolitionist Society, are extremely exaggerated, unjust, and offensive to the character of the Spanish authorities in that island, against whom such grave accusations are brought, founded on no other sources than gratuitous assertions and vague conjectures, wanting therefore the necessary validity to be taken into consideration.

I can assure you that, in General Tacon's time, the emancipated negroes were distributed in the same manner as is now the case, amongst individuals who dedicated them to the arts and offices, and instructed them in the tenets of the Christian religion ; but that General arranged that, in order to obtain a liberated negro, a contribution of seventeen hard dollars towards the support of charitable institutions and public works should be deposited in his office.

But as this consignment gave rise to suspicions that some very subaltern *employés* might take other presents, this contribution was abolished, and he directed that, in the distribution of emancipated negroes, those persons should have the preference who, possessing the necessary qualifications, should prove, by receipts from the depositaries of public institutions, that they had rendered some service, or contributed voluntary donations, applicable to the funds destined to these purposes.

General Tacon's successor, the Prince of Anglona, followed the same system, and represented to this office, upon various occasions, particularly on the 31st of July, 1840, that the first thing looked to was the personal qualifications of the individual who took a negro under his charge, the donation not being considered sufficient when the qualifications were not so.

Thus it is, that frequently a negro is only given to an individual without taking the donation into any account, there being sufficient proofs of the morality and responsibility which are required for taking charge of the liberated negroes.

To the severity with which this system, adopted and continued to the present day by the Captain-generals, and approved of by her Majesty's Government, has been observed, is unquestionably the cause why the negroes so very rarely complain to the first authority of the island, as they can do whenever they choose, of the individuals to whom they are entrusted; and those who have made complaints have found the relief and justice which they solicited.

Those negroes who have promptly arrived at a state capable of earning their subsistence, without dependence upon anybody, have received their letters of emancipation, confirming to them that freedom which they had already acquired under the stipulations of the treaties.

Others, unfortunately the greater number, are idle, or so stupid, that it would be a burden on our conscience to leave them to themselves, because it would turn out to their own detriment, and to that of the community in general at Cuba. But, notwithstanding this, the Captain-general of Cuba has directed a formal list of the emancipated negroes to be made out, in order to begin giving them the certificates of emancipation, according to the order in which they finish the term of their consignment or apprenticeship with the individuals to whom they were entrusted. By this means, all will be provided with their certificates of emancipation, since so much has been said about this formality, which will only be omitted under those circumstances where it is indispensable that they should remain under the care of some individual or public establishment.

His Highness the Prince of Anglona was succeeded in the office of Captain-general of Cuba by Don Geronimo Valdez, a person of a very different character, who

> " Disdained
> To soil his fingers with base bribes, or wring
> From the hard hands of peasants their vile trash
> By any indirection."

In the first days of his government it was, no doubt, difficult for General Valdez to overthrow a system which had long been established; which the equally disinterested General Tacon had left as he found it, causing the money to be accumulated, not for his own benefit, but for public purposes, and which had thus taken deep root, not merely within the walls of his palace, but in the habits and manners of the entire population; more especially as, in the case of the Prince, his predecessor, the law was enforced, which requires a retiring Captain-general to remain for three months near the seat of the government he has just vacated, for the purpose of meeting any charge of malversation that may be brought against him.

In answer to an address presented to General Valdez, soon after his accession to the government, his excellency distinctly admitted that the malpractices complained of were of frequent occurrence during the Vice-royalty of several of his predecessors, and he endeavoured to effect a compromise between the slave dealers and the rest of the community, by allowing to the one a term of six months to wind up their affairs, and promising to the other, at the end of that time, the absolute and complete suppression of the slave-trade.

In due time, the cause of the unfortunate emancipados was revived, as exemplified in the case of our sturdy *aguador*, who was already the father of an interesting family, the mother of whom was the favourite slave of a person of kind feelings and respectable station, making no objection to the gratification of the earnest desire of the woman and the mother, who, better instructed than the emancipado, had been suffered to receive the light of religion and morality, and was most anxious to have her connection hallowed by the blessing of the church.

Expecting, through this channel, to promote the liberation

of Gavino, and, through him, of the unhappy class to which he belonged, the Consul caused simultaneous applications to be made to the master of the slave, and to the task-mistress of the emancipado, requesting their sanction to the performance of the marriage ceremony; and, strange to say, although no difficulty was met with, on the part of the legitimate owner of the slave, who was legally entitled to interpose his *veto*, a stern refusal was encountered from the mistress of poor Gavino.

This refusal, however, enabled the Consul to present the condition of the emancipados in a point of view so striking, to the pure-minded General Valdez, as greatly to facilitate the process, still too slow, of their practical liberation. And, in the meantime, he practically yielded the point of Gavino's marriage, by referring it to the priest of the parish in which the mother of his children resided; by whom, indeed, it was declared that Gavino was still a pagan, incapable of receiving the nuptial benediction; but, being in reality a well-disposed person, the padre exerted himself so well, that, in the course of three months, with the willing aid of her who felt the deepest interest in the event, the poor emancipado was declared to be a good Christian, and, on the same day, in the face of the church, although still in the lowest rank of servile degradation, became the head of a Christian family.

It was, of course, impossible that this state of things could last. The good padre, moved by a scene so touching, joined his influence to that of the Consul, and the certificate of emancipation, which had been signed by the British and Spanish Judges, in the Court of Mixed Commission, more than sixteen years before, and had remained as a deposit in the office of the Captain-general ever since, was restored, with an excellent grace, by the good Captain-general, to poor Gavino, whose joy and gratitude knew no bounds. He could with difficulty bring himself to believe that no service of his would be accepted for the boon he had received so unexpectedly. For the Consul, the better to obviate cavil, had never even seen him till the hour of the marriage ceremony, when he had the pleasure of giving away the bride. But poor Gavino very soon set to work, with good heart and good will, to earn the freedom of his wife, whose master interposed no difficulty, and their joint efforts, in the course of a few months, accomplished the manumission of the whole of the family.

This was the beginning of that end which has not yet arrived. It is true that a few hundreds of the most feeble, and, in a pecuniary sense, of the most worthless of the emancipado class, have been suffered to come to Jamaica at the expense of this island;* but, as if Spanish authorities were morally disqualified from doing anything in an honest and straight-forward manner, a considerable proportion of the persons who have been sent here, in pretended acquittal of their solemn obligation to secure to this class of persons the practical enjoyment of their freedom, have really belonged to a much more numerous category, consisting of persons who have either been born free, or have acquired a legal right to the boon by gift, bequest, or purchase, and, for some reason or other, have become unwelcome to the authorities, who, by this dexterous substitution, accomplish the double purpose of foiling, *pro tanto*, the just claims of the British people, and of sending into exile, free of cost, a certain number of individuals, suspected, by a tyrannical Government, of discontent or sedition.

Some estimates have been formed of the number of persons, belonging to the class of emancipados, who may still be living in Cuba, in this lowest state of bondage; but, for the most part, they appear to have been derived from erroneous

---

* Up to the month of October, 1849, this practice has been continued by small parcels, and at distant intervals.

and imperfect premises. They assume, for instance, the highest rate of mortality which is known in countries where the slave-trade supplies the deficiencies which are constantly arising in a population where the sexes are not distributed in their usual and natural order ; and, in the presence of so many deaths, they make no allowance for the births, which, in some degree or other, must evidently serve as a counterpoise.

But there are several reasons for doubting the accuracy of these calculations. First of all, the emancipados, for the most part, have been detained in the immediate neighbour-hood of the Havanna, for the convenience of the Captain-general and his subordinates, in watching over the vested interests they have so unrelentingly asserted in this peculiar species of property; and, as there happen to be no sugar plantations within the range convenient for this sort of surveillance, the emancipados have thus escaped the most destructive description of toil to which slave labour is usually applied. And, secondly, a great number of them are treated, like our friend Gavino, the water-carrier, as street porters, volante drivers, labourers on the wharves, or at the railway stations, and are thus left in the possession of as much freedom as is consistent with the payment of a daily stipend to the task-master, who, in some cases, will exact a much larger sum from his victim than was required from our friend the water-carrier, if he happen to possess some pro-ficiency in skilled labour of any sort, as, for instance, in the manufacture of sweetmeats or cigars.

It is difficult, however, to understand why her Majesty's Government, the Consul, the Commissioners at the Havanna, or any other British officer, should quietly content themselves with mere estimates, or calculations, of the probable number of emancipados still living in a state of servitude under Spanish dominion, seeing they are so clearly entitled to demand a strict and circumstantial account of the whole number, in virtue of the provisions already stated in detail; from which it is clear that the Spanish authorities, and the case is the same with regard to Brazil, can only escape in one of three ways:—1st. By producing evidence, to the satisfaction of the British authorities, of the death of each emancipado, if a male; of herself and her issue, if a female. 2ndly. By similar evidence, renewed every six months, that the male emancipados, and the females, with their issue, are living as persons of free condition, absolved from all constraint, on Spanish or Brazilian territory. Or, 3rdly. By the fact, that these authorities, Spanish or Brazilian, have, *pro tanto*, relieved themselves from their responsibility to her Majesty's Government, by having handed over a certain number, of established identity, to some competent British authority.

With regard to the cases of the Portuguese and Brazilian emancipados we are not so well informed; but to them, of course, the same principles must apply, as the nature and spirit of the obligation to recognise and protect them as persons of free condition, are the same, although the words may not be identical. And that their case has not been neglected will clearly appear from the following correspondence on the subject:—

Viscount Palmerston to Mr. Ouseley.

Foreign Office, March 12th, 1841.

With reference to former correspondence respecting the negroes liberated by sentence of the Mixed Court of Commission at Rio de Janeiro, I observe that it does not appear from your despatches that you have hitherto been able to induce the Brazilian Government—first, to agree to a set of regulations, which might secure to those negroes who have been emancipated by sentence of the Mixed Commission that freedom which has hitherto been withheld from them; and, secondly, to conclude a convention, by which the negroes who might hereafter be emancipated should be transferred to a British colony, where their permanent liberty would be secured.

I have, in consequence, to desire that you will present a note to the Brazilian Government, stating that strong representations have again been made to her Majesty's Government, that the negroes who have been emancipated by sentence of the Mixed Commission at Rio de Janeiro do not enjoy that freedom which the Brazilian Government is bound by treaty to secure to them.

Her Majesty's Government, therefore, propose, and earnestly request of the Brazilian Government, that all those negroes may be brought before the Mixed Commission, according to a nominal list, in order that the Commission may ascertain, by personal examination of each of them, whether they are in a state of entire and perfect freedom, so that any restriction which may exist upon the liberty of any of them may immediately be made to cease. You will press this proposal in the most earnest manner upon the Brazilian Government.

You will add, that arrangements will be made by you for sending off to the nearest British colony such of these liberated negroes as may be willing to go thither; and as the condition of slavery has been entirely abolished in those colonies, the negroes who may be sent thither will be perfectly sure of retaining their liberty.

You will further earnestly urge the Brazilian Government to agree that all the negroes who may, in future, be emancipated, by virtue of the convention between Great Britain and Brazil, shall, immediately after emancipation, be delivered over to British authority, to be sent to a British settlement; and you will state to the Brazilian Government, that her Majesty's Government will cheerfully bear the expense of the arrangements for transferring the liberated negroes to a British colony. I herewith transmit to you, for your information, a copy of an instruction which I have addressed to her Majesty's Commissioners at Rio de Janeiro upon this subject.

I have to desire that you will concert with her Majesty's Commissioners the arrangements necessary to carry the abovementioned measures into effect.

For this purpose you will select a proper officer to receive the negroes from the Mixed Court of Commission; you will settle with the commander of her Majesty's receiving ship "Crescent" the means of accommodating the negroes on board that ship, until a passage can be procured for them to a British colony; you will send them, under proper custody, to such British colony, stating, in a letter to the Governor thereof, the circumstances under which they are sent, and recommending them to his care.

You will send me an account of the expense incurred in the execution of these measures, together with the vouchers for the same; and you will draw for the amount thereof upon the Lords of her Majesty's Treasury, giving to their lordships and to me notice of the bills.

I am, &c., &c.,

(Signed)   PALMERSTON.

Mr. Ouseley to Mr. Aureliano.

British Legation, March 21, 1841.

It is with great regret that the undersigned is obliged to represent to Senor Aureliano, that under former administrations, and even up to the present time, the Africans nominally liberated by the Mixed Commission have, in fact, with perhaps a few exceptions, not reaped the benefits of the humane efforts made in their favour; and that the regulations for their advantage and protection, the credit of issuing most of which is due to his excellency himself, when formerly in office, have been systematically evaded.

It is with pain that the undersigned mentions the extreme misconduct of certain officers, in whose charge these Africans have been placed in the Caza de Correcçao and elsewhere, in the personal maltreatment of the unfortunate Africans, and the general abuse of their trust.

These Africans have, it is positively asserted, instead of being placed with responsible persons of good character, been literally sold to individuals, and taken to estates in the interior, and simulated certificates of their death, or the substitution of those of other deceased negroes, been restored to conceal these shameful transactions.

Aware of the humane disposition of Senor Aureliano, and

of the benevolent intentions of the Government of which he forms a part, especially as regarding the wrongs inflicted on the natives of Africa by the cupidity and cruelty of those engaged in the slave-trade, it is with confidence that the undersigned applies to the imperial Government to put an effectual end to the criminal abuses that have been too long perpetrated with impunity against those who have a right to the mutual protection of the two Governments.

The employment, by the imperial Government or its officers, of these individuals, or the apprenticeship of the Africans only to persons of responsibility within reach, and under the observation of the authorities, but, more especially, a general registration of each individual African, with the appointment of a visiting magistrate, and a protector of the liberated Africans, would go far to ensure the efficacy of the protective measures in their behalf.

The registration resorted to in the West Indies, previously to the total abolition of slavery in her Majesty's possessions, was found of the greatest practical benefit.

The undersigned ventures to make these suggestions, as it is clear to every one acquainted with this matter, that, by the present system of treating the liberated Africans in Brazil, the beneficent views of either Government have not been attained.

The undersigned further has the honour to submit to the consideration of the imperial Government, that the Mixed Commission might, with propriety, be charged with the protection of the liberated Africans, who, as a rule, ought never to be employed at a distance from this capital. The Commissioners being in immediate communication with the supreme Government, their beneficial interference might be rendered effectual in securing the *bonâ fide* good treatment, and ultimate complete emancipation of the apprenticed negroes.

The imperial Government will, doubtless, agree with the undersigned as to the impossibility of allowing the humane and costly efforts for the freedom and advantage of those Africans, rescued from the felonious traders in human beings, to be set at nought by the connivance and complicity of those who abuse the trust confided to them ; and the undersigned looks forward, with confidence, to whatever measures Senor Aureliano's enlightened judgment will enable his excellency to put in force for the better protection of the Africans, when entrusted to the care of the Government of this empire.

The undersigned avails, &c.,

W. G. Ouseley.

Mr. Aureliano to Mr. Ouseley.

Palace, Rio de Janeiro, June 19th, 1841.

The undersigned, &c., acknowledges the receipt of the note which Mr. Ouseley addressed to him on the 16th inst., in which, after saying that strong representations have been made to the Government of her Majesty the Queen, alleging that the negroes emancipated by sentence of the Mixed Commission of Rio de Janeiro do not enjoy that liberty which the Brazilian Government is bound by treaties to secure them, he concludes by declaring that he has received instructions to propose :—1st. That all the blacks who have been emancipated by that tribunal should be presented before the Brazilian and English Mixed Commission, in order, according to a nominal list for the purpose, to examine whether they be in a state of complete and perfect liberty, and to cause to cease immediately any restriction which might exist on the liberty of any of them. 2ndly. That prompt arrangements should be entered into, in order that such emancipated negroes as desired it should be sent to the nearest British colony ; and likewise, in order that all the blacks who may in future be liberated, in virtue of the convention subsisting between the two crowns, should be immediately delivered to the British authorities, to be sent to an English settlement, his Government willingly obliging itself to bear the expenses necessary for their transfer.

The undersigned abstains, for the present, from duly replying to the first proposition of Mr. Ouseley, because he

requires from the Minister of Justice the information necessary to this end, it being his duty, however, now immediately
to declare to Mr. Ouseley—first, that these representations
and accusations are, for the most part, exaggerated, and
originate in malevolence; secondly, that it is possible that
one or another of the individuals to whom the services of
these negroes have been confided may have committed some
abuse, as happens in every part of the world, since, where
there are men and laws, there exists, more or less, some
abuse of the latter. As regards the second proposition,
however, it is his duty to signify to Mr. Ouseley, in reply,
that he is about to forward his note to the Brazilian plenipotentiary, the Senator Lopez Gama, in order to take it
into consideration in the negotiation which he has to enter
upon with the British plenipotentiary, respecting other proposals made by Mr. Ouseley, as this is the most regular and
promptest manner of proceeding with one now newly made
by him.

The undersigned, &c.,

(Signed)   Aureliano de Souza E. Oliveira Continho.

Viscount Palmerston to Mr. Ouseley.

Foreign Office, August 23, 1841.

Sir,—I have received, and laid before the Queen, your
despatches of the 18th and 21st of May last, relative to the
condition of the Africans who have been liberated by decree
of the British and Brazilian Mixed Court of Commission at
Rio de Janeiro, and made over to the care of the Brazilian
Government.

I entirely approve of the note which you addressed to the
Brazilian Minister, on the 18th of May, stating that you
would " suspend the delivery to the Brazilian authorities of
any Africans hereafter liberated by the Mixed Court until,
at least, such arrangements were made by the Brazilian
Government as may secure the ends which both Governments declared they had in view, in concluding the convention for the suppression of traffic in men, and in framing the

regulations necessary for the due execution" of that convention.

For the convention states, that the negroes emancipated by sentence of the Mixed Court shall be delivered over to the Government in whose territory the Court which shall have judged them shall be established; but they are not to be so delivered for the benefit of that Government, but for their own; not to be employed or sold as slaves, but to be employed as servants or free labourers, their liberty being placed under the guarantee of that Government.

In regard to negroes emancipated from Brazilian slave ships by sentence of the Mixed Court at Rio, this stipulation has been notoriously violated by the Brazilian Government, and by its authorities. These negroes do not enjoy that liberty which the Brazilian Government engaged to guarantee to them; and they are not employed as free labourers, but are in the condition of slaves.

Under these circumstances, her Majesty's Government cannot any longer be parties to the injustice which the Brazilian Government commits towards these negroes; and I have to instruct you to inform the Brazilian Minister that her Majesty's Government cannot deliver over to the Brazilian Government any more free negroes, to be treated as slaves; and that, therefore, until the Brazilian Government shall show that it faithfully executes its engagements towards emancipated negroes, all negroes who may in future be brought to Rio in a captured Brazilian slave ship will be retained on board the " Crescent" receiving ship, till the slave ship has been condemned; and then, instead of being delivered over to the Brazilian Government, will be sent to a British colony.

In communicating this arrangement to the Brazilian Minister, you will point out to him, that if the Brazilian Government contend, as an excuse for not having performed their engagements, that the custody of these negroes would be a burden to the Brazilian Government, were that Government faithfully to execute the engagements it has undertaken by the convention, then the Brazilian Government cannot feel any objection to the arrangement, unless it makes some undue advantage of the negroes, in violation of the stipulations of the convention.

I have further to desire that, in carrying this measure into effect, you will follow the instructions given you in my despatch of the 12th of March last, as to the removal from Rio of such of the emancipated negroes, already in the Brazils, as might be given up to you by the Brazilian Government, in compliance with the request of her Majesty's Government.

A copy of this despatch will be sent to her Majesty's Commissioners at Rio de Janeiro, for their information and guidance; and the Lords of the Admiralty will be requested to instruct the officers in command of her Majesty's ships, on the Brazilian station, to take, in concert with you, the necessary measures for carrying this arrangement into effect.

I am, &c.,

(Signed) PALMERSTON.

Viscount Palmerston to M. Montezuma.

Foreign Office, August 27, 1841.

The undersigned, &c., has the honour to state to M. Montezuma, &c., that, by the convention of the 23rd November, 1826, between Great Britain and Brazil, for the suppression of the slave-trade, it is stipulated that the negroes, emancipated by sentence of the Mixed Courts, should be delivered over to the Government in whose territory the Court which shall have judged them shall be established; but they are to be so delivered, not for the benefit of that Government, but for their own benefit; not in order to be employed or sold as slaves, but in order to be employed as servants or free labourers, their liberty being placed under the guarantee of such Government.

But with regard to the negroes emancipated from Brazilian slave ships by sentence of the Mixed Court at Rio, this stipulation has been notoriously violated by the Brazilian Government, and by its authorities. These negroes do not enjoy that liberty which the Brazilian Government engaged to guarantee to them, and they are not employed as free labourers, but are in the condition of slaves.

Under these circumstances, her Majesty's Government cannot any longer be parties to the injustice which the Brazilian Government commits towards these negroes, and her Majesty's Government cannot deliver over to the Brazilian Government any more free negroes to be treated as slaves.

The undersigned, therefore, has the honour to request that M. Montezuma will state to his Government, that until that Government shall show that it has faithfully executed its engagements towards the emancipated negroes, all negroes who may in future be brought to Rio in a Brazilian slave ship, captured by one of her Majesty's cruisers, will be retained on board the " Crescent " receiving ship, till such slave ship shall have been condemned ; and then, instead of being delivered over to the Brazilian Government, they would be sent to a British colony.   And the undersigned has to add, that instructions to this effect have been given to her Majesty's representative in Brazil, and to the Board of Admiralty.

The undersigned has, in conclusion, to observe, that if the Brazilian Government contend, as an excuse for not having fulfilled their engagements on this subject, that the maintenance of these negroes, in a state of real freedom, would be a burden to the Brazilian Government, and that, consequently, that Government cannot faithfully execute the engagements it has undertaken by the convention, then the Brazilian Government cannot feel any objection to the intended arrangements, nor can it object to comply with the request, already made by her Majesty's Government, that all the negroes who have hitherto been declared, by sentence of the Mixed Court at Rio, to be free, shall forthwith be handed over to the British Government, to be removed to a British colony ; and her Majesty's Government cannot persuade themselves that the Brazilian Government will be induced to decline to comply with these two requests, on the ground that it makes an undue profit or advantage by selling, or by giving, as a present to private individuals, the services and labour of such negroes for a limited number of years, because such a proceeding is a direct violation of the engagements of the Brazilian Crown.

The undersigned avails, &c.,
(Signed) PALMERSTON.

We must now return to the details of the Jamaica movement, so auspiciously begun in Spanish Town on her Majesty's birth-day. Scarcely had the announcement of that meeting appeared in the newspapers, when another requisition was published, calling a meeting of the inhabitants of the parish of St. George, who claimed the honour, it appears, of having made a step in the same direction two years before, and were not a little jealous of losing their precedence. The St George's meeting took place at Buff Bay, on the 1st June, and the proceedings were communicated in the following letter :—

Mr. Grosett to Mr. Turnbull.

St. George, Jamaica, 4th June, 1849.

SIR,—I have the honour of transmitting to you a series of resolutions passed at our recent public meeting relative to the foreign slave-trade, and to the enforcement of the slave treaties made between Great Britain and other nations.

In conformity with the fourth resolution, I take the liberty of requesting that you will make such use of them as you may consider most conducive to the objects had in view.

I remain, &c.,
(Signed) J. R. GROSETT, Custos.

To the Hon. John Rock Grosett, Custos of St. George.

St. George, May 18, 1849.

SIR,—We, the undersigned proprietors, magistrates, clergy, and others, the parishioners of St. George, having observed in the public prints that a meeting of the principal inhabitants of Kingston and Spanish Town is to be held in the latter city on Thursday, the 24th current, "for the purpose of inviting the inhabitants of Jamaica to consider the effect produced on this country by the non-observance of the treaties for the suppression of the slave-trade by which Spain and the Brazils are bound to her Majesty, and of devising such a measure as may tend to promote at once the great interests of humanity, and the relief of the intertropical possessions of the British Crown from the deep distress in which they are now involved," beg leave to remind your Honour that at a meeting of the parishioners, held here in 1847, at which you presided, the following resolutions were agreed to and passed, viz.—

8. "That the continuation and great increase of the foreign slave-trade (especially now that the importation of slave-grown sugar and coffee is not only permitted but promoted in British ships, for consumption in the British market) is becoming an intolerable grievance.

9. "That a memorial on the subject, addressed to the Right Hon. Lord Palmerston, her Majesty's Secretary for Foreign Affairs, be prepared, and that the one now read be adopted; and that his Honour the Custos be requested to forward it to his excellency the Governor for transmission."

We, therefore, request your Honour will convene a meeting of the parishioners, for the purpose of taking into consideration the above important question, and co-operating with the influential persons whose names are attached to the requisition addressed to the Custos of St. Catherine; and also to inquire into the fate of the memorial alluded to.

Henry Mason, J.P.	R. J. Robertson, J.P.
W. P. Crichton, J.P. & M.D.	Francis Guscott
Robert Dunbar, M.A.	Edw. Skyers
Frederick Grosett, J.P.	Edwin Carter
Wm. Williamson, J.P.	Isaac Silvera, Sen., J.P.
John Fowles, Sen.	William Kirkland
John Fowles, Jun.	George Touche
C. T. Rapkey, M.R.C.S.	Charles T. May, Rector.

Charles W. Grosett, J.P.
James Henderson
Robert Kirkland
Jos. Brough, J.P.
Isaac Silvera, Jun.

D. Osborn, Island Curate
H. Brown, I. Curate of
Portland
A. H. Bowswell
D. Campbell.

In accordance with the above requisition, I hereby convene a public meeting, to be held at the Court-house, Buff Bay, on Friday, the 1st June, for the purpose therein mentioned.

J. R. GROSETT, Custos.

At a public meeting, held by requisition at the Court-house, St. George, June 1, 1849, the Hon. John R. Grosett in the chair, the following resolutions were unanimously agreed to, viz. :—

" 1. That at a public meeting held in our Court-house, September, 1847, the following memorial, relative to the foreign slave-trade, was adopted, and transmitted to Lord Palmerston, viz. :—

" *To the Right Hon. Lord Viscount Palmerston, Her Majesty's Principal Secretary of State for Foreign Affairs.*

"The humble Memorial of the Proprietors and Magistrates of St. George, Jamaica.

"Your memorialists address your lordship in consequence of the following resolutions, adopted at a public meeting held in their Court-house, Buff Bay, on the 18th September, viz. :—

" ' That the continuation and great increase of the foreign slave-trade (especially now that the importation of slave-grown sugar and coffee is not only permitted but promoted in British ships, for consumption in the British market) is becoming an intolerable grievance.

" ' That a memorial on the subject, addressed to the Foreign Office, be prepared, and that the one now read be adopted and transmitted.'

" In making this address, we feel the more emboldened,

knowing that your lordship has always been a steady and
decided opposer to slavery, especially of the foreign slave-
trade; for the abolition of which, by treaties with foreign
nations, your lordship's abilities have frequently been exerted.

" We, however, complain of the flagrant infraction and
violation of those treaties, by reason of which we are now
seriously injured, in consequence of the great advantage
which the foreign planters, especially those in Cuba and
Brazil, enjoy over us in Jamaica, by obtaining cheap and
almost illimitable labour, through the fraudulent introduction
of negro slaves. It appears, and has been stated in Parliament, that above forty thousand negro slaves, even last
year, were surreptitiously imported into the Brazils, and it is
well known that thousands have been annually imported, for
years past, both there and into Cuba. There is no reason to
suppose that, under the present system, those numbers will
decrease, but, on the contrary, that the slave-trade will be
stimulated, and will greatly increase, now that the slave-owner
not only finds permission, but encouragement, to send his
slave-labour produce to England for British consumption.

" It will be impossible for us, as British planters, to withstand so unequal a competition, especially deprived, as we
are, and have been, of all adequate supply of free labourers,
in consequence of which our plantations are going to decay,
and many entirely abandoned. As practical men, and as
men interested in the utter extinction of foreign slavery, we
consider no means would be so effectual as to enable us to
undersell the foreigner; for which purpose facilities ought
to be given to us as British subjects, and difficulties imposed on
the slave-grower. We, therefore, consider ourselves and our
fellow-colonists entitled to ask facility of procuring labour,
by the introduction into Jamaica, at the national cost, of as
many free labourers as shall equal the number of slaves
furtively introduced into Cuba, on an average of the last
three years; and, as regards *difficulties* in the way of the
Brazilian and other foreigners, we ask a strict enforcement
of all treaties made with foreign powers for the suppression
of the slave-trade; and also a strict enforcement of all Acts

of Parliament, with additional penalties, if necessary, for the prevention of British capital being invested or employed in upholding or promoting slavery in foreign countries.

" We do not enter into other grievances, such as duties and impost, but confine ourselves to that branch which arises from slave labour, and emanates from foreign countries. We, therefore, address your lordship as being at the head of the Foreign Department, rather than her Majesty's Secretary of State for the Colonies, to whom, if our memorial were of a general nature, it would seem to have been more properly transmitted.

" In conclusion, your memorialists respectfully request your lordship to take into consideration this their memorial, adopted at a public meeting held by requisition.

" 2. That since the above period our representations have been disregarded, and the evil we then complained of as an intolerable grievance, has since increased.

" 3. That the various treaties for the suppression of the slave-trade having been entered into by the United States, May 15, 1820; by Great Britain, March 31, 1824; by Buenos Ayres, November 15, 1824; by Brazil, November 23, 1826; by Austria, Russia, Prussia, 1841; by Portugal, 1842, whereby the slave-trade has been declared piracy, the encouragement now given by Great Britain to the importation and consumption in the home market of foreign sugar and coffee, produced by the labour of Africans surreptitiously introduced and worked as slaves, is calculated to create suspicion, on the part of foreign nations, that the British Government is not sincere in the desire of putting down the foreign slave-trade, and is, moreover, highly detrimental to our interests.

" 4. That the above resolutions be forwarded by the Custos to the President of the Chamber of Commerce, with a request to transmit them to their agent in London, in aid of any instructions the Chamber may have given on the subject, and that copies be also sent to the gentlemen forming the Mixed Commission in this island.

" 5. That these resolutions be published twice in the 'Dispatch' and ' Morning Journal.'

(Signed)   " J. R. GROSETT, Custos."

Henry Mason, Esq., then moved that the Rev. Charles T. May do take the chair, when a vote of thanks was unanimously passed to the Hon. John R. Grosett, for his able and impartial conduct as chairman of the meeting.

Her Majesty's Commissioners to Mr. Grosett.

Mixed Commission Office, Kingston,
7th June, 1849.

SIR,—We have the honour to acknowledge the receipt of your letter of the 4th inst., addressed to Mr. Turnbull, containing a series of resolutions, passed at your recent public meeting, relative to the foreign slave-trade, and to the enforcement of the slave treaties made between Great Britain and other nations.

And we hasten to assure your Honour that we shall not fail to bring the subject under the notice of her Majesty's Government.

We have the honour to be, Sir,
Your most obedient servants,
(Signed)   D. TURNBULL,
A. R. HAMILTON.

The Hon. J. R. Grosett,
Custos of St. George, Buff Bay, P.O.

Her Majesty's Commissioners to Viscount Palmerston.

Jamaica, 7th June, 1849.

MY LORD,—We have this day received a letter from Mr. Grosett, Custos of the parish of St. George, transmitting to us a series of resolutions, passed at a recent public meeting in that parish, with reference to the foreign slave-trade, and to the enforcement of existing treaties between Great Britain and other nations on that subject. And we take the liberty of enclosing a copy of the letter, and its enclosure, for your lordship's consideration.

We have, &c.,
(Signed)   D. TURNBULL,
A. R. HAMILTON.

Viscount Palmerston to her Majesty's Commissioners.

Foreign Office, July, 30th, 1849.

GENTLEMEN,—I have received your despatch, No. 14, of the 7th ultimo, in which you address a copy of a letter, addressed to Mr. Turnbull by Mr. Grosett, enclosing a series of resolutions, agreed to at a public meeting held in the parish of St. George, Jamaica, setting forth the grievances to which the inhabitants of that island are subjected by the continuation of the foreign slave-trade, and by the habitual violation, on the part of Spain and Brazil, of the treaties for the suppression of the slave-trade by which those powers are bound to Great Britain, and requesting Mr. Turnbull to make such use of the resolutions as he might consider most conducive to the objects had in view.

I now transmit to you, under flying seal, a letter which I have addressed to Mr. Grosett, in reply to the resolutions above referred to, and I have to desire that, after perusing it, you will forward it to that gentleman.

I am, with great truth, &c.,

(Signed)   PALMERSTON.

Viscount Palmerston to Mr. Grosett.

Foreign Office, July 27th, 1849.

SIR,—I have the honour to acknowledge the receipt of a series of resolutions, passed at a public meeting recently held in the parish of St. George, Jamaica, setting forth the grievances to which the inhabitants of that island are subjected by the continuation of the foreign slave-trade, and by the habitual violation, on the part of Spain and the Brazils, of the treaties for the suppression of the slave-trade by which those powers are bound to Great Britain.

I have to express my regret on finding that the memorial which was addressed to me in September, 1847, and which is embodied in the present resolutions, was, by an oversight at the time, omitted to be acknowledged by me, although I did not fail, immediately on the receipt of that memorial, to give such renewed directions to her Majesty's naval authorities as the case appeared to require.

I now further beg leave to state to you, for the information of the parties interested, that the subject of their representations has engaged, and continues to engage, the earnest solicitude of her Majesty's Government, and that her Majesty's Government are sedulously directing their attention to the attainment of the object which the inhabitants of Jamaica have so much at heart.

I am, &c.,

(Signed)   PALMERSTON.

Spring Garden, St. Andrew's, 2nd Sept., 1849.

SIR,—I have much pleasure in forwarding to you a despatch from Viscount Palmerston, dated the 30th of July, transmitted under flying seal to her Majesty's Commissioners, in acknowledgment of a series of resolutions from the parish of St. George, on the subject of the enforcement of the slave-trade treaties, which you did me the honour to entrust to my care, in the month of June last.

Her Majesty's Commissioners have received by this packet two separate despatches from the noble Secretary of State, in relation to our Jamaica proceedings on this subject, which serve to confirm the confidence they previously felt that her Majesty's Government would follow up the steps we had taken to promote the enforcement of existing treaties with perfect cordiality.

I remain, &c.,

(Signed)   D. TURNBULL.

The Honourable J. R. Grosett,
    St. George's.

The next meeting in succession was that of the parish of Clarendon, which was held at Chapelton, on the 16th of June, and was distinguished by the boldness of the language of several of the resolutions, by one of which it was announced that the climate and soil of Jamaica are as favourable for the production of sugar and coffee as those of any other country, and that its inhabitants are quite prepared for competition in the markets of the world with the natives of Cuba and Brazil, provided that the stipulations of the treaties made between those countries and Great Britain were as faithfully observed by them as they have always been by the subjects of her Britannic Majesty. One of the speeches delivered at this meeting, although coming from a man of peace, establishes a striking contrast between the present mode of dealing with the infractions of our treaties with foreign powers for the suppression of the African slave-trade and that which took place in 1816, when the Dey of Algiers, having violated a similar engagement for the suppression of the trade in slaves of a paler complexion, Lord Exmouth was sent there to remind him of his promise, and exact its performance.

PUBLIC MEETING AT CHAPELTON, CLARENDON, JUNE 16.

A meeting was this day held at the Court House, pursuant to the requisition presented to the Custos on the 30th of May. Shortly after twelve o'clock it was moved that the Honourable Edward Thompson, Custos, do take the chair, which he accordingly did.

The Chairman then proceeded to state that the object of the meeting was to address her Majesty the Queen, and to petition both Houses of Parliament that measures should be taken to enforce the long-standing treaties between the Government of Great Britain and those of Spain and Brazil for the total abolition of the slave-trade. He urged forcibly on those present the necessity which pressed on every member of the community to raise his voice against the continuance of this horrible system, and he stated, that however ruinous it might be to the proprietors, whose estates, exposed to the competition of slave labour, might be thrown out of cultivation, that it would be attended with consequences still more deplorable to the black population; that they would relapse into a state of barbarism, and that the benefits intended them, by conferring freedom upon them, and which they were already partially enjoying, would be entirely lost. He then drew a picture of the horrors to which their brethren in Cuba were exposed, worked for sixteen or eighteen hours every day, under fear of the cart whip, and at night, when their task was over, shut up alone in barracoons, and denied the natural society of women; in short, they were treated as so much stock, and used up with as little compunction. It was to remonstrate against this disgraceful state of things, and to call upon those who had authority to do so, to put an end to it by enforcing the treaties he had referred to, that they had met there that day. If those treaties had been observed from the time they were passed, he believed that all the slaves in Cuba would be now free; and if they could only prevail upon the English Government to insist upon their fulfilment henceforth, he, for one, should have no fear of our being able in this country to compete with those of any other country. But he was satisfied of the impossibility of our competing successfully, with the fair and moderate share of labour which we could command since freedom, against the sixteen or eighteen hours of toil extorted, as he had already stated, by the lash. The object of this meeting, it would therefore be seen, was of the utmost importance; and, he fully believed, that if they only united earnestly and steadily in pressing this subject upon the British people, they must be successful. The spirit which formerly existed in England upon this subject was only dormant, and we must rouse it. He remembered the feeling which existed in England on this subject in the year 1829, which led to the extinction of slavery in this island, and other British West India possessions. Then, every one felt that his course was right, and he could not believe that what had been pronounced right in 1829, could be deemed wrong in 1849. He would not further occupy their time, as the gentlemen who would move the several resolutions would explain to them the object of each, and he would, therefore, call upon the Rev. Dr. Stewart, the rector of the parish, to move the first resolution.

The Rev. Dr. Stewart said—I rise, Sir, in answer to your call, to move the first resolution, which I will read—

" That the treaties formerly made, and still subsisting, between the British Government and the Governments of Spain and Brazil, whereby it was declared that all future traffic in slaves by their respective subjects should be deemed an act of piracy, have been constantly and openly violated by the people of Cuba and Brazil; that this traffic has latterly increased to an alarming extent; and that all measures hitherto adopted for its prevention, whether by means of Mixed Commissions, or by armed cruisers stationed on the coast of Africa, have signally failed to accomplish this object."

Having done so, he proceeded—I have attended many public meetings in this place since I became rector of Clarendon; and although every one of them had some object of importance and utility, in none did I feel such anxious interest as I do in the meeting now assembled. On other occasions, we advocated or deprecated measures calculated to increase or retard our prosperity, as the case might be; but now, Sir, we approach the discussion of a measure of such vital importance, that on the success of the appeal, which I have no doubt we shall agree in making, will depend, in a very great degree, our existence. It has come, very nearly, to a case of life and death. It is a source of satisfaction, even under the depression which has come on us, that, in pleading our own cause, we are at the same time advocating the cause of a large portion of the human family, which has long been the object of violence and injury. We pray for the liberation of prisoners and captives, and for judgment on behalf of the desolate and oppressed, in the most grinding way to which these terms can give expression. You and I, and some others now present, attended the meeting in Spanish Town on the Queen's birth-day, which was the first step in the movement we are now met to forward, and which, to his honour, was presided over by the Lord Bishop of the diocese. If the advice of some persons had been followed, that meeting would not have been held—at least, it would not have been led and conducted in the happy manner in which it was managed. We all rejoice that the movement began under such auspicious circumstances. I am, certain, Sir, that you and the gentlemen whom I now address, in common with those who composed the first meeting, have yet to learn that it is not the duty of the Church, from her head to her humblest member, as well as of the ministers and members of all sects and bodies of religionists, not even confining it to Christians, to stand forward in the cause of justice and humanity. If doing this excite the displeasure of those who bear rule and possess power, we can only regret that it is so. Honest and true men are not to be deterred by such considerations. But I hold a different opinion of the sentiments of our gracious Queen, and those whom she has engaged to carry on her Government. If the latter have neglected the interests, or injured the cause of the West Indies, I cannot believe they have done so because they love injustice and oppression, or that they will be insensible to the united and ardent appeal of every grade and class in this afflicted community. Since the meeting in Spanish Town, the information has reached us that, even had we been apathetic or indifferent about the matter, our opponents were up and doing. In the House of Commons, the so-called liberal party, little more than a month ago, sought to procure the repeal of the law which renders the treaty with Brazil at all available, and which would enable her Majesty's Government to respond to the call we are now making for the total abolition of the slave-trade. The nature and bearings of the treaties have been fully explained to the public here, on recent occasions, and it is unnecessary to repeat what has been so well said by others. It may, however, be somewhat interesting to refer, for a short time, to the arguments adduced by those who so unworthily sought to append to the measures of free trade, already enacted, a free trade in mankind—liberty to steal and make slaves of all who have not the means of resistance, without censure or restraint. I think the exposure of the unsoundness, to say no worse of these arguments, must add strength to the cause we have in hand. One argument used by Mr. Milner Gibson, the mover of the measure, was, that however philanthropic men may now condemn the slave-trade, and shudder at its horrors, England herself practised it within a few years past. Well, so she did; and how does that justify the fact? England, in days gone by, practised many strange and unwarranted courses. Her class legislation, and her penal laws, in many instances, excluded the least gleam of light from the dark and gloomy enactments. But, not to enter on such recollections, we cannot forget that a very few years since, down to a later period than the abolition of the slave-trade, the law of England declared, that if a prisoner indicted for felony, &c., refused to plead, he should be laid on his back, a stone or heavy weight placed on his chest, and he be fed on water until he yielded by pleading "guilty" or "not guilty," or, continuing obstinate, until he died. Is it because this, or any similar measure, steel boots, racks, and thumbscrews were, in past days, according to English practice, that they are to be justified if practised in our days? And will the once evil course of those who have gone before justify us in quietly looking on at the atrocities practised in the capture of slaves, the horrors of the middle passage, and the crushed life of unbearable toil and violence, which finishes in untimely and miserable death? Again, we are told the slave-trade and slavery were abolished in the British dominions—not by foreign intervention, but by the influence of moral and religious sentiments which gradually prevailed, but which took at least thirty years before the cause was crowned with success. The facts, with regard to England and Spain and Brazil, which render this argument unavailing are carefully kept out of sight. Indeed, if there be any peculiar influence in a period of thirty-one years, between the proposal and success of the measure, it has already been exceeded in both the countries referred to. The treaties with Spain and Portugal, also, were commenced in 1817, thirty-two years ago; and, in the treaty with Portugal, Brazil, being in 1817 under the same Government, was included. If, by throwing off the mother country, Brazil, during the interval, repudiated the Portugal treaty, she renewed it in her own case as soon as her independence was recognised. The thirty-one years, then, and more, have elapsed. But the reason why the friends of freedom in England could afford to wait was, they yearly, monthly, daily, during the thirty-one years, saw their cause advanced. Fresh adherents quickly and numerously increasing their numbers, and thinning the ranks of the slavery upholders, raised their hopes, and rendered success certain. Let us inquire what chance exists that sentiments of morality and religion are likely to prevail over the evil propensities of plunder and avarice in Brazil and the Spanish colonies? The terms religion and morality in those countries are words without meaning. Let any one who has visited these countries, or any of them, speak. Were it necessary that I should outrage decency in unveiling truth, I might describe the worse than beastly, the most unnatural aspect which the system of slavery in those countries presents, which makes them the representatives, in the middle of the 19th century, of the cities of the plain, upon which the Lord rained brimstone and fire out of heaven, nearly four thousand years ago. Then, Sir, we are told that the enforcement of these treaties is at variance from the due operation of international law, and infringes upon the rights of independent nations. The absurdity of this statement is most forcibly put by Lord Palmerston. He says, the people who rely on this as an argument, found it upon a confusion of international piracy with conventional piracy, and this confusion leads them to think that their argument is sound. "There is," says his lordship, "a piracy which is by the law of nations cognisable by all nations, consisting of acts of violence and plunder upon the high seas : which is proved by an overt act—but which, when committed, and the parties taken in the fact, is punishable summarily, without any international convention. But that is not this case. The slave-trade is not piracy by the law of nations in that view of it. It may be made piracy by convention, or by the law of any particular country. Now, in this case, two nations agreed that it should be piracy. Great Britain and Brazil made a convention, by which any act of slave-trading by any subjects of Brazil (the Spanish treaty is the same) should be deemed and treated as piracy." Can any statement be more plain? And yet we are told, that asking Brazil and Spain to enforce its own law, and carry out its own solemn engagement, is a violation of international law—

not resting upon what may sometimes appear undefined claims, but upon a calmly entered on treaty, and that it is an encroachment on the rights of independent nations. Although the case is simple, let us advert to it on the showing of the advocates of free-trade in slaves. When they talk of international law—can they mean that the nations of Africa have no claim to be included within its pale? and when the privileges of independent kingdoms are discussed, have the African governments no right to participate in them? Is it because they are ignorant they are to be maltreated, or encouraged in ill-treating each other? Is it because they are incapable of protecting themselves that they are to be the unregarded victims of avarice, and the unpitied subjects of outrage? Are all her delicacies of feeling, as regards the rights of independent kingdoms, and all her sympathies in reference to international law, to be profligately wasted on the man-stealer and the man-killer, while the miserable victims are wholly disregarded! The supposition is horrible—the fact cannot be so. It is added, to give weight to such arguments, that the effects of the law to carry out the treaties were to carry the subjects of the contracting parties to the abolition of the slave-trade before tribunals which were foreign to them, and subjecting them to rules and regulations of which they had no knowledge—tribunals where no Brazilian (I may add, or other foreign) counsellor or judge had any *locus standi*. Does Mr. Milner Gibson, for self and fellows, give us, as regards the case of the stolen slave, a description of his position as to his knowledge of the rules and regulations he is subjected to, and the nature of the tribunals which control his destiny, and the *locus standi* of his counsellors and judges in the slave courts of Cuba, Porto Rico, and Brazil? Well, Sir, the last argument I shall refer to is "the great difficulty which the executive of that country had to contend with, in inducing the public voice to consent to such an act for carrying out such an engagement." This is worse than all which preceded it. As regards the inclination of these Governments to carry out their own treaties, hear my Lord Aberdeen in 1845:—" With rare and short exceptions the treaty had been by them systematically violated, from the period of its conclusion to the present time. Cargoes of slaves had been landed in open day in the streets of the capital, and bought and sold like cattle, without any obstacle whatsoever being imposed upon the traffic. Our officers had been waylaid, maltreated, and even assassinated while in the execution of their duty ; and justice, in such cases, if not actually denied, had never been fairly granted. No doubt much had happened, in the course of the last ten or twelve years, which would have justified, and almost called for an expression of national resentment ; but her Majesty's Government had no wish save to provide for the effectual execution of the treaty as stipulated for by the first article." And now, Sir, hear my Lord Palmerston :— " It was not controverted, that not only from the time of the actual passing of the convention, but from the time of the passing of the law in Brazil, in virtue of the convention, the Government of Brazil had pursued one uninterrupted course of violation of that treaty." Think you, Mr. Chairman and gentlemen, that such testimony as this leaves a doubt that there is no difficulty between the Government and the people about the carrying out of the treaty? They are all of the same spirit, and must all be treated in the same way. But, Sir, I am old enough to remember that, in former days, there were white men who were held in slavery on the northern coast of Africa—a sort of retaliation for the exploits in slavery carried on by Christians in other parts of the same continent. In my school-boy days, I remember to have read the history of the abolition of that slavery somewhat to this effect : Lord Exmouth having, in 1816, command of the Mediterranean fleet, concluded a negotiation with the States of Barbary for the liberation of all Christian slaves in their dominions. His lordship had scarcely returned to England before it was discovered they had violated all their engagements. We heard nothing in those days about England herself being guilty, although she was then, and for eighteen years after, a slaveholder. We were not talked to about international law — the insulted feelings of independent governments—or the difficulty in persuading the people to allow the observance of treaties made by their rulers. The arguments used, and the course pursued then, were very different. Lord Exmouth returned to Algiers, having sent in a flag of truce without effect, and followed it by the most destructive bombardment perhaps ever known, and thus the treaty was rendered efficient, and that sort of slavery totally abolished. It could not be, Sir, that I, who by my sacred profession am a man of peace, and who desire ardently that the day may soon arrive, not only when wars shall for ever cease, but when man shall no longer take the life of his fellow-men by judicial sentence, could wish to witness or hear of a similar scene,—I do not believe it would now be necessary. I cannot, however, believe that England is less opposed to slavery than she was three-and-thirty years ago. I cannot believe that now, when class legislation has nearly passed away, that she would recognise any difference between the claims of the black slave and the white one. I see that the attempt to legalise slavery in the British Parliament was equally opposed by the members of the late and the present administrations, by Sir Robert Peel and by Lord Palmerston. I learn that out of the whole British House of Commons only thirty-one persons, the representatives and the adherents of the Manchester cotton spinners, could be found to support the monstrous proposition. For these causes, in connexion with others, I believe a united and decided appeal to the British Government will bring about, by whatever means may be necessary, an enforcement of these treaties— and this, I trust, will at once be made. The period for the extinction of slavery has come—the fiat is gone forth, and it is now only a question of, I believe, limited time, if the people of this free empire will but do their duty. Every one of us has a place to occupy, and a task to perform. We must not cease to urge on those who rule our Christian empire, and our voices must speedily produce the destined effect. This unnecessary and fearful evil must be abated, and one of the triumphs of Christianity will be manifested, inasmuch as in the accomplishment of her plans of benevolence and renovation the degradation of an injured race shall cease,

and the captive shall be made free. I beg heartily to propose and support the resolution I have read.

Mr. F. Lowe seconded the resolution, expressing his
hearty concurrence in it. It was unanimously adopted.

The Honourable R. D. Thomson, who rose to propose the
second resolution, said, that the statement contained in the
resolution seemed to him perfectly true, but that it was not
on that account the less important. The people in England
seemed to think that we wanted protection—now this resolution declared that we were perfectly prepared to compete
with all the world; that all our natural advantages were
equal, and that, under such circumstances, he had never
known Englishmen beaten by the skill, industry, or capital
of any foreigners. All we asked was to have the treaties
fairly enforced, and then, without discussing the free trade
principle, as it was termed, we were quite ready to accept it.

2. " That the climate and soil of this island are as favourable
for the production of sugar and coffee as those of any other country; and that its inhabitants are quite prepared for competition
in the markets of the world with the natives of Cuba and Brazil,
provided that the stipulations of the treaties made between those
countries and Great Britain were as faithfully observed by them as
they have always been by the subjects of her Britannic Majesty."

Mr. A. Rose seconded this resolution, which was unanimously carried.

Mr. Louis Mackinnon proposed the third resolution,
which was seconded by Mr. Edward Ewbank, and adopted.

3. " That it is only by means of the importation of slaves that
the inhabitants of those countries are enabled to undersell the
planters of this island in the various markets of the world; and
that, if they are permitted to continue this course, there is no
doubt the supply of the English market itself, when the duties
shall have been equalised, must of necessity fall into their hands,
their sole advantage over us arising out of their habitual violation
of treaties that we have strictly fulfilled."

Mr. Henry Crewe, in rising to propose the fourth resolution, declared his hearty concurrence in the object of the

meeting, and his firm conviction that this country could compete with any other in the cultivation of tropical produce, if relieved from the unequal competition with slave labour.

4. " That if it be deemed inexpedient by the British Government to insist absolutely and unconditionally upon the observance of these treaties, it is, at all events, but equitable to make the right of selling their produce in the British market, now conceded to the subjects of Spain and Brazil, dependent upon their adherence to those engagements entered into by their several Governments with Great Britain."

This resolution having been seconded by Mr. Thomas Heath, it was carried.

Mr. M. S. Farquharson then moved the fifth resolution, stating, that it had only just been put unexpectedly into his hands.

5. " That this meeting is of opinion that an appeal to the British Government and people has become more than ever necessary, in consequence of an attempt lately made in the British House of Commons, on the motion of Mr. Milner Gibson, to abrogate the treaty on this subject with the Brazilian empire."

This resolution was seconded by Mr. F. Jarman, and adopted.

The Reverend Dr. Stewart then moved, which was agreed to, that the memorial, which was read, should be presented to her Majesty the Queen, and that the Chairman be requested to sign it on behalf of the meeting ; and that the resolutions passed should be embodied in a petition, to be signed by the inhabitants, and sent to the two Houses of Parliament; and that the petitions be entrusted to his Honour the Custos, who is about to proceed to England, with the request that he will take the best means of having them presented and supported in the House of Lords and Commons.

It was then moved that the Custos do leave the chair, and that Louis Mackinnon, Esq., do take the same, which having been done, the thanks of the meeting were unanimously voted to the Honourable E. Thompson for his readiness in convening the meeting, and his conduct in presiding over it.

Mr. Thompson returned thanks, and having expressed his gratification at the harmony and unity of feeling which had prevailed at the meeting, and the interest manifested in it by all parties, said, that now the business of the meeting was over, he would beg to call attention to a suggestion that had been made as to the propriety of sending home a competent person, as well on the part of this island, as of the other colonies, to arouse the sympathies of the people of England on the subject of slavery; that a mere trifle subscribed by each person would enable us to do this, and that the enlisting the body of the people at home in our cause would be the most effectual mode of accelerating the time when this accursed traffic should utterly cease. He agreed with the Rector that its days were numbered—its doom sealed—but it was the duty of every one who heard him to accelerate the period of its extinction.

The meeting then separated.

On the 19th of the same month another great public meeting, with the same objects in view, was held in the populous parish of St. Andrew, of which the city of Kingston was formerly a part. At this meeting the Rev. Alexander Campbell, the rector of the parish, presided, and having taken the chair, on the motion of the senior magistrate, delivered the following address :—

" Gentlemen, long as I have lived among you, you could not have fixed on an individual less qualified by experience for fulfilling the duty which you have done me the honour to devolve upon me ; for, in truth, this is the first time, during my long residence in Jamaica, in which I have occupied the chair at any meeting, except at times in those of my brethren of the clergy. But little as I am gifted, either by nature or experience, for the duties of the office to which you have now been pleased to call me, I do not decline it, because the present is no ordinary occasion, because it is a most holy movement in which we are about to join, and one in which

I deem it the especial duty of the clergy, after the example of their venerated diocesan, to perform their appointed part. It is not simply the cause of slavery against which we are now to raise our voice, but against slavery in union with the horrors of the slave-trade. The abolition of slavery is with us but a thing of yesterday, and perhaps some of us might get little credit for our sincerity, in giving expression to the repugnance we feel against it; but the horrors of the slave-trade belong, I may say, to a past generation, forgotten almost by the oldest of us; and the long interval of nearly forty years that elapsed before its abolition was followed by that of slavery, and which, I rejoice to think, was not altogether neglected, nor unsuccessfully employed in preparation for the blessings and duties of freedom. Gentlemen, it is not against free trade, nor against anything else that ought to be free, that we are now to raise our voice, but against crime, and against traffic in human beings. But these things will be better and more effectually told you by the several gentlemen who are about to address you, and therefore I will not longer detain you."

The Reverend C. H. Hall, Island Curate, from the mountainous districts of the parish, being called on to move the first resolution, which was to the following effect:

" That it is necessary to denounce, and this meeting does solemnly and unanimously denounce, the inhuman traffic of slaves carried on by the planters of Cuba, Porto Rico, and the Brazils, contrary to the provisions of the treaties with the Spanish and Brazilian Governments, destructive to the happiness of mankind, and in defiance of the laws of God and the institutions of all Christian nations:"

observed — Mr. Chairman, this resolution states that it is *necessary* to denounce, and, acting on that necessity, does denounce the inhuman traffic in slaves carried on by the planters in Cuba and other parts of the world. And truly, Sir, the wide-spread ruin in the British colonies—the fearful extension of that gigantic evil the slave-trade—which, whilst it accumulates fresh impulse through our weakness, increases

by that very success our difficulties, together with the almost
complete stagnation of public opinion in England on the
whole question,—truly, Sir, I say all these circumstances combined, demonstrate the necessity, and justify the efforts now
making to renew that warmth of British sympathy for the
unfortunate, once existing, and which, called again into action,
may compel a faithful performance of the various treaties on
the slave-trade question, by the different foreign Governments enumerated in this resolution. We meet here, not
alone on the ground of our pecuniary interests being affected,
but because the higher, nobler interests of humanity and
justice demand our strenuous exertions. In 1807 the British
Government put an end to the slave-trade, prohibiting all
her subjects from engaging in it; and, seven-and-twenty
years after its repudiation of this glaring national iniquity,
the movement was followed up by the total abolition of
slavery throughout the British colonies. The cause of
freedom, *then*, was holy, just, and good—the battle in its
favour, at *that time*, earnest, vigorous, and strong, and greatly
is it to be regretted that the issue of so promising a cause has
not been as favourable—the result by no means as successful
as its advocates anticipated, and its merits justly deserved;
for, despite the great efforts of the friends of freedom, the
slave-trade has steadily increased, and flourishes more vigorously than ever in the neighbouring countries of Cuba, Porto
Rico, and Brazil. And to what causes may a result so
unfortunate, after the exertion of so much energy—the
expenditure of so much treasure and blood—be ascribed?
England's cupidity and apathy. She has culpably permitted,
nay, forced us into an undue competition with the owners of
slaves—thrown open her markets to their produce, and thus
placed the honest man in unfair opposition to the thief, to
the certain encouragement of the one and the as certain
discouragement and ultimate destruction of the other. She
has fallen from her high position of active antagonism to
slavery—her zeal in the righteous cause has abated—the
Christian fervour that animated and actuated her is gone—
and now, to stimulate her lukewarmness and reanimate her

expiring interest and zeal in a question of such paramount importance to ourselves and to the sons of Africa, it has become necessary for us to take up the cry of condemnation once so loudly sounding from her shores—reiterate it, until the reverberation shall reach her ears, and remind her that the " traffic of slaves, carried on by the planters of Cuba, Porto Rico, and the Brazils, contrary to the provisions of the treaties with the Spanish and Brazilian Governments," is still the same inhuman, accursed thing which it has ever been. This resolution denounces slavery as being contrary to, and in defiance of, the laws of God and the institutions of all Christian nations. It is true that religion in the beginning seems to have sanctioned slavery. The Hebrew law permitted under certain modifications its existence (but even then, under the Mosaic dispensation, the *man-stealer* was deemed worthy of death), and the Christian religion, cautious in its interference in political matters, pronounces no explicit condemnation on its sinfulness ; for we observe St. Paul, in sending back Onesimus to his master, intercedes for the pardon of the *slave* without any disapprobation of *slavery*. But notwithstanding the seeming toleration of this crime by an apparent tacit acquiescence on the part of Christianity, of which many have not failed to take advantage, contending that " Christianity was never intended to make any alterations in the civil conditions of men," slavery is nevertheless as opposed to the genius and spirit of Christianity as any system can possibly be. The Christian religion inculcates as essential the noble and divine principle of *love;* a mark by which we may know aright whether we be actuated by a divine spirit. It promulges the royal law, " do unto others as you would be done by," and slavery, on these comprehensive and imperative principles, must be expunged from the face of every *Christian nation;* for it contravenes the very groundwork of their faith. Who would like to endure the hard bondage of the slave? Who then ought to be instrumental, directly or indirectly, in riveting the chain upon the captive? *None!* And in obedience to that divine law of love which comes from God, and without which we are nothing it must be pronounced, in the language of this resolution, that the hateful system of slavery, is " in defiance of the laws of God and the institutions of all Christian nations." Great Britain perceived this, and recognising the paramount obligation of the great Christian doctrine of love for the whole human family, she abolished the slave-trade and, subsequently, slavery in her own dominions. But what has been the tenor of her subsequent legislation? In a great measure to paralyse and nullify her past exertions. A worldly cupidity has prevented her acting fairly towards those who, embracing the same principles, and yielding to her wishes, justly looked for some encouragement and protection at her hands, under the pressure of the difficulties inevitably attendant on an experiment unexampled in the history of nations. That encouragement and protection she has withheld—and what is the consequence? Whilst the slave-trade progresses and thrives by her policy, and slave owners are enriched by her liberality—we, her free children, are suffering most severely—religion, morality, our social state, all threatened; and if, Mr. Chairman, Great Britain persists in this same course, it needs no prophet to foretell a dark night coming on, when, everything holy and good driven from among us, we shall be compelled to leave our native country and seek subsistence in other lands. I feel great satisfaction in proposing this resolution. Let it not be said that suffering pecuniary interests alone induce us to bestir ourselves; that we, because colonists, have no claim to the feelings of brotherly love, no regard for the interests of humanity;—I claim for myself, I claim for this meeting, I claim for this island generally, some portion of those holy feelings of Christian love and brotherly kindness imperatively due from man to man.

Mr. Stephen W. Mais, a magistrate of the parish, seconded the resolution, which, having been put to the meeting, was passed unanimously.

Mr. Edward Jordon, also a magistrate of the parish, said—This resolution, which has been put into my hands to be moved, has reference to the slave-trade and to the large amount annually expended in keeping the naval squadron on the coast of Africa. It is as follows:—

" That notwithstanding the British Government annually expends one million and a half of money, and sacrifices many valuable lives in its endeavours to suppress the slave-trade by means of a naval squadron on the coast of Africa, that trade still continues to be carried on with increased vigour, whilst its horrors are multiplied tenfold, and the plantations of Cuba and the Brazils are regularly re-stocked with slaves."

Mr. Chairman, it is hardly necessary for me to say anything in support of a resolution of this kind. We all know that the slave-trade has been carried on, on the part of certain nations, notwithstanding the existence of treaties between them and Great Britain for its suppression; and, if the accounts which we often receive are to be believed, there is no doubt that that trade has fearfully increased. The resolution states, that notwithstanding the British Government annually expends one million and a half of money, and sacrifices many valuable lives in its endeavours to suppress the slave-trade, that trade continues to be carried on with vigour. England, it must be admitted, has never hesitated, for a single moment, to expend her money in the attempt to put down this trade, and she has even spilt her best blood in that attempt—she has never hesitated to select from her officers, men of undoubted skill and energy to guard the African coast. It is true that the efforts made for the suppression of that trade have not succeeded, and that it has increased tenfold, and he feared was very likely to increase thirtyfold. Notwithstanding the large number of victims who have been annually sacrificed to European cupidity, he was of opinion the number would have been greater, but for the presence of the squadron in question; the trade continued, and the efforts used had failed in checking it as effectually as could have been desired. We are not, however, he said, to lose hope because the traffic has not been diminished. If any adequate idea could be formed of the number of persons who are annually taken from the coast of Africa, notwithstanding the presence of the

squadron on the coast, it would be seen that the meeting had
abundant cause to regret that the treaties for the suppression
had not been carried out.   He admitted that the policy of
Great Britain, in keeping the squadron on the African coast,
was an excellent one, but contended that her conduct on the
whole was contradictory, and indeed incomprehensible. How
any nation could expect that the slave-trade could be put an
end to, when the inducement to carry it on had been increased, he could not understand.   That trade, he observed,
continues, not because the masters of the slave vessels or the
crews of them derive any pleasure from the mere conveyance of Africans from the coast to the countries in which
they were sold into slavery.   It was not from any pleasure
which employment of that kind afforded to those engaged in
it, but from the love of gain—the desire for the money made
by the purchase and sale of their fellow-men that the inhuman traffic was entered into.   We know very well, he
observed, that smuggling is carried on in almost every
country, notwithstanding the existence of laws for its prevention, and that it will be, so long as the gain is sufficient
to cover the risk.   Those who are engaged in it tell us, or
used to do so, that one safe venture out of three is sufficient
for this purpose, and leaves an inducing profit.   And so it is
with the slave dealer.   He is encouraged to engage in the
slave-trade because it yields him a handsome pecuniary
return.   If the price of a negro in Cuba and Brazil be £100
sterling, he can afford to lose two out of every three cargoes
purchased by him (and it has been said, by some, four out of
five)—that price being increased to £150, will he not be
able to bear the loss of six out of every seven?   The price
of sugar being low in Europe and the Continental markets,
the price of slaves is also low in Cuba and Brazil.   The
former is the barometer by which the slave owner and slave
dealer regulate their movements.   And if, when sugar was
low, the slave dealer could carry on his traffic, the price
even then being sufficient to induce him to incur the risks,
how much stronger the inducement to do so when it has
increased and is high?   If England, by the alteration in

the sugar duties, raised the price of slave-grown sugar, and there can be no doubt of the fact, is it not evident that she induced the desire to produce more of the article—increased the demand for the labour necessary for that purpose—and of consequence afforded an additional stimulus to the slave-trade? She imposes taxation on her own people, to the extent of one million and a half annually, ostensibly for the purpose of putting an end to the slave-trade, and her Ministers expend that amount of British gold every year for this purpose on the one hand; whilst, on the other hand, with astonishing fatuity, they adopt measures which give an extraordinary impetus to that very trade, by largely increasing its profits. How any man, or set of men, can hope or expect to put an end to the African slave-trade under these circumstances, or by such means, he confessed himself incapable of understanding. The desire for gain, the love of money, is the cause of the trade. Great Britain increases, stimulates that desire by allowing the foreigner—the slave owner—to enter her markets on the same terms as her colonies—as ourselves. Were the treaties enforced, and the supply of labour cut off, the production of sugar in slave countries would soon be reduced. It may be kept up for a short time, by over-working the slaves, but this is an evil which will cure itself. The harder these are wrought, the sooner they will die; the slave owner knows it, and in proportion as the number of tons of sugar increase, in the same proportion will the number of slaves decrease. So long, however, as the Cubans and Brazilians can draw fresh supplies of slaves from Africa—can obtain cargoes of human cattle—so long will they continue to increase their cultivation, tempted to do so by the prices they obtain for their produce in *our* mother country. He happened to be in England when the last Sugar Duties' Bill passed, and met, in a counting-house in Birmingham, a gentleman connected with estates in Cuba. That gentleman was perfectly cock-a-hoop at the prospect of gain which that measure opened up to him. What hope was there that the rapid extension of sugar estates in Cuba would cease, so long as encouragement was thus given to increased production, and of consequence to an increased demand for slaves, and increased energy and vigilance in prosecuting the slave-trade? It was perfectly natural that men who did not consider it sinful to engage in that trade, or to own slaves, would, so long as it was profitable, purchase and sell or hold them. And, taking this view of the question, it did not appear unfair to ask Great Britain to impose such a duty upon their produce as would entirely exclude it from the English markets. He believed that England had been and was sincere in the desire to put down the slave-trade. The maintenance of the squadron on the African coast, and the expenditure of a million of money annually, were evidences of that desire. But to do this, and to admit slave-grown sugar into the British markets, was grossly inconsistent. Either let her openly throw her philanthropy overboard, or cease to pursue a course which had the effect of neutralising her best efforts, and of encouraging the trade. He could not believe that she would do the former—that her humanity was so entirely lost and gone. It was a fact, nevertheless, that there were men in England who plainly and distinctly advocated the policy of withdrawing the squadron, and leaving the slave traders to pursue their occupation without hindrance or molestation. And it was still more surprising that such a course was urged on motives of humanity. These parties would permit the slave dealers to resort to the African coast, and the man-stealer to pursue his avocation in peace and quiet; they would have the slave-trade rampant, because it is humane—it is philanthropic to do so. It was because he believed there existed an amount of humanity in the mother country amply sufficient to ensure the enforcement of the slave-trade treaties that he had consented to move the resolution. And if England will act with energy and determination—if she will prove to the world that she is determined to be consistent—she will not fail to enforce the treaties in question. He would be sorry to say anything which could be considered as reflecting upon her Majesty's Ministers, but there did appear to him to exist, on their part, a

decided unwillingness to enforce them—nay, more, a disposition rather to encourage than to put down the traffic. He
was constrained to say that the desire to obtain cheap sugar
had induced them to pursue a course which had placed the
consistency and the honour of England, and the interest of
the colonies, in a most perilous position—and which was
calculated to ensure a supply of a cheap commodity without
reference to, and irrespective of, the means by which it was
produced. The West Indies had suffered and were still
suffering—their condition, instead of improving, was becoming every day worse. Nor was there any prospect of a
change for the better. We see estate, he said, after estate
being thrown up and their proprietors prostrated by the
storm. It was needful that those who were suffering should
put forth some effort to produce a change—should make
some attempt to obtain the aid of the British people in this
matter. From the Ministry, said Mr. Jordon, emphatically,
I expect nothing; from a particular section of the free
traders—and certain politicians—from the mere man of the
world or of business, who regards the matter simply as one
of pounds, shillings and pence—we have very little indeed to
expect. Our appeal must be to the friends of humanity—to
the philanthropists of England. We must endeavour to
rouse that feeling which brought about the emancipation of
slavery in these colonies—the anti-slavery portion of the
public. Their leading men have long been inviting us to
join them in pressing this very important subject upon the
consideration of her Majesty's Government. But we have
been careless, lukewarm, and indifferent. When the Sugar
Duties' Act was before Parliament, and they essayed to
prevent its passing, the West Indians—the parties most
deeply interested—either quietly looked on with their arms
folded, or lent their aid to Government in carrying the
measure. A stern necessity, however, now drives us to
exertion—and I trust this meeting will be followed up by
others in every parish of this island—that we will show that
we have some little energy—some vigour remaining, and
are willing to bring them into exercise, in making at least

one effort to recover our lost ground and to better our condition.

Mr. John Fowles, junior, another magistrate of the parish, said,—I feel great pleasure, Mr. Chairman, in seconding the resolution. The present occasion opens a wide field for reflection, for we have all come here to assist in mitigating the sufferings of the slave-trade. In the year 1834, when her Majesty's Government emancipated the slaves, the Marquis of Normanby, who was then at the head of our affairs, said—" Slavery has received its death-blow—that accursed system must fall, and you will receive the thanks of your fellow-men on the other side of the water, and they will record their concurrence of your conduct." This was his declaration, and it was supposed that he would have exerted himself on our behalf; but we have found that he, in common with others in England, have encouraged the foreigners, and have actually upheld them by a policy which is vicious, and must bring down retribution on the heads of the British people. I am quite at a loss to understand the policy of the British Government. While we were endeavouring to do all in our power to assist ourselves, after the act of emancipation had passed, and to do good to our peasantry, the British Government stepped in, and with one fell swoop annihilated our actions. Sir Robert Peel, who had extended his hand to extinguish slavery, stood up in his place in the House of Commons, and declared we could get no protection. My hon. friend, Mr. Jordon, has related to you an anecdote, and I remember a similar case in England, where I met a gentleman who talked loudly against the horrors of slavery, while at the same time his house was engaged in furthering the slave-trade, and when he was spoken to on the subject, his answer was, "That's not me, but my house." I hope, Mr. Chairman, we shall do all in our power to put down this atrocious, this abominable slave-trade. I feel certain that if all of us were to lend a helping hand in carrying out the object for which we have met, that some good results would be effected.

The second resolution was then put and passed.

Mr. Osborn, member of Assembly for the parish of St. Andrew, said—Ladies and gentlemen, in coming forward to offer for your adoption the third resolution, I shall have a very few observations to make to you. I had been preparing a few ideas, but I find that the rev. gentleman, who has so ably addressed you, has taken them from me, and my friend, Mr. Jordon, has also drawn upon them. Upon reflection it does not, however, appear strange that all of us should express ourselves to the same effect, although in different language, upon so important a subject as this. The English prices current is the social, the political, and the moral barometer of this country, and it appears to be pointing downwards, and must therefore fill us with gloom and apprehension. When we view the depressed state of things, we are naturally weighed down with anxiety, to know how long we shall be able to afford our families the necessaries of life. If we go to our sugar estates or coffee plantations, we find the planter labouring under gloom, dread, and misapprehension. Go into our mercantile houses, and you will find the clerks and their masters sitting idle. Go into the shop of the humble artisan, and you will find him sitting idle. Agriculture is failing, and trade is dull, and this state of things is extending itself even to private families. Our carts are no longer seen going home filled with the good things of this life. This is known to the ladies, for if they go into the pantry it is seen empty—if they go into the kitchen, pans and kettles, which were used for culinary purposes, are seen hanging up. These are facts which we see daily, and which we are practically experiencing ; and if there should be a man present not experiencing such a state of things, all I can say is, that he is more fortunate than his fellow-sufferers. The resolution which I am called upon to propose is this :—

" That under the present system of British duties, if the planters of Cuba, Porto Rico, and the Brazils are permitted to evade the treaties entered into by their respective Governments with Great Britain, for the suppression of the slave-trade—are allowed to import slaves in unlimited numbers from Africa—and are suffered to enforce from their slaves sixteen hours of labour out of every twenty-four—the planters of this thinly populated colony cannot, with any hope or prospect of success, continue to cultivate their estates, or to arrest the downward tendency of the affairs of this fine and once prosperous and important exporting island to a state of hopelessness and irremediable ruin."

Now, then, you have heard the resolution read, and if you call to mind what has been advanced by the Rev. Mr. Hall and my friend, Mr. Jordon, who has carried you to Cuba and Brazil, nay, further, to a counting-house in Birmingham, you will see that there remains little or nothing for me to say. I may, however, call to mind the decided manner in which the English nation settled the question of slavery; and we are all agreed in the opinion that slavery was a curse, and every passage of Scripture was invoked for the purpose of carrying out a principle which was good. The English nation declared with one voice that slavery was inconsistent with Christianity—that it was inconsistent with that doctrine which said, "If any man says he loves God, and hateth his brother, he is a liar." Pamphlets after pamphlets were published, and the doctrine was reiterated, and the declaration was repeated, "Whatsoever ye would that men should do unto you, do ye also unto them." It was impossible that any Christian would act upon this principle, and coerce his fellow-creature. The Christian people of England have declared that man should not be the slave of man—that the Almighty never intended that man should hold his fellow-man in bondage; and having adopted this principle, appeals were made to the people of this island, who yielded up their slaves, and the British people gave us twenty millions of money to compensate us for the loss we had sustained. They not only paid us this, but they voted adequate sums of money to guard the coast of Africa; they also entered into treaties for abolishing the slave-trade and slavery in other countries. Upon this, we all felt particularly well satisfied, until they set to work diligently, and undid what they had done. You have seen what an extraordinary revulsion of feeling has taken place in the British people, from which cause we find all classes suddenly thrown into poverty and want. We have done nothing to provoke this; we have not been a rebellious people—we have always been a loyal people; but no one can tell how long this will last. The question is one of great importance—what is to become of these countries, and the people inhabiting them? The produce of slavery is admitted freely into England, to the disadvantage of the free producer, and the sliding-scale of duties which they gave us is fast sliding from beneath our feet. There can be no doubt that sugar, made by men who are compelled to work sixteen hours in the day, like cattle, can be sold at a cheaper rate than by the planter who cannot obtain labour for more than six or eight hours. Some persons have said that we can compete with the slave-labour sugar, but I cannot understand how this can be done, when the labourer works as he likes, and when he likes. I have never heard it explained yet, and I consider it perfectly Utopian for us to be told so. I think I need hardly trouble you with any further remarks, ladies and gentlemen; I will therefore quit you for a few moments, while I address a few remarks to my friends below. You (continued Mr. Osborn, addressing the labourers present) are not employed at such rates of wages as you ought to be, and the reason is evident. If sugar and coffee are shipped home, and they continue to lay down in the warehouses, the proprietors cannot get money to carry on their estates. You see estates thrown up, covered with weeds and bush, and you are not asked to clear it, because they cannot pay you. Many of you think if you plant cocoas you could eat some and sell some, and by this way you could get on easily. In the times of slavery a man was allowed one Saturday in two weeks, and that was considered sufficient to enable him to attend to the cultivation of provisions for his family. If one day is enough, what is to be done with the other days? The planter cannot send home yams and plantains, for before they reach half way they would be good for nothing; and if cane and coffee cannot sell, what is to be done? This is the question which induces you to see all classes mixing up here; the state of things has become perfectly distressing, and we are obliged to be content with half-diet, and if it continues longer we may be brought to quarter-diet. However great our distresses are, we are sometimes enabled to make a good appearance, but this cannot continue, and we must unite as one man to tell the British public that we are willing to be loyal, but that we cannot, for the sake of loyalty, continue any longer to starve. Let us tell them that we are willing, as children, to perform our duty as such, but that they too have duties which must be performed. We cannot starve for the sake of loyalty—we cannot die without trying to save ourselves. By the sweat of our brow we are to eat our bread, and we are willing to do so, but the interests of the calico manufacturers will not permit us to do so; they seem determined to keep us from earning our livelihood, but we must boldly lift our voices and tell them, you shall not any longer prevent us from doing so. We must assume a high position, and know whether we are to be sacrificed for the purpose of spreading the principles of free trade.

Mr. G. W. Gordon, one of the magistrates of the parish, and a member of Assembly, in seconding the resolution, said—I have a word or two to say on the subject of my abhorrence of the slave-trade and slavery, and I hope that this meeting will be followed up throughout the island, to demand the enforcement of these treaties. I rely upon British honour and British justice, and therefore it is that I hope the same favour which has been extended to others will be extended to us. We have struggled through the difficulties which we have had, in competing with the slave-stealer, and I feel it is only necessary that we should bring the matter prominently before the British people, and we will soon discover a perfect development in our favour. We are, Sir, affected by the introduction of the sugars of Brazil and Cuba into the English markets—we who have been slaves, and who have had a boon conferred upon us; because no sooner was this boon granted, than a measure of oppression has been put upon us. I have no doubt that upon a proper representation we shall be fairly heard; we must cry loudly against the curse of slavery, the accursed traffic in human flesh; we must take courage, and I feel convinced that our cry will succeed; we must appeal to their humanity—to that charity which is due from man to man. I feel, Sir, that on the subject of slavery I grow warm, and therefore I must content myself by seconding the resolution.

The third resolution was put and passed.

Mr. Bristowe, also a member of Assembly and a magistrate, moved the fourth resolution. He said—The resolution which has been put into my hands shows—

" That it is expedient to urge upon the imperial Government, in the most emphatic manner, the necessity of insisting upon the immediate fulfilment of the treaties for the suppression of the slave-trade by the Spanish and Brazilian powers, in order that the emancipated colonies of Great Britain may be enabled to meet and overcome the competition of the slave dealers and planters of Cuba, Porto Rico, and the Brazils, in the home and other European markets."

I could have wished that the important resolution entrusted to me had been placed in more competent hands, and with some one of those many enlightened individuals whom I have the pleasure of seeing around me; but as it has been confided to me, I will endeavour to bring it under your consideration as briefly and plainly as possible. My honourable friend, Mr. Osborn, told this meeting at the commencement of his speech that he did not intend to occupy your time and attention very long, but his speech has, as usual, been somewhat lengthy, although much too interesting to be tedious or disagreeable. I have really and truly but little to say upon the subject under consideration, nor can I give even that with the force and eloquence which are required to render it interesting to the meeting. Holding as I do, however, strong opinions upon the violation of these treaties, and believing that the abominable traffic they were intended to put down, to be contrary to all law, human and divine, and opposed to the best interests of humanity, and to the progress of civilisation throughout the world, I will not shrink from the performance of the duty imposed upon me—that of asking the meeting to urge upon the imperial Government to compel, with arms if necessary, the performance of obligations and treaties entered into in the most solemn manner by the Spanish and Brazilian Governments for the purpose of suppressing a frightful and immoral evil. I will place the question in a somewhat different light to that in which it has been placed, by the learned and eloquent speakers who delivered their sentiments at the great meeting recently held in Spanish Town, as well as by those who have spoken before me on this occasion; and I will endeavour to show, amongst other things, that it is a breach of contract, highly prejudicial not only to England, but to the West Indian colonies, and a precedent for other nations, replete with mischief and disaster. There were all the elements in the treaty of 1817, entered into with his Catholic Majesty, of a good and valid agreement, and which would be held binding, if entered into on any of the ordinary transactions of life ; there were the parties to the contract, the consideration, and the promise; and it is a fact patent to the whole world, that the consideration of £400,000 was paid by England, and that the contract on her part was fairly and honourably completed. What, then, is to be said or thought of a nation that enters into an agreement—a contract for a sacrifice, if they please to call it such—and receives a consideration for an act to be done one day, and on the next repudiates the agreement, and denies the obligation ? Or, what is to be said or thought of that other nation which permits itself so to be cheated, and then laughed at and insulted into the bargain, whilst its own people are suffering from the non-observance of that contract which was partly entered into for their benefit and advantage? I know there are many and serious difficulties in the way, but Great Britain has the power to enforce the observance of the treaties; and in mercy to mankind, and in justice to her own suffering colonists, I say she is bound to exercise that power. Let her at once declare her determination to treat slave traffickers as pirates, and let her act upon that determination, and hang up the first batch of them as an example to others, and in two or three years the trade which now excites so much of our horror and disgust would be put an end to. Treaties and diplomacy are a mockery when the shackles of slavery are rattling in our ears on every side. I believe the Government of Great Britain to be actuated by just principles and moved by noble impulses; but I think she does appear to be too indifferent at times to the best interests of her colonial subjects, and profoundly, if not wilfully, ignorant of their real wants and necessities. Let her take warning in time. Canada presents at this moment a frightful picture of colonial disquiet and confusion—God grant that it may not turn into anarchy and complete disorganisation, to be speedily followed up by separation from the parent State. Colonies will not submit, in these times, to be governed either negligently or ignorantly; and I say it is the policy, as well as the duty of every parent State, to study the requirements of the people in distant dependencies such as this. I know this, Sir—that nothing but an enlightened and liberal policy, and a remission of the duties at present imposed upon our island staples (a subject I merely allude to for illustration, nothing more), together with the honest fulfilment of the treaties referred to, can possibly impart prosperity to this naturally fine island. I know, Sir, that— to use a legal metaphor—the case at present is, " British revenue and endurance *versus* colonial existence," and I do hope and believe that the imperial Government will deal justly and fairly in the matter. When individuals entered into agreements they are bound—in all countries where law is known and respected at all—to observe and to keep to them, and the same general principles which bind individuals to the performance of their contracts, will apply with respect to the contracts of nations. This is a maxim to deny which would be to strike at the roots of moral, as well as social and political order; but Spain and the Brazils did practically abjure the maxim, and they ought to be compelled to perform those agreements for which the money of England had been paid. I think, Sir, that the shield of

England, with the lion rampant so proudly emblazoned
upon its front, has been stained, and the honour of Great
Britain wounded, in the late affair of Sir Henry L. Bulwer
with the court of Spain ; an affair which, I believe, originated with, and arose in some measure out of, the non-observance of these very slave treaties.   I feel somewhat ashamed,
as an Englishman, to admit that the lion of England was
kicked by the Minister of her most Catholic Majesty of
Spain, and that the kick went unresented, and the insult
unavenged, although it was universally admitted that abundant cause was shown for a vigorous exercise of British
power, not only in vindication of her own national honour,
and in support of her own Ministers, but also in order to
enforce those treaties, the non-observance of which is operating so prejudicially against her own emancipated colonies.
His Catholic Majesty knew perfectly well what he was
about, or the Spanish Government of the day did, when the
treaty of 1817 was entered into ; and to compel its fulfilment
would be no injustice to Spain, whilst it would be compul-
sion acceptable to the whole civilised world, and would
accomplish what the treaty had in contemplation—namely,
the absolute annihilation of the most revolting traffic that
ever disgraced the commerce of nations.   Our own glorious
act of emancipation has been in some degree rendered
nugatory by the non-observance of that and other treaties,
and it is a matter of necessity that they should at least be
enforced and observed.   I am not one of those sanguine
persons who imagine that everything is to be attributed—
all the evils we are suffering here are to be traced—to the
non-fulfilment of the treaties alluded to; but I do think that
many of them are to be attributed to that source ; and, at
all events, it is not consistent with the honour or interest
of England, to suffer them any longer to be evaded—to be
evaded too, by whom, and by what powers and people?
It makes my blood boil, as an Englishman, and almost
curdle, as a human being, to reflect upon the insults endured
by Great Britain, from paltry, petty slave-owning States, and
to think how dead she has shown herself to the exhibition

of all the vile doings of the slave dealers. But I hope and
trust these things will no longer be endured. It is with
sorrow, and almost with shame, that I am forced to admit,
that whilst the planters of Cuba and Brazil are realising
enormous profits for their staple productions in the markets
of England—the fruits of slave labour—the planters of this
island are suffering ruin, almost starvation, by being brought
into this unnatural competition, and I must say that I deeply
sympathise with them in their present cruelly depressed
condition. It is absurd to suppose that the planters of
Jamaica can successfully compete with the planters of Cuba,
in the present comparative condition of the two islands.
In Cuba, the planter can command slave labour to an
unlimited extent, and work each slave for any number of
hours; whereas, in Jamaica, the planter cannot command,
as it is generally believed, a sufficiency of labour, and that
which he could command was given only for a reasonable
period (and very properly so given) of each day. Happily
for the people of this island, the great act of emancipation
put a stop to compulsory labour amongst them; but it is
obvious that if the compulsory labour of countless numbers
in foreign States is to be brought into open competition with
the labour (however good and effective) of a limited number
of free men in Jamaica, the persons employing the latter
must of necessity go to the wall; and the complete destruction of the employers' interests would naturally involve, and
carry along with it, the best and most vital interests of the
employed, and, indeed, of all ranks and classes of the community. It is of great importance to this island, Sir, that
the treaties of which we have heard so much should be fulfilled, and I hope the petition to Parliament and the memorial to her Majesty will meet with the hearty sanction and
support of all classes, and of people of all shades and
denominations of belief and opinion. It is due to humanity—
it is due to the British colonists—it is due to the great name
of the British nation and people, that the accursed system,
with its host of united horrors and atrocities, should be put
down; and I hope that the whole force and power of the

empire will be put forth, in order that the treaties for the suppression of the slave-trade might be enforced—the fetters be struck from the limbs of the slave—and the disgusting trade in human beings be at once and for ever put an end to.

Mr. John R. Brice, coroner for the parish, in seconding the resolution, said, that the mover of it had been so elaborate and emphatic that he was at a loss what to say, and would content himself with merely seconding it, which he trusted would be carried with acclamation.

The Rev. Duncan H. Campbell, the rector's curate, proposed the fifth resolution :—

" That this meeting unanimously approves of the resolutions and sentiments adopted and promulgated at the public meeting held at Spanish Town, on her Majesty's birth-day, and which was so propitiously presided over by the Lord Bishop of this diocese; and that the memorial to her Majesty, and the petitions to the two Houses of the imperial Parliament, agreed to at the public meeting held in Spanish Town, on her Majesty's birth-day, be adopted, and that a committee be appointed to procure signatures to the petitions."

He said, Mr. Chairman, I accept, not without some diffidence, the honour you have conferred, in selecting me to propose the resolution which I now hold in my hand. I presume not to attribute such an honour as any personal compliment to myself, but rather to that laudable desire which has been evinced, and which, I trust, will continue to pervade the whole future course of this mighty movement— a desire of associating the clergy with the benevolent object of the meeting. And you, gentlemen, will concur with me in saying, that while your cause will lose nothing by *our* willing and steady co-operation, we do not transgress the strict bounds of our peaceful vocation in yielding ourselves willing co-operators in your philanthropic labours. It would be difficult now, in June, 1849, to present the evils and wrongs of slavery under any new or unknown aspect—it would be impossible to describe, with additional power of language, the horrors of a system, which seems to possess this unnatural quality, inherent and peculiar to itself, that the more familiar the more execrable it becomes. I do not intend now to occupy the attention of the meeting by retracing ground which has already, both here and elsewhere, been so successfully trodden. Suffice it to say, that we see before us an evil of the most appalling magnitude—an evil, not proceeding from unseen, unknown causes, but originated and propagated by human agents, to satisfy an inhuman avarice—we see before us a system of unparalleled atrocity and cruelty, at which Christianity shudders, and human nature recoils; and we see, at the same time, a remedy by which the system may be annihilated, and all its cruelties suppressed. I allude not now to any preventive African coast squadron, all of which, mournful experience declares, have only squandered away the wealth of England, ignobly exposed the lives of her seamen, and most fearfully increased the sufferings and privations of the unhappy victims of their protection; but I allude now to a safe, sure, practicable remedy—a remedy founded on the easy carrying out of existing treaties, which have been honourably entered into, but most dishonourably violated—a remedy which is embodied in the petition that I am now to invite you to sign. And shall we, gentlemen, having within our reach means by which slavery, that hydra-headed monster slavery, may be for ever crushed and demolished—shall we sit down in apathy and indifference, or shall we not rather bind ourselves in solemn combination; shall we not go forth, resolved neither to desist nor to return, until the battle has been fought and the victory been achieved? We shrink not now from any consequences. Far be it from me—a man of peace—to breathe aught of the language of strife; but if the church's prayers may be offered for success in lawful war—if her prelates and priests have consecrated banners that have gone forth and returned victorious before the armies of England, in the battles of the Lord and of their kings—surely in such a cause as this, if (which God forbid) carnal weapons must be put on, and a righteous war undertaken, surely the church's prayers will not be unavailing, nor her

blessing unfruitful. Gentlemen, I invite you all to join on
our side, for in this matter we contend not as single, solitary
individuals. This is a cause which ennobles, as it is itself
ennobled by, the very weakest instrument which is engaged
in it; so that of each one it may be said, that "the race
is not to the swift, nor the battle to the strong." We came
not here as isolated individuals, but links in a mighty chain
stretching onwards beyond the reach of present vision. We
have here a common life, common interest, a progressive
destiny, and one common reward, so that the very humblest
who is associated with us, participates equally with the
greatest in the glorious results which must eventuate from
our determined combination. Yes, gentlemen, we stand here
on the threshold of a work which must be completed; we
constitute the second meeting engaged in a cause which must
not, may not, shall not, be abandoned, until it has attained
its final successful consummation. Gentlemen, the resolution
speaks of the meeting " so propitiously presided over by the
Lord Bishop of this diocese." Need I say how personally
gratifying it is to me to be made the organ of expressing
this spontaneous sentiment of the meeting towards my
rev. diocesan. You do but justice in anticipating propitious results from his lordship's co-operation. I am at
liberty to say that this meeting, so far as it accords with the
objects of its predecessor, has the bishop's fullest good-will
and support; and I am warranted in adding that his lordship is even now adding weight to our cause, and furthering
the objects of our association, through his influence with the
spiritual peers in the imperial Parliament, where we are
about to petition. Thus, gentlemen, the movement has
received the impress of a religious and Christian spirit, and
for this reason, on behalf of myself and my reverend brethren now present, I tender our hearty good-will and zealous
co-operation.

Mr. David J. Alberga, a gentleman of the Hebrew persuasion, in seconding the resolution, said—It is, indeed,
propitious that I should be selected to follow in the wake of
the rev. gentleman on a subject which some of the speakers

considered a strictly Christian one, but I feel pleasure in
being engaged in a movement in which the whole human
race is concerned—the traffic in human blood being repug-
nant in the present day to all sects and persuasions; and
although I might differ with regard to religious tenets, there
can be no difference in desire to relieve the sufferings of the
oppressed, and to extinguish the sale and barter of human
beings. I expect, Sir, much good from the various influences which are brought to bear against the inhuman traffic,
and the desire to suppress it, and when we have also the
ladies countenancing such a cause—the ladies, whose influence is as the genial zephyr which cheers and invites to
expansion every flower it breathes upon—can we despair of
success? I regret that I cannot agree with my friend, Mr.
Jordon, as to the advantage of the blockading squadron,
because I think it could not be denied that it had failed in its
object, and that it was inseparably associated with other evils
of a more apparent character ; that, in point of fact, it tended
to increase rather than diminish the horrors of the traffic.
The frightful misery and death to which the armed suppression of the slave-trade gave rise on board the slavers was
most affecting ; the fact was, that the skill, arrangement, the
daring energy, and personal impunity of all parties engaged
in the slave-trade, have been found to be more than a match
for any squadron of cruisers that can be employed on the
coast of Africa ; in that service they are stimulated by the
profits, and regardless of the horrors they occasion. I shall
give an instance of the successful prosecution of this detestable traffic. The commissioners at Rio Janeiro, in a late
report, mention the name of one Manuel Pinto de Fonseca,
who had stated publicly that his gains in 1844 were £150,000.
I perfectly agree that nothing short of a declaration by the
great powers, making the slave-trade piracy, will be sufficient to rid humanity of its guilt and horrors. The ministerial policy of the present day towards the fast decaying
West India colonies, reminds me of an Arabian proverb,
which says, "that the barber learns his art on the orphan's
face." So it was with the Ministry; their present legislation

appeared to be, to acquire wisdom by experiments on our distresses.

The following gentlemen were named a committee for the purpose of carrying out the fifth resolution :—Rev. C. H. Hall, Edward Jordon, Robert Osborn, John Bristowe, and Thomas A. Cargill, Esqrs., and Rev. Duncan H. Campbell.

Mr. Edward Jordon proposed the sixth resolution, which was seconded by Mr. John Gordon :—

" That the committee appointed under the fifth resolution do correspond with parties in the several parishes likely to take an interest in the question of the enforcement of the treaties with Spain and Brazil, for the abolition of the slave-trade; to invite their attention to the proceedings in Spanish Town, on the 24th May ; and to point out the necessity of their adopting the memorial and petitions passed at that meeting, and of procuring signatures to the latter."

Dr. William Pine moved the seventh resolution, which was seconded by Robert Smith, Esq., the senior magistrate of the parish :—

" That as soon as a sufficient number of signatures be obtained in this parish, the lists be handed over to the chairman, for the purpose of being transmitted to his lordship the Bishop, to be appended to the petitions to both Houses of Parliament, agreed to at the meeting in Spanish Town, on the 24th ult."

Robert Smith, Esq., was then called to the chair, the thanks of the meeting were accorded to the Rev. Mr. Campbell, and the meeting broke up at about three o'clock.

The parish of Saint Ann's, the next in order, held its meeting on the 20th of June, under the presidency of the senior magistrate, Mr. Rose, who, on taking the chair, delivered the following address :—

The able and eloquent manner in which the subject, on which we have met this day, has been discussed by the right reverend prelate, and other distinguished individuals, at the general meeting in Spanish Town, and at the meetings in the parishes of St. George and St. Andrew, must be so fresh in your recollection, that my travelling over the same ground, and attempting to follow in their footsteps, is a task as unnecessary as I feel myself unequal to it. I shall not, therefore, trespass on your time by a lengthy address; but I cannot refrain from congratulating the inhabitants of this my native parish, who have ever been conspicuous for loyalty, patriotism, and public spirit, on having proved, by this demonstration, that they are equally so in the cause of humanity. I feel much gratification at the presence, on this occasion, of so many ministers of our sacred religion, as they must feel a lively interest in the welfare of mankind in general, and be zealous advocates of measures, the object of which is the total suppression of the iniquitous traffic in human beings. I am highly gratified, also, by the attendance of so large and respectable a portion of our labouring population, as that not only evinces their just sense of their interests being identified with those of the higher orders, but also, their desire of uniting with them towards relieving their suffering brethren in the foreign colonies from the galling yoke of slavery,—a consummation which I confidently expect, and I hope that I shall live to see the odious term " slave " expunged from the vocabulary of the universe. I shall conclude by recommending that all extraneous matter be avoided which might tend to interrupt the harmony and order which have characterised the public meetings in this parish, at which I have had the honour of presiding. I shall now be happy to receive any resolutions which have been prepared for this occasion.

Mr. Charles Royes, a magistrate of the parish, having been called upon, said that he had the honour to propose the first resolution to the attention of the meeting, and, having read it to the following effect—

" 1. That this meeting has to deplore the progressive deterioration and utter ruin of the agricultural and commercial prospects of this island, and the subverted confidence of capitalists, as the results of the unnatural competition with slave-cultivated countries, into which she has been forced by the acts of the parent State : "

—he proceeded to observe that it was needless for him to enter into the causes which had produced the disastrous state of things to which this resolution referred, as they were well known to have been brought about by the unnatural competition to which we were exposed with countries which were cultivated by slave labour, and he therefore contented himself with calling on the meeting to support the resolution he had read.

Mr. R. H. Holworthy seconded this resolution, which was unanimously carried.

Rev. B. Millard, in proposing the second resolution, said, that it was a source of gratification to him to find so numerous an attendance at a meeting having for its object the destruction of slavery throughout the whole world, and by acting with unanimity on the subject, slavery, which is a curse, would cease. The subject was one which did not require any lengthened speech, nor did it require any eloquence to prove the destructiveness of the slave-trade, or the injury it did to the finest feelings of human nature, and he dwelt with much force on the horrible cruelties exercised on the weak, unfortunate Africans; he showed, in striking and emphatic language, how children are torn from their parents, husbands from their wives, friends from each other; in short, the undeniable evils to Africa and humanity of which the traffic is productive. The speaker then glowingly and feelingly went on to prove that slavery is inimical to the moral and spiritual interests of the enslaved; that so long as slavery existed, religion cannot enter; that Bibles are not permitted to be brought into Cuba for the use of the slave, and in the Havanna the Spanish Government had seized and destroyed all the Bibles they found—their introduction was by stealth. The accursed system of slavery, said the rev. gentleman, destroys the finest feelings of the heart, and the sweetest affections, and so long as it exists we shall have an immoral instead of a moral being, and religion cannot flourish; but darkness must give way before light, and he hoped that the efforts we were now making would be the death-knell of slavery.

Mr. Millard then read the resolution:—

"2. That this meeting regards the African slave-trade and slavery as opposed to humanity—productive of the worst evils to Africa—degrading to all engaged in the traffic, and inimical to the moral and spiritual interests of the enslaved."

The Rev. B. B. Kingdon, in rising to second the resolution, said, he had come there that day for the purpose of showing his sympathy for the cause for which they had met, to assist in protecting the interests of his adopted country, and to endeavour to avert the evils that slavery is producing. He was a member of the Anti-Slavery Society, and had been so from his youth—that great body having bound themselves to support all movements that tended to abolish slavery; and he must in justice say, that the Society had been asleep, but not extinct, and that meetings of this description would tend to awaken their feelings with greater intensity. The slave-trade was an unnatural traffic. It had been rumoured that this movement had been suggested by the British Government, and the Attorney-general stated in his speech, in Spanish Town, that the Ministry of England feels the importance of the inquiry; and this opinion was strengthened by the fact that, in the House of Commons, on a debate on Mr. Milner Gibson's motion to rescind the treaty with Brazils of 1845, the motion was negatived by a majority of 4 to 1. Sir Robert Peel and Lord Palmerston, men of opposite political tendencies, voted against it. He was aware that a cloud was hanging over us—all was very dark, sad, and gloomy, and although he saw no rainbow, yet he still thought that he could, amid the gloom, see some of its colours. Hitherto meetings had been held, but there was a want of unanimity among them; they had not before met for one object; but in the meeting which he was now addressing, there was a *oneness*, it was no *party meeting*, it affected all classes; we were all in one boat, and must sink or swim together: and he believed that our united voices would be listened to in England, and be productive of benefit to the cause that we had met to advocate. He would suggest that we should have petitions from every congregation in the parish. He was the only individual from his district who was present, but he was assured that uncontrollable circumstances prevented others attending; it was from no want of sympathy on their part in the objects of the meeting. He was not in the habit of making speeches in public; but as a minister of religion, and as an old member of the Anti-Slavery Society, he could not refuse to support and second the resolution placed in his hand, which met with his hearty concurrence.

The resolution was put and carried.

The Rev. John Clark, Presbyterian Minister, said that he had the two following resolutions to propose :—

" 3. That this meeting has learned with deep regret, that, notwithstanding the long-continued and costly efforts of the British nation to suppress the African slave-trade, it is carried on by the subjects of Spain and of the Brazils to an enormous extent, and under circumstances of aggravated atrocity and horror; and that during the last two years it has been prosecuted with increased vigour and activity, owing to the British markets being thrown open to the slave-grown sugars of Cuba, Porto Rico, and the Brazils :

" 4. That this meeting records its conviction, that it is the duty of the British Government to demand of the Governments of Spain and of the Brazils, the fulfilment of the treaties into which they have entered for the suppression of the African slave-trade, and to insist on the liberation of all who have been illegally introduced into their territories :"

and observed, that it had just been stated that the anti-slavery feeling is to a great extent asleep in England; but he hardly thought that correct, as recently a memorial had been presented to the Queen, imploring her to use her influence to abolish the slave-trade, and public meetings were being held to implore the British Government and British Parliament to enforce the treaties with Spain and the Brazils. He agreed with Mr. Kingdon that there is a disposition to do all that is possible towards the extinction of the slave-trade, and that it would be necessary to keep this one object in view. He admitted with deep regret the deplorable state of the island, that distress was prevalent, and bankruptcies and insolvencies were daily taking place, the people compelled to work for very low wages—and all this brought about by the competition of slavery with our free labour; but we had higher objects before us than merely taking the pecuniary view of the matter; there were multitudes of our fellow-men reduced to degrading and horrible slavery. The slavery that formerly existed in Jamaica was bad enough, but there was no comparison between that and the slavery of Cuba, Porto Rico, and the Brazils: he held documents in his hand to prove this. Since the British Government had determined to abolish slavery, 4,000,000 of our fellow-men had been stolen, and 8,000,000 more had been destroyed in the attempts and efforts that had been made to procure slaves to supply the slave markets. England entered into treaties with Spain and Portugal for the entire abolition of the slave-trade, and the sum of £100,000 was paid by England to Spain for this purpose; but, notwithstanding the treaties, the slave-trade had been carried on for the last two years with greater vigour and atrocity. From the years 1840 to 1845, the average annual number of slaves introduced into the colonies of Spain and Brazil has been 32,000; in 1846 and 1847 the quantity was double, or 64,000; and last year there is every reason to believe that the number had greatly exceeded this; besides nearly 20,000 who annually perish on the passage. The speaker then adverted to the evils of slavery, and he did so in very vivid language; he then proceeded to inquire, how can England insist on the fulfilment of the treaties? how can England compel Cuba and Brazil to refrain from encouraging the slave-trade? Shall it be by war? His profession, as a minister of religion, made him averse to war: he was opposed to guns and swords, as a means of enforcing right: there was a moral power to effect this; but England might go to war, and overcome her enemies, and might compel them to put an end to slavery. She might double her steam navy—she might punish all engaged in the traffic as pirates, and hang every man found on board; but would that be wise, and would it be best calculated to ensure the correct observance of the treaties?—It would be doing evil that good might arise. He would not recommend any of these courses, because he was against war; but England had the power of suppressing the slave-trade and slavery by other means. Within the last three years slave-grown sugar has been admitted into England at a rate of duty which renders its production remunerative; prior to that time, up to 1846, there was a heavy duty laid on sugar produced by slave labour, which amounted almost to a prohibition; in that year a law was passed lowering the duties, and which eventually will enable the slave colonies to export their sugars to England at the same rate of duty as Jamaica and the other free colonies—it will, therefore, be hardly worth our while to cultivate sugar in Jamaica, unless we are placed on an equality as to labour. And in illustration of this he would ask, if two men had an article, one of whom paid a fair price for it and the other had stolen it, who could sell it the cheapest? He was a free-trader, so long as free trade was based on justice; but in this case we had to compete against the forced labour of the slave of sixteen hours a day, when our own people worked but eight hours per day. Unless some remedy is speedily applied, our sugar cultivation would have to be abandoned altogether, and free England would derive its supply from slave labour. The course the British Government should pursue is to prohibit the importation of slave-grown sugar into England, as when she buys the produce of slave labour she encourages slavery. But there was still a strong feeling in England against slavery, and there are thousands who would not use slave-grown sugar, as they believe in doing so they sinned against the great God. He believed in a God of justice and mercy, and that slavery and the slave-trade could not much longer exist. He spoke not of the poor slaves: the horrors of their position were too well known—the cruelties they endured were well understood—they had no safety. And what did the supporters of slavery gain?—money; but that will carry a curse with it—a stain of guilt would follow their ill-gotten gains. He would not be satisfied until slavery and the slave-trade were abolished from the face of the world.

The Rev. J. Curtis, in seconding the resolution, said that he had not attended the meeting to take an active part, but merely to evince the interest he took in the subject, and that he fully concurred in all that had been said by his beloved friend, the Rev. Mr. Clark.

The resolutions were unanimously adopted.

The Rev. Mr. Thompson moved the fifth resolution, to the following effect:—

" 5. That in the event of the Spanish and Brazilian Governments refusing to fulfil their solemn engagements for the abolition of the slave-trade, the British Parliament be implored to pass a law prohibiting the introduction of all slave-grown sugar into the British markets."

He said, that in consequence of the lively interest he took in the subject before the meeting, he had attended it, so as to mark his approbation of the efforts that are being made to ameliorate the condition of the slave. He did not expect to be called on to move a resolution, but one having been placed in his hands, he would read it to the meeting. He strongly advocated the necessity of calling on the Spanish and Brazilian Governments to fulfil their solemn engagements for the suppression of the slave-trade, and that, in the event of their refusal so to do, that the British Government do pass a law prohibiting the introduction of slave-grown sugar into the British markets. He dilated on the injustice of being exposed to an unnatural competition with slave labour. The rev. gentleman then graphically called the attention of the meeting to the effects of such competition, and the impending ruin which was stalking around us. He forcibly appealed to the labouring population—as to their comforts being abridged, their wages reduced, their future happiness threatened—and proceeded to argue in support of the resolution. He also expressed the pleasure with which he had read the proceedings at the general meeting in

Spanish Town, and of his entire concurrence in all that was done there, and concluded by exhorting the meeting to unite for the purpose of carrying out the objects contemplated by the meeting.

Mr. C. Fletcher seconded the resolution and said,—that after the excellent speeches that had been made by the speakers who preceded him, little was left for him to say; he therefore seconded the resolution, assuring the meeting of his cordial assent to all that had been done to carry out its objects.

Carried unanimously.

Mr. M. Solomon proposed the sixth resolution.

" 6. That a committee be appointed to co-operate with the committee of the general meeting held in Spanish Town, and that the resolutions and memorial agreed to at that meeting be adopted, and signatures obtained thereto, and then forwarded to his lordship the Bishop, to be attached to those that are to be laid before the Houses of Parliament, and that the following gentlemen be named as such committee :—The Rector, Rev. John Clark, Rev. B. B. Kingdon, Charles Fletcher, Esq., Charles Royes, Esq., Rev. T. C. Rose, Rev. B. Millard, Rev. E. S. Thompson, Rev. T. Curtis, Rev. T. Gould, Rev. J. Young, Rev. J. Hodgson."

Mr. Solomon then said, that he was gratified that the rev. gentleman who proposed the fifth resolution had concurred in and approved of what had been done in Spanish Town, in respect to the subject for which we had assembled, and he should call on the rev. gentleman and the meeting to affirm the resolution which he had the honour of proposing. The resolutions passed at that meeting were so excellent, that they required no comment or observations from him to render them acceptable to this meeting.

Mr. C. Stewart seconded the resolution, which was carried unanimously.

We regret exceedingly that we are unable to do justice to the very excellent speeches made at this meeting. They were listened to with great attention by the people, and the speakers were greeted with much applause during their addresses. The meeting was a most orderly one, and redounds much to the credit of our labouring population for the manner in which they conducted themselves.

The next in succession was the parish of Westmoreland, where a numerously attended meeting was held at the Court House, Savanna-la-Mar, on Friday, the 22nd of June, to take into consideration the non-observance of the treaties for the suppression of the slave-trade by the Governments of Spain and Brazil.

There were present, his Honour the Custos; the Rector; the Hon. H. A. Whitelock; T. R. Hylton, Benjamin Vickars, Thomas Jelly, W. Johns, James Jenkins, George R. Gow, David Mason, Daniel Sinclair, and G. B. Videl, Esqrs.; the Rev. Edw. Galbraith, and many other gentlemen, together with the greatest number of the labouring classes ever collected at a public meeting for several years past.

The business of the day commenced by his Honour the Custos reading the requisition; after which,

Mr. Benjamin Vickars proposed that the Rev. Wm. Mayhew, rector for the parish, do take the chair; which proposition was seconded by Thomas Jelly, Esq., and carried.

The Rev. Chairman then, in an eloquent speech, directed attention to the subject-matter of the requisition, after which,

J. Jenkins, Esq., proposed that Mr. Joseph Dolphy be requested to act as Secretary for the occasion, which being seconded, was agreed to.

The following gentlemen (most of whom came prepared) were then nominated a committee to prepare resolutions:— The Hon. Thos. McNeel, Custos; the Hon. H. A. Whitelock; Benjamin Vickars, James Jenkins, David Mason, I. N. Vaz, G. B. Vidal, Esqrs.; and the Rev. Edward Galbraith; who, after a short absence, returned into the Court House, and the rev. Rector resumed the chair, when the following resolutions were unanimously agreed to:—

The first resolution was moved by the Hon. Thomas McNeel, Custos, and seconded by the Rev. Edward Galbraith, as follows :—

" Resolved, That this meeting desire to denounce most solemnly and emphatically the inhuman traffic in slaves, as carried on by the planters of Cuba, Porto Rico, and Brazil, in flagrant violation of existing treaties with the Spanish and Brazilian Governments— as subversive of the happiness of mankind—as a disgrace to the civilised world, and in defiance of the laws of God."

The second resolution, as follows, was moved by Thomas R. Hylton, Esq., and seconded by Dr. Thomas Jelly :—

" That the vast expenditure of treasure and the sacrifice of many valuable lives, in endeavouring to suppress this diabolical trade by the squadron kept on the coast of Africa, have not prevented the traffic being carried on with increased vigour within the past two years; and the augmentation of the number of slaves, on the plantations generally of Cuba and Brazil, during that period, has been carried to an almost incredible extent."

The third resolution was moved by the Hon. Hugh A. Whitelock, and seconded by I. N. Vaz, Esq., as follows :—

" That it is a matter of fact that the slave population of Cuba and Brazil (from the preponderance of male slaves imported, as well as from the cruel system of management pursued by their owners,) requires renewal every ten years. That it is also a fact, and known to Lord Palmerston, that one-third of the slaves now in Cuba are virtually free under treaties made with the Spanish Government, for which treaties Great Britain paid a very large amount of money. That it does appear to this meeting monstrous that such a circumstance should be known to the British Government, and British humanity should be put at defiance by an open recognition of a flagrant violation of treaties made in furtherance of so laudable a feeling."

Mr. Benjamin Vickars moved the fourth resolution, which was seconded by Dr. Mason, and is as follows :—

" That the emancipated colonies, labouring under most serious disadvantages, are by the present system of the British sugar duties, brought into open competition with the foreign slave grower in the English markets; and so long as the Spanish and Brazilians are permitted to evade the treaties entered into between the Governments of their respective countries and Great Britain, for the suppression of the slave-trade, and openly to import slaves in unlimited numbers from Africa, the planters of this island cannot, with any hope or prospect of success, continue their estates in cultivation, against such unjust and unnatural competition."

The Hon. H. A. Whitelock moved the fifth resolution, seconded by Cuthbert P. Butter, Esq., as follows :—

" That it is needless to pay a million and a half annually to blockade the African coast, and at the same time to offer a bonus by stimulating slavery and the slave-trade by the consumption of slave-grown produce, to the destruction of free-grown produce, and to the ruin of the freed and other inhabitants of the emancipated colonies."

Mr. James Jenkins moved the sixth resolution, seconded by G. R. Gow, Esq., as follows :—

" That reduced as the inhabitants of this colony are to the most dire distress, it is expedient to implore the imperial Government to insist upon the rigid fulfilment of the treaties for the suppression of the slave-trade by the Spanish and Brazilian nations, with a view to relieve our fellow-creatures from the unmitigated horrors contingent upon the abominable traffic in human flesh, and to enable the emancipated colonies to enter upon a just and equitable competition with their foreign rivals in the European markets."

The seventh resolution, as follows, was moved by Benjamin Vickars, Esq., and seconded by C. P. Butter, Esq. :—

" That this meeting desire to express their unanimous approval of the resolutions and sentiments adopted and promulgated at the public meeting in Spanish Town, auspiciously presided over by the Lord Bishop of the diocese; and that the memorial to her most gracious Majesty, and the petitions to both Houses of Parliament, have our warmest and unqualified concurrence, and that a committee be appointed to procure signatures to the petitions, and forward the same to his lordship the Bishop."

The eighth resolution, as follows, was moved by the Hon. H. A. Whitelock, and seconded by his Honour the Custos:—

" That petitions from the parish of Westmoreland, carrying out the resolutions of the day, be sent to Parliament, and that a committee be appointed to frame them, and transmit to such members of the Houses of Lords and Commons as they may think meet."

The following gentlemen were then named such committee:—The Rector, the Rev. E. Galbraith, David Mason, and James Jenkins, Esqrs.

The Rector having left the chair, the Hon. Thomas McNeel was called thereto, when

The Hon. H. A. Whitelock proposed the thanks of the meeting to the Rector for his urbanity in the chair; which was seconded by Benjamin Vickers, Esq.

The Rev. Chairman, in returning thanks, said it was a pleasure to preside over a meeting where but one feeling prevailed.

The meeting then separated.

ILLEGAL REMOVAL OF NEGROES FROM THE BAHAMAS INTO CUBA.

Before proceeding with the report of the great public meeting held in Kingston on the 25th of June, let it not be forgotten that there is another and a numerous class of persons now held in slavery in Cuba, who have, if possible, still stronger claims on British sympathy and protection than even those unfortunate emancipados.

During the period of agitation and alarm on the subject of emancipation, which prevailed in the West Indies for some years anterior to the act of 1833, the owners of slaves in the Bahama Islands, who had never been very prosperous either as planters or salt rakers, were induced, from their near proximity to Cuba, some to emigrate to that island, with whole gangs of negroes, and others to sell their slaves, with a view to their involuntary and illegal removal to a country where the system was not so near its term, as it evidently was, under the flag of their own country.

These illegal operations were in general performed clandestinely; but some of the gentlemen concerned, relying with too much confidence on the retired position of their estates on some distant island, when they felt as if they were beyond the reach of observation, and when they certainly were not subject to any immediate control, embarked their slaves openly in the face of day, and carried them, or sent them, to the nearest market in Cuba or Jamaica. There is evidence on record of speculations of this kind, when the living cargo has been carried from one port or one island to another, and sold by retail, just as an American ship-master on a trading voyage would sell, swop, or barter an assortment of notions.

Encouraged by the first instances of success, this species of emigration proceeded at such a rate as pretty nearly to depopulate a considerable number of the out-islands of the Bahama group. At length it was brought so prominently under the notice of the authorities at Nassau, in the island of New Providence, that in the case of one of the principal offenders, Mr. Forbes, a criminal proceeding was instituted, and a true bill for a felonious abduction was found by the grand jury of the island, in virtue of which he was declared to be an outlaw; and having made good his retreat to a plantation he had purchased in Cuba, he was thus deterred from ever showing himself again in any part of the British dominions.

By the act of 1806, which came into operation on the 1st of January, 1807, abolishing all slave-trade under the British flag, the removal of slaves from a British to a foreign possession was declared to be illegal; and the mere fact of the embarkation of a slave in British waters, with the intent of removing him to any foreign settlement or pos-

session, was declared to be a felony, and *ipso facto* to work
the forfeiture of such slave to the Crown.

By way of exception to the rule, it was provided by the
same statute that if a slave owner should himself have
occasion to travel, he might, by a certain prescribed form of
entry at the Custom-house of the place from which he
embarked, entitle himself to carry with him, for the sole and
express purpose of acting during the voyage as personal or
domestic servants, two slaves for himself, and two more for
each member of his family who might accompany him on
the occasion. In this way a door was opened for the most
flagrant evasions of the law itself, of which several of the
Bahama emigrants did not scruple to avail themselves.

In the case, for instance, of Mr. Forbes, his principal gang
of negroes were settled on the little island of Exuma, from
whence, to the number of one hundred and twenty, they
were carried off in a body to his plantation, near Cardenas,
some thirty miles from Matanzas, without asking or obtaining the shadow of an authority for their removal. But Mr.
Forbes had also a private residence at Nassau, in which he
had a family of illegitimate children, with their mother at the
head of the establishment, with the usual and convenient
title of housekeeper. In this domestic establishment there
were a number of slaves, fourteen of whom were suffered to
embark under the eye of the Custom-house authorities, on
pretence of their being required during the voyage, to act
as personal attendants on Mr. Forbes himself, his female
housekeeper, and their five children.

It was this public proceeding at Nassau which directed
the attention of the authorities to the simultaneous abduction
of the principal gang of negroes, belonging to Mr. Forbes,
in the distant island of Exuma. Attention was first drawn
to this particular case by that worthy and zealous officer,
Dr. Madden, who, after acting for some time as a stipendiary

magistrate in Jamaica, was removed from thence during the currency of the apprenticeship system in the British West Indies, to discharge the more important functions of Superintendent of liberated Africans at the Havanna, an office which fell under the patronage of the Colonial Department.

On the resignation of Dr. Madden, and by the concurrent appointment of the Foreign Minister, Viscount Palmerston, and of Lord John Russell, the Colonial Secretary, this office was united, for the first time, and under separate commissioners, to that of her Majesty's Consul, who, soon after his arrival, sought an opportunity of inquiring into the condition of those abducted negroes on the spot.

The arrival at the Havanna of a distinguished traveller, Mr. Goff, who had so far made his way back towards England, on one of his extraordinary circumambulations of the globe, presented a convenient and agreeable occasion for seeing something of the interior of the country, and of accomplishing an object prescribed by a sense of duty. A day was fixed for the journey, and the greatest care was taken that Mr. Goff's passport should be perfectly *en règle*. This document was of somewhat formidable dimensions, being the same he had obtained at the Foreign Office in London, before starting on his journey eastward, and which had carried him through the Chinese empire, and across the American continent, through the States of Mexico, as far as the Havanna. It is not usual for a foreign Consul, in travelling in his own consular district, to make use of a passport. His person is presumed to be known, his uniform affords *primâ facie* evidence of his identity, his right to visit his fellow-subjects entrusted to his care is unquestionable, and the exhibition of the *exequatur* of the Supreme Government to which he is accredited, is more than equivalent to any local passport. On this principle, and thus provided, the Consul had repeatedly visited various parts of the country, at the instance of his fellow-subjects who claimed his assistance, complaining not unfrequently of unjust and unwarrantable imprisonment.

The steam boats which ply for passengers between the Havanna and the outports of Cuba, are notoriously employed as accessories to the slave-trade, in facilitating the debarkation of the illicit cargoes, diminishing the risk of capture near the coast, and occasionally saving a good many lives. The masters of these steamers are very generally retired slave captains, selected, probably, on account of their experience in this peculiar branch of duty.

On the occasion just referred to, Mr. Goff and the Consul embarked at the steam-wharf without any obstruction. The vessel had more than her usual number of passengers, because, on her stated day of sailing, immediately previous, she had, for some reason or other, been absent from the station, to the disappointment of a great number of persons. When the dinner hour arrived, the ex-slave captain, all bedizened with finery, took his place at the head of the table, and insisted on installing the two Englishmen, in what he considered the seats of honour, on his right and left. In the course of the entertainment, one of the strangers inquired, in a tone of raillery, what accident had occurred to prevent the sailing of the steamer on the previous Saturday; on which the captain burst into a furious passion, not with the questioner, but at the incident he proceeded to describe; beginning with a declaration that he had been treated most scandalously; saying that he had consented, at the first signal, to get up his steam, and run down to leeward, in which direction a well-known clipper from the coast, much behind her time, had been observed beating up. His part of the duty had been performed most successfully; but, although the adventure must have been exceedingly profitable, and although he had fully expected to receive a hundred doubloons for the service, in consideration of the disappointment his passengers had suffered, and the consequent damage which the interests of his vessel had sustained, the scoundrels had fobbed him off with thirty !

On nearing the port of Matanzas, after the passage money had been levied by a subordinate functionary, the captain, who upon his other onerous duties accumulated those of an agent of the police, made his tour of the passengers, and required from each of them the delivery of his passport, for the purpose, as he said, of reporting them at the office of the Lieutenant-governor, when they would be returned on application.   Against this arrangement it was in vain to demur, and Mr. Goff's passport was left, like the rest, in the hands of the ex-slave captain.

The two Englishmen, on landing, procured horses at their hotel for an evening's excursion; and were told, on their return, that the Town-major and two military gentlemen were then in the house to inquire for them, and that they had been waiting there some time.   On making his bow, the Town-major stated he had received information that two English gentlemen had arrived that afternoon from the Havanna without any passport, and that it was his painful duty to take notice of the great irregularity.   To this the obvious and natural answer was returned, that the whole of the passports, Mr. Goff's among the rest, had been delivered to the commander of the steam-vessel, by whom they had been authoritatively demanded; and if there existed any doubt on the subject, it was required that that person should immediately be sent for.   This the Town-major did not think necessary, and retired, with his military friends, to consult, as he said, the Lieutenant-governor on the subject. Returning to the hotel, in the course of the evening, the Town-major declared that the Lieutenant-governor was not satisfied with the statement made to him, and declared that neither Mr. Goff nor the Consul could be permitted to proceed to Cardenas, in the morning, as they proposed. An interview, that evening, with the Lieutenant-governor was declined by his excellency, on the ground of urgent business; but he sent a message to say that his excellency would be happy to receive the two gentlemen at twelve o'clock the following day. At that hour the steamer would be at sea, on her return to the Havanna; and it was therefore required that her captain should be detained, but this was not acceded to.

Seeing the turn which the affair had taken, Mr. Goff consented very kindly to remain at Matanzas alone, and to watch its denouement, allowing the Consul to return to his arduous official duties at the Havanna.

The result was not very creditable to the Lieutenant-governor, who was known to be deeply engaged himself in slave-trade practices. At the hour appointed his excellency was pleased to receive Mr. Goff in his cabinet, with an air *très affairé*, seated at a writing-table, with piles of papers heaped upon it. After desiring Mr. Goff to be seated, he opened the conversation by declaiming on the enormity of a stranger in a foreign country presuming to travel without a passport. To this Mr. Goff did not fail to make a proper reply; and while peering about the room, and along the heaps of papers on the table, he espied something just under his excellency's hand, at the bottom of a pile, very strongly resembling the black leather envelope of his passport, which was in the form of a pocket-book, and from the great length of his journey had become exceedingly voluminous. Making sure of his point, while yet engaged in earnest .conversation, Mr. Goff stretched forth his hand, and, upsetting the pile of papers, laid hold of the prize, which proved to be exactly what he was seeking for. Pointing out to his excellency the *visa* for Cardenas, which had been added to the passport at the office of the Captain-general at the Havanna, Mr. Goff observed that it was his intention to proceed on his journey, as soon as he could obtain the means of conveyance; but to this the Lieutenant-governor objected, declaring that, after the suspicions which had arisen on the subject, he could not consent to it. This result was pretty much what the Englishman expected, but the time which the adventure had occupied was not entirely lost, either to the traveller or the Consul.

Not very long afterwards a young mulatto, with all the air of a Spaniard, but speaking English with fluency, made his appearance stealthily, at a late hour in the evening, at the private residence of the Consul, which was outside the walls of the Havanna, and stating that he was a British subject, named James Thomson, born at Nassau, New Providence, came to claim the protection of her Majesty's flag. On a careful investigation of his case, it turned out that his statement was true, and that, in the same year with the act of abduction for which Mr. Forbes was then an exile and an outlaw, he had been carried off from Nassau, with a number of his brothers and sisters of mixed blood, by an American named Norris, who had married his half-sister, the legitimate daughter of his father, a merchant in Nassau; and that Norris, having established himself as a merchant in the seaport town of Gibara, near the eastern extremity of the island of Cuba, and within twenty leagues of Ragged Island, one of the Bahama group, he had there reduced his wife's mulatto relatives to slavery, retaining some in his own service, and hiring out or selling the rest.

On growing up to man's estate, James Thomson, being of a bold and resolute disposition, made sundry unsuccessful attempts to escape to Ragged Island; and hearing at length that a new Consul had arrived at the Havanna who would be likely to afford him protection, he had the courage to undertake a journey of five hundred miles, travelling chiefly by night, and at length, by the help of the stars, which often served him as a guide, he made his way into the presence of the Consul, who, for greater security, thought it his duty to receive him on board her Majesty's ship " Romney," a dismasted hulk, then stationed at the Havanna for the reception of liberated Africans.

A more minute inquiry into the personal history of James Thomson and his family disclosed a great number of facts, resembling, more or less, the cases of wholesale abduction committed by Forbes, or the minor felonies of Norris, and determined the Consul, as soon as an opportunity should present itself, to visit the spot and investigate the facts in person.

This opportunity occurred much sooner than at the time appeared to be probable. On the last advent to power of Sir Robert Peel's administration, the Earl of Aberdeen, in pursuance of the conciliatory policy which his lordship thought it convenient to observe towards Spain, sent out a new Consul to the Havanna, leaving his predecessor in possession of the separate office of Superintendent of liberated Africans, the tenure of which the Colonial Secretary, Lord Stanley, did not think it immediately necessary to alter. But this last was an office which had never been recognised by the Spanish authorities, and did not afford that protection to the incumbent which is universally conceded to a Consul, even in countries having fewer pretensions to civilisation than the colonial dependencies of Spain.

Before ceasing to be Consul, the Superintendent had been frequently warned by some of the best men at the Havanna, among whom he had many devoted personal friends, that his life, even then, was far from being safe ; and they earnestly counselled him, as soon as the new Consul had arrived, either to return to England, or, at all events, in the meantime to

take refuge on board the " Romney." Having resolved on
this latter course, he remained there a sufficient length of
time to admit of his receiving the relief from an irksome
position which he earnestly desired ; and not having heard
from Lord Stanley on the subject, at the end of four months
he resolved on proceeding to the Bahamas, for the purpose
of completing the investigation he had already begun, on the
subject of the felonies and abductions already referred to.

On his arrival at Nassau the Superintendent of liberated
Africans addressed himself to the local authorities, from
whom he met with all possible encouragement and assistance
in the prosecution of his inquiry, more especially from
Lieut.-governor Nisbett, Mr. Attorney-general Anderson,
Mr. Chief-Justice Lees, and Mr. Justice Gahan. In pursuit
of the evidence he required, he made the tour of the whole
Archipelago, visiting all the localities from whence abductions
were known to have taken place; and, having armed himself
with some hundred and fifty depositions, stating the various
facts in the minutest detail, he addressed himself to the
resident Spanish Consul, Senor Maura, accompanied by the
Honourable the Chief-Justice, and, after some show of hesitation, obtained a passport declaring his official title, as her
Britannic Majesty's Superintendent of liberated Africans in
Cuba, and stating, more in detail than is usual in such
documents, the special nature of the object he had in view in
visiting the eastern department of the island of Cuba.

These preliminary arrangements being completed, the
Superintendent, in the same hired vessel in which he had
just made his tour, presented himself before the fort which
commands the entrance of Gibara, and having caused the
usual signal to be hoisted, he received a communication
from the shore, on which he expressed a wish to be presented
to the chief authority. This officer, who bore the local
rank of Commandante-de-armas, or Fort-major, came down

to the beach in person, and after many demonstrations
of civility invited the Superintendent to his private residence in the town, when, after examining the passport
of Mr. Consul Maura, who is reported to have made an
immense fortune by the monopoly he has secured of the
trade between the Bahamas and the neighbouring ports of
Cuba, the Commandante introduced the Superintendent to
the ladies of his family, engaged him to dinner at the usual
early hour of the country, and leaving him then, went out,
as he said, to enter the passport on the archives of the fort.
The Commandante did not return till three o'clock, the hour
appointed for dinner, when he brought with him a person in
plain clothes, whom he introduced by name ; and referring
to the object of the Superintendent's visit, as stated in the
passport, he expressed his great regret that, in his subordinate
position, he could do nothing to promote the object himself,
but earnestly recommended his guest to proceed to the city
of Holguin, a place of 10,000 inhabitants, which was the
residence of a Lieutenant-governor, about thirty miles distant,
who alone had the power of rendering any assistance to the
proposed inquiries of the English Superintendent.

In the issue, this arrangement, although not intended in
the least degree to facilitate the proposed investigation,
was, in the absence of any wish to promote it, the very best
thing that could have happened to accomplish the end in
view. The district of country, which is situated between
Gibara and Holguin, had been reclaimed from a state of
nature within the previous twenty years, and had been
originally peopled by a colony of emigrants from the
Bahamas. Well informed as to the relative or topogra-
phical position of the various plantations, from the written
evidence he carried in his travelling bag, the Superintendent,
without deviating from the beaten track, had no difficulty in
marking down his game, so as to be able to bag it on his

return; an object which he could not conveniently attain on going afield, because the worthy senor, who attended him in the nominal capacity of a guide, proved to be the chief officer of police ; and they had not left the house of the Commandante more than ten minutes when they were joined by six infantry soldiers, fully armed, and mounted on horseback, who were explained by the guide, who carefully maintained his incognito, to be necessary for the protection of the travellers, the country being, as he said, infested with brigands. Before starting, the Commandante was asked to restore the Superintendent's passport, but he excused himself by saying he had left it, from forgetfulness, in his office, and that it would be carefully preserved and restored on its owner's return. These incidents had already disclosed the fact, that the Superintendent was not a free agent : but he did not care to discover his sentiments on the subject to his guide and guardians, lest his immediate position and its capability for realising or rectifying his previous information should be damaged by it.

The road being no better than a bridle path, the guide took the lead, the Superintendent with his servant followed, and the rear was brought up at a respectful distance by the soldiers in Indian file. According to the custom of the country, the guide made some civil remark to every one he met; not unfrequently drawing bridle for the purpose, and expressing himself very generally in English. This example was naturally followed by the Superintendent, after the customary interval between the ranks had been restored ; and it was very soon established in the clearest possible manner that even the half-seasoned Africans were acquiring a knowledge of English in preference to Spanish, and that, in point of fact, he was travelling through what was practically and substantially an English colony.

From the leisurely pace at which they moved, it was

considerably past midnight before the travellers reached
Holguin ; and, in answer to an inquiry for the locality of the
best posada, the guide observed, in a tone of something like
authority, that his orders were to go in the first instance to
the residence of the Lieutenant-governor, General Nevarro.
Against a conclusion which was evidently foregone, it was
vain to remonstrate; and the guide having roused the
household from their slumbers, was promptly ushered with
his charge into his Excellency's bed-chamber. Provided
with a light inside the mosquito netting, the General broke
open the seal of a packet of papers handed to him by the
guide ; and, after reading a letter contained in it, demanded
of the Superintendent, in a tone of severity, how he dared to
enter the country unprovided with a passport. The scene
between Mr. Goff and the Lieutenant-governor of Matanzas
was thus about to be re-enacted, but in a manner still more
truculent, as will presently appear. From the very opening
of this extraordinary interview, it was pretty evident that
General Nevarro did not feel himself on very sure ground.
In the midst of it he got out of his bed, put on his dressing-
gown, and knocking gently at a door of communication with
an adjoining chamber, called out, repeatedly, in a loud
whisper, "Fulgencio! Don Fulgencio!" This Christian name,
being somewhat uncommon, attracted the attention of the
Superintendent, who knew it to be that of Colonel de las
Salas, the confidential secretary of the Captain-general, and
a person of the highest honour and integrity, to whom he
was personally known, having frequently met him at the
hospitable board of General Valdez. On General Nevarro
being admitted into Don Fulgencio's room, it became evident,
to those left in that of General Nevarro, that a very earnest
conversation was going on inside, although the words were
not distinguishable. At length, from an interlocutory
whisper, the tone changed to that of *reading*, when the

Superintendent could plainly distinguish the words of his own passport, which, according to the Commandante at Gibara, had been accidentally left behind; and, according to General Nevarro himself, had never existed.

Presently after, the Lieutenant-governor returned into his own room, when he was joined by several military gentlemen, in full uniform. One of them addressed himself to the Superintendent, saying he had orders to conduct him to a lodging for the night; and walking out together, after calling at several military posts, no doubt to enable the sentinels on duty to identify the person of the stranger in case of need, he was carried out of town to a barrack, where a European regiment was stationed, and where he was forthwith installed as a prisoner.

Provided with a camp bed, and his travelling bag for a pillow, he was awoke, before daybreak, by the sergeant-major of the regiment, who said he had the Governor's orders to examine his baggage; and after sundry comings and goings, demurs and remonstrances, the parley ended in a capitulation. The papers found in the travelling bag were declared to be the object in request, which, according to the sergeant-major, it was the intention of the Lieutenant-governor to send on to the Havanna, for the inspection of the Captain-general. In that case it was suggested that there could be no reasonable objection to their being sealed up in the presence of the sergeant-major, and addressed to General Valdez. This concession being made, the papers were carefully packed up in three successive envelopes, the first being addressed to their owner; the second to her Majesty's Consul at the Havanna; and the outer one, in due form, to his excellency the Captain-general, with a strong letter of remonstrance against the proceedings adopted by his subordinates at Holguin and Gibara.

In his barrack-prison, the Superintendent was placed, *en*

secret, and was not suffered to communicate with any one but the officer on duty for the day; on whose hospitality he was compelled to depend, faring sumptuously on some occasions, on others, reduced to the shortest commons, according to the good-will or the means of the individual. Every successive change brought some fresh gossip from without, as to the probable fate of the prisoner. The prevailing opinion, duly reported to the party immediately interested, was, that having landed at Gibara without a passport, he was to be treated as a spy, and carried out next morning, to be shot on the nearest rampart.

Having ascertained that Don Fulgencio, the guest of the Lieutenant-governor, was really the secretary of the Captain-general, and that he had been sent to Holguin, to inquire into the previous conduct of General Nevarro, the prisoner found means to forward a letter to Colonel de Salas, appealing to his honour, as a gentleman, to authenticate his personal cognisance of the fact of the existence of the missing passport, as well as of the prisoner's identity, as a subject and an officer of her Britannic Majesty.

The answer to this appeal was brought, on the instant, by the gallant officer in person, who made no sort of difficulty in doing all that he was asked to do, assuring the prisoner that General Nevarro had been overruled in the design he had formed of committing an atrocity which might have led to serious international results; that he had thus filled up the measure of his offences, and that he, Colonel de Salas, having brought with him a discretionary power from the Captain-general to displace General Nevarro, and to leave the colonel of the regiment, Don Raman Conti, in charge of the government, he, Colonel de Salas, had resolved on carrying General Nevarro and his prisoner back with him to the Havanna, in the " Congreso " war-steamer, daily expected at Gibara.

From this moment, the prisoner's position was very much altered for the better. On the following morning, he received a personal visit from the new Lieutenant-governor, Colonel Conti, who was good enough to express his great regret that any British officer should have been exposed to so much inconvenience ; that, for his own part, he would have been glad to have afforded the Superintendent all the assistance in his power, in investigating the cases of the Bahama-born negroes, held in slavery on the plantations in the neighbourhood, but that, after giving the whole subject his best consideration, he did not feel himself at liberty, at the first moment of his taking charge of the government, to do more than report the case for the decision of the Captain-general. In the meantime, his excellency declared, with evident sincerity, that, subject to this condition, it would give him great pleasure to make the Superintendent's stay within his command as agreeable as possible ; that all he required was, that the Superintendent should undertake to be on board the " Congreso," at Gibara, on the third succeeding day ; and that, in the meantime, he had selected an officer of his regiment, Senor Maestre, distinguished above the rest for his known enthusiasm in favour of Englishmen, although he did not speak their language, to be in attendance on the Superintendent from that moment, until his embarkation at Gibara. Don Raman Conti excused himself for withholding the original passport of Senor Maura, the Consul at Nassau ; but furnished the Superintendent with something which proved infinitely more valuable, consisting of an authenticated copy, with his own seal and signature at the bottom, as Zeniente Gobernada ; for when presented, next day, to the manager of an English plantation, it had a magical effect in silencing all opposition to the inquiries which the Superintendent proceeded to institute.

Senor Maestre, on being introduced, did all in his power

to confirm the favourable impression thus created by his friend and colonel. He was ready to start at a moment's notice, and proved, by his whole deportment, how honestly the choice had been made.

In the course of the same afternoon the two gentlemen, followed by a single unarmed servant, found themselves in the district of Candelaria, in the midst of the English plantations. Their first visit was paid to Mr. Driggs, the proprietor of a considerable sugar plantation, with whom resided his widowed mother, Mrs. Bellerby. Here the strangers were received with a cordial welcome; and, during their stay, there arrived a party from the adjoining plantation of the late Captain Izing, of the 2nd West India Regiment, comprising several members of that officer's family. The whole aspect of the case confirmed, in the clearest manner, the information previously received; and Mr. Driggs very kindly agreed to accompany his guests, the following morning, on their way to the more distant plantation of Mr. Wood, a barrister, at Nassau, who formerly held the office of Attorney-general, and still enjoyed that of Queen's Advocate in the Government of the Bahamas.

On the arrival of the two strangers at Mr. Wood's plantation, they were received by a brother of that gentleman, whom they found acting as manager, and who, when the object of the Superintendent's visit was explained to him, called in the assistance of two other Englishmen, his subordinates in the management.

The Superintendent stated to these persons that the object of his visit was to inquire into the actual condition of a number of British-born subjects, residing on that estate, who were reported to be held there in a state of slavery; and he requested that the head-man, Daniel Rolsall, might be sent for, that he might be interrogated on the subject.

After some conversation, in the course of which the Superintendent stated that, when recently in Nassau, he had stated to Mr. Wood, in the presence of Mr. Justice Gahan, that it was his intention to visit this plantation, and that he had requested to be furnished with an order on his manager, not only to facilitate the investigation on which he proposed to enter, but to sanction the removal to New Providence of such of the persons held in slavery in Candelaria, as might eventually be proved to be entitled to their freedom. To this application, it was frankly added, that her Majesty's Advocate, with a smile of incredulity, which might have been intended to apply either to the seriousness of the Superintendent's intentions, or to the probability of his success, replied by a firm but civil refusal.

Mr. Wood, the manager, in more awe, apparently, of the Spanish officer, Senor Maestre, than of the English Superintendent, who were both in full uniform, attempted, at first, to make light of the application; but a marvellous change came over Mr. Wood's features, and those of his overseers, when, at the opportune moment, the formidable Spanish document, bearing the seal and signature of the new Lieut.-governor, was presented, declaring, *in gremio*, not only the style and quality of the bearer, as her Britannic Majesty's Superintendent of liberated Africans, but stating most explicitly, in good Castilian, that the specific object of his visit to the eastern department of Cuba was to inquire into the actual condition of a number of her Majesty's subjects, born in the Bahama islands, who had been reported to her Majesty's Government to be held in slavery there.

On a repetition of the demand, in a tone of increased firmness, that the head-man, Daniel Rolsall, should immediately be sent for, to undergo a course of interrogation as to his own actual condition, as well as that of his brothers, six in number, and the other British-born negroes, residing on the estate, the manager, making a virtue of the supposed necessity, caused the head-man to be introduced; and his declaration having been committed to writing, in the presence of the whole party, and in a form precisely similar to that of those which were then on their way to the address of the Captain-general at the Havanna, the best confirmation was afforded of the general truth of the facts which it had become so desirable to establish.

In the act of folding up this fresh document, the Superintendent proposed to Mr. Wood, the manager, that Daniel Rolsall should accompany him on board the "Congreso" to the Havanna, and from thence to Nassau; but to this Mr. Wood objected, until he had an opportunity of consulting the new Lieutenant-governor on the subject, which he proceeded to do at once, leaving his residence in the company of his unwelcome visitors, and starting for Holguin, while they turned their horses' heads in the direction of Gibara.

In that seaport itself a great deal remained to be done, in furtherance of this investigation. The friends of James Thomson, the masculine assertor of his right to possess his own person in freedom and in peace, were by this time at Nassau, waiting anxiously for some intelligence as to the probable fate of his unhappy relatives. His white sister of the pure blood, now the widow Norris, received the Superintendent's visit with great apparent courtesy; but was decidedly firmer than Mr. Wood, of Candelaria, in her resistance to his demand for the restoration of her enslaved relatives to their freedom. The subsequent circuit of other quarters of the town, where British-born negroes were known to be held in slavery, produced a sensation which, after the lapse of seven years, is not even yet, perhaps, entirely obliterated. The Superintendent's last visit in Gibara was to the Commandante-de-armas, to whom he applied for a boat, to carry him on board the "Congreso," and ventured to make a little merry at the expense of the Commandante on the total failure of his diplomacy.

In due time the party re-assembled on board her Catholic Majesty's steam-frigate, including General Nevarro, his late prisoner, and Colonel de Salas. The Commander was exceedingly civil, and gave up his own cabin to the stranger. The voyage to the Havanna did not last many days; and after an unsuccessful attempt to put the Superintendent in the wrong, his papers were restored to him, with the seal unbroken; and his person was placed under the nominal protection of the Consul, with an intimation that his longer stay in the island of Cuba would not be tolerated. The next steam-packet carried him back to Nassau, to complete the work he had undertaken; and he had the satisfaction to be the first to announce to her Majesty's Advocate that he might very soon expect to see his head-man, Daniel Rolsall, restored to the freedom of which he had been so long unjustly deprived.

This singular expedition has been denounced as Quixotic and foolhardy; but it has not been altogether fruitless. James Thomson rejoined his deliverer at Nassau, attended him from thence to England, and afterwards to Jamaica, where he has served the Lord Bishop and other persons of distinction. Mr. Wood's head-man, Daniel, after acquiring a competent knowledge of his right to the enjoyment of his freedom, had fallen below zero as an exchangeable commodity, and might possibly indoctrinate his fellows with some inconvenient notions on the subject of their actual condition, and the claims they might justly pretend to. So the head-man was sent back to New Providence, where he now is; and five of his nearest relatives were despatched to Jamaica, by way of Santiago de Cuba. Of these five, only four reached this land of liberty, the fifth having died in the prison, where they were all placed in deposit, until the arrival of the packet afforded a suitable means of conveyance. One of the four survivors, Bill Relsal, found his way home to New Providence; another, John Relsal, discovered that his mother had been carried to Demerara, and joined her there; a third, Nat Relsal, by trade a carpenter, is still living in Jamaica; and the fourth, Cuffer Relsal, having entered the service of her Majesty's Senior Commissioner, has remained with him for the last five or six years, in the vain hope of its leading to the recovery of his wife Eve, their ten children, and an unknown number of junior descendants.

It is to be feared that her Majesty's judicial advisers are not perfectly agreed as to the legal condition of this unfortunate class of persons; but it is to be presumed, from the tenor of the following despatch, addressed, by her Majesty's Minister at Madrid, to the Spanish Secretary of State for Foreign Affairs, that a view of the subject highly favourable to the cause of liberty was entertained at head-quarters at the time it was written :—

Mr. Aston to the Secretary of State.

Madrid, September 9th, 1841.

I am directed further to state, that there are many British subjects now held in slavery in Cuba, and as it is impossible that her Majesty's Government can permit any British subjects, be their colour what it may, to be held in slavery in a foreign country, her Majesty's Government claim and demand, as a right from the Government of Spain, that all such persons shall be immediately released, and shall be placed on board the " Romney," under the care of Mr. Turnbull, the Superintendent of liberated Africans, in order to their being sent back to Jamaica, or such British colony as they may choose to go to.

I have to observe, that the fact that any such persons may happen to have been slaves in a British colony, at the time when they were taken from thence and carried to Cuba, can make no difference in the matter; because, in the first place, their removal from a British colony as slaves was illegal; and because, in the next place, they would now have been, by law, free, if they had remained in a British colony; and it cannot be admitted that their illegal removal to a Spanish island should deprive them of that liberty which the law of England has conferred upon them. I have in conclusion to state, that her Majesty's Consul at the Havanna has been instructed forthwith to take all the steps that may be necessary for finding out all the British subjects in Cuba, who are thus illegally detained in bondage, and to apply to the Governor for the release of all persons whom he may discover to be so detained. And her Majesty's Government request that the Government of Spain will immediately send the most positive orders to the Governor of Cuba to afford to her Majesty's Consul every possible facility in pursuing his investigations, and to deliver over to him all persons who may appear to be British subjects, and to be so detained in bondage.

I avail, &c.,

(Signed) ARTHUR ASTON.

We now proceed to offer our report of the great public meeting held in Kingston, on the 25th of June, which was second only in importance to that which had taken place in Spanish Town, on the Queen's birth-day. At the instance of a very numerous body of requisitionists, the meeting had been summoned by Mr. Hector Mitchell, the mayor; and, on being assembled—

Dr. Ferguson rose, and expressed his regret that, in consequence of indisposition, his Honour the Mayor was unable to attend and preside over the meeting. He was sure this would be also regretted by the people of Kingston, who had on all occasions the pleasure of seeing their meetings presided over by his Honour, with that impartiality which they all admired. In the absence of the Mayor he had much pleasure in moving that the Rev. Dr. Stewart be requested to take the chair.

Mr. Donald Campbell, an eminent solicitor, rose, and said he had much pleasure in seconding the motion.

The motion was carried by acclamation, and

The Rev. Dr. Stewart proceeded to the chair, and said— Ladies and gentlemen, I feel sensibly the honour you do me in desiring that I take the chair, in the absence of the venerable Mayor of Kingston. But while I express my regret for that absence, and its cause, you must permit me to tell you that I think your chairman would have been better selected from among the great body of gentlemen of influence and talent who now surround me. The character and object of our being here together are so well known, indeed they have been already so eloquently set forth, at the great meeting in Spanish Town, by the distinguished prelate who presided on that occasion, that I feel any additional observations on my part would be altogether superfluous. I therefore call upon Edward Jordon, Esq., to propose the first resolution.

Mr. Edward Jordon, member of Assembly for Kingston, and one of the editors of the *Morning Journal* newspaper, said that the first resolution which he had the honour to propose was to the following effect :—

"That amidst the ruin and desolation which are everywhere apparent in these emancipated colonies, there is no man in this assembly—there is not one in ten thousand anywhere—who seriously desires the reinstatement of his fallen fortunes through the restoration of slavery or the slave-trade. The statutes of freedom, which have placed the British people on the glorious eminence they now enjoy among the nations of the earth, are recognised, by those who suffer from them, to be as irreversible as the laws of the Medes; but it is nevertheless demonstrated, as the uniform result of the experience acquired during the long interval which has elapsed since the dates of these statutes, that so long as the sugar planters of Cuba, Porto Rico, and Brazil, in defiance of the laws of their respective countries, and of the treaties by which their Governments stand bound to her Majesty, are permitted to resort to the coast of Africa for the means of strengthening their hands and increasing their profits, it is hopeless, in countries so thinly peopled as Jamaica, for the proprietors of the soil to persevere in its cultivation."

He could hardly expect that the general statement which the resolution contained, and with which it commenced, would be taken for granted—that the emancipated colonies are in a condition of ruin and desolation—and, therefore, it was necessary for him, for the information of those to whom these statements might go forth, to make a few observations. He had no personal knowledge of the condition of the other West India colonies, but he was in the habit of receiving, monthly, the journals published in them. In those journals the state of the several places was set forth, and that state appeared to him very similar to our own. But, supposing that no accounts had been received from them—no complaints heard—the meeting would be justified in assuming that their condition was similar to ours, from the fact of their labouring under similar disadvantages. In the first place, they were, with the exception of Barbadoes, thinly populated —in the next, their proprietary were non-resident—and lastly, they depended upon capitalists in the mother country for the means of carrying on their cultivation. These circumstances had, in the altered policy of the mother country, brought ruin and desolation upon us, and, he repeated, they might reasonably be assumed to have produced a like effect in the other emancipated colonies. But circumstances alter cases —our own ruin and desolation are alleged, and he might be asked what evidence he had of the fact? The first proof he should adduce was the report of a Committee of the House of Assembly, appointed, in 1847, to inquire into the depressed state of agriculture in this island. The evidence taken by that committee was on oath, and he knew of his own knowledge that the Chairman, a gentleman now present, devoted much time, and took great pains in the inquiry. In the report which it had made to the House the following statements would be found :—

"That since the passing of the British Slave Emancipation Act, of the 653 sugar estates then in cultivation in this island, 140 have been abandoned, and the works broken up, containing 168,032 acres of land, and having then employed in their cultivation 22,533 labourers.

" That those properties, now extinct, produced, in the year 1832, 14,178 hogsheads of sugar and 5,903 puncheons of rum.

" That since the same period, 465 coffee plantations have been abandoned, and their works broken up, containing 188,400 acres of land, and having employed in their cultivation, in the year 1832, 26,830 labourers."

Since this report was made, in December, 1847, a number of other estates, both sugar and coffee, have been abandoned ; and, were an inquiry now instituted into the state of agriculture in the island, the picture would be found even more sombre than it was at the time just mentioned. But, independent of the facts contained in the report from Mr. Barclay's committee, we have our own knowledge and experience of the state of things at present. In this city great distress prevails, and I believe this to be the case in the other towns in the island. Desolation was to be seen in the number of the untenanted stores and houses. It is only necessary to walk along Port Royal-street, where our great commercial establishments are situated, to be satisfied of the state of things there ; and if we go into the other streets, and the upper part of the town, the number of unoccupied houses is enough to alarm us. Some few years ago it was difficult to procure a decent residence. The late fire destroyed a portion of the city, and increased the demand for habitations. The inquiry which had suggested itself to him was—what had become of the people who formerly inhabited these houses ? The population of the city was not less, he believed, than it was, and there was no other conclusion left, than that two or three families, from their altered circumstances, were now forced to occupy the same premises. With regard to Port Royal-street, he believed that but for the continued drought—the absence of all moisture—that moisture which was essential to vegetation—Rippinham's prediction, that grass would grow in that street, would long since have been verified. In the country, things were not much better. The agricultural labourers in many parishes were suffering severely. Their condition might be inferred from the fact, that in some parts they are glad, it had been said, to labour for sixpence a day. The parties who not long since refused to accept less than one shilling and sixpence for a fair day's labour, are now compelled to accept one-third of that amount. Nothing could more clearly show their altered circumstances. Then there were the small proprietors of land. These were reduced, in many instances, to great distress; and some cases had occurred in which, as had been stated in another place by a friend, they could not find their way into their own houses, the land being overgrown by bush. But it might be inquired how had this ruin and desolation been caused? Without meaning to exculpate ourselves from blame, or to deny that there has been great neglect on our part, those evils may fairly be charged against the British Government. It was the Home Government which first forced slavery upon us. It was Government which gave us a protected market and monopoly prices for our produce, and afterwards suddenly abolished them, and produced the present state of things. With unpaid labour, a protected market, and monopoly prices, large fortunes were for a long time made. Money was plentiful, and the result was extravagance on the part of the absentee proprietors—the West India nabobs, who, in the mother country, not only vied with princes, but even royalty itself—and in the colony the same extravagance prevailed among all classes, from the attorney down to the overseer. The former not only spent their large incomes, but involved themselves in debt; and, encouraged by the West India merchants, ate the calf, so to speak, in the cow's belly. This state of things continued, and extravagance and disregard for money became general, until the Government first put an end, and righteously, to the slave-trade; and then, also righteously, to slavery; and, last of all, changed its commercial policy, and passed the Sugar Duty Act of 1846. It was then that the proprietor, deeply involved in debt, found that he could no longer obtain the needed advances, and was without the means of carrying on his estate or continuing cultivation. Without means he must pay for labour, whilst he ceases to have either a protected market, or the monopoly prices upon which he had been accustomed to rely. But in this condition of ruin and desolation, the resolution states, no man desires the restoration of slavery. There are some humane religious men who, considering that slavery is sinful and unjust, would be sorry to see it restored. There are others, who would object to its restoration, because it is a system fraught with evils. Slavery engenders pride, wastefulness, and carelessness. It also prevents improvements which would prove beneficial. I remember, said Mr. Jordon, visiting an estate in St. David, in 1819, and seeing a plough lying in the yard, which, although it had never been used, was corroded by exposure to the elements; and on asking the overseer why it had not been used, as it is in England and Scotland, the reply was, the stumps and stones prevented the use of it. The unpaid great gang, and second gang were there to dig the cane holes with the hoe, and the plough was disregarded. But freedom came, and, a friend of his being in the management of the estate, the stumps had disappeared, the stones had vanished, and the estate, which could not be ploughed in 1819, was being, he believed, ploughed in 1849. Slavery was also opposed to education and religious instruction. It kept the people degraded, demoralised, and barbarised. The consequence was, that we had a peasantry who were ignorant of their duty to their employers, to themselves, and to society. They knew nothing of the connexion between the employer and employed, and could only be acted upon by their selfishness; they could only be moved by the prospect of gain. And now, said Mr. Jordon, that extraordinary efforts are called for, and ought to be made, to educate and religiously instruct them, we are without the means, and cannot respond to the call. Slavery renders life and property insecure. We had an instance of this in the outbreak to Leeward, some years ago, when many lives were lost, and much property destroyed. Those outbreaks produced the abolition of slavery. It was found that it was becoming dangerous—that it had lasted just as long as it safely could, and that it must be put an end to. For these reasons, few persons would desire its restoration, even though it promised some temporary advantage. The resolution further states, that so long as the sugar planters of Cuba and Brazil are permitted to resort to Africa for slaves, it is hopeless for the planters of this island to persevere in cultivation. If, by this, it is intended to be insinuated that slave labour was cheaper than free, he should demur. He held the directly contrary opinion. The advantage of the slave owner was, that he had the labour when he wanted it, and could apply it as he pleased. The cost of slave labour was not to be estimated simply by the amount paid for the slave and for his maintenance and clothing. There was the expense of the military establishment, necessary to uphold the system. The natural tendency in man was to desire freedom, and the slaves of Cuba would very soon burst asunder the bonds that bound them, but for the large standing army which Spain kept up. Add the cost of that army to the other expenses, and slave labour would be found to be dearer than free. The slave owner, acting upon the principle of the stage-coach proprietor, worked his human cattle to death. The average life of a slave in Cuba was seven or eight years. The late Lord George Bentinck had stated in Parliament that it was seven. This fact would give some idea of the manner in which the slaves were worked in that island. But this course was pursued because the Cubans knew that they could draw fresh supplies from Africa. Cut off those supplies, and they would soon have to change their policy. The evil would speedily cure itself. In the conduct of the labourers in this island we have another instance of the evils of slavery. In that State the people were taught that one day in a fortnight was sufficient, devoted to the cultivation of the soil, for the maintenance of a man and his family. Was it surprising that upon their emancipation they felt that they were independent of their employers and their money wages, and that, upon discovering that they could till the

soil more profitably on their own account, they should refuse
to labour for others?   The present state of things was in a
great measure the result of the conduct pursued by the
Government, and it was only right that we should ask it,
now that it had put an end to the English slave-trade—to
slavery in these colonies—and had changed its commercial
policy, that it should insist upon the treaties being regarded,
and an end put to the foreign slave-trade, from which we
have suffered, and were continuing to suffer so severely.

Mr. Vickars, a black gentleman, member of Assembly
for Spanish Town, said—Mr. Chairman, I was disposed to
enter largely into the present question, but after the very
able speech which we have just heard, and the handsome
manner in which the mover of the resolution has introduced
it, I shall merely content myself by seconding it—which I do
most sincerely.   It is to be regretted that what we are now
seeking was not done contemporaneously with the abolition
of slavery ; but I say, Sir, it is better late than never, and I
trust that our efforts will have a due effect upon the British
Government, and that that which we desire to obtain will
soon be granted.

The resolution was then put and carried.

Mr. Alexander Barclay, Receiver-general, and Custos
Rotulorum for St. Thomas in the East, said, that in moving
the second resolution, which had been put into his hand, he
should detain the meeting with only a very few observations.
The objects for which they had met were emphatically the
cause of outraged humanity and the cause of freedom ; and
to those great objects he hoped the meeting would address
themselves, abstaining from the canker subject of politics,
or dwelling upon the sufferings of the island, as if self-
interest was the only, or the main object they had in view.
How severe these sufferings were, over the length and
breadth of the island, and among all classes, few had more
ample means of knowing than himself; but into that distressing subject he would not enter at present.   If any good
was to result from that meeting, and others of a similar
character, and good he hoped would result from them, it

was by stirring up agitation on the other side of the water, by again arousing a feeling, which he hoped was only dormant, against the abhorred slave-trade and slavery. The resolution put into his hand was to the following effect :—

" That if these treaties are not to be regarded as a mockery of the African race—as a stultification or a satire on the principles or professions of the high contracting parties, and as a snare for the Colonial Legislatures who consented to emancipation—it is, in the opinion of this meeting, the imperative duty of her Majesty's Government, by all the means at their disposal, to require and enforce their exact and faithful observance."

He had no reliance on any Government, no matter what party was in power, taking action in a case of this kind, unless impelled by the public voice. A brief reference to the past would show this. When the African slave-trade was at its greatest height, the British Government not only was active in respect to its own colonies, but under the Assiento treaty became the carriers of slaves for the Spaniards. At a subsequent period, when the Assembly of Jamaica, to its honour be it said, made an attempt to regulate and restrain that trade, what did the Government do? It wrote out, through its mouth-piece, Lord Somers, to say, that no obstruction would be permitted to a trade so beneficial to the nation. In 1807, when the trade was ultimately abolished, was that done by the spontaneous act of the Government? No, it was forced upon the Government by an out-door pressure, of which Mr. Wilberforce was the head. So in like manner was the Emancipation Act carried—scarcely a city, or a town, or even a village in the United Kingdom that did not join in the cry for a termination of slavery. Thus in like manner must it be now ; that powerful voice, which has done so much already, must be again raised to complete the work that remains. It will not be done otherwise. That the selfishness of human nature continued the same now as it was in the time of Lord Somers, about one hundred years ago, there was very convincing proof by the last English packet which reached these shores, giving an account of a proposition made in Parliament, which had substantially for its object, to give free scope to the Brazilian slave-trade, in order to give the same free scope to the cotton trade of Manchester. It affords some ground of hope that this proposition met so few supporters in the House of Commons, and failed. Turning to another view of the subject, it appeared to him impossible that England could long remain in her humiliating and inconsistent attitude, with one arm raised against the slave-trade, and with the other holding out boons for its encouragement. Equally difficult was it to believe that the three greatest powers in the world would long continue to enact what looked very much like a farce, or child's play, in maintaining expensive armaments on the coast of Africa, to capture the Cuban and Brazilian slave vessels found outraging treaties, which those Governments might so easily be called upon to fulfil. The proceeding seemed so strange that one could not help doubting if those great powers were really in earnest; and, looking to the connection between cause and effect, one was led to suspect that on the part of France there might be some jealousy of England—that England was biased by the profits of the Cuban and Brazilian sugar and cotton trade, while American ardour in the cause was cooled by the state of slavery yet maintained among themselves. Whatever the causes might be, it was quite clear these three great powers, instead of placing watch vessels on the African coast, under the Spanish and Brazilian treaties, might easily, if they were in earnest, and would act together, take a more short and efficient course of compelling the fulfilment of these treaties. He had said, in the commencement of his observations, that this great question should not be urged by the people of Jamaica as one of self-interest—it was nevertheless proper that the calamitous condition of the island should be put forward on much higher grounds—the cause of African freedom, in which so many benevolent minds had taken a deep interest. In St. Domingo its failure was attributed to the violence, bloodshed, and anarchy with which it was accompanied. In the

British colonies the great change was effected under the law, and, thanks to the ministers of religion of all classes, without disorder, or the shedding of a drop of blood. Here, then, was a fair field of hope.—Shall it be slighted by favour to the man-stealer? Are the fertile fields of Jamaica doomed to become as desolate as those of St. Domingo? And is the last hope of African civilisation thus to be cast to the winds? Justice and Heaven forbid! With these few observations he would move the resolution.

Mr. R. J. C. Hitchins, member of Assembly for Kingston, said,—Rev. Sir, in rising to second this resolution, I find that little has been left me to say by Mr. Barclay. That gentleman has so ably treated the subject, that he has left little for me to add. I must, however, crave the indulgence of this numerous and respectable meeting, to declare my conviction, that unless the observance of the treaties be enforced with Spain and Brazil, all that England can do will be of no avail; and further, that unless England does seriously insist on the enforcement of these treaties, the whole world will declare that her assumed philanthropy was nothing better than hypocrisy and a trick to encourage her own trade. It will never be believed that a nation like England, whose history presents so many examples of jealousy with regard to the fulfilment of treaties — a nation which has resorted to war and bloodshed for the merest trifles with respect to the observance of treaties—could be sincere in her present conduct. Every one must remember the very trifling cause for the hostilities which resulted from some quarrel ᵃ   ᵃ cutting of logwood in the Bay of Honduras. Every one must be aware of the wars of immense length in which England has been engaged about the capture of some small sugar island; and yet England allows slaves to be landed within sight of our shores, in direct contravention of solemn treaties, while she suffers our fields to be desolated by means of the scourge of slavery. That those unfortunate people who have been smuggled into Cuba have a right to be free, no one can deny; but, for every slave smuggled into Cuba, a golden ounce is paid to the

Government of that island. This may appear outrageous, but it is so, and the fee is paid. Great Britain chooses to allow it, and sells the wares and merchandise of slavers, which furnish the means for the purchase of more slaves. And unless the slave-trade be abolished, how can we expect it to be otherwise? But we must call on all persons, on women as well as men, throughout the length and breadth of Great Britain—we must call on all to aid in the work—we must carry petitions to the foot of the throne, to the House of Lords and to the House of Commons. When our legislature abolished slavery, they did so under the security of a solemn compact with England. Our legislature has carried out our part of he engagement, while England has neglected hers. All that we can now do, therefore, and I think it will be untiringly done, is to agitate, agitate, agitate! and to call on all who possess any influence whatever, to assist in the effort to abolish the iniquitous slave-trade.

The resolution was then put and carried.

Dr. Macfayden, an eminent physician in Kingston, proposed the third resolution, as follows :—

"That the plan which was embodied by her Majesty's principal Secretary of State for Foreign Affairs in the draft of a convention with Spain, and which was transmitted by Viscount Palmerston to her Majesty's Minister at Madrid, on the 25th day of May, 1840, as appears from the papers on slave-trade, presented in that year to Parliament by her Majesty's command, is, in the judgment of this meeting, practical and feasible; and if now urged on the Spanish and Brazilian Governments with suitable energy, it would prove beneficial and effective in extinguishing the slave-trade, and in enabling the emancipated colonies of Great Britain to survive and withstand the competition in the home and other markets of the world, on the equal terms to which they are about to be exposed by the operation of the Sugar Duties Act of 1846."

He said, Mr. Chairman, ladies, and gentlemen, in every community there is a class who, from the nature of their calling, or from their position in society, are not expected to take a prominent part in public affairs. The scene of their duties lies amid the calm and privacy of domestic life, and they seem to quit their proper sphere when they venture on the notoriety of a public display ; yet there are occasions, in times of general calamity and distress, when even such are called on to overcome the repugnance they may feel, and to contribute their aid to that of others for the advancement of the common weal. Thus we read with admiration, in the narratives of besieged cities, that when the danger was imminent and the leaguer pressed sore, ministers of religion and delicate females served on the ramparts to repulse the assaults of the enemy. Our situation differs from theirs in many respects, yet there is a resemblance in the general suffering and distress, with apprehensions for the future, calculated to alarm and to rouse the most indifferent to exertion. Calamities, not less disastrous than those of war, have befallen us. For a number of years we have had a succession of misfortunes ; and privation, and stinted means have been experienced more or less in every family. Our interests have been made the sport of party politics—the spirit of enterprise has been crushed, and the productive resources of the country crippled. In the language of Wordsworth—

> " The land is stricken to the heart ;
> Many rich
> Have sunk, as in a dream ; among the poor,
> And of the poor many have ceased to be,
> And their place knows them not."

Nor can we console ourselves with the thought that the worst is past, and that the tale of our misfortunes is completed. Ours is ruin, in a state of progress, and not even the shrewdest can calculate how or when it is to terminate. Under such circumstances it becomes every one of us to be on the alert. Our cause cannot be desperate until we have lost all hope, and given ourselves up to apathy and supineness. Let us depend on our own energy and self-reliance, and as the evils which press upon us are avowedly great, so also must be the exertion with which they are to be met. Above all, let us cherish cordial co-operation and union, so essential to success in combined effort. We have been called together to-day for the purpose of representing the injury we suffer, as British subjects, from the violation of treaties entered into by the British Government with Spain and Brazil for the suppression of the slave-trade. We have, doubtless, many other grounds for complaint, founded on our interests being overlooked or neglected, or direct injury inflicted by the legislative acts of the imperial Parliament. This is one, however, which is palpable and undeniable, and it has been considered that we are more likely to succeed by bringing this prominently forward, than to have the effect of our representations weakened by dividing the attention among several objects. Let us, in the first place, take a short review of the different treaties entered into by Great Britain for the suppression of the slave-trade ; treaties which have never been properly enforced, but have been allowed to remain as a dead letter, or have been systematically violated by Spain and the Brazils. The first engagement entered into by Spain was in 1814, and produced a royal ordinance prohibiting Spaniards from engaging in the slave-trade, except for the supply of the Spanish possessions. There was a further treaty, in 1817, in which his Catholic Majesty engaged that the slave-trade should be abolished throughout the entire dominions of Spain on the 30th May, 1820. It was further stipulated that England should pay the sum of £400,000, as a compensation to Spain for the losses that might be sustained from the intended abolition of the trade. This was followed by empty professions on the part of Spain, of her readiness to fulfil the conditions of the treaty, and repeated remonstrances on the part of Great Britain at the manner in which the treaty was notoriously and flagrantly violated. At length, in 1835, another treaty, the most efficient for the purpose, was entered into by the late King of England and the mother of the present Queen of Spain. In this it was stated, " that the slave-trade was hereby again declared on the part of Spain to be henceforward totally and finally abolished in all parts of the world." By this treaty it was ordered that Mixed Courts of Justice be established for the adjudication of disputed cases. I need scarcely say that this treaty has not been observed by Spain, for slaves continue to be imported into Cuba, though in a less open and shameless manner than formerly. It was in 1840 that the convention alluded to, in the resolution which I have the honour to move, was proposed by Lord Palmerston to the Court of Madrid, at the suggestion of one whom we all esteem (Mr. Turnbull), and who is now present. It is to be regretted that the proposal was not then carried out. We trust that ere long we shall be more fortunate, so that he, at whose humane suggestion it was proposed, may at length witness the successful results of his benevolent exertions. The Brazilian treaties are of a similar tenor, and there has been a similar want of faith in their observance. I may, in the first place, mention, that when the Brazilian Government declared its independence, it acknowledged itself to be bound by the treaties which Portugal, the mother country, had contracted with foreign powers. Now, among these treaties were several entered into for the abolition of the slave-trade. In 1826, negotiations were commenced for the entire abolition of the slave-trade, and a treaty was signed with Great Britain, stipulating that the carrying on of such trade, three years after the date of the treaty, by Brazilian subjects, would be deemed and treated as piracy. Had the Brazilian Government acted in this with good faith, there cannot be a doubt but that the slave-trade would, long ere this, have been abolished in that part of the world. They never, however, intended to observe the treaty. On the contrary, they made application, in 1828 and in 1829, to have the time specified in the treaty extended. In the meantime, the abominable traffic continued to be carried on : papers continued to be granted sanctioning the practice. Every impediment was thrown in the way of the fair working of the Mixed Commission, and masses of human beings continued to be imported and consigned to bondage, contrary to the Brazilian laws founded on this treaty. At length, in 1843, the British Government intimated that it would remain for her Majesty to take alone, and by her own means, the necessary steps to carry into full and ample effect the humane object imposed by the convention of 1826. It is upon this resolution that our Government have since been acting, and it was for the repeal of this treaty, and to give the Brazilians a free-trade in slavery, that Mr. Milner Gibson recently made a motion in the House of Commons. Let us now consider the injury inflicted on the West India colonies by the non-observance of these treaties. Formerly, the productions of these countries were excluded from the English market by prohibitory duties ; now they are admitted into direct competition with ours. This competition, though otherwise unjust, we might meet, were there no slave-trade to furnish them with an unceasing supply of labour. The facility with which loss of labour can be supplied, renders them prodigal of human life. The great object of the Cuba planter is to make his sugar at the lowest possible cost, that he may undersell all others in the market. His power over his slave, even when abused, is unchecked and uncontrolled, reaching almost to that over life, and the extent of his cupidity is the only limit for the labour that is to be exacted. The free labourer, in Jamaica, is expected to give, as a day's labour, what his strength is equal to. But it is different with the slave. What ! though life is shortened, and death comes ere long to the relief of the wretched, the slave market is at hand, and a fresh victim can at once be procured. It would be otherwise, were there no fresh slaves to be procured. Self-interest would induce the owner to look after the welfare of his slave, and he would refrain from exacting a task, to which the human frame is unequal. Were there no slave-trade, the Cuba planter would no longer boast that ten shillings per cwt. was a remunerating price ; he would agree with his brother planter in Jamaica, that sixteen shillings is the very lowest that sugar can honestly be made for. We now come to the question, how is Great Britain to enforce these treaties ? In private life, when a man faithlessly refuses to fulfil his engagements, measures are taken to compel him. It would be a cause for regret that war should be resorted to for this purpose. Yet England has gone to war for a less justifiable cause. In 1798, she made war against Denmark, bombarded Copenhagen, laying nearly the whole city in ruins, and destroying a vast number of the inhabitants; and all this to establish the right of searching neutral vessels. This was a most unrighteous war. But it would be different with a war undertaken to compel cruel and lawless men to observe their agreements, and to abstain from violence and crime, and to rescue the weak and the helpless from the blood-stained hands of the oppressor. What we complain of is, that England has never appeared to be sufficiently in earnest in demanding the observance of these treaties. Remonstrances have been made; but, in many instances, no answer appears to have been returned. We fear, if some decided step is not speedily taken, that the cause of humanity for a length of time will suffer. A very different spirit from the present actuated the counsels of Great Britain, when these treaties were drawn up. The voice of the nation was then to be heard pleading loudly for the rights, and in denunciation of the wrongs of the oppressed of our species. Now, Mammon is the god of their idolatry; the exigences of commerce outweigh the rights of humanity, and the opinion gains advocates, that to secure a more extended market for our manufactures, the slave-trade must no longer be fettered. It was in this spirit that the Sugar Bill of 1846 was passed. I talk not of the ruin of individuals, and the desolation of families, and the poverty and distress it has brought on this island; but I would point out the fresh impetus it has given to the slave-trade, and the hundreds of thousands of the sons and daughters of Africa, whom it has torn from their homes, and consigned either to watery graves, or what is far worse, to a bondage wretched beyond conception. There is one effect following the enforcement of these treaties which is rather startling. All imported as slaves into Cuba or Brazil, since the signing of these treaties, are illegally held in bondage, and are entitled to freedom, according to the laws of these countries, founded on these treaties. When you recollect that 75,000 slaves were in 1848 imported into Brazil, all of whom are by the laws free, you may imagine what a large proportion would be liberated were justice enforced. A notice to this effect from Lord Palmerston, in proposing a convention in 1840, produced the greatest alarm among the authorities at Madrid, as well as the slave owners in the Havanna. The Americans also, in the proposed annexation of Cuba, have been struck with the difficulty ; for after the judgment pronounced in the case of the " Amistad," it is plain the law authorities would pronounce for the right to freedom of these people ; and thus our western friends, in taking possession of the coveted island, would find already there the materials for a free black republic. Ere I draw to a close, permit me to express my conviction, that were the slave treaties enforced, the planters of Jamaica would successfully compete with the slave owners of any country. This is a beautiful island — favoured in soil and climate—surpassed by few in natural advantages. All that is wanted is, to use a sporting phrase, a fair field and no favour—that is to say, free us from competition with those who are backed with the slave-trade, and we ask no protection. In the meantime, let us be true to ourselves and cease to despond ; let not cultivation be abandoned too hurriedly ; and let us give time to a good Providence to work in our behalf. Let the peace of Europe be once restored, and there will be a vast increase in the consumption of sugar. To be convinced of this, look at France, where there is a high duty to protect beet-root sugar. Though the population is double that of England, there is two and a half times less sugar consumed. Doubtless, ere long, monopolies of every kind will be abolished, commerce will be free to all, and the markets of the world will be opened to our produce. In concluding, let me remind you, in the words of Wayland, an American writer, that " So far as I am able to discover, the most important conditions on which the productiveness of any society depend, are industry and frugality, virtue and intelligence. Possessed of these, no nation, with the ordinary blessing of God, can long be poor. Destitute of either of them, whatever be its natural advantages, no nation can ever long remain rich. Patriotism, no less than religion, would therefore teach us to cultivate these habits in ourselves and in others, and he is the purest patriot who cultivates them most assiduously."

Mr. Osborn, member of Assembly for St. Andrew's, and one of the editors of the *Morning Journal*, rose amid shouts and applause. He said—Mr. Chairman, were I to follow in the course laid down by the gentleman who has preceded me, and who has so elegantly, so nervously, and so ably described the history of the treaties entered into with Great Britain for the suppression of the slave-trade—were I to say that the arguments of that gentlemen leave nothing for me to do, I would be saying what was correct. The worthy Doctor, as well as those others who have preceded me, have so ably enlarged on the subject, on grounds so extended, and in a manner so instructive, that I feel myself in my proper place in this humble corner. (Mr. O. was at the south-east part of the Court-house.) But I find that one circumstance has been overlooked by all the speakers, and that in the absence of the ladies, and the very small attendance which we have, no allusion has yet been made to the matter ; and I, therefore, may be permitted to offer a few observations. I must say, Sir, that it is with some surprise that I see so few ladies here to-day, especially when I know that Kingston can at any time turn out her fifteen hundred. Whether the ladies are feeling the practical effects of the Sugar Bill at home or not, I cannot say. Perhaps they do not like to come here, and join in our doleful song ; but I confess, Sir, that I should have been more happy to have seen them taking at least the piano part in this discussion, if not by speaking, at least by looking on. Having expressed regret at their absence, I must go on to say that I cannot see why they are absent ; but I suppose we must give them credit for having stayed at home to perform those domestic duties which assist us to float smoothly down the current of life. I dare say their time is engrossed by their home duties, and we must make every allowance. The resolution is so long, Mr. Chairman, that I will not read it, as it has been already read, and you have all heard it. But it seems to me that I am expected to say something, and I will make it as short as I can. The Doctor, who has preceded me, has made, as I before said, so plain a statement of the treaties, and the manner in which they have been shamefully neglected by Great Britain, whose influence and power are strong enough, and whose cause is strong enough, to enforce the carrying out of those treaties which England paid for, that I have little more to add. England is quite strong enough to enforce them ; but the slave-trade is winked at by the British Government ; no one can deny this—and why ? Because its disallowance would do an injury to the cotton trade. The political part of this subject has already been so ably treated, that I will not occupy your time on that ground ; I could not do it so ably. But when I see, Sir, so large an assemblage of persons interested in these matters, I may, perhaps, be excused in indulging a little in my own ideas. I say, then, that I consider it an imperative duty, imposed by Providence on the mixed races, to do all in their power for the suppression of the slave-trade. If anyone here is ashamed to acknowledge that he is descended from the African race, I stand here to confess that I am a descendant of Africa. There is no mistake at all about it. Nature never intended that there should be any mistake. The mark has been placed upon me, and will remain with me until I go back again. Any one can see it, and if they cannot see it, why they may feel it. I therefore consider it imperative on us to express our deep abhorrence of a system by which thousands of our fellow-creatures are annually destroyed. I contend, Sir, that there is happiness in ignorance. The carrying away of slaves and their posterity is a wrong done to Africa, and wherever their descendants are to be found they should come forward and give expression to the abhorrence which every well-regulated mind must feel, and desire to express. The horrors of the slave-trade have been already ably depicted. You already know the numerous instances of kidnapping young girls from the bosom of their mothers. I would ask many present if they have ever seen how cattle are packed up on board ship—how they are wedged together on the deck—how they are bruised and cut in the landing, and how they have died from those causes? Even so has it been with our maternal ancestors. Those Christian feelings which such enormities called forth were expressed throughout England. She was determined that such atrocious acts should not be committed by any nation under the sun; and, as has already been told you, she paid £400,000 to Spain as a bonus for the abolition of this shameful traffic, and that Africans might be left alone in their own country. Spain promised and engaged to do these things, but she has since neglected her engagements and refused to carry them into effect, and Great Britain, who has so often assisted Spain, now hesitates to enforce the treaty. The question then arises, what is the cause of this neglect? How are we to account for it? Is it possible that a reaction has taken place in the minds of Englishmen? Can it be possible that they have ceased to be the same honourable, religious, and moral people that they formerly were? Can they have recently discovered that there is a pleasure in slavery? Can they have found it right to take a man from his home and friends, drag him from his family, and place him in a state of slavery — to make him the slave of a man unknown to him, and of that man's children? If the British people have suffered this revulsion of feeling, they have astonished us, and astonished the world. It is in vain to say that they have not done it themselves, and that they reprobate the system. We say, you have paid for the abolition of a system which is contrary to the law of God and man, and if you still have the will, as you have the power, it is your duty to see those treaties carried out. Having, Sir, cursorily glanced at the manner in which the people of Africa are brought to slaveholding countries, I will not dwell on the unmanly and brutal, not alone mercenary, but brutal spirit, which induces these acts. Let us suppose that we were a people steeped in ignorance, and that our neighbours could come here and take you, Doctor, or any lady from her husband, into a state of slavery, what would be our feeling then? And it is only by putting ourselves in the position of these unfortunate people that we can arrive

at the horrors of the inhumanity which is practised upon
them. Without wishing to dwell on the iniquitous middle
passage, where, out of seven hundred persons, not more than
three hundred ever arrive at their destination, let us imagine what must be the misery of persons who attempt to
throw themselves into the yawning waters which roll beneath
them, in preference to suffering the horrors of their position?
What must be the feelings of people who would attempt
that melancholy resort? I know, Sir, that they have been
made blind—that they have been deprived of the sight which
the Almighty gave them — that they have been maimed,
because, knowing that they were born free men, they desired
to throw themselves into the mighty deep, to escape the
melancholy fate which their persecutors had prepared for
them. Has the British Government not declared the solemn
principle that man never was intended to be the slave of
man? Has it not declared slavery to be incompatible with
Christianity? Has it not decided that the system should
die? Then what is the meaning of this inconsistent conduct?—of this supineness and indifference on the part of the
most powerful nation on the earth? The answer is, the
interests of the manufacturers of cottons and prints are at
stake. For their benefit the British Government has sacrificed every feeling of honour, as if there were not a God in
heaven, who would confer advantages on men, without their
stooping to such unrighteousness. Now, Sir, having addressed myself to the first part of the resolution, I will attend
to the second part, in doing which, I shall be as concise as
possible. I believe, Sir, that all persons are aware that this
is exclusively an agricultural country; all our wealth, as is
the case with many other countries, lies in our soil. In
some places, where trade and manufactures are so extensive,
no immediate injury would be felt by the neglect of agriculture; but our island is exclusively agricultural; and it
has been shown, by the test of experience, that we are unable
to manufacture such articles as woollen goods, paper, and
the like; we have, therefore, nothing to rely on but our soil,
and if our soil and its produce are not remunerative, in the

name of heaven what is to become of us? We see the
slave-trade not only permitted, but fearfully reacting on us,
to our disadvantage, in a manner which forces the agri-
culturist to abandon the soil. If the work of abandonment
is to continue—if, year after year, sugar and coffee estates
are to be thrown out of employment, how, I ask, is all this to
end? If property after property is to be abandoned, every
man must see that we have nothing left us but to fall. My
friend, in an early stage of the proceedings, made allusion to
a remark of mine, that people cannot find their own doors in
consequence of the bush which hides them. I tell you,
gentlemen, that this is a fact; many persons are obliged to
search among the bush for the entrance to their doors,
because their estates have been so long abandoned, agriculture having ceased to be remunerative. The labourers are
feeling it wonderfully. I heard one, on Thompson's piazza,
say, "If the Lord does not have mercy upon us, I don't
know what we shall do." This question, therefore, Sir,
concerns all classes in the community. As for the workmen,
I am told that there are upwards of 500 in the city, who, in
spite of their endeavours, can find nothing to do. We
would give them employment, but there is no money to pay
them. There are many persons, as my friend Mr. Jordon
has told you, who can remember the difference of Port
Royal-street in former days. I am not an old man, as the
ladies will tell you, and yet I can remember drayloads of
doubloons passing up and down Port Royal-street. I will
not say I am a young man, but I am a middle-aged
man — I see the Doctor (Ferguson) smiling, but I dare
say he recollects it—but now we cannot find a cheque,
no, not even red cheques.* Those who used to call them
"red rags" are coveting them now, but there are none to be
had. What, then, is to become of us? There is universal
desolation. The ladies feel it in the absence of many comforts, and the gentlemen in the emptiness of their pockets.
We are also told that schools are being shut up. Parties

* In allusion to the small notes issued on the security of the island
treasury.—Ed.

who go over the country find schools shut up from the want of means to carry them on. Then, I ask, who are to take our places when we are dead and gone? How is the rising generation to be brought up? How are our agricultural youngsters to be reared? A boy's father may have now a table and a knife and fork; but if there be no work, and the table gets broken, father and son must sit on the ground, and if there be no knife and fork, they must eat with their fingers. All civilisation and progression must cease and be prostrated. Can a man be said to be in a state of progressive civilisation who has no table, no knife and fork? There is now no capitalist, nor any one else to help us. While I am speaking, Sir, there are dozens here around me who are practically feeling what I have detailed. Many once had table-cloths, and good furniture, which are all worn out, and who have not the means of supplying new ones. What can be done? We can only look up to our Almighty Father, while we appeal to Great Britain for protection. We must unite to tell them that it is neither lawful nor just that our people should be made to starve, for the benefit of another population. We are willing to be loyal and good subjects, but while we are so, we feel that the parent Government has its duties also. We are neither a foreign nor a conquered people. We have never been a rebellious, but always a loyal people, and our records can establish that fact; but it is right that we should be permitted to do that which the Almighty intended all men to do—earn our bread by the sweat of our brow. I will not detain the meeting any longer, Mr. Chairman; I beg to second the resolution, as it is too long for me to read.

The Rev. S. Oughton, Baptist minister, of Kingston, on rising to propose the fourth resolution, was received with loud cheering. He said—Mr. Chairman, ladies, and gentlemen,—The resolution which has been entrusted to my care reads as follows:—

"That as the interests of human freedom and of African civilisation, the maintenance and welfare of all voluntary intertropical industry, and the social progress of our emancipated population, are, in this great question, so intimately blended, as to be no ʟonger capable of separation or distinction, it becomes desirable and expedient that all past differences should be forgotten, and that, meeting on the same platform, the man of business and the philanthropist—he who is seeking his own advantage, and he who loves his neighbour as himself—should henceforth make common cause with each other in promoting the extinction of the slave-trade, and the extirpation of slavery throughout the earth."

There is much (said the rev gentleman) in this resolution which is interesting and important; the subjects comprised in its introduction demand our gravest consideration, and claim our most untiring exertions; and I might be justified at once in entering upon their discussion, but as that method of proceeding has characterised the addresses of every pre-ceding speaker, who from the commencement of these reso-lutions have steadily followed their course even to the close, and as I sometimes like to indulge in a little harmless originality, I shall pursue a course the very opposite of theirs, and shall begin my speech with the end of my resolution. In adopting such a course I think I am justified by the overwhelming importance of the subject it presents, which is nothing less than the extinction of the slave-trade, and the extirpation of slavery throughout the earth. This is a con-summation so devoutly to be wished, that every other loses its importance when compared with it. Yet think not, Sir, because I speak thus, I do not love Jamaica, and feel no interest in its prosperity. Jamaica is to me a spot more endeared than even the land of my birth, or any other spot in the whole geography of this earth. Jamaica is the land of my adoption—the land where some of my happiest years have been spent, around which my most delightful asso-ciations gather, beneath whose sod several of my dear children sleep, and with whose future history and happiness I trust those who still survive will be identified. But, Sir, much as I love Jamaica, I love justice more, and therefore do I hail with emotions of peculiar satisfaction a resolution whose end and aim is the total extirpation of slavery, and the universal freedom of the whole human family. In this respect, Sir, I listened with regret to the addresses of some of the gentlemen

who preceded me; it appeared to me most extraordinary
that, with those gentlemen, the slave-trade was almost inva-
riably coupled with Jamaica's poverty, as though they could
not feel for the sufferings of the slave, except as they themselves were made to suffer, and that there were no avenue
by which their sympathies could be approached but that of
their own pockets. Sir, I should blush for my sympathies
did they spring from such a source. To feel aright we must
separate the condition of the slave from our own, instead of
identifying them with each other. We must feel for the
slave because he is a man. We must feel for the slave
because he is an oppressed, afflicted, down-trodden man, the
victim of avarice and cruelty, shut out from all the comforts
and enjoyments of this world—the innocent and hapless
inheritor of contumely, injustice, and suffering. For this
cause, Sir, (continued Mr. O.) we feel for the slave, and for
this cause, too, I feel for myself, to think that it is to the race
from which I am descended the peeled and spoiled sons of
Africa have received this wrong; and just in proportion
as I pity the slave—just in equal proportion do I experience
shame for my country, which was the first to wrong and
spoil him, whilst, until the present hour, African slavery has
been more identified with civilised and Christian European
nations than any other on the face of the earth. Sir, deeply
as I feel interested in the welfare of Jamaica, I would not
dare to purchase it at such a price as slavery involves;
rather would I that we had poverty with righteous freedom,
than wealth with an unrighteous bondage; and if the terms
of returning prosperity were a return to slavery, I would say
down with slavery. If slavery could restore the strange
phenomenon of doubloons dragged through our streets by
truck and dray loads, as mentioned by a gentleman just now
as having been once the case in this city, I would still say
down with slavery, and rather let us enjoy poverty with a
conscience unpolluted by guilt, than wealth stained with the
blood of the poor and the oppressed. Thus much (said the
rev. gentleman) for the end of my resolution; it is high
time that I should now direct your attention to its beginning.

There is much, Sir, in this resolution that accords with my feelings; it comprehends two most interesting subjects—liberty for all mankind, and unity amongst ourselves; it opens with the interest of human freedom and African civilisation; thence it proceeds to " the welfare of all intertropical industry, and the social progress of our emancipated population." These, it declares, are blended together, and dependant on each other, and to promote them we are invited to forget all minor differences and heartily to co-operate. I could not but observe, when the resolution was first given to me, how these subjects gradually sunk from generalities to particulars, and from the more extended and general good it descended to the special and particular benefit; but is not that the natural and proper course, and ought we not at all times to seek our own advantage from that which contributes at the same time to the general welfare? With respect to human freedom, it is an object for which every honest and Christian heart must pant; it is God's highest earthly gift, and man's most treasured inheritance. But, Sir, human freedom has been, and is, even now, invaded. In Cuba, slavery exists in all its horrors; and even in Brazil—that land which itself, not many years ago, exhibited so much impatience of control, and, determining to be free, tore itself from the paternal Government of Portugal—even Brazil still holds slaves, whilst both are even now the promoters and perpetrators of the cruel and accursed traffic in human flesh. With such a system as this, desolating its country and coasts, who can hope for the civilisation of Africa? How can we expect that Africa should be civilised, when there is no security for either life, connections, or property? How can we expect that the African should ever strive to gather around him either social comforts or domestic delights, when his homestead is not secure from invasion and destruction for a single day, and when, as he retires to rest each night, he cannot tell lest, before the morning dawns, the wife of his bosom may be abused or murdered, his innocent babes slaughtered, and he himself carried away into an exile and bondage worse than death itself? No, Sir, the African slave-trade and African civilisation are incompatible with each other, and the one must cease to exist before we can hope to see the other flourish.   Besides, Sir, a country's civilisation depends upon a country's industry; but how can industry thrive when the flesh and bones of men are the most valuable material in its commerce? But let that demand cease, and the attention of Africa will soon be aroused to find some other and less objectionable articles of trade.   The Rev. Mr. Townsend, a missionary from Africa, at a meeting of the Church Missionary Society in London, last month, confirms this opinion; he tells us that the subject is one of common conversation amongst the chiefs of Africa, who complain that they are not encouraged to traffic in anything but human beings. They say: "The white men press us with their goods; they come and say, take our goods, and give us slaves for them; and whenever an African is told that an Englishman is desirous of extending a lawful traffic, he says, why don't you extend it to our country? If you will sell us your goods for cotton instead of slaves, there will be an end to the traffic in slaves, and you will have the traffic in cotton in its place." Here, then, we learn (continued Mr. O.) it is manifest that the abolition of the slave-trade is not only the surest means to produce African civilisation, but also to advance human freedom in its most extended sense. Abolish the slave-trade, and Africa will soon become a large cotton exporting country; whilst America, cut off from a considerable portion of her trade in slave-cultivated cotton, may learn that slavery is not only a wicked, but an unprofitable pursuit, and, if not moved by better principles, be shamed into honesty, and from interest learn to be just. And if human freedom and African civilisation depend for their existence on the destruction of slavery and the slave-trade, our intercolonial industry and the local improvement of our emancipated population are not less dependant. The British West Indian colonies are entirely restricted in their commercial intercourse to the British nation; it is to their markets alone that they can look for the sale of their productions, and, cut off from this source of industry, there appears to be no other in which they can hope to be usefully and profitably employed. And can it be expected that the cultivation of our staples can proceed, unless they yield a fair remunerating profit to the producer—for who would toil and labour, only to grow poorer by his industry? Would the manufacturers of Birmingham and Manchester do so? Would they invest their capital and industry in the production of hardware and cottons, unless they hoped to obtain a fair return for the investment? But this we cannot hope for, whilst slavery and the slave-trade are encouraged. The sugars of the freemen of Jamaica can never compete in the markets of England with the slave-extorted productions of Cuba and Brazil; thus our hope of intertropical industry is cut off, and the mainspring of our commercial greatness broken. And, Sir, if the staple productions of our country ceased to be articles of commerce, what hope have we that the other branches of manufacture and art can be maintained? Ours, Sir, is an agricultural country: we have no other sources of wealth, no other means of obtaining money to purchase the comforts or even the commonest necessaries of life. What, then, will become of our masons and carpenters, our shoemakers and tailors, and all those who minister to social comfort and refinement in this land? No, Sir, destroy our agricultural interests and we are a ruined and undone people, whilst all hope of social progress would be a delusion, too Utopian to be expected. There was a time when I enjoyed the most sanguine expectations that Jamaica would ere long enjoy no inconsiderable portion of social, moral, and religious distinction. When, eleven years ago, the former slaves of Jamaica entered on the full possession of their rights and liberties, who could observe the sudden impulse given to their improvement, without cherishing the most sanguine expectations of their future elevation? When the negro first cast off the shackles of his former bondage, he seemed to spring, with almost superhuman energy, into the atmosphere of social and moral improvement, and I fondly hoped that his progress would be commensurate with his beginning; but, alas! where is that hope now? Since the fatal Bill of 1846, it has become extinguished, and the position of our population has been retrograde rather than advancing; where plenty once reigned, nothing but poverty is now experienced. Estates have been thrown out of cultivation, and people thrown out of employment, whilst, as a natural consequence, the inhabitants of our towns have been made to share in the distresses of our agricultural interest. In this city hundreds of industrious people are without work to earn their daily bread. I, Sir, know a man who for more than thirty years maintained himself and family in this city in comfort and respectability by his trade, as an upholsterer, but who from failure of employment has been reduced to poverty, and driven to the mountains to cultivate a miserable piece of land, in order to escape starvation. This is not a solitary case; hundreds of others have been driven to the same expedient, and our city is desolate. Another proof of social advancement in a country is the prosperous condition of its educational and religious institutions, and what a mournful picture in this respect does our island now present! Within the present year the Wesleyan Society have been compelled to abandon no less than twenty of their schools. The society to which I belong has been reduced to the same sad alternative, and we are not alone—ours have been but types of every other religious society, whilst chapels have been closed, and ministers, ruined and broken-hearted, have been compelled to leave these shores and return to their native land. And why all this ruin?—why all this desolation? Because slavery and the slave-trade continue to exist, and England has become their patron. Oh, Sir, slavery is a bloody crime—it is the scourge of man, denounced by God, and must be abhorred by all good men. It was only this day that I glanced over the report of the extent to which the slave-trade has been carried during the last eight years. And what has it accomplished during that period? No fewer than 444,876 slaves have been deported from Africa; of these 111,019 perished during the middle passage, and

333,007 were sold into slavery in Cuba and Brazil, whilst 31,180 were captured by our British cruisers. Oh, Sir, let others say as they will, I love to see the British flag engaged in such a cause—it is an honour to my country, and most fervently do I pray that it never may be unfurled in an object less humane and praiseworthy. But we must not forget the fact, that whilst 31,180 were saved by British humanity, 111,019 were doomed to suffer a dreadful death, amidst the horrors of the middle passage, in order to gratify Cuban and Brazilian avarice and cupidity. And are we to be quiet whilst such atrocities as these are enacted? Will you, within whose veins the blood of Africa runs, be quiet, whilst your countrymen and your kindred are thus inhumanly murdered? (Cries of " No, no.") Yes, and I say no. The history of the African slave-trade is written in tears of blood, and it is our duty to arise and blot it out for ever. Oh, Sir, the worst is not told yet. England—my heart swells with shame and anguish as I mention it—England shares in the guilt of their traffic. England encourages and supplies this trade, and justice compels me to say that England is as guilty as Cuba or Brazil. It has often occurred to my mind (said the rev. gentleman) that the traveller who was robbed and ill-treated on his way between Jerusalem and Jericho, was no bad type of the people of Africa; they have indeed fallen amongst thieves, who, although of different nations and languages, have nevertheless agreed in this, that it was an easy victim, and that they were determined to enrich themselves at its expense; and if it be asked who they are, I say that they are Cubans and Brazilians, who steal their children to sell them into a cruel bondage on the one hand; and they are the Birmingham and Manchester manufacturers on the other, who provide material for the accursed traffic, and grow rich by supplying the articles by which the poor victims are purchased, and the shackles by which they are bound, whilst as yet no compassionate Samaritan has been found to stanch her bleeding wounds and minister to her welfare. But, Sir, England must be aroused to a proper sense of her position, and to the faithful discharge of her duty in this matter. There was a time when England stood forth nobly in the cause of humanity and freedom, and Jamaica was obliged to sit at her feet and receive her lessons. Now the case is altered, and Jamaica is compelled to stand forth to teach justice and humanity to England, and I hope she will at least be not less willing to learn than she found her colonies. Sir, I will not attempt to conceal the fact, that our duty and our interest in this matter go hand in hand, nor can I conceive that such a circumstance can be advanced, fairly or justly, as an argument against our object; if the principles we advocate were just in 1834, when they involved so much loss to the proprietors of Jamaica property, they are not less equitable now, when their being carried out will tend to revive and restore their ruined fortunes. The only question that remains is, how can this be accomplished? I believe, Sir, that in military tactics the same method is not always pursued, in order to accomplish the same end. If the citadel of an enemy is to be obtained, there are two ways by which it may be done—the first is, by storming, and taking it by a *coup de main;* and, Sir, if this method were necessary to destroy slavery in its strongholds, England would be at no loss for means to accomplish it; it would require but little effort of her gigantic and almost irresistible power to crush such paltry adversaries; it needs only for England to assume an attitude of determination, and utter the language of authority, in order to hush them into silence, and compel them to be faithful to their engagements. The fact is, Spain and Brazil have obtained impunity in their faithlessness, not from their power but from their very insignificance; they were considered too contemptible to deserve our notice, or, long ere this, the haughty Spanish dons would have been brought to their knees, and the blustering Brazilians would have dwindled (if such were possible) into less than their natural and proper dimensions. But this course, however effectual it might be, is one which, as a Christian minister, I can neither approve or recommend. War is at all times a doubtful course of policy, and certainly ought never to be adopted until every other means have been tried and proved ineffectual ; and we have other means within our power, less objectionable in their character, and equally certain in their success. I would not storm the citadel of slavery, and take it by force ; I would beleaguer it, and starve it into a surrender. I would adopt the Apostle Paul's method for abolishing laziness—starve it into industry, or else out of the world. If they will steal men in spite of all our efforts, one thing we can do, and that is, to have no share in the abominable transaction. The disgrace and con-demnation will then be all their own. We can only partake in the shame in proportion as we share in the spoils. Let Great Britain resolve to be no partner in such a nefarious traffic, and she will be no partner in the crime. Let her resolve not to taste, touch, or handle the accursed thing, lest she be involved in the guilt, and liable to the awful responsi-bility of her conduct. I do not, Sir, advocate this upon the principle of protection for our commerce. I ask not for favour, but for justice ; I seek not that England should be partial, but I demand that England be honest. With the fair and equitable cultivator, in whatever part of the world he may dwell, we are willing to compete, but we are not willing to compete with men who obtain their productions at the price of the bones, and sinews, and blood of our fellow-creatures. Let Cuba and Brazil abolish slavery and the slave-trade, and then is England welcome to open her ports for the unfettered introduction of their produce. And this, I believe, Sir, would have been soon accomplished. But for the fatal Bill of 1846, I believe that slavery would by this time have been nearly or quite destroyed. I have it on the authority of the public documents of the commissioners in those countries, that so highly did the planters and merchants of Cuba and Brazil estimate the importance of the British markets, that they seriously entertained the idea of abolishing slavery, in order that they might be open to their trade. Sir, England has satisfied their desires ; England has opened her markets to Cuba and Brazil, but not to reward a righteous act of emancipation, but to encourage and sustain an atrocious system of slavery. I say, again, we do not ask protection; give us, as my friend Dr. Macfayden has said, a fair field and no favour, and it shall be seen that Jamaica can and will produce her staples as cheap as Cuba. But, Sir, it is too bad to ask the honest producer to compete with the man who obtains his goods by robbery and spoliation. I have no doubt that when the report of this meeting reaches England, there will be found not a few who will endeavour to detract from its influence and evade its arguments, by endeavouring to impugn the motives of those who have been engaged in it. Sir, the impugning of motives is an old device of the enemy, and is as mean, cowardly, and dishonourable as it is unjust. Who is he that has a right to sit in judgment upon the motives of his fellow-man? To usurp the place of God, and dare to decide upon the hidden feelings of the soul? If you, Sir, a Christian minister, express your sympathy for the sufferings of the slave, and your abhorrence of that system which perpetuates them, by what right dare I, or any man, to impeach the integrity of your statements, and charge you with hypocrisy? I say not this because I entertain any alarm lest my motives will be suspected. My sentiments on the anti-slavery question have been too consistently maintained, and too long and publicly declared. I have suffered too much in that cause to render me obnoxious to suspicion now; still, as some at this meeting may be charged as acting rather from interested than benevolent motives, I feel it my duty, in their name as well as my own, indignantly to denounce so unjust and dishonourable a method of evading the force of a great and all-important question. But who are the men to impeach our motives? Are they the Cobdens, or the Brights, or the Gibsons? Are they those gentlemen who grow rich by making the gaudy trinkets, and trumpery muskets, or flaunting cottons, by which the traffic is carried on? They, Sir, at least, ought to be chary how they attribute motives, when their trade has, by its late increase in articles for slave traffic, been augmented, since 1846, no less than £200,000 per annum. I would advise them, at least, not to talk about motives, lest they should be met by the bitter retort—" Fool, first take the beam out of thine own eye, then shalt thou see clearly to take the mote out of thy brother's eye." But, oh, Sir, they can afford to judge, and stigmatise, and sneer at us; they are prospering, while we are sinking into ruin—they are rich, whilst we are poor—they are, therefore, honourable men, and can call us ill names, for, as the poet says—

> " Wealth makes the man, and want of it, the fellow,
>   The rest is nought but leather and prunella."

Can we wonder, then, that the honourable member for Manchester (Mr. Milner Gibson), honourable, Sir, by courtesy, could have dared to bring forward a resolution to rescind the former order of Government for the suppression of the slave-trade, and boldly to advocate free trade in flesh and bones? I did not wonder, Sir, when I heard that Manchester had profited so greatly by that trade; but I was surprised and grieved when I saw Mr. Bright—a man so long associated with that distinguished body of Christian philanthropists (the Quakers) and descended from a long and illustrious line of members of that persuasion, mixed up in that disgraceful transaction. I felt for the humbling position he occupied, and the disgrace he had brought upon his profession, and think that he must have felt it too. Not one moral or religious sentiment did he use throughout the whole course of his speech; his argument was money, from the beginning to the end. First, he told us of a trade with Brazil worth £3,000,000 per annum; secondly, of British capital invested in Brazil to the amount of £4,000,000 or £5,000,000 more; thirdly, the insecurity of British property in that country; and lastly, the terrible fact that British goods were in danger of being raised from 15 to 33⅓ per cent. import duty; and these were the arguments of an English Quaker for free trade in slaves. Sir, if he had been a member of my church I would have excommunicated him; and I cannot but think that, as a Quaker, he deserves to be put out of the society and compelled to wear a collar to his coat, and have the brim of his hat cut to more moderate dimensions, so long as upon such principles he advocates a trade in human flesh and blood. But, Sir, Mr. Bright did not stop there; he went further, and not content with giving his voice for the removal of all restrictions on the Brazilian slave-trade, he even ventured to taunt Lord Palmerston with what he called his " philanthropic crotchet," because he defended those restrictions. Sir, I honour that nobleman for his philanthropic crotchet; and I believe that Mr. Bright will find, if the matter be fairly put to the people of England, that there are tens and hundreds of thousands who have the same philanthropic crotchet as Lord Palmerston. Men of noble heart and stern integrity, who would shudder at the bare thought of such base and guilty conduct, and if called upon to pronounce a verdict would sustain the views of that distinguished nobleman, with a majority of the nation as proportionably great as that which crushed the unworthy motion of Mr. M. Gibson in the House of Commons. Some allusions (said Mr. Oughton) have been made to the ladies. I rejoice to find that in this country they take so deep and lively an interest in these proceedings ; they well deserve the sympathy of the more tender and humane sex, and I trust they will also obtain their valuable co-operation. In England the ladies are alive to the subject and exerting themselves on its behalf. And why should they not do the same in Jamaica ? Their sweet voices never sound so harmoniously as when raised in behalf of the poor and the needy and they who have no helper, and in such a cause no earthly voices are so omnipotent. I told my congregation (continued the rev. gentleman) last Sunday, that I should have petitions at the doors of my chapel next Lord's day, and invited the women to sign them as well as the men ; and why not ?—cannot women feel for the poor slaves as well as men ? Are not women as much interested in human freedom and happiness as men ? And are not the women as much disgraced by slavery as men ? Yes, Sir, they are : British colonial slavery was first introduced when a woman (Queen Elizabeth) sat upon the throne of England, and the very sex feel compromised by the fact. But I thank God, that if, under the rule of one British Queen, slavery was permitted to commence its hateful existence, in the first year of the reign of another British Queen (our own beloved Victoria) slavery in her dominions was crushed to death; and now, throughout the length and breadth of her vast empire, there is not one of her countless subjects who does not enjoy his natural birthright, liberty, as a man, and his civil and religious privileges as a British subject. And it needs only that we be active and energetic in this good cause to secure even greater triumphs. The Anti-Slavery Society at home are with us heart and hand in this matter, and only wait for our cordial co-operation to enter on a new crusade for universal liberty. Yes, liberty to Brazil! liberty to Cuba! and last, but not least, liberty to Africa! Yes, only let England be true to her profession, true to her principles, true to her duty, true to her conscience, and true to her God, and then, before our virtuous, just, and beloved Queen (whose reign was ushered in by the advent of a partial freedom to the enslaved African) shall close her mortal career, and descend from her throne of earthly royalty, to ascend, I humbly trust, a brighter throne in heaven, and lay aside that crown which now does not so much adorn her, as she by her virtues adorns the crown, to have placed upon her brow a diadem of glory—then, before that day shall arrive, her history shall be distinguished by the advent of a more extended deliverance, the emancipation of every slave beneath the sun, and the proclamation of universal freedom.

Mr. Daniel Hart, a gentleman of the Jewish persuasion, and member of Assembly for St. Mary's, being called upon to second the resolution, said — Mr. Chairman, after the very eloquent and able speech which has just been made by the reverend gentleman who proposed the resolution which I have the honour to second, I feel that no further remarks are necessary to recommend it to the meeting. I have great pleasure in seconding it, and am sure it will be cheerfully adopted.

The resolution was then put, and carried by acclamation.

Mr. Wm. Girod, then editor of the *Despatch* newspaper, but since of the *Colonial Standard*, and member of Assembly for St. George's, rose and said—Sir, the resolution which has been placed in my hands was intended to be left to the more able care of the illustrious General de Santa Anna, on whose behalf it falls to my lot to offer an apology for unavoidable absence. I have, therefore, at very short notice, been requested to stand in his place, and to propose this resolution in his stead. But I must first observe, that the matter could scarcely have been put into better hands than into those of this distinguished General, who was for a long time at the head of one of the greatest republics — indeed, with the exception of the United States, the greatest republic in America. The greatest boast of Mexico is, that its institutions are based on universal freedom. It is an almost fundamental principle of the republic that slavery cannot exist within the limits of its territory. In this respect, Mexico furnishes a bright example to the neighbouring republic, and if Mexico cannot boast of her naval armament, she can at least point with pride to this moral example which the United States will do well to follow; for though the United States might have emblazoned on their Declaration of Independence the inherent right of every man to be free, they still think it right to encourage and uphold slavery in the Southern States. Therefore, it is most fitting that the resolution which I am about to read should have been proposed by one who so long wielded the destinies of free Mexico. The resolution is as follows :—

" That it is also desirable that the views of this meeting should be brought under the notice of the inhabitants of the recently emancipated foreign colonies, and more especially of the French, Danish, and Swedish possessions in these seas, together with the free States on the Continent of America, suggesting to them the advantage of engaging their respective Governments to co-operate with that of her Majesty in the negotiations with Spain and Brazil which this meeting recommends."

—It is worthy of remark, Mr. Chairman, that among the various islands in the Archipelago there is not one, excepting those belonging to Spain, in which slavery exists. Denmark and Sweden, some time since, abolished slavery in their colonies, and France, in the establishment of that political freedom, which she supposes herself to have gained by her late revolution, has not confined its extension to her own internal affairs, but has almost simultaneously granted freedom to her colonies. It now, therefore, becomes our right to call on the foreign colonies to sympathise with us in our present movement. A few days ago, a gentleman placed in my hand an extract from a conservative paper, published in December, 1841, from which I will content myself with extracting the leading paragraph. It is as follows :—

" On Monday last, a treaty upon the subject of the slave-trade was signed by the representatives of Russia, France, Austria, Prussia, and Great Britain. By this memorable document the slave-trade is declared piracy, and additional efficiency is given to the mutual right of search. A nobler act than the conclusion of this treaty could scarcely have characterised the commencement of a Tory administration. The five signatures that were appended to this treaty at the Foreign Office on Monday have, we trust and believe, completed the death-warrant of the cursed system to which it relates."

Now, Sir, if the death-warrant of the slave-trade was, indeed, signed in the Foreign Office in 1841, it may be fairly said, after mouldering for five years in the archives of Downing-street, to have been formally repealed in 1846. I unfortunately stand here and see that prophecy, which a Tory administration gave rise to, bitterly falsified in the subsequent history of the slave-trade. Of the four nations which signed that treaty, France only was interested. In fact, it may be said that wherever legitimacy existed, all have joined, except Spain, to put down the detestable slave-trade—while Spain alone assists in its support. Sir, it seems impossible, in the present state of public feeling in favour of extended liberty, that this one nation can be permitted, in defiance of honour and honesty, thus to break her faith. It is not to be doubted that England is alone quite strong enough to insist on the observance of treaties made with her; but if England supposes that for diplomatic reasons

other nations would object to her proceeding against Spain,
she should remember that other nations have signed these
treaties, and that England still has their signatures on record ;
and I am persuaded, Sir, that no nation in the world would
uphold Spain in so unprincipled a violation of her engagements.   It therefore becomes our province to ask the aid of
other colonies, and to induce them to urge on their Governments to unite in insisting on the fulfilment of these treaties.
Sir, one resolution which has been passed to-day alluded
to the convention of 1840.   I think that justice has scarcely
been done to Lord Palmerston in this matter, for I believe
that noble lord to have been anxious to carry out the measures which he officially proposed to Spain.   There is one
gentleman now present, who knows, and can affirm that
Lord Palmerston has always been most anxious for the suppression of the slave-trade, and who can also tell you the
effect in Cuba of that desire on the part of his lordship.   I
have here, in a late number of the " Anti-Slavery Reporter,"
an extract from a communication addressed by Mr. Commissioner Turnbull to the Foreign Office, which will serve
to show the effect which the very mention of this convention
had in Cuba ; and I think there can be very little doubt that,
had it been followed up, we should not have found it necessary to assemble here to-day, in order to claim from Great
Britain the enforcement of these treaties on the part of Spain.
—The paper from which I read is a memorial presented, at
the latter end of last year, by the Anti-Slavery Society, on
the same subject on which we are now assembled, and one
paragraph of that memorial is as follows :—

" The Spanish Government did not deny the claim of this
country ; they became alarmed, because they were convinced that,
at length, measures would be taken to give effect to existing
treaties ; and the alarm spread to Cuba, and for once, something
approaching a sincere desire was expressed by the corporate bodies
of that island, as well as by individuals of wealth and position,
that the slave-trade at least should be wholly discontinued.   The
effect of your lordship's demand on the Spanish Government is thus
described by Mr. Consul Turnbull, in a despatch to your lordship,

dated August 31, 1841:—'I have the satisfaction to be able to assure your lordship that since the date of my last communication, on the subject of the popular movements in this island in favour of the suppression of the slave-trade, that movement has been accelerated in a very remarkable manner, by the arrival of an intimation from the supreme Government in Madrid, that her Britannic Majesty's Government had demanded the emancipation of the African slaves introduced into the Spanish West Indies since the date of the first of the existing treaties for the suppression of the slave-trade. It is generally believed that the Captain-general has been instructed to obtain the most authentic statistical information as to the number of slaves introduced into the island during the period in question, and, in point of fact, it is known that his excellency has addressed himself on the subject officially to several of the public or corporate bodies of the island, and also to a number of private individuals; but from the selection of witnesses and parties that has been made, from whom to obtain the means of answering the inquiries of the Regency, it is evident to all the world that his excellency is resolved, if not to keep his Government in the dark, at least to furnish it with the means of making, as far as in his power, such a representation to your lordship as will serve, if anything will, to defer the evil day, which has been so long impending.' "

This despatch was written in 1841, and at that time there was in power the same Tory Government whose first proud act was to make anti-slave-trade treaties with foreign courts, of whom only one was in the smallest degree interested in the question. But, in 1842, we find Lord Aberdeen saying as follows:—

"In a despatch from Lord Aberdeen to General Sancho, dated February 12th, 1842, his lordship says: 'The undersigned requests that General Sancho will acquaint her Highness the Regent, that her Majesty's Government do not intend at present to press upon the Government of Spain the question of a convention, for the purpose of examining generally into the condition of the negroes in Cuba: and that her Majesty's Government learn with pleasure that the Spanish Government have issued orders for preventing the fraudulent importation of negroes as slaves into Cuba, contrary to the engagements entered into by Spain with Great Britain.' "

Now, Sir, unfortunately for us, and unfortunately for the cause of humanity, those promises have been relied on ever since. The Foreign Office has been satisfied with the promises of Spain not to permit the slave-trade, and yet it is notorious that the government of Cuba receives a golden ounce for every slave imported into that island. I think, Sir, the groundwork has been already laid, and if that convention was properly carried out and joined in by foreign courts, the contraband traffic must speedily be put down. Let us, then, call to our aid in this good work the free people of the other emancipated colonies, to which end I have to solicit the consent of this meeting to the resolution which I have just read to them.

The Rev. Duncan A. Campbell, domestic chaplain to the Lord Bishop of the diocese, on being called upon to second this resolution, observed that he entirely concurred in its terms, as well as in the observations by which it had been supported by the honourable and learned gentleman who had preceded him. At the same time he was desirous of supplying an omission which appeared to him to have occurred, with reference to the gentleman so pointedly alluded to by the mover of this resolution. The exertions of that gentleman in this holy cause were well known to this meeting. It was known how he had perilled his life in promoting it; how he had entered the lion's den, deprived them of their prey, and brought away the victims to this land of liberty, to bear testimony to the fact that thousands of British-born negroes are at this moment held in slavery in Cuba, appealing in vain to the sympathy of the British people to assist them in the restoration of their birthright. That gentleman bears on his escutcheon the glorious legend of " I saved the King," won by the chivalry of some remote ancestor. But in these days of refinement, when it is no longer the fashion for kings to descend into the lists, and expose their persons in tournament or bull-fight, let us suggest to the fountain of honour, as the appropriate guerdon for what he has achieved, that his shield should henceforth bear the legend of " I saved the Slave."

The Rev. Mr. Radcliffe, of the Established Church of Scotland, in proposing the sixth resolution, said,—Mr. Chairman, the resolution with which I am entrusted is as follows :—

"That the Chairman and the movers and seconders of these resolutions be requested to act as a Standing Committee of the inhabitants of Kingston, any three to be a quorum, with power to add to their numbers, for the purpose of promoting, by all the means in their power, the great object which this meeting has in view."

On reading this resolution, when put into my hand, I at once felt there was one of two things before me—either to merely read the resolution, under the persuasion that there was no need for a set speech to recommend its adoption, or that, from its very nature, it gave me the privilege of speaking *de omnibus rebus et quibusdam aliis.* I have been rather disposed to interpret it according to the latter construction; and therefore, Sir, with your permission, I shall for a short time take advantage of the privilege thus afforded, to speak about everything and something else. The burden of this resolution, as you perceive, is the appointment of a committee for the object specified. I feel, indeed, however, that the resolution requires on my part explanation, rather than argumentation. The appointment of committees— especially provisional ones—for the last eighteen months, or so, has been rather a serious thing. To all and sundry, therefore, to whom it may concern, we wish it distinctly to be understood that we contemplate nothing in the shape of disloyalty, or anything savouring of revolution. So much for explanation. And yet, Sir—pardon the wish—I am anxious for a revolution, not of blood, but of the condition of things here—a revolution whereby we would see wealth again flowing in its accustomed channel; by which those once comfortable, but now ruined, would be again blessed with competency; by which the estates of the country, now overgrown with bush, would assume the hue of agriculture; and a revolution, Sir, above all, by which the hideous system of slavery—even as Dagon before the Ark— would crumble, prostrate and powerless, before the genius of universal emancipation. I rejoice therefore, Sir, that a committee is to be, I trust, appointed, in order to carry out the object contemplated ; and I do so on this ground, that that which is everybody's business is nobody's business. And now that a committee is to be appointed, I feel that it is highly necessary that they should know something of the nature of the difficulty before them, and the line of conduct they should therefore adopt. I know no way whereby I can better convey my idea of their duty than to take my own state of mind, when coming here about six months ago, and then, comparing it with the belief I entertain now, to mention what was at least a portion of the experience which has led to my conviction, or conversion if you choose. I come from the land of candour (Mr. Radcliffe is evidently an Irishman), and therefore do I not hesitate to say that I had impressions very different, when coming here, to what I have now, as to the whole question of Jamaica's complaints and Jamaica's wrongs ; I know, therefore, what is the state of mind of people generally at home— I know now how incorrect it is, and therefore do I now proceed to mention what I believe must be done by the committee, in order to lead not one, but millions, to an equally correct conviction. Beyond all doubt, the very first thing you must do, is to make the people of England believe that you are suffering distress, and that your stories of woe are not exaggerated. There is an understanding, let me tell you, with many at home, that the purses and pockets of Jamaica are, and have been, suffering from plethora, and that it would be well to bleed them ; nay more, they are persuaded that it would require a good long drain to bring them to anything like exhaustion. You must convince the people of Britain to the contrary ; tell them that hundreds are in want of bread—that agriculture cannot be prosecuted for want of means—that Port-Royal street, which was once an important station for the commercial affairs of Europe, is now almost deserted—and that every one who can, is leaving this country as one of incipient beggary and subsequent desolation. Allow me, Sir, to refer to one fact which weighed greatly with me; in fact, which came over me almost with the light of a revelation. I had gone down to the office of that highly respectable firm of Messrs. M'Whinney, Hendrick and Co., and after conversing for a time with Mr. M'Whinney, I went out at the west side of the premises—there was lined along the street a large number of the sorriest hacks I ever saw, with a number of leaders or drivers, the most miserable I had ever witnessed, all of which hacks had flung over their galled backs little dirty bags, filled with something, I knew not what. I asked my friend what all this meant? " Oh!" said he, " these are the cultivators of coffee, and those are little bags of coffee they have brought in for sale!" I saw it at once. The property was passing out of the hands of those who once had thriving estates, and the miserable remnant was getting parcelled into little patches. The respectable proprietary of the country were fast going away, and along with its poverty was the tendency to original barbarism. This is the state of things now, and Britain must know it; nay, must be told, that it is solely by her non-enforcement of those treaties of which you have heard this day, that her own sons and subjects cannot stand in the competition with compulsory labour. But, Sir, were it merely a thing of pounds, shillings, and pence, I should not have felt myself called on to take part in the present meeting. A higher interest is at stake; even the great cause of humanity and religion. Pardon me if I indulge a little in speaking of my personal feelings. Before coming to this country, I had thought that, of all other places, Jamaica was to be considered the great scene of the working out the social experiment of emancipation. I knew how difficult anything of that sort was. I knew it from experience—from knowledge of the human mind, and, above all, from the dealings of God with his people of old. Centuries of oppression had wrought such degradation, that, in the nature of things, the race which came out of Egypt furnished no materials for a race of independent freemen— therefore were they permitted to die out in the wilderness. I knew all that, and was prepared, with no disinterested feelings, to watch the progress of social improvement in this land of my adoption. I cannot tell you, Sir, how rejoiced I was when my excellent friend, the Receiver-general, at the late meeting at Spanish Town, gave shape and body to what was to me a dim speculation. It is on this wise:—If I could describe, as Mr. Oughton has this day described Africa, I would say that she has often appeared to me weeping for centuries of unremedied degradation, and refusing to be comforted, because her sons and daughters had been so ruthlessly torn away. Still, in the midst of all did I hope, even the mighty—the glorious—the redeeming hope, that Africa's sons, learning the blessings of liberty and religion in this country, the land of their former bondage, might, at no very distant day, return with hearts full fraught with filial and sanctified affection, and that Jamaica might thus have the distinguished happiness of breaking Africa's chains, and of bringing to her the higher liberty—even the liberty by which Christ makes his people free. These were my speculations. They are gone! Gone! all my imaginings as to what will be done for that land! Her sun has only risen to meet a disastrous eclipse! Go, then, ye gentlemen of the committee, and speak as earnest men to Britain ; tell her that she has arrested social improvement—that the emptying of schools, and the closing of churches, are the consequences of her fatal legislation—and, after she may be disposed to luxuriate in the cheapness of intertropical produce, tell her it is on the tremendous condition of sacrificing the cause of humanity in Jamaica, and of extinguishing the nascent hopes of Africa's emancipation. I feel, Sir, that perhaps I am taking too much on me, in thus lecturing the committee; I am one, I believe, myself, so of course I am included. Let me therefore say, then, one thing incumbent on the committee, and that is, in a spirit of faithfulness to tell Britain of her guilt. I am persuaded that many in Britain, like myself until lately, are ignorant of the sanction which England has been giving to slavery, by her connivance at the non-fulfilment of those treaties. Her legislators know it, her Corn-law League men know it, and yet, so far from a shout of condemnation from one end to the other being raised, there is a palliation for such monstrous conduct. Sir, though not an Englishman by birth, I rejoice in the glory of Britain. Her Majesty possesses not a more loyal subject. I have been thankful, even proud, that go where you will, there was the encirclement of England's power, like a qualified omnipotence, to protect one from insult or injury. Sir, the pride I entertained is turned of late into shame! She is now as degraded as America. Tell her, then, of her guilt and degradation—say to her that its existence and prosperity cannot live together—she must expel the Achan before she can obtain heaven's blessing. Let me now ask you, Sir, and the committee, and this respectable, unanimous, and earnest meeting, have we ground to be discouraged? For my part, I have great hope. Speaking after the manner of men, I have great hope in the first place from the circumstances of the times, and their influence on the ministry. I think you will all agree with me that the ministries of England for some time back have been—I was going to use a fine word—compressible—I prefer another, a stronger one, *squeezeable;* yes, Sir, we all know they are *squeezeable.* None can resist the *vis à tergo.* There is quite enough to squeeze them now. Ireland is quiet. Why? It is on the principle of making "solitude, and calling it a peace." The Canadians refuse to be quiet. The inter-tropical islands are ready to join any that will lead them to prosperity and peace. This is an uneasy state of things. Far be it from me to say anything which would seem to insinuate Britain's decrepitude. No, Sir, her old heart still beats like a cannon. Long may it do so! but it is impossible that an empire can flourish when there is such general discontent. Therefore, Sir, do I feel that some hope arises out of this very evil. But, Mr. Chairman, I should be the last to utter anything like bravado; it suits neither my disposition or profession. Therefore, under God, have I greater hope in the honesty, the justice, the honour of the English people.— Tell your story as it is—agitate, agitate, agitate! My hope, too, rises higher when I think of the affectionate character of

our beloved Queen. On her decision would I risk the whole
matter. Imagine, then, such a man as Mr. Cobden, or even
Mr. Bright, with aspect solemn and demure, taking their
stand before her Majesty. They tell their story :—" Please
your Majesty, we have by our exertions done much for your
Majesty's subjects. We have earned them the boon of
obtaining sugar at one half-penny or one penny per pound
cheaper." Before her Majesty pronounces her acknowledgment of their services, I can imagine a gentleman like
yourself, personally dignified, and officially respectable,
interposing and uttering, with the accents of truth and
mercy, such a remonstrance as the following :—" May it
please your Majesty, it is admitted that this boon has been
obtained ; but we beseech your Majesty to remember at
what expense — at the expense of ruining your colonial
subjects—at the expense of retarding the great cause of
liberty and humanity—at the expense of the dishonour of
your Majesty's crown and kingdom !" What think you
would be the decision? Full well do I feel that standing
with the dignity of a Queen, and swelling with the affection
of a mother, her answer would be—

> " Dash down the cup of Samian wine,
>   A land of slaves shall ne'er be mine."

In conclusion, Sir, I do not apologise for appearing here
to-day. I could not, in justice to my own feelings, have been
silent. I thank you very sincerely for the patience with
which you have heard me, and beg that this resolution may
be unanimously adopted.

Mr. W. W. Anderson, member of Assembly for Portland, and a solicitor in Kingston, said he felt great pleasure
in seconding the resolution which had been so ably proposed
by the Rev. Mr. Radcliffe.

Mr. E. C. Mowat, member of Assembly for Hanover, and
a solicitor in Kingston, proposed the seventh resolution :—

" That the memorial to her Majesty the Queen, and the petitions
to the two Houses of the imperial Parliament, now read, be adopted,
and that the Chairman be authorised to sign the memorial to her
Majesty on behalf of this meeting."

He then read the memorial, and added some few observations urging the necessity of enforcing the treaties.

The Rev. Rabbi Solomon Jacobs rose to second the resolution. He said—Mr. Chairman, ladies, and gentlemen,— Scarcely had I taken my seat in this vast assembly, to hear some of the eloquent speakers give expression to the indignation and abhorrence felt by them, and the public generally, at the atrocious and inhuman traffic of the slave-trade, when I was requested to second what you have just heard read, and so ably dilated on; and scarcely, Sir, had I considered the nature of this resolution, than, without deliberating on the deep importance and sacredness of the question before this meeting, I unhesitatingly consented to lend my feeble voice in uniting to excite public sympathy and universal commiseration with the painful and heart-rending condition of the children of Africa. But, Sir, when I reflect on my deficiency—when I take into view the mighty interests involved in this great and holy cause, and the very limited powers I am able to bring forward in furtherance of so solemn and so worthy an object, I almost regret having taken upon myself a task which would have been better served by others, more gifted than I am with the requisite ability to promote the freedom, civilisation, and happiness of the manacled slave. There is, however, one thing, Sir, which counterbalances any diffidence I may experience upon this point, and which at once stimulates me to come forth on behalf of the injured and oppressed. I am, Sir, a descendant of a race who were themselves the victims of the direst cruelties and oppression, but whose galling fetters were rent asunder by the mighty and benign intercession of a gracious and omnipotent God; and, Sir, I feel that I should be wanting in gratitude to Him, did I not come forth now as the vindicator of freedom, when Africa's groans assail our ears. I should be violating my duty as a man, if I did not feel and express my feelings for my fellow-beings; and I should also but poorly carry out those duties which, as a minister of religion, it is my province to support. And, Sir, when I behold your reverend and dignified person filling that seat, spreading a halo around us all, I am encouraged and induced to co-operate with the ministers of every other faith to assist in destroying the infamous and odious traffic in human flesh. Sir, I feel that I breathe the breath of an Englishman, and there is something free and independent in that. I am a British subject, and from his earliest infancy a British subject is taught to loathe tyranny and oppression. It is this very abhorrence we all feel which we have come here to-day to exhibit. Englishmen have hitherto considered slavery a sin in the sight of God; and I say that we need no argument at present to be convinced that slavery is a most heinous one. Let us, Sir, divest the question before us of anything like argument. What we are dealing with, is a question of right. We need no subtle reasoning to show us that it is absolutely infringing on the rights of our fellow-creature, to drag him forth from his home, his wife, his children, and dispose of him in the most cruel manner, to satiate the cupidity and avarice of another. Englishmen have used the strongest efforts to prove their abhorrence of this vile abomination. They have for years insisted that it was a gross iniquity—their sense of indignation has been manifested by something more than words—they have expended money, sacrificed life, made treaties with other powers, who have sworn, many of them, a solemn oath, to which British subjects freely and voluntarily subscribed, that they would not pollute their palate with sugar tainted with the blood of the slave. Treaties were ratified between England and other nations where slavery existed; and English health has been exhausted, and English blood freely spilt, on the shores of an unhealthy climate, all in assurance that they were sincere in their anxiety for the slave. Eloquence which drew tears of pity from every eye—eloquence which had the power of making men abandon their own immediate interests for the welfare of the human race, flowed from the lips of pious and zealous advocates of human rights; and the whole country, as if with one voice, cried aloud against the inhumanity perpetrated on Africa. Here, then, Sir, lies all the argument. We can turn back and look to all that was done, and now simply repeat it, as the best and most rational argument for petitioning her Majesty and the two Houses of Parliament to enforce her treaties with Spain and Brazil; and we can likewise call upon the British people to remember their solemn asseverations, and not now to violate what they once called God to witness they would never be guilty of. Sir, I feel that we need do no more than portray the actual position of things, and make Great Britain remember what she has enforced on these shores, and her honour will not slumber; her sympathy will again be excited, and her odium and contempt will again find vent in unmeasured terms against the cruelties and miseries consequent on the slave-trade. I say, Sir, it is impossible that England can have forgotten what energy she employed to exclude slave-grown sugar. What, Sir, will the philanthropists tell us it is no longer a sin to do that which was before so loudly condemned? No, Sir, a few avaricious men who seek to increase their wealth at the sacrifice of human life may — but England never will. Let us tell our fellow-subjects on the other side of the Atlantic, that the day is not very remote when they professed their deep abhorrence at the mere mention of slavery, and in the most solemn manner protested that the use of slave-grown sugar was a wicked and gross abomination in the eyes of God. Let us, Sir, I say, tell them all this, and if England has not sunk from her high and exalted pinnacle of moral integrity, she will force Parliament to pass such measures as will raise her in the sight of God, and in the eyes of nations, for her honesty and consistency. Sir, although I do not possess eloquence to render the cause in which we have engaged the justice it deserves; although my powers of speech are but poor and meagre, when compared with the very elaborate addresses that have so energetically been made by the various speakers who have preceded me; yet I feel something equally as powerful and as deep, which excites me to follow in the train of this holy undertaking. The cause before us, Sir, requires no better, no stronger, and no livelier eloquence than the eloquence of feeling, which speaks warmly and

enthusiastically in every heart. Every eye which this day
witnesses our proceedings indicates that soft eloquence of
feeling, which is far, infinitely superior to any language
which human oratory can express; and it is my earnest hope
and trust, Sir, that every man, woman, and child throughout
this island will convey this pure eloquence, by the signature
of their names to the appeal and memorial, which will be
brought before the graceful diadem of England's empire;
depicting before her commiserating soul the cruelty and
miseries in which the slaves of Cuba and Brazil are plunged,
and the utter prostration to which her own liege subjects
have been reduced, through the impetus given to a further
encouragement of the slave-trade. Sir, can there be anything, indeed, more inconsistent than the conduct of Great
Britain to us? Why, Sir, to prove her philanthropy, she did
more than any nation ever did; she spared no means to abolish
slavery on these shores, and in other colonies where the British flag is proudly hoisted, in token of their allegiance to her
most gracious Majesty. But, Sir, while our fellow-subjects
in Great Britain have assumed a high tone of humanity, and
made it a sin to use sugar grown by slaves here and in the
other British islands, they encourage the detestable traffic in
favour of the foreigner. This is one of the most inconsistent
acts they could be guilty of, and the nations must laugh at
their vaunted philanthropy. But, Sir, I cannot believe that
England will not retrace her steps—I will not believe that a
nation which has employed such vast resources, such unabating
zeal, such incomparable energy, to emancipate the negroes
in her own colonies, was in league with the foreigner, so that
sugar might be a little cheaper. No, Sir, England's humanity is unshaken; but she is, alas! a prey to influences at
times, which work on her credulity, and deceive her. It is,
therefore, Sir, our province to open her eyes to the cheats
and deceptions of which she has become a victim, and I
therefore agree, Mr. Chairman, with the terms of the seventh
resolution, that petitions should be presented to the two
Houses of Parliament, and a memorial to the Queen, so
that the voice of sympathy and commiseration with the

slave may again resound throughout the length and breadth of the land ; as in those days when every heart in England beat with warm and benevolent impulses for the enslaved negro. I do not despair of success. Let our appeal go forth, and notwithstanding all the calumny that may be invoked against us by the Manchester fraternity, I say let our appeal go forth, and I fear no unsuccessful issue. Sir, I can very well picture to myself the smile of irony that will dance first on the lip of the famous Cobden, and be imitated by his coadjutors, the Brights and the Gibsons of sacred memory. I think I hear the man of Manchester exclaiming, " Behold here a revulsion of events ; Jamaica, which was herself the seat of this infamous and cruel system ; Jamaica, whence issued forth the cries, the groans, and the piercing shrieks of the fettered negro ; Jamaica, which gloated on the blood and sinews of the slave ; she for whom, in conjunction with the other islands where this detestable and atrocious bondage existed, we were obliged to raise the enormous sum of twenty millions sterling, in order that they might be induced to abandon their guilty commerce—she now has become humane and pathetic." But, Sir, the ironist may laugh and deride our efforts. We can, however, refer to the indisputable evidence which will prove our sincerity. Sir, it is, we may say, matter of history—and the records of our local legislative Assembly can testify the truth thereof—that Jamaica craved the imperial Government (before England was moved with a holy abhorrence for slave-sugar) that the slave-trade might cease on our fertile shores ; hence our appeal now against slavery is a consistent, a true, a sincere one, and we can proudly refer to the time when the slave-trade was considered no sin in England, and yet Jamaica sought its abolition ; and we can say to those who are now most anxious to propagate it, behold here the contrast! We adhere now to what our ancestors professed then ; but you—you first spoke fine words of humanity, and emancipated the slaves, the property of your own countrymen, and now consider it no moral violation of right, and principle, and justice, to import the production of slave labour in return

for your manufactured goods. We can tell them this—we
need not droop our heads, we can raise them—and, with the
satisfactory assurance that we have right, justice, and consistency on our side, can smile at their unworthy insinua-
tions. Sir, I confess that I was seized the other day with a
species of indescribable astonishment in beholding the unblushing effrontery of the right hon. Milner Gibson, in
attempting to obtain leave to bring forward a motion for the
repeal of the statute which throws certain obstacles in the
way of the Brazilian branch of the slave-trade, although, I
must say, that nothing coming from that quarter ought to
surprise me. Why, Sir, the right hon. gentleman, without
any remorse of conscience, does nothing less than ask the
British Government to allow slavery to exist, and pre-
sumes to argue that the slave-trade, according to the
terms of the treaty, is not piracy, and hence would make
it appear that Great Britain has been the guilty party in
destroying the lives of those who are apprehended on the
seas engaged in this vile traffic. This is the philanthropy
of the Free-Trade Association ; and it is lamentable to
think that a desire to abolish every restriction upon so
odious a system, and to give free scope to the insatiate
avarice of the slaveholder, should find an echo in no less a
paper than the *Times*. That paper, which is commonly
called "The Thunderer," has, in an article upon the subject,
endeavoured to lead the public mind to second the views
of Mr. Milner Gibson. The *Times* wishes the country to
suppose that it is only by removing every restriction
upon the slave-trade, by no longer employing our squadron
on the coast of Africa, that slavery will cease to exist. With
a precipitancy that may scarcely be considered the effort of
a sane understanding, the *Times* draws the inference that,
because Cuba is contiguous to America and Jamaica, the
spirit of freedom which exists in these places will communicate itself to Cuba, and that without our enforcing an observance of the treaties, slavery is doomed to perish. This, Sir,
is the reasoning of the *Times*. But it is an inference bad
in itself, and drawn from a very rotten foundation. What

are the bases from which this is drawn? Why, certainly nothing less than this: declare men to be thieves, remove every obstacle in their way, have no magistrate, no police, do not raise your voice against crime, and men will become honest of themselves—and this is equally the reasoning of the *Times*. Do not consider yourselves bound to enforce the treaties; do not interfere with Spain and the Brazils; take their sugars, enjoy the produce of slave labour, though it has consumed life in the process of its production; disregard everything you have said and done, and slavery is doomed, because Cuba is contiguous to America and Jamaica! Now, let me tell you, Sir, the inference I draw from the premises of Mr. Milner Gibson's notice of motion,—that, if ever the treaties should be abandoned, and slavery encouraged, a new impetus will be given to the trade, and, notwithstanding the proximity of Cuba to America and Jamaica, instead of being doomed, it will expand, with renewed horror and increasing gloom to the benighted race of Africa. It is monstrous to think to what extent men will go to carry out a selfish object. Why, Sir, to find vent for the overstocked markets of the manufacturing districts of England, Manchester ingenuity has discovered a legal flaw in the indictment. In the year 1849, the Manchester philosophers have, like most acute lawyers, detected a loop-hole in the treaties of Spain and the Brazils, and like those laws of the land through which a coach and four, it is said, may be driven, have ingeniously found a space wide enough to suffer all the Spanish and Brazilian slave-ships to sail unmolested. What is the cause of all this? Do you suppose that there really is any ground for saying the treaties are null and void? No; it is this:—When the advocates of free-trade were told that the colonies would be ruined if they did not enjoy that small protection which would enable them to reciprocate the advantages with the manufacturers of England, at that time the treaties were perfectly valid and legal, and humane and proper; but now that the pernicious consequences of free-trade are felt at home—now that our markets, the markets of the colonies, are shut up to British manufactures, we find

the Gibsons and the Brights, and the Cobdens, all full of
legal technicalities, quoting text and law books in justification of the mercenary and sanguinary men engaged in the
loathsome traffic in human flesh. I blush at the assertion
that there are people in the great senate-house of England
who would discard a sense of human right to serve their own
immediate views; but I blush more deeply at the line of
conduct pursued by Lord Palmerston when Mr. Gibson
brought forward his views before the House. Lord Palmerston's reply has thrown the public mind into a state of sus-
pense. He said that he did not consider it prudent, on the
part of that gentleman, to have brought forth his measure
now, when a committee was sitting on the subject, who
would bring in their report, and the House would have
proper data to go upon. I say, Sir, this reply is most vague
and unsatisfactory; it leads the public mind to imagine that
the abrogation or enforcement of those treaties will depend
on the committee's report. But what has the public—what
has Lord Palmerston—to do with that report? Has the
time so long elapsed when the treaties were signed, and when
all England paid for these very treaties? What care we
what construction may be put upon slavery, now we know
that we have paid for its abolition? And Lord Palmerston
should therefore have taken higher grounds, and have
denounced anything like an attempt to influence the House
in favour of slavery. He should not have made any reference to the committee then sitting, but should have referred
to a higher one, which is that of the public voice, which cried
out against—and the public purse, which contributed immensely for the suppression of slavery. I say this should
have been his conduct; but I fear, Sir, that unless we
heartily co-operate in bringing the real condition of things
before the bar of public opinion, the men who seem to
delight in the dismemberment of every wise and hereditary
institution, will again seek to introduce a measure which will
irrevocably seal the fate of Africa. Let us, therefore, Sir,
unite, and invoke Divine Providence to aid us in so inclining
the heart of her gracious Majesty, that she may direct her

Ministers to carry out the object of our memorial, and with these imperfectly expressed remarks, Mr. Chairman, I have great pleasure in seconding the resolution.

The resolution was then put and carried.

The Rev. Mr. West, Wesleyan minister in Kingston, proposed the following resolution :—

" That his excellency the Governor be respectfully requested to transmit the memorial to the Queen, through the Secretary of State for the Colonies, for presentation to her Majesty, and to lend his aid in recommending the object of the meeting to the attention and favour of her Majesty's Government."

He said,—Mr. Chairman, ladies, and gentlemen,—When the resolution which I hold in my hand was sent to me, and I saw that it was marked No. 8, being aware that resolutions have always movers and seconders, and sometimes supporters, I could not help thinking that the relationship I should bear, as a speaker to this meeting, would be something like an Irish cousinship—begging my friend Mr. Radcliffe's pardon—a relationship so important as to render it a matter of very little consequence whether I had anything to say on the subject of it or not.   And I can assure you, Sir, and you, too, gentlemen, that—while I yield to no one in my abhorrence of the detestable traffic which has been the subject of animadversion to-day—when the cause of the injured has been so ably advocated as it has been at this meeting, it is as gratifying to me to sit among the listeners as to take a place among the speakers. It has been remarked to-day, that in consequence of the impoverished state of the people of this island, nineteen Wesleyan day-schools have been closed. It may, perhaps, be thought by some, that the closing of those schools was not so much owing to the impoverished state of the colony, as to an unwillingness, on the part of the Society in England, to afford that amount of assistance to the Wesleyan missions here it had been in the habit of doing ; but I have the means of knowing, Sir, that the amount of money expended by the Wesleyan Missionary Society at home on its missions in Jamaica for the current year, is greater than it has been accustomed to expend for several years past. The Society was driven to the alternative of closing some of its schools, or of withdrawing its missionaries, closing their chapels, and scattering their flocks; and, attaching greater importance to the labours of the missionary than to those of the teacher, the former alternative was chosen. Sir, the movements that have taken place in this island, since the long-to-be-remembered meeting of Spanish Town, show that when a good example is set them, the people of Jamaica know how to follow it; especially, some one may be disposed to add, when, of the advantages that are likely to result, there is a prospect of their coming in for a share. And really, Sir, I can see no great objection to that. The reflex benefits of the great movements of the day form by no means the most insignificant items in the estimates of the movers. The inhabitants of Europe and America would not have such facilities for travelling as they enjoy, if those who furnish those facilities had not an eye to personal emolument; and if the people of Jamaica have discovered that, by tearing off the manacles of the slave, and separating the links of his chain, and placing him in the position of a man, and awarding him the dignity to which he as a man is entitled, they can promote their own interests, and better their own circumstances, I see not that they are to blame. It is all very beautiful to talk about motives of purely disinterested benevolence, but I cannot help thinking that such motives are more frequently talked about than brought into active operation. If the people of Jamaica can benefit themselves while they are benefiting the slave, I think that they have a right to do so. After all, Sir, I believe that the people of Jamaica really compassionate the slave; that they hate slavery for its own sake; that they regard it as unjust, as cruel, as outrageous, as atrocious, to tear the unoffending African from the land and home of his fathers, subject him to the horrors of the middle passage, and draw him and his offspring to hopeless bondage; and I believe, Sir, that were it left with the people of Jamaica to wipe out the blood-red blot of slavery from the world, they would do it, though they had to do it at a sacrifice. America, although there is no reference to it in my resolution —America has been mentioned to-day in connexion with slavery, and it is to be lamented that America, that makes a boast of its liberties, should be found among those who are the perpetrators of slavery. I was standing on one of the wharves of this city, a short time ago, when a friend of mine said, " How significant is the American flag : do you know what is meant by its stripes and stars? I'll tell you; they mean that the Americans give stripes to their negroes by starlight." That, it is true, was but an interpretation with which his imagination had supplied him; but it is to be feared that it exists in fact, and that the light that beams from the stars of America is a too frequent witness of the stripes that are inflicted on its slaves.* It would not be right for me to occupy your time any longer; I will only add that, as the Rev. Mr. Campbell has already observed, we have everything to encourage us to go on. The undertaking must succeed—the time must, and, we believe, will soon come, when " slave " shall be a " name in ancient books met only; " when the nations of Africa shall take their proper stand among the nations of the earth, and when the people of Cuba—Cuba, whose foliage is moved by the breezes that wave our own, and whose shores are lashed by the waves that lash our own—when her people shall all be free—when, by its now suffering population, the horrors of slavery shall be lost amidst the blessings of freedom, and the bitterness of their grief shall be forgotten in the exuberance

* This allusion reminds us of the epigram on the star-spangled banner, written, in a moment of inspiration, by our lamented friend, the author of " The Pleasures of Hope : "—

" United States, your banner wears
    Two emblems :—one of fame ;
Alas ! the other that it bears
    Reminds us of your shame !

" The white man's liberty in types
    Stands blazoned by your stars;
But what's the meaning of the stripes ?
    They mean your negroes' scars ! "—EDITOR.

of their joy.   With these remarks I beg to move the resolution.

Mr. G. W. Gordon, being called upon, said—Mr. Chairman, I merely rise to say that I feel much pleasure in seconding the resolution so ably proposed by the Rev. Mr. West.

The resolution was then put and carried.

Mr. Leaycraft, a merchant in Kingston, and afterwards treasurer of the fund for promoting the object of this publication, said,—Mr. Chairman, in presenting to the notice of the meeting the resolution with which I have been entrusted, I feel that it is alike *unnecessary*, as at this stage of the proceedings it would be *untimely*, for me to make any remarks on the great question of consideration of the day.   Already has the meeting been addressed by most able and eloquent speakers, as to the just and merciful and material consideration involved in this movement, and already has the meeting responded thereto, in giving their consent unanimously to the resolutions which have been submitted to them, " to petition the Queen and Parliament to adopt the necessary measures for the effectual suppression of the slave-trade." It would be superfluous in me, therefore, to make further comment thereabout.   But, Sir, I crave the indulgence of the meeting for a few moments, whilst I endeavour to press upon them the great importance of the resolution which I shall have the honour of submitting to them—so important in its bearing on the proceedings of the day, that *without it* all that has been done is useless, and the resolutions which you have passed will be impotent.   Too truly, unfortunately, is it said, that the measures that emanate from all our public meetings in Jamaica, *die with their birth.*   We are too apathetic and listless, and lack the necessary energy to bring them to a successful issue by following them up. But not so, Sir, let it be with this great measure, headed by our respected Bishop, and seconded and supported by the members of the learned professions, and by the agricultural, commercial, mechanical, and labouring population throughout the island.   A movement, in the success of which are

involved justice and mercy to others, and existence to ourselves. Not so be the fate of this movement, and yet such
will be its fate—so will also perish, as its predecessors, other
public measures in Jamaica, *unless* you not only sanction, as
I hope you will, my resolution, *but* collectively and indi-
vidually support it. The purport of the resolution which I
hold in my hand, is to urge upon the Standing Committee
the necessity of enforcing, in a suitable manner, our claims
on Parliament and the people. But I venture a step
further, and call on you all to take a part in so doing, by
your personal influence and correspondence, to enlist the
sympathies and exertions of your friends, and the British
public and all philanthropists in the support of your object.
Remember, in the success of your cause there are great
attainments — liberty to the enslaved and existence itself
to yourselves. I beg leave to propose resolution the
ninth :

" That the Standing Committee be requested to take the necessary measures for the presentation of these petitions in a suitable
manner to Parliament, and for engaging such further support to
their objects, in the two Houses, and from the public press, as may
be attainable."

Mr. Kelly Smith, an emancipated negro, said—Mr.
Chairman, I crave a few moments' indulgence from this
respectable meeting, for the expression of a few words, in
seconding the resolution which we have just heard, and
which has been so ably introduced. It is, Sir, with unusual
energy and heartfelt joy that I watch the progression of this
philanthropic movement. All who regard the position of
our fellow-men in Africa, look to England for a fortification
of those principles which decreed freedom. They look to
her because she is more enlightened, and being more enlightened, therefore more culpable for her present conduct,
if her sympathy for the African is not to extend beyond
what she has already manifested. What shall it profit us, if,
while we live, we see our brothers starve? our neighbour
gasping for food? Yet such has been the lot of the libe-

rated African since the late acts of the British Government.
Is the mere name of emancipation to be the " be all, and the
end all," of British philanthropy? Such an idea would dim
the lustre of her Majesty's diadem, once the brightest in the
world. The late acts of England to her colonies are a
disgrace to the British Crown, and a stain which will be
remembered by generations yet unborn; for it will be told
how England emancipated the slaves, and took from them
the means of obtaining bread for their families. England
has sacrificed principle to expediency, and is now starving
the many for the monopoly of the few, and to the detriment
of the West India planter. It is time for us to go further—
to tell our wants, and to demand sympathy for our deplorable and forlorn condition. Let us bravely recommend
them, as did the Apostle of old, to " repent." Let them not
shut their eyes to the fact, that there is yet time to save the
last grain, the last drop of the people's love—forasmuch as
the people are dying for want of bread, the condemnation
of England must be greater, because of her enlightenment.
Before the law of 1846 was passed, foreign coffee was
admitted through the Cape of Good Hope into the British
markets; this coffee was allowed to go home, and to be sold
to the detriment of the British planter. As soon as this was
known, our step-dame Government capped the climax of
her injustice by the iniquitous enactment of the law of 1846.
Jamaica, Sir, has since tottered, and is still tottering towards
its final fall. We are told, Sir, to compete with slave
countries. As well may the child compete with the giant.
We, who have been just emancipated, are cast down—we
cannot find employment. The mortgagees have laid hold of
the money, and we cannot go on with cultivation against
such competitors as Cuba and Brazil. It is time to tell the
Government that this cannot be tolerated. Thousands of
voices must be raised, until they meet the ear of her Majesty.
We must petition, and let us all unite to pray that the
hearts of our rulers may be inclined to good. Then will the
news alarm the slaveholding planters of Cuba and Brazil,
but it will be gladdening to all hearts in this our unfortunate

country. I thank you, Sir, for your indulgence, and I beg to second the resolution.

The resolution was then put, and carried unanimously.

Mr. W. Titley then rose and proposed the following resolution :—

" That the thanks of the meeting be respectfully offered to his Honour the Mayor, for the trouble he has taken in bringing us together, and to the Rev. Dr. Stewart, for his conduct in the chair."

Mr. J. Leaycraft seconded the resolution, which was carried unanimously.

The meeting then broke up.

The memorial from the Kingston meeting to her Majesty the Queen, having been transmitted by the Chairman in the usual course, through his excellency the Governor, has been acknowledged in the following terms :—

King's House, October 8, 1849.

SIR,—I have the honour, by the direction of the Governor, to put into your hands a copy of a despatch which has been received from the Secretary of State for the Colonies, in reply to the Governor's despatch, in which his excellency transmitted at your request, in July last, the memorial of certain inhabitants of Kingston, which accompanied your letter to his excellency of the 5th of July.

I have the honour to be, Sir,

Your obedient humble servant,

T. F. PILGRIM, Sec.

The Rev. Thomas Stewart, D.D.,
    Rector of Kingston.

(COPY.)

Downing-street, 19th August, 1849.

SIR,—I have to acknowledge the receipt of your despatch of the 7th ult., No. 69, forwarding a memorial addressed to her Majesty, at a meeting of the inhabitants of the city of Kingston, Jamaica, praying for the enforcement of the

treaties between Great Britain and the Governments of
Spain and Brazil, for the suppression of the slave-trade.

I request that you will inform Dr. Stewart, who presided
at this meeting, that I have laid this memorial before the
Queen, and that her Majesty was pleased to receive it very
graciously.

You will further acquaint Dr. Stewart that the matter will
receive the serious attention of her Majesty's Government.

I have, &c.,

(Signed)   GREY.

The Right Hon. Sir C. E. Grey,
&c., &c., &c.

The reports of the other provincial meetings are at once
too numerous and too voluminous to be given *in extenso*.
Where so much has been said, the chief wonder is that there
should have been so little repetition ; and, in the *embarras
de richesses*, the Editor's difficulty has been to make a satisfactory selection. On the 29th of June two great meetings
were held, the one at Montego Bay, under the presidency of
the venerable Archdeacon Williams, the other at Manning's
Town, the Hon. Mr. Cooke, the Custos Rotulorum of St.
Mary's, in the chair.

GREAT PUBLIC MEETING AT MONTEGO BAY.

The meeting advertised to take place in Montego Bay
was exceedingly well attended by all classes of the community, including a considerable number of ladies. The
Venerable the Archdeacon, in opening the proceedings,
said, he fully felt and appreciated the great compliment that
had been paid to him, in placing him in the chair at a meeting
of the kind ; he might call it a great meeting, because of the
nature of the objects which had induced it. It was, besides,
not one of a political nature, nor yet one in which the local
interests of the parish only were concerned—no ; it was one
in which the interests of thousands—of tens of thousands—
aye, of millions of our suffering fellow-creatures were con-

cerned; and, in such a great and godlike cause, he was exceedingly happy to render any service in his power. This was the first meeting over which he had presided, and he felt much pleasure at seeing it constituted of all classes, complexions, and creeds. Sincerely did he pray that God's blessing might be with the work which it had set before it, and prosper its progress in their hands. Though they were as a drop of water compared to the mighty ocean, yet, nevertheless, their efforts he hoped would not be entirely useless, in their endeavours to gain the rights and immunities of free men (such as we all now possess) for those of our fellow-men who are still held in bondage. The subject had been some time before the public, it had been ably discussed in the newspapers, and he had little else to do than mention that they were there assembled to petition our gracious Sovereign Queen Victoria and the Imperial Parliament to enforce the treaties that had been entered into with the Brazilian and Spanish Governments, to endeavour to effect the enfranchisement of those wretched beings who are held as slaves by the subjects of those Governments, in direct and shameless contravention of the terms of those treaties. The petitions would be addressed to those who would give their ready sympathy to their brethren, and who felt, and had a deep and abiding interest in emancipation, and whose assistance and co-operation they could doubtlessly rely on.

The Venerable Chairman then called upon the Hon. G. M. Lawson, the Custos of the parish, to propose the first resolution. His Honour then rose, and addressed the chair as follows :—Sir, the first resolution to be proposed to this meeting has been put into my hands for support; and when I look to its nature, my feelings tell me how happy I should be were I able to do justice to it, could I recount in language sufficiently forcible the blessings of which it speaks ; but as I lay no claim to oratory, and have not even been in the habit of addressing public bodies, I shall have to crave much of your indulgence for offering merely a few introductory remarks upon it. Tranquillity, combined with friendly intercourse, it sets forth as being the present condition of this colony; and in expressing our thanks for this social state, it asserts that it has been secured by equal political privileges having been granted to all its inhabitants. And, Sir, when I cast my eyes around me, and observe the different classes which compose this assemblage—all meeting for one purpose —and bring to my mind the diversity of interests, whilst we are all, equally, beset by difficulties—is there not reason, I ask, to be thankful—to rejoice—that peace and good will should prevail amongst us, and that the possession of those rights which mankind should hold in common has procured them for us? Surely there is; and I hope we all see that, our laws being just, our happiness depends in a great measure upon ourselves. I indulge this hope—in fact I do more than hope—I trust that it is so, and that as we advance in our relations with each other we shall the more fully perceive how incalculable are the benefits we derive, not only by being so governed, but also from having our feelings thus influenced. I say again, that there is reason to be thankful for the social intercourse which now exists amongst the inhabitants of this island,—a condition which ought to be well observed by those States and dependencies in which slavery is upheld, and should lead them, confidently, to follow the example which has been set them by Great Britain and her former slave possessions. What excuse can they offer for not doing so? With us—if our steps had been imperceptibly progressive, the records of history would have furnished similar examples, while the remarks of even warm advocates of the great change, characterising it as "a frightful experiment," would have given colour to delay. But no. Humanity threw aside everything of that kind, and nearly at one stride cast herself into the open field of freedom. I would, then, repeat my question, and by doing so ask, more especially, what will they say, who, in addition, encourage and carry on the slave-trade? We all know their reply. I will not mention it—let shame cast her mantle over it. Hateful, however, as this view of the subject appears, how shall we designate the movements now, of a party in England, who give a stimulus to this horrid traffic because it affords them a cheap article? But will they be permitted to continue doing so? Can we imagine that those feelings, which for ever effaced slavery from every statute book throughout the British territories—which, only a few years ago, raged from one end of the kingdom to the other, branding with odium and disgrace all who opposed them— will remain at rest, amidst the multiplied evidence of the enormities going on? No. There are spirits who called them forth, then, in the cause of freedom; and if they have been stilled by the force of a party, they will revive with power so much the more, and, in annihilating this odious traffic, cover its supporters with their merited ignominy. Treaties had been entered into by Spain and by Brazil with Great Britain for the extinction of this trade, and large sums of money have been paid to them as an equivalent, on the supposition that they might lose by its discontinuance. Notwithstanding this—notwithstanding the solemn obliga- tions into which these two States have entered, the horrors of the middle passage are greater than ever, and are wholly attributable to them. It is cheering, however, to think that it may soon cease. A very eloquent speaker (the Rev. Dr. King), in addressing the meeting lately held in Spanish Town, told them that slavery is doomed — that its defenders know that it is—and now its end is only a question of time. He calls for the blow to be given, which, to use his own words, "shall shake the Colossus on its pedestal, and ere long bring it to the dust." Spain and Brazil, I would then say, should take timely warning. They have refused to erect a monument for themselves, having freedom as its capital; but let them not wait for this blow—a blow which must humble them amidst the crash. Rather let them attempt, ere it be too late, to grace their fall by abolishing the slave-trade, and commencing the good work of emancipation.

The Rev. Walter Dendy, in rising to second the resolution just submitted, said, he felt much and sincere pleasure to be present at a meeting like the present; the large attendance at it manifested the interest that was taken by all classes of

the community in the great object which it was their desire
to further. He would have felt much greater pleasure,
however, if a meeting of this nature could possibly have been
convened under other circumstances, and regretted it had not
been in other and happier days. In a colony suffering under
great agricultural and commercial distress, it would appear
to those so disposed to view it, that the agitation resulted
from the sordid promptings of a grovelling spirit of self-
interest, rather than as a spontaneous effort, awakened to
exertion—the effect of a pure and exalted humanity. He
thought, and possibly he might be singular in so thinking,
that God had purposely brought us to feel agricultural and
commercial distress, to awaken us to that duty which was
always ours, but which we had so long neglected. It most
assuredly was the duty of Jamaica *free* to agitate for freedom,
for persons who had passed through affliction were those
who could best sympathise with others who might be suffering ; those who had endured and knew the horrors of bondage
could best feel for those who were still bondsmen, and it
became us not to relax our efforts, if by our exertion we
might ultimately cause the downfall of the system in Cuba,
Porto Rico, and Brazil. The British Government had
endeavoured to effect this with its accustomed generosity, by
paying a large sum of money as indemnification for the estimated loss, and this, too, was eagerly taken by the Government to which it had been offered; and, though so shamefully
receiving money to do that which was on her part but an act
of justice, had added to her disgrace by not fulfilling that
which she took money to do,—an act as degrading to her as
it would be in a judge to take a fee for giving a righteous
decision, deciding, despite even that, wrongfully. It had
been shown, by competent authority, that 555,834 persons
had been landed in those countries since the treaties had
been made ; and if so many had been landed under the knowledge of *authority*, how many thousands more must have
perished in the horrors of the middle passage, and found
their untimely grave in the bosom of the waters, was a question which time alone could truthfully solve ! Treaties made

between nations must be carried out, not with powder and ball,—no, a moral influence must be set at work, to induce the violators to keep their pledged faith, and non-intercourse with such countries must be the retaliatory means to produce the desired result. Jamaica, awakened to a knowledge of her duty, will send her memorials to the foot of the throne; her voice, strong and loud, will awaken echoes which will reverberate throughout Cuba, Porto Rico, Brazil, and in slave-cursed America too! She will stand up and declare that emancipation is not what its enemies have represented it—a failure! In the enjoyment of that first of social blessings, civil peace, the truth will be evinced—the fact that we need no police-guard to watch over our lives, nor iron locks and bars to protect our treasure and shut out the dreaded knife—in a manner to evidence the greater happiness of our position. Could *they* dare hold a meeting like this? No! And while internal peace had been secured, the best friends of emancipation might be proud of the result. It was true that there was no progress in education, and it was also lamentably so, that morals and religion had received some check in their onward course, but these resulted from transitory causes, and he thought he saw better days in store for Jamaica. Many among us excuse their supineness by saying, " it is not our duty, it is the minister's duty, it is the magistrate's duty, it is the duty of those who are in and have authority;" but they were wrong, for it was alike the duty of all; we should every one of us throw our influence in the scale, in the legitimate endeavour to advance the morals of the community; and, as God has been pleased to place Jamaica in the foreground of emancipation, so ought our exertions to be pointed to the maintaining her in that proud pre-eminence. We might possibly never have control over the markets of the world, nor exercise any influence in its commercial relations, but we might promote and establish among ourselves happiness and peace, which would fully counterbalance such loss. Then shall we find that " the Lord of hosts is with us : the God of Jacob is our refuge."

The resolution was then put, and carried unanimously.

Mr. Robert Dewar said—It devolves upon me to propose the second resolution, and in doing so it is with mingled feelings of joy and sorrow. I rejoice that for the first time in St. James's I address an anti-slavery meeting. Well I remember, when I came here, sixteen years ago, that slavery was rife, and now we meet here alike, the sons and daughters of England, and in a meeting so largely and respectably attended, with but one common object. I feel sorrow at the necessity of so meeting, in being forced, as children of England by adoption, birth, and education, to complain of her injustice—there was much to sorrow for in this! By no one is England more steadily honoured than myself, and I hope that our petitions will reach the throne. Treaties between nations, Sir, are like bonds entered into by individuals, and England having paid the consideration (in one instance of £400,000) Spain and Brazil should be made to fulfil their portion of the contract. Mr. Dewar here read the resolution :—

" It is the opinion of this meeting that the effect of admitting slave-grown sugars into the British dominions, on equal terms with those of the emancipated colonies, has been to augment the amount of human suffering ; and we lament that, owing, in some measure, to the unequal competition we are compelled to sustain against slave-trading and slave-holding countries, the agriculture and commerce of this island have been reduced to a most deplorable condition."

I think the difficulty lies in our inability, fully and emphatically, to detail our grievances. Coinciding entirely with much which had fallen from Mr. Dendy, I was prepared to go the whole length with him, and ask if any one among them all rejected the emancipation act? But I regret to find that Mr. Dendy had such a Utopian idea as to expect that religion and morality would be upheld and increased in a community sinking in its commerce and agriculture. No ministers, however efficient, could expect this. God works by means, and where were the stipends to come from—the schoolmaster to be paid? Surely we must look to our agriculture and commerce. Now, I will endeavour to prove, not by statistical details, for they are tedious, but by a slight sketch, the influence the Sugar Duty Bill of 1846 has had upon our productiveness. In 1834 we exported 68,000 tons sugar; in 1840, 25,000; and in 1845, 37,000 tons, being an increase of 1845 over 1840, of fifty per cent., and this was mainly induced by the confidence the colony had in the fostering care of the mother country; and in 1849, he might add, the best calculations only gave, as the probable amount likely to be exported, the minimum quantity yet exported of 23,000 tons, with a prospect of a still reduced quantity in 1850. Now, Sir, the year since the emancipation which had witnessed our largest export was in 1845, and Jamaica was better in its moral and social state than it is in 1849; it was a melancholy fact, and it was melancholy, too, to trace the cause of the effect, to that delusion now dominant in England, called free-trade, which was a misnomer,—not free-trade in its extended signification, but the free-trade of a class with the foreigner. England has been completely *chloro-formed* with this poison, and has drunk deeply of the infernal decoction. Freedom in trade, as interpreted by those who now translate the public sentiment of England, is freedom to the manufacturers of that country to trade with the slave-holders, on terms advantageous to their now privileged class, and to ride rough-shod over the shipping, agricultural, colonial, and every other interest not identified with theirs. Looking retrospectively to 1831, we find England philanthropic, generous, and just. In 1846, sordid and unjust, and she reverses her policy and commits a political adultery with Spanish and Brazilian slave produce, while she at the same time professed to feel a virtuous affection for her free colonies—admits the principle that the freeman could not compete with the slave, and yet determines that he shall; but what is that, Sir, so that the iron and cotton manufacturers be the gainers? I feel pride in England as a son of hers; I glory in her Protestantism, and feel that she is a God-honoured country; when I contemplate the beauties formerly associated with Britannia's rule—when I looked and saw her strong right arm sustaining the scales of justice, to enforce and temper it, while she held also the sword of mercy; when I saw that she herself was sustained—propped by the bales of merchandise—when I looked at the dim distance, and saw her own goodly ships hastening to pour the wealth of either Ind at her feet—and further, saw her fields redundant of cereal riches, and the plough contributing its growth of glory to the halo by which she was surrounded —then, indeed, I saw her true to the motto of her banner— the hitherto unsullied flag—*Ships, Colonies, and Commerce!* Now, alas! I dread the description of the picture she presents—still surrounded by the attributes she once possessed, how utterly perverted are their uses! Those scales, which even-handed justice herself envied, are now thrown recklessly aside—her sword of mercy rusty and broken at the hilt—her bales of merchandise containing but the blood-red calico, the price of the slave—her ships dismantled; and, instead of the Blue Peter at the fore, the Union Jack half-mast high, and the broom at the mainmast denoting they were for sale; her fields, once so luxuriant in their returns to her bold peasantry, now lying unweeded and deserted—the plough and harrow encrusted with dirt, and eaten by rust; and instead of the generous and noble lion at her feet, we now see an ostrich, that bird of the desert, typical of her neglect of her progeny. The poor creoles who in the distance are in waiting, humble suppliants at her hands for justice, are impatiently waived off for another time, and another hearing; while favours are lavishly distributed to the foreigner, among the most prominent of whom are the Brazilian and Cuban slave-sugar manufacturers! To complete this truthful, melancholy, and wretched picture: for an evidence of our commercial depression we need but look at our harbour, where, instead of, as formerly, eight or ten square-rigged vessels, there is now lying but one solitary brig, all on one side, too, as though she sympathised in our forlorn condition; and now let me beg you to accompany me through this town, and look at its roofless and decaying houses, its deserted streets, and see if its sad and solitary aspect does not look as though an earthquake, a plague, or a pestilence, had marched in desolation through the land; yet farther on, and accompany me to the country—doubtless many know of this, but I may be excused enlarging on this head; for, as I am a proprietor of the soil, and a native, and one who had his every interest bound up and centred in Jamaica, to whose fate I had nailed my flag—I might be excused. I do not mean to make a comparison of the estates in their present condition, to what they were in slavery; far from that : but to that time, when we trusted in England—when agriculture appeared to have regained some of its pristine strength—I mean in 1845, during Lord Elgin's administration—what a contrast with the present! Now there is no spirit in the cultivation—look where we will, nothing meets the eye but implements abandoned, cultivation neglected, houses unroofed, gates unhung, walls broken down, and all these things the results of a heartless legislation. A few years ago this parish counted eighty-three estates in full cultivation, now we have twenty-seven abandoned, ten in process of abandonment, and of the forty-six remaining many would be eventually so. Such are the facts of our position. In former days no one thought of selling his spare mill; it was kept reserved for any contingency which might arise. Now, I have myself sold mine to supply an order received from Cuba, and have yet another order for a similar article from the same place; besides, I have an order from a neighbouring parish to charter a vessel for the States, to carry fifty tons of iron, a portion of the last remains of what were once flourishing sugar properties, and these, I fear, are but indices of the other parishes throughout the island. I cannot see, I confess, how England is benefited by the Sugar Duties Bill of 1846, which has given so great an impetus to slave labour, because she only exports £4,800,000 to the slave countries of Brazil, Cuba, and Porto Rico. I must, however, hope, that as God, in his providence, raises men for the times, and does not adopt the times to men, some spirit now slumbering may be waked who will in all respects be equal to the exigency. Let us also take courage, and learn a lesson of self-dependence; let us acquire energy, for you know creoles are proverbially lazy, apathetic, and indolent — I can take the liberty of telling you so, as I am one myself; and let us endeavour to be something else than mere " hewers of wood, and drawers of water," and eaters of cocoa and plantains. Let me tell you all, there is nothing degrading to the best among you, in holding the plough and tilling the fields, and that I do not know any place or country where the labourers are better off—indeed, none where they are so well off; and this arises from your immediate and intimate connexion in the cultivation of sugar, which gives continuous employment. You are, therefore, much interested in keeping up the estates, and, as far as you can, preventing their abandonment. I must thank you for the indulgence you have shown me, and the attention with which I have been listened to, and have much pleasure in submitting the resolution to your notice. (Mr. Dewar's speech was received with repeated cheers.)

Mr. Dendy rose to explain. Mr. Dewar has stated that I had advanced something Utopian, on the subject of morals, religion, and education depending on agriculture and commercial prosperity. What I did say was, " if we are doomed to fall in commerce and agriculture, we will have a corresponding rise in the moral and social scale." But I shall not detain the meeting further than by saying, " Let the people praise thee, O God : let all the people praise thee. Then shall the earth yield her increase ; and God, even our God, shall bless us."

The Rev. Mr. Reid rose to second the second resolution. The rev. gentleman said, it is literally impossible for any person, taking a correct view, and forming a proper estimate, to resist the conviction that the present state of the island is, as the resolution expresses it, " truly deplorable," and threatening all ranks, professional, commercial, and agricultural, with the direst and most distressing calamities. Whatever difference may obtain as to the causes, near and remote, which have been instrumental in producing the crisis, there can be but one opinion as to the existence of the fact, and but one feeling and sentiment expressed, to wit, sincere sorrow and unfeigned lamentation. I can sincerely unite with the resolution in the utterance of heartfelt grief on account of the prevalence of those evils which are causing sad countenances and anxious spirits; men's hearts are failing them through fear, and daily watching for events about to transpire, in the flattering hope that they will prove advantageous. It is in every aspect a source of deepest regret that the lately emancipated colonies should have been placed in competition with those countries which are cultivated by the labour of slaves; for in that case the prosperity of the former must entirely depend upon the latter not being able to extend the trade, or increase slavery. It is a principle, incontrovertible, in commerce, that the value of goods in the market will depend upon, and be regulated by, the original cost of the article; so that, as long as slavery is carried on and increased according to demand, the competition must be unequal and unsuccessful. Instance the fact, that the profits, for 1844, of Manuel Pinto de Fonseca, engaged in the slave-trade, amounted to £150,000! While we ought to employ all constitutional and moral means to remove the causes of the unequal commerce, we ought, as a people, most industriously and perseveringly to exert ourselves, to the fullest extent of our capabilities, to lessen the evils and protect ourselves against complete and ultimate ruin. The cause of the present distress is a very complicated one, and certainly slavery, with its natural and legitimate fruits, as it once existed in this island, has had a full share in inducing our present calamities. It has ever appeared to me, that since the period of emancipation the different classes in our land have not felt and acted towards one another as being to all intents and purposes members of the same body, engaged in the same cause, the success of which securing the prosperity of all alike, and the failure of which involving all in one common calamity. I believe it is a fixed law in the economy of our common Parent, that the united interests of a nation are bound up in the well-being of each part, and that the real advantage of the one is never promoted at the expense of the other, but in all cases the very reverse holds true. In this country there do not exist separate and distinct interests, even in appearance— there being but one source of productiveness, one means of advancing the pecuniary prosperity of the inhabitants; and as in the wreck of a ship all suffer equally, inasmuch as each loses all, so if the production of the staples fail, all classes will suffer—the labourer as well as the planter—the professional and commercial men equally with the former. It is not only the duty, but it would be to the personal advantage of all, to do their very utmost to raise the culti- vation of the soil to the highest state of perfection. It ought to be the direct effort and honest boast of every resident in the island, to have the country producing and exhibiting all its capabilities and unfolding all its available resources. Let the motto be, cultivate, cultivate ; the more produce the greater reward; the more labour the greater return—the more we export the larger in amount will be our importa- tion and consequent benefits. This resolution does not intro- duce the principles of free trade—we are not met to discuss that question; nor does it call upon us to denounce the admission of slave-grown produce, as a new principle adopted by the Government of 1846. The resolution has been care- fully worded, and it calls upon us simply to express our opinion that the admitting of slave-produced sugars on equal terms with free grown, has increased the amount of human suffering, and that we lament the competition to which the emancipated colonies have been subjected with slaveholding communities. The augmentation of human suffering referred to in the resolution is caused by the increase in the slave-trade and slavery. Let me show what the trade is, by a few quotations from the work of the immortal Buxton. This subject may be viewed in the first seizure — march to the coast — detention on the coast—the middle passage, and what has been termed the seasoning :—

Of 1000 victims to the slave-trade, one half perish in the seizure, march, and detention 500
Of 500 consequently embarked, one-fourth, or 25 per cent., perish in the middle passage 125
Of the remaining 375 landed, one-fifth, or 29 per cent., perish in the seasoning....................................... 75

                                    Total loss.................. 700

So that 300 negroes only, or three-tenths of the whole number of victims, remain alive at the end of a year after their deportation; and the number of lives sacrificed by the system bears to the number of slaves available to the planter the proportion of seven to three. Then applying this calculation to the

Number annually landed at Brazil, Cuba, &c., which I have rated at 150,000
Of these one-fifth die in the seasoning 30,000

Leaving available to the planter.............................. 120,000
The number of lives annually sacrificed, being in proportion of seven to three 280,000
This amount may be verified in the following manner:—
Taking the annual victims at 400,000
One-half perish before embarkation 200,000

Embarked 200,000
One-fourth in the middle passage 50,000

Landed 150,000
One-fifth in the seasoning 30,000

Available 120,000

        Annual victims of Christian slave-trade......... 400,000

Proceeding in like manner with the Mohammedan slave-trade, we find the numbers to be—

Exported by the Imaum of Muscat 30,000
Carried across the desert..................................... 20,000

                                                            50,000
Loss by seizure, march, and detention....................... 50,000

Annual victims of Mohammedan slave-trade.............. 100,000
    Ditto   Christian   ditto   400,000

            Annual loss to Africa............ 500,000

All this suffering confined to the flesh and blood of the
victims of this nefarious traffic, and inflicted by countries
calling themselves Christian, professors of that religion
which has for one of its grand purposes the leading men to
be guided by the law of love.—" Do unto others as ye would
that they should do unto you." Reflect upon the amount of
mind degraded, ruined, and completely destroyed. The
Redeemer has said, " What shall a man give in exchange
for his soul?" How awful to contemplate the loss of 500,000
beings annually! The image of God, defaced and murdered, so many times every year, for the purpose of making
a little sugar, and enabling certain individuals to luxuriate
in a style of wasteful extravagance, which imparts no good,
but evil to themselves. This is besides slavery itself, with all
its wretched attendants. Slavery is bad; radically bad in
all circumstances, but especially where backed by the trade.
In Brazil and Cuba the most sensual and wicked passions of
the human heart are developed and gratified, without the
slightest restraint; and motives of humanity and a regard to
future consequences are swallowed up in downright and
unblushing selfishness—their motto being " work the negro
to death and supply his place from the market,"—regard
neither life nor death, the present nor the eternal interests
of the slave, if cursed gold can be gathered. But let us
take encouragement. Brazil and Cuba are not in a condition to supply the sugar markets of the world. Their
present position is one of dreadful peril, and any day a
crush may come and sweep away at once, and for ever,
every vestige of slavery, and throw them into competition
with just principles. It is literally impossible that the
system of trading in "the bodies and souls of men" can
endure much longer ; and this country is in far more
favourable circumstances to pursue the cultivation of sugars
with advantage than any of the slave countries, when once
the system is abolished. The impression cannot be too
deeply engraved upon our minds, that the deliverance,
salvation, honour, and ultimate prosperity of the island, is
placed to a great extent in our own hands; and that by a

diligent, patient, persevering course of industry, we may fully realise the enjoyment of prospects which, to indulge at present, might be considered the height of delusion; and cherishing hopes thus inspired, we would sincerely pray, God bless Jamaica in all her interests, political, commercial, agricultural, and religious. " Then shall our land yield her increase, and God, even our own God, shall bless us." (The rev. gentleman was loudly cheered.)

Mr. Lewin rose and said :—Mr. Chairman, it has occurred to me, during the time I have been sitting here, that whatever conclusion we may come to in reference to the object of our present meeting, we shall be taxed with partiality. I see occupying the place of advocates and jurors those of that portion of our race who are remarkable for benevolence and compassion, and it will be said, what but a favourable result was to be expected in a cause involving the deepest feelings of humanity?—But, Sir, it is not merely to the feelings that I intend to appeal on this occasion. My case requires the co-operation of the judgment, and, before I conclude, I hope to convince the ladies who have honoured us with their presence, as well as the vast multitude who now compose this assembly, that the issue of my case stands upon so firm a basis that the verdict must be in my favour. This, Sir, may be called, essentially, an anti-slavery meeting, in the language of Mr. Dewar, and, as such, it becomes us to indulge in reminiscences of those who have gone before us in this glorious work. This month, the month of June, commemorates a period of sixty-two years since that celebrated and noble-minded man, Thomas Clarkson, with Granville Sharp, and ten others, formed themselves into a committee for effecting the abolition of the slave-trade, which was then legalised in the British dominions. It was the first concentrated and organised effort that was made for the purpose. You are aware, Sir, that after twenty years of incessant and energetic labour, with that ever-to-be-remembered philanthropist, Wilberforce, as their leader in Parliament—the exertions of this little band were crowned with glorious success, and still more significant tokens of Divine approbation. Sir, in the perseverance of a mighty cause was the fact, that that good man, Thomas Clarkson, who died three or four years ago, at the age of eighty-seven, was permitted to behold the abolition of slavery itself in the British dominions, after having spent a life of sixty years of unceasing and indomitable energy in the work he had undertaken. The problem which he solved theoretically at the Cambridge University in 1785, when studying for orders as a clergyman of the Church of England, comprised in the words, " *Anne liceat invitos in servitudem dare*,"—translated, " Is it right to make slaves of others against their will ? "—as the academical essay of that year, he was graciously allowed to see practically affirmed in his long, consistent life, by the famous enactment of the law for the emancipation of the slaves in the British colonies.   Why need we then, Sir, despair of success, if from a small beginning like that which I have been describing, there have been such stupendous results ?   Let us take courage and go forward in this cause, and be assured, Sir, that if our petitions are presented in a hearty and devoted spirit to the Sovereign of the Universe, as well as the sovereign of England, the God of heaven will give prosperity to our endeavours, and we shall soon see this great work of humanity accomplished, and the monster evil entirely destroyed.   Mr. Lewin then read his resolution :—

" That, at no period during the long-continued and costly efforts of Great Britain for that purpose, have the treaties and conventions on the part of the Spanish and Brazilian Governments for the abolition of the slave-trade ever been faithfully and unreservedly executed—but, on the contrary, these Governments, by connivance and evasion, have permitted its continuance in the most horrible and aggravated form ; and no amelioration is to be expected so long as slavery exists, and the British dominions allowed to be the unrestricted emporium for the slave-labour produce of Cuba, Porto Rico, and Brazil. This meeting would, therefore, earnestly urge that the British Government should demand from the Spanish and Brazilian Governments the liberation from slavery of all Africans, and their descendants, illicitly introduced into their respective colonies and territories; and should they attempt to evade the demand, that measures be taken to exclude their produce from the British markets, until slavery itself be abolished by them."

He said, it called upon him to show that treaties existed between Spain and Brazil on the one hand, and Great Britain on the other, and that these treaties have never been honourably carried out. For this purpose, he referred at large to the treaty of 1817, and subsequently to conventions and decrees on the part of Spain, and also the treaty of 1826, and decrees on the part of Brazil, abolishing the slave-trade, and declaring it piracy, and that none of the subjects of these Governments should be engaged in the trade, under severe penalties, Spain after May, 1820, and Brazil after March, 1830. Mr. Lewin then read from official documents to prove that the authorities of Cuba and Brazil had openly given countenance to the infernal traffic, and that Lord Palmerston and Lord Aberdeen had themselves charged the Brazilian legislature with an express avowal of its breach of faith, and that the trade, ever since the treaties to abolish it, had continued to flourish under the connivance of the authorities, and in the face of all engagements, however solemn. Mr. Lewin said, some friends had taken objection to the use of the word " *treachery* " in his resolution, and to satisfy them he had substituted the word "*evasion ;* " but he believed that those gentlemen, as well as the whole of this assembly, must admit that, from the official despatches he had been reading, both the Spanish and Brazilian Governments have been, and are, guilty of base and infamous treachery. It was no use to make a compromise of language, when conduct of so disgraceful a nature was involved. Mr. Lewin said, that having established, for the information of the assembly, that treaties were in existence, and that they had never been honestly executed, he would now proceed to elucidate that portion of his resolution, which asserted that the slave-trade had been continued in the most horrible and aggravated form. He read the account given of a Brazilian vessel captured by one of her Majesty's cruisers, the *Cygnet*, with 556 slaves on board, describing the severities practised, and showing that they were, both male and female, branded on their shoulders, arms, and breasts, with initial letters of individuals for whom they had been shipped, and to whom they belonged. He also read a most graphic and horrifying detail of the sufferings of the middle passage, as given by Captain G. Mansel, R.N., to " the Select Committee of the House of Commons, for the final extinction of the slave-trade," last year. It showed the wholesale murder of thousands of human beings on the coast of Africa, to relieve those engaged in the slave-trade from the expense of feeding the slaves, when there was no immediate prospect of embarkation. The plan of literally packing the slaves—the way in which they are jammed together—the emaciation of their physical powers from this mode of stowing them—the disgusting condition in which they remain for days — the little food which, from these circumstances, they are enabled to receive —the putridity of dead bodies laying sometimes three or four days before they were discovered, and the decomposition which ensues rendering it almost impossible to remove the bodies in an entire form, together with the immense loss of life during the passage and at landing, from disease contracted, and the waste of the system on the voyage—were delineated in terms not to be misunderstood or doubted. Mr. Lewin said, these are the means by which the cultivation of sugar is carried on in Cuba and Brazil, and in consequence of the Parliamentary Bill of 1846 an impetus had been given to the cruelties of the slave-trade and slavery. He said, the statistics respecting the slave-trade showed that from 1840 to 1845 the average importations into the Spanish colonies and Brazil were at the rate of 32,000 per annum. In 1846 they increased to 64,000, and from that period they have been increasing to 100,000, giving now what they were in the rifest time of the brutal traffic. He referred also to the increase of sugar production under these Governments, since the passing of the Bill lessening the duties and tending

to equalise them. He showed that in 1846 Cuba exported
190,000 tons of sugar, and that in 1847 and 1848 she exported about 269,000 tons each year. That the exportations
from Brazil in 1846 were 302,000 cwts., and in 1847 they
increased to 702,000 cwts. He said, these were awful pic-
tures and indications of the slave-trade and slavery, and that
these horrors would be augmented, so long as the British
dominions were allowed to be the channel for the consumption of slave-manufactured sugars. He said, now that the
right of visit and search, on board vessels bearing the Brazilian flag, and of holding Mixed Commission Courts in that
empire, had ceased, the trade would be carried on by the
subjects of that Government with increased vigour and bar-
barity ; and thus it is said to be necessary for the British
legislature, in accordance with previous policy, to adopt the
enactment 8th and 9th Victoria. How deplorable was it, he
said, to see a Government, like that of England, abandoning
the high ground she had always maintained in the cause of
humanity ! She had not been sparing either of her means
or talents in that noble work. She had paid Spain £400,000,
in 1817, to indemnify her for the losses of the slave-trade,
and such was the earnestness of England in this matter, that
in 1814, three years anterior to the treaty already mentioned,
she offered the Government of Spain £800,000 at that time,
to abolish the slave-trade in five years. It was refused, but
the Spanish King pledged himself that measures should be
taken for the abolition. The generosity of our noble nation,
in giving her money for the rights of humanity, was not confined to Spain. In 1815, she paid £300,000 to the Portuguese Government, and remitted at the same time the
balance of a debt of £600,000 due by her. These were
splendid sacrifices in the cause of justice, and they are but a
few of the many she has made in this great work of human
happiness. I wish, Sir, he said, that she was ruled by the
same principles now. It was said that the policy of the
British Government is regulated by the wants of the people
of the United Kingdom. So far as sugar is concerned, if
excise statistics be true, it would appear, that in 1847,

besides the stock on hand, and free-labour sugar from other countries, the quantity, in that year, from the British East and West Indies amounted to 290,000 tons, and the consumption in the United Kingdom was 289,000 tons ; thus showing a surplus of 1,000 tons from the free colonies of Great Britain.   I am led, therefore, to the inference, Sir, that it is not for the individual benefit of the people of England that foreign slave-grown sugars are admitted, but on account of the enormous revenue, amounting to millions of pounds, derived from the duty on the article.   I feel that this cause wants but a strenuous advocacy, in the person of some gifted spirit like that of William Knibb.   The great secret of his success, in the cause of emancipation in these colonies, with the people of England, Scotland, and Ireland, was that he had seen the enormity of the system he described. If some spirit like his were to arise from Cuba and the Brazils, and make known the horrors of the slave-trade and slavery, as it is to be seen in those countries, to the people of our mother country, who would doubt the fate of the question?   May we not hope, Sir, that the time will soon come when gentlemen who have been engaged in the planting line, like some of those I see around me, and whose knowledge of the horrors of slavery would afford them better means of description than I possess, will go forth in the land of their birth, with retired fortunes, and advocate with fervency the cause of the oppressed African ?   Let them take Zachariah Macaulay for their example.   His hand had been stained in the crime of slavery ; but when conviction came upon his mind, he hesitated not, with a singular magnanimity, to become one among the renowned benefactors of Africa.   He was an active and zealous member of the " African Institution," formed in 1812, for the civilisation of Africa, but whose work was rendered abortive on account of the foreign slave-trade proving to be too formidable an enemy.   However, Mr. Macaulay continued to his death a sincere anti-slavery man.   Let his example ennoble the minds of others, and whatever may have been their previous views, the change of sentiment will be regarded, by right-thinking men, only as the result of those operations of conviction which convert the heart in morals and religion from a debased to a purer condition. You will, Sir, permit me to observe, that this is no new position to me. I belong to a class of men who have, for a series of years, in this country, been endeavouring to oppose slavery in every form and shape, and to improve the condition of the slave; and, whatever may have been our errors in the course we pursued, I trust, now that we are enabled to see matters through a different medium, our motives will be duly appreciated. It is with great pleasure, Sir, that I see you occupying this place. Though I have had the honour of becoming acquainted with you only during the last month, I have known for many years how indefatigable you have been in instructing the descendants of Africa. I became acquainted, twenty years ago, Sir, with an instance of your teaching, in the moral rectitude of a daughter of Africa, an offspring of slavery. I did not come here, Sir, for the purpose of dealing with the commercial or agricultural interests involved in this question. My advocacy is of the cause of humanity and justice, and it will be a pleasing reflection to you, Sir, that, as you say it is the first time you have appeared in so public and prominent a manner, that appearance is to sustain the glorious work of humanity, which is so intimately connected with your particular vocation. And now, Sir, recurring to my resolution, I must recommend this meeting to adopt the suggestion it contains. A million and a half of money is said to be expended yearly, in keeping up the British squadron for the suppression of the slave-trade. The captures which that squadron has hitherto made, have amounted to but four per cent. per annum in the number of persons stolen from Africa; and when you reflect upon what I have already stated, together with the fact mentioned by the Rev. Mr. Reid, from Mr. Buxton's book, that about two lives and a half are lost in procuring one slave, I say, Sir, there is no dealing with this question in an ordinary way. In Cuba the slave-trade is well known to be a source of considerable gain to the heads of departments there. The Captain-general is selected from a long but insignificant list of generals. Without patrimony, and without practical or theoretical administrative knowledge, and no fixed or safe principles of morality, he is appointed to the government. Scarcely has he taken possession of it, when two or three hundred slaves arrive, for which he receives his bag, containing as many ounces of gold. Then there arrives another and another, and thus the traffic to him becomes a continued and abundant source of wealth. The unexpected accumulation of so much gold dazzles and seduces the loose principles of the soldier, who contemplates, for the first time in his life, such an amount of money. He forgets at once his military renown and ancient Castilian purity, and becomes the sordid creature of lust and avarice. Amidst all this, what are we to expect but connivance and treachery? When men will pursue dishonest courses, and no change can be effected in their habits, the line of conduct should be to have nothing to do with them. For these reasons I impress upon this meeting to urge upon the Government of Great Britain, to say to the Spanish and Brazilian Governments, " Execute the virtuous intentions of your treaties, or we shall refuse to take your products into our markets, wrung from the bloody labour of your slaves." With these remarks, Sir, I take leave to propose the resolution.

This speech was listened to with great attention, and concluded amidst loud cheering.

Mr. Ralph Brown said—Sir, the duty of seconding this resolution devolves upon me, and I cannot but feel thankful to the gentleman who has just sat down, for having so ably and so fully enforced and explained it, as to leave to me a short and easy task to perform. You have had set before you a faithful picture of the horrible atrocities of the slave-trade, and of slavery in Cuba, Porto Rico, and Brazil; and I am sure that your sympathies have been powerfully excited on behalf of the wretched beings who are subjected to the cruelties which you have heard described. Mr. Lewin said that he would have been better pleased if some of the old planters had come forward with such a description as their own experience might enable them to give; but I may venture to affirm, on behalf of the planters, that they entertain no less abhorrence of slavery than he does, and would be equally ready to set forth the evils of the system, were they as well accustomed to speak in public as he is. He may, however, congratulate himself on that account, for it serves to make the coruscations of his own genius shine brighter by the contrast. But, Sir, there is another portion of our fellow-creatures who are quite as deeply interested in the proceedings of this day; I mean our own lately emancipated fellow-subjects, whose fate and fortunes are indissolubly bound up with our own. If at any time, Sir, as Mr. Reid has stated, the various classes of West India society thought, or acted as if they thought, that they had distinct and separate interests to maintain, that time has passed away. The delusion is dispelled, for the misfortunes which have well-nigh overwhelmed us all, must, at least, have stamped this conviction on the mind, that we must either stand or fall together! Dr. King, and other gentlemen, at the late Spanish Town meeting, have so graphically portrayed the lamentable condition of our commerce, and of our agriculture, and the consequent distress universally experienced, that any attempt on my part to dilate upon that subject would be a needless occupation of your time; but I am sure I may confidently appeal to every soul who hears me, to bear me out in the declaration, that we all do feel the calamities which they have so eloquently described. Our own sad experience testifies, that instead of being able adequately to maintain institutions for the moral and religious instruction of our own labouring population and their offspring, we have the melancholy anticipation of schools being abandoned, and places of worship closed! Surely, Sir, the people of England never contemplated such a result from their costly and persevering efforts to establish freedom here! Doubtless they expected that the objects of their solicitude should be raised in the scale of society—that they should not only become useful members of the community in which they live, but should be qualified also to enjoy all the blessings of Chris-

tianity. If we can only succeed in convincing them that the
cause of their probable disappointment in these respects lies
in that very encouragement which they are giving to slave-
grown produce, and in the open violation, by the Spanish
and Brazilian Governments, of solemn treaties (the observance of which it is in their power to compel), depend upon it
that the same spirit of justice will animate John Bull, and
make him rush to the rescue alike of the freeman and the
slave. Already is the same spirit displaying itself among the
ladies of England, which distinguished them so much in the
cause of freedom some twenty years ago. It is but lately
that I read in the public prints more than one spirit-stirring
address from a lady, urging her own sex to give no rest to
their husbands, brothers, and friends, till they shall have
completely extinguished slavery. And who can doubt the
effect of such an agency on their husbands, brothers, and
friends? I would venture it against even that of the late
William Knibb himself, Sir, if he were still living. May I
not congratulate you, Sir, on seeing so many ladies here to-
day? I am sure I only express the sentiments of the whole
of the male portion of this meeting, when I say that we are
rejoiced to see them. It is, indeed, an occasion on which
their presence does them honour, and betokens the amiable
qualities of their hearts ; and I trust, Sir, that we may look
upon it as a most favourable augury of success for the object
which we have in view. One word as to the cupidity which
has been attributed to the people of England for their love of
cheap sugar; I do trust that no expression of anything like
a vindictive feeling towards the people of England will go
forth from this meeting. It is pleasing to observe, that
throughout the island, wherever similar meetings have been
held, the most unbounded loyalty has been displayed towards
our beloved Queen Victoria, God help her! And in this
respect the parish of St. James will yield to none. Even of
the Government we desire to speak respectfully, though we
cannot but feel that we have been hardly used ; but, above
all, Sir, let us cherish feelings of friendship towards the
people of England, in the confident hope that they will

afford us that aid which, under Providence, will soon
remove those evils of which we complain. With these few
remarks, Sir, I beg most cordially to second the resolution.

Mr. Brown resumed his seat amidst much cheering, and
the resolution was then put, and unanimously adopted.

The Rev. Mr. Moss rose to propose the fourth resolution,
in doing which, he said he thought he could best promote
the objects of the meeting, at that late hour, by just submitting it to its notice.

The Rev. Mr. Hewit seconded it, and, in doing so, said,
he hardly deemed it necessary to follow the example set by
Mr. Moss, and he must say he felt great pleasure at seeing
the part taken by the planters, and would congratulate them
on the feelings which had been expressed on their behalf by
Mr. Brown, who said he was unaccustomed to speak in public.
Why, if they had such a beginning, what would the end be
like? The poor parsons would have to hide their " diminished heads," and sink into the shade. Immediately after
the emancipation, a wrong feeling had taken place, and a
particular class was considered as hostile to the general
interests of the colony—legislation tried to restore its prosperity, and promoted immigration, which was to be a
panacea, but the costly efforts in that direction had failed too.
Indeed, immigration was a perfect failure, but he thought
they had come to the right point at last. Much had been
done to the benefit of this now prostrate colony, but ineffec-
tually, and he thought it so resulted because we were suffering as a community, in the sight of God, from the sin which
prevails in it! Some say the planters have ruined the
country—some say the labourers had ruined the country—
and some say the Baptist parsons had ruined the country.
The truth is, they had all a hand in it. But let us henceforward be united, and raise a loud note, which would reach
the shores of England, that we were determined slavery
shall be abolished—it would find an echo there. He could
not help thinking what a strange day this was! Revolution
was rife in Europe. Denmark and Prussia, Germany and
Italy, had had theirs ; but when he thought of an anti-slavery

meeting in the Court-house of Montego Bay, he would say, that we too had had a glorious revolution. Why, if the walls of the buildings and the streets of the town could speak, they would cry "Bravo, bravo!" They would bid them go on in their good work and prosper! He hoped there would be a revolution like this in Cuba, and in Porto Rico, and in Brazil, and even in America too—not a bloody revolution—not one accompanied by horrors—but one brought about and accomplished by the moral agency which might be brought to bear on the question. It wanted but a few Knibbs, and Burchells too, to go forth into these lands and proclaim the destruction of slavery! A great deal had been said about the people of England's inconsistency in wanting slave-grown sugar because it was cheap; but it was difficult to be consistent, and he wondered if all there present had not on some article made by slave labour. If we would do as we ought, we must smoke no more cigars, for they are entirely the production of slave labour, and we must have no more cotton. He hoped sincerely the petitions would have effect, and that our beloved Queen would give instructions to her Ministers (for it was in her power to do it) to forbid the production of slave-grown sugars. Our interests are identified with those of the planters—with them we stand, or with them we fall. The labourers, too, must stand and fall with them; and we voluntaries also; for you know, Sir, (said the speaker, addressing the venerable Chairman with rather an arch expression of countenance,) we voluntaries can't get our salaries except the labourers have employment, and it is only the planter who can furnish it; so that one and all of their interests were intricately interwoven and identified one with the other. He hoped always to witness the prevalence of unanimity among them, and would now beg most cordially to second the resolution. It was accordingly put and carried unanimously.

The fifth resolution was then moved by the Rev. John Howard Moore, as follows:—Mr. Chairman, a resolution has been put into my hands to move at this meeting, to which I am altogether unprepared to speak. I have just

now been so busily and anxiously engaged in scenes and
duties of so dissimilar a nature, as completely to deprive me
of time, and unfit the mind for giving this resolution proper
consideration. I am fortunate that it is such a one as it is,
for had there been involved in it any of the financial or
statistical concerns of the island, my short residence here,
and my ignorance of Jamaica affairs, would completely
unfit me to speak of them.—Therefore, as my present speech
will be purely extemporaneous, I trust you will grant me
the indulgence which these facts and my country (for I am
an Irishman) demand. The first thing the resolution states,
is, "that the memorial now read be accepted and forwarded
to the secretary of the Anti-slavery Society." This is the
medium through which we purpose forwarding our petitions
to her Majesty the Queen, and the two Houses of Parliament.
I think the medium an excellent one, and cannot agree with
a speaker who preceded me, in his fears that our petitions
will never reach the throne. It might be objected that
very many here were opposed to this Society, and that at one
time this Society was antagonistic to them. Time works
great changes, and I am sure I see several in this room upon
whom it has had its effect; and if now you have come round
to have the same view as this Society, I cannot see why you
should not avail yourselves of its assistance. Besides, if you
select any member of either House of Parliament to bring
forward your petitions, however enlisted he may be in your
cause, he may be inadequate to the task assigned to him.
But, if you intrust your petition to this Society, whose members are on the spot, and have been long and anxiously
engaged in the abolition of slavery, they will be able to select
one who is competent to advocate the claim set forth in
your memorial. Again, if those who have been opposed to
each other become reconciled, we find that either side will
use all diligence and exertion in carrying out every wish or
request made by the other. And so with this Society. You
were once opposed to it; it will now rejoice in your changed
sentiments, and will, I have no doubt, take every pains that
our petitions shall arrive at their proper quarter and desti-

nation. While the resolution proposes the Anti-slavery
Society as our medium with the Queen in Parliament, it
proposes that our chairman, the Archdeacon, shall be the
channel of communication with the Anti-slavery Society.
This I conceive to be a good selection; it will give tone
and influence to our proceedings, and will show that the
question you have taken up is one which occupies the minds
of those who have the best interests of the people at heart.
I was, at one time, of opinion that a meeting of this sort was
not a proper or becoming place for clergymen to appear, or
take a part in; but I have changed my opinion, and fully
agree with the words of our right reverend diocesan, that
attendance at such meetings, and espousal of their objects,
" would neither stain the judicial ermine, nor sully the
episcopal lawn." I am sure, Mr. Archdeacon, you need not
fear for your surplice. The only point I have further to
speak on, is the clause of the resolution—" that we request
the Society to adopt measures for the strenuous advocacy of
the prayer of the petition." The best way we can urge this
upon the Society is by our own earnestness, zeal, and importunity. If any of you come to ask a favour of, or look for
some public situation from a gentleman—if you did so coldly
and indifferently, you would never obtain it; but if you
besought and entreated him, and were importunate, and
would not be put off, your request would be granted, if it
were but to get rid of your importunity. Since I came to
this meeting, I have heard and seen many things to remind
me of my own country. The meeting itself does. I have
seen repeal meetings—great monster meetings, one hundred
times larger than this—for the purpose of agitating for
repeal; in the same way should we agitate—the whole island
should be agitated for the fulfilment of those treaties which
were formed with Great Britain for the abolition of slavery
—until the voice of this agitation should roll across the
broad Atlantic, and thrill the very hearts of the people of
Britain, causing the hands of the supporters of slavery to
fall powerless, and giving stimulus and energy to the friends
of freedom and the slave. I do not agree with Mr. Lewin,

and his moral force argument. He says, " If Cuba, and Porto Rico, and Brazil will not fulfil their treaties, we will withdraw from them—have no further dealings with them, and exclude their sugars from our markets," &c. Now, I would only like to know, if I borrowed ten pounds of Mr. Lewin, and refused to pay him, would he quietly drop the matter, and let me keep his money ? Would he say to me, " Go away, I will never lend you money again—I will have nothing more to do with you ?" No, he would bring me into a court of justice—put the law in force against me, and punish me for my attempt to swindle and defraud him. Now, a clergyman should be a man of peace, and I trust I am a man of peace ; but my sentiments are these :—If the Governments of Brazil, Porto Rico, and Cuba, will not listen to our petitions, and the remonstrance of the British public, then,—I might be wrong,—but I would bring the wooden walls of old England to bear upon them, and would extort from them, by the thunder of British cannon, what they refuse to the justice of our petitions and entreaties. (This sentiment appeared to create on the large assemblage the impression that the rev. gentleman had suggested the only agency which would be effective.) Let me add, Mr. Chairman, that I feel much pleasure in being present at this meeting, and fully concur in the design for which it was convened, and now beg to move the resolution.

The rev. gentleman resumed his seat amidst prolonged cheers.

The resolution was seconded by Isaac Jackson, Esq., and carried by acclamation.

The venerable Chairman then vacated the chair, when it was proposed by W. H. Knott, Esq., seconded by H. E. Groves, Esq., that the Custos do take the chair, and that the thanks of the meeting, which were eminently due, be tendered to the Venerable the Archdeacon, for his conduct in the chair and his presidency over the meeting. The motion was carried unanimously. It was suggested that some other mark of respect should be shown to the rev. chairman, when the persons assembled rose, with one accord, and stood for some seconds, while the chairman acknowledged the compliment by bowing.

Thus concluded the first anti-slavery meeting, held with unanimity of purpose, in the parish of St. James.

REQUISITION FOR A PUBLIC MEETING AT ST. MARY'S.

To the Hon. A. D. Cooke, Custos Rotulorum of the Parish of Saint Mary.

St. Mary's, June 18th, 1849.

SIR,—We, the undersigned inhabitants of this parish, respectfully request that you will be pleased to call a general meeting of our fellow-parishioners at an early day, to consider and discuss the same important subjects which occupied the attention of a large and influential public meeting, holden in Spanish Town, on Thursday, the 24th May last, viz.,—" The effect produced on this country by the non-observance of the treaties for the suppression of the slave-trade by which Spain and the Brazils are bound to her Majesty, and the devising of such a measure as may tend to promote at once the great interests of humanity, and the relief of the intertropical possessions of the British Crown from the deep distress in which they are now involved."

R. Robinson, Rector	George Sank
J. W. Grey, J.P.	O. Phillips, V.M.
A. Girod	Thomas McCulloch, J.P.
E. R. Da Costa, J.P.	Henry Rigg, J.P.
Michael Levy, V.M.	M. Kelly, J.P.
Benjamin Palmer	David Day, Baptist Minister
J. B. Goffe	William Evans
John Philpotts, J.P.	John Cowan, Presbyterian
Robert F. G. Page	Minister
H. B. Shaw, J.P.	Nathaniel Wilson, V.M.
James Hinton	A. C. Duncker
William Haughton, J.P.	J. Ward, jun.
Henry Lindo	T. Rankin
A. Sank	E. H. Huston
Robert Clemetson, J.P.	C. Redmond

A. J. Lindo, J.P.

Richard Harrison, J.P.

Thomas Grey

David Ferguson, M.D.

John Simon

Robert Faichney, J.P.

Frederick Lindo

J. B. Livingston

Heneage Girod, Island
    Curate

C. Jones, J.P.

Abm. De Souza, V.M.

Alexander Lindo

John Churnside

William Gray

Charles Barnet

E. T. Guy, J.P.

Henry Sergeant

P. Morgan, J.P.

J. A. M. Davidson, Island
    Curate

John Simpson, Presbyterian
    Minister

J. M. Jeffrey, J.P.

John Campbell, Presbyterian
    Minister

W. E. Cruickshanks, V.M.

Henry Ergas

James Finlay

E. Donallan

W. L. Thompson

John Morrison

Henry Westmorland, J.P.

W. Litherland, J.P.

In compliance with the foregoing requisition, I appoint
Friday, the 29th June instant, for holding the above meeting.

(Signed)   A. D. COOKE,

Custos Rotulorum, St. Mary's.

The attendance at the St. Mary's meeting was likewise
very numerous, and comprised, with few exceptions, all the
influential gentlemen of the parish, with the clergy of all
denominations, and large numbers of the peasantry, many
of whom were afterwards heard to express themselves highly
gratified by the occasion. It gives us pleasure also to notice
the presence of the ladies, which has of late become quite a
new and pleasing feature in our debates.

Among the gentlemen present were noticed :—The Rev.
R. Robinson, Rector of the parish; the Rev. John Camp-
bell, Presbyterian Minister; the Rev. John Simpson, Pres-
byterian Minister; the Rev. Heneage Girod, Island Curate;
the Rev. David Day, Baptist Minister; the Rev. John
Davidson, Island Curate; the Rev. J. Cowan, Presbyterian
Minister; the Rev. Mr. Teale, Baptist Minister; James
Stewart, Esq., J.P.; Michael Kelly, Esq., J.P.; J. W.

Gray, Esq., J.P.; W. Litherland, E·q., J.P.; W. Jeffrey, Esq., J.P.; Thomas McCulloch, Esq., J.P.; Oliver Phillips, Esq., Vestryman; Richard Harrison, Esq., J.P.; P. Morgan, Esq., J.P.; W. Haughton, Esq., J.P.; H. Bigg, Esq., J.P.; H. Walsh, Esq., J.P.; A. J. Lindo, Esq., J.P.; E. B. Da Costa, Esq., J.P,; A. Hire, Esq., J.P., Metcalfe; W. Pine, Esq., J.P., St. Andrew's; A. De Souza, Esq., V.M.

Shortly after 12 o'clock, the hour appointed, his Honour the Custos was moved into the chair by J. W. Jeffrey, Esq., J.P., and his Honour then rose and opened the proceedings of the day with the following prefatory remarks : — The object for which we are met to-day has been so often and so eloquently handled by men of the highest talent in the island, that many in this large assemblage require no explanation from me on the subject; these will, I hope, bear with me, while I deem it necessary to address a few observations, in plain and familiar language, to the immense concourse of our fellow-parishioners, the labouring classes now present. It is known, my friends, to you all that the great island of Cuba, within our sight, holds at this moment an enormous black population, in the most abject state of slavery that ever man was subjected to. It may not, however, be as well known to you, that while Great Britain was giving millions to wipe away every trace of slavery in her own colonies, she was also spending her treasures with praise-worthy generosity in effecting treaties with Spain and Portugal, for the immediate and total suppression of the slave-trade in those countries, and for the ultimate abolishment of slavery altogether. Now, my friends, it is notorious to the world that these solemn pledges have been totally disregarded—have been disgracefully broken; and that, at this moment, the slave-trade and slavery are carried on in Cuba and Brazil, in their most hideous, inhuman, and unnatural forms. It is therefore to petition our beloved Queen, her Parliament, and the people of Great Britain that we are met here to-day, to pray that England shall at once demand of the Spanish and Brazilian Governments the fulfilment to the letter of these treaties, and to state

openly and firmly that, until these just demands are attended to—until these her legal rights are enforced—England's dignity is not maintained, while the results of Spanish
and Brazilian perfidy are encouraged in her markets, to the
disgrace of the British nation, and to the ruin of her loyal
and unoffending colonists. I rejoice, my friends, to see that
the good leaven of the great Spanish Town meeting has
raised in Saint Mary the entire body of the people; all sects
and creeds, all classes and colours—even the ladies, I am
proud to see, have come from their retirement, gracefully to
sanction, strengthen, and dignify our meeting by their presence, and all join in calling on England, Christian England,
to listen to our prayer, and to obey forthwith the dictates of
humanity, of justice, and of duty.

The Rev. Heneage Girod then rose, and spoke as follows
—Mr. Custos, ladies, and gentlemen—It devolves upon me
to take the initiative on this occasion, by having had the first
resolution allotted to me to propose; but why, considering
the relative position I occupy in the parish, my modesty will
not allow me to account for. However, before making the
few observations I have to offer, I will read the resolution
to you :—

"That this meeting, composed of loyal subjects of every class
and colour, and without distinction of creeds, rejoices in the fact
that England has taken the lead amongst the nations of the earth,
in exerting her philanthropy and power for the destruction of the
monstrous wrongs of slavery and the slave-trade in her own
dominions."

Sir, in consequence of the prominent lead that has been
taken by the Lord Bishop, in originating this movement, it
is, I believe, expected that the clergy generally will contribute their support to it likewise. It is for this reason I am
here this day to take a part, humble though it be, in the
requisition to his Honour the Custos, lest, by my absence, I,
as one of the clergy, should be accused of being lukewarm
in a matter of so much concern as the occasion of our
meeting undoubtedly is; otherwise I should not have cared

to run the risk of having the cry of "political parson" raised against me. And I am glad to be able to notice another fashion that has been set and followed upon this occasion, rendered thereby somewhat auspicious,—I mean, the appearance of so many ladies in our deliberations, whose sympathising hearts are ever open to compassion for distress, whenever and in whatever type it is exhibited. But, Sir, I am reminded that it is not in a political point of view we are led to regard this question. A great moral principle is involved, which, and which alone, is to be invoked; and when I see not only the clergy of the Established Church, but ministers of other denominations, and persons of every creed and colour, assembled to do justice to our cause, you may rely upon this, that whatever divergence in opinion may unfortunately exist between us in other matters, there is none whatever in this, and that we all are unanimous in the belief, that the present agitation is essentially necessary in the crisis which this and the other West India islands have at length reached. And it is to be hoped, nay, the inference is pretty strong, that these circumstances combined will carry along with them some weight. And yet, after all, when we come to reflect upon the vast array of talent which has been brought to bear upon this subject by the English clergy, and by the champions of the anti-slavery party, without much good result, it is to be feared that our advocacy, which is comparative weakness, will fail in accomplishing its desired end. True it is that, in consequence of those strong appeals, the British Government made an effort, and have come to expend annually a sum of one million sterling for the suppression of the slave-trade, having previously abolished slavery in their own possessions at a very large sacrifice. Were I to attempt to sketch you an outline of the causes which led to this, it would require me to wade through the political changes which alternated the mother-country for many years preceding the great event itself. I should have to introduce you to the British Parliament, where the humane champions of freedom pleaded not only as orators, but as Christians, the cause of the slave;

and where they ceased not, year after year, to plead this holy cause, till justice and humanity prevailed, and sympathy took hold of the hearts of Christian men and women, and they declared that there should be no longer slaves, at least in their own dominions. But the glory thus achieved has been allowed to be tarnished; for what was it but discouraging slavery in their own possessions, and encouraging it in those of their neighbours, when afterwards they are found patronising and consuming the sugar manufactured by the unholy toil of the oppressed slave, when they had just before repudiated it, pharisaically so, when made here by a similar process? What was it, too—(the ladies will, I am sure, excuse the allusion I am about to make to their sex, from the occasion which calls it forth)—what was it but rank hypocrisy, when pious and elderly spinsters declared that it revolted against their too delicate feelings to use our sugar thus made, and that somehow or other their tea never tasted sweet when sugared with the article? It was, in fact, in their estimation the accursed thing from which they would in anywise keep themselves. But now a lop-sided policy has enabled them to purchase it a penny or two cheaper in the pound, they feel no such squeamishness. According to the emphatic and significant language of the *Times*, all the time England is conniving at slavery in one country she is professing to suppress and resist it in another. In the one hand she extends filthy lucre, with the other she launches out the thunderbolts of war. In the one hand is temptation, in the other intimidation. It was, I believe, in 1826 that a convention was established between Great Britain and the Brazils — (that with Spain having been concluded many years before)—the first article of which was to the effect, that from and after the year 1830 it should be unlawful for that country to carry on the slave-trade, and that the carrying it on, directly or indirectly, should be deemed and taken as piracy. It is well known how these treaties have fared. Our meeting here to-day assures us it is well known that these countries have not performed what they engaged by solemn compact to do. And it is on this account, and feeling the ruinous effect of this non-fulfilment, and because the British Government, having both the means and the power, have not yet seen fit to enforce them (*sic volo, sic jubeo,* I suppose, is always their motto); it is, I say, on these accounts, that this country, conjointly with the other inter-tropical islands, raises her voice against the flagrant injustice thereby entailed. Considering the belligerent character that attaches to the noble lord, the Foreign Secretary, it is perhaps not a little surprising that his lordship has not voted this infraction a *casus belli*—not that I would seem to be advocating war principles, for I am sure if her Majesty's guns were only seen bristling at Rio, Cadiz, or the Havanna, the object would be achieved without any bloodshed. Notwithstanding, however, this apparent neglect or delay, call it which you like, I think there is cause of rejoicing in the position which Britain has assumed on the great question of slavery. And my humble opinion is, that whether she is governed by a Whig or Tory ministry, she will not suffer her colonies to be ruined. Her ministers may have legislated upon a mistaken policy—they may have been deceived and led astray by pet theories, or become too much absorbed in abstract principles; but if they shall see, as they must have begun to do, the bad effect of their legislation, I am confident they will vary their policy — when they find our orchards and plantations sinking one after another to decay, and our "hanging gardens" deciduous, they will halt in their destructive course, and give a helping hand to restore their wonted vegetation. And I yet anticipate that it will be eventually shown that in the estimation of the British Government our interests are not so small as to become involved in the maxim, "de minimis non curat lex." I will, Sir, with your permission, read a short extract from Lord Palmerston's speech, where his lordship, after stating the grounds upon which he resisted the motion of Mr. Milner Gibson for the repeal of the Brazil Act, concluded by observing, "that notwithstanding the feeling that seemed to exist in the minds of some persons, of indifference to the slave-trade, he could not allow himself to think that the majority of that House would declare themselves adverse to those principles which had so long done honour to this country, or that they would, now that they had made great progress in putting it down, give their sanction to the opinion that this country was indifferent to the continuance of that atrocious and abominable traffic." We are called upon, gentlemen, to consider the effects produced upon this and the other islands by the non-observance of certain treaties. I imagine it is not to satisfy each other on that point, or in fact to convey any fresh intelligence at large, but simply to tell the British nation that such a state of things exists as cannot longer be endured, unless she steps in to redress our evils, which have now become crying. Distress is now so generally felt by all classes, that people have begun to trace cause and effect; but as it has been echoed from one meeting to another, and from one end of the island to the other, and will no doubt be amply unfolded to you to-day, it would be uselessly occupying your time were I to attempt to delineate its features; its broad outlines have been filled in by more competent hands. In spite, however, of this general prostration, and the ruinous wants thereby engendered, I have great faith in the high hope that good may come out of our meeting; and I do not forget that I am a citizen of the world—that every interest which is right, just, and proper, is an interest with which I am identified. I rejoice, therefore, that we are come together. There has been a great deal of misunderstanding between different parties in Jamaica. We have in our several turns been misrepresented, but I think if sympathy shall now be ripened into cordial co-operation for the future, the country is saved, and good will be done. When our distresses shall furnish matter for history, I am persuaded that by not relaxing ourselves in what is good, we shall secure peace and prosperity to the neighbourhood in which we live, and to the island at large. I trust to see the time when the breath of heaven, that plays on the face of the earth, shall go over the earth, and never fan the face of a slave. Slavery is doomed; Revelation condemns it; human policy condemns it. I trust all will

condemn it.   And if Britain shall ask, What are we to do?
we answer, enforce the treaties you have entered into with
Spain and Brazil, by remonstrance and by every other means
you can use; and if these fail, what then?   Cannon balls?
No! But let England close her markets against them, and
that will do more than all her cannon balls can do.   I am
well aware that cannon balls going through a man's house
may be a very convincing argument, and more so if one go
through his head, but in this matter I believe them to be
unnecessary.   If peaceable means be used, moral force will
prevail, and a bloodless victory will be secured.

Mr. Philpotts, in seconding the motion, said—It has been
apportioned to me, your Honour, ladies and gentlemen, to
second the resolution proposed and so ably commented
upon by the rev. gentleman who has just sat down; not but
that I feel myself inadequate to the task of expatiating as
eloquently upon the topics suggested in it as they merit;
not but that I know, right well, a more able advocate than
myself might have been enlisted in this cause.   It is, indeed,
Sir, a matter fraught with much satisfaction to me to behold
such an assemblage as the present, composed, as it is, of
men of all classes, creeds and complexions, forming so large
a portion of the community of this once prosperous parish.
We all are, your Honour, if I rightly understand the particular object aimed at by this resolution, to endeavour to
excite once more the latent energies of the people of Great
Britain,—I term them latent, inasmuch as they appear to
have fallen asleep over the task of emancipation which they
but a short time since set themselves to perform.   We are
here to add one cry to the thousand supplications that have
been or ere long will be laid before the Imperial Legislature
by the inhabitants of these colonies, and to educe, once more,
if possible, that spirited and vigorous determination, under
the influence of which, but a few years since, England was
enabled to crush the demon of slavery throughout her dominions.   I believe, Sir, there is none here who would willingly
detract from or attempt to lessen the glory which England,
on that occasion, earned for herself; but there are many here

who will coincide with me in thinking that the people of
the mother country are bound by every tie of conscience
and honour not to halt, but to prosecute the crusade they
have pledged themselves to, against slavery, and never to
be satisfied, or imagine they have performed their work, so
long as one African can be bought or sold on his native coast.
I feel justified, Sir, in asserting that there are thousands of
the middle classes in England who are not only willing
but able to put down slavery throughout the world, and I
anticipate that period when I say that nations yet unknown
will extol and envy the glory England will have earned for
herself; whatever be her fate—whatever the future may
have in store for her,—whether it be her lot still to maintain
her present proud supremacy among nations, or whether it
be her doom, like others that have gone before her, to sink
into oblivion or insignificance—still, Sir, so long as the
records of one generation are handed down to another by
the pen of the historian—so long as there exists one man
whose heart warms at the revival of a virtuous deed—this
act of Great Britain will be blazoned forth in the annals of
fame, and shed undying lustre on her memory.

The Rev. David Day, in proposing the second resolution,
said—Your Honour, ladies, and gentlemen—In moving the
resolution which has been entrusted to me, I feel myself
placed in a delicate and somewhat painful position; not that
there is anything in this resolution I can object to, but there
is, I believe, existing in the minds of most persons, a love for
their native country which can scarcely be eradicated from
the mind. If there appears to be anything like blame or
at least suspicion cast on England, I can only say,

"England, with all thy faults, I love thee still."

There is in this resolution much to call forth our love to
Great Britain; she is spoken of as having gained to herself
glory, and the resolution attributes her chief glory to works
of humanity, justice, and benevolence. We have heard of
the glory of the British arms, of countries subjugated more

frequently than of advantages gained by subjugation; of
names famous in history for the blood which they have shed.
The language of the resolution places the glory of Britain
on a far better basis; and I imagine that the glory which
belongs to such men as Wilberforce, Clarkson, and others
that might be mentioned, is, that their names will be immortalised when monuments and marbles shall have crumbled
to dust, and, I hope, immortalised in the principles and
practices of the British Góvernment. I am very glad to
speak of justice and benevolence as the chief glory of
England. I am but little acquainted with other parts of
the world; but we find that England stands pre-eminent for
her justice, liberality, benevolence, and kindness. There
is no country where civil and religious privileges are enjoyed
to such an extent—where the poor are so well cared for,
and provided for, as in England,—(would to God they were
taken as much care of in Ireland!) We find that England
abounds with benevolent institutions for instruction—both
secular and religious education; and the chief glory of
England consists not in her navy or army, or her achieve-
ments in war, but in kindness to the needy and the oppressed, and long may she wear the crown of glory that she
has on her head. We do not meet to censure England,
much less to place ourselves under the flag of stars and
stripes. No; but we meet for the purpose of diffusing
information amongst ourselves, and to gather around us the
sympathies of our fellow-parishioners, in the difficulties
and dangers by which we are beset. I think we have
a right to complain that England has not dealt fairly
with us, and I think it is our duty to tell England so.
We prove our affection to our fathers and mothers, when
capable of judging of their conduct, by gently reminding
them of their faults, and we do only our duty if we ask
them to persevere in a good work which they have begun.
England has earned glory; other nations have stood by and
looked on. America has never yet arrived at that point of
moral courage as to induce her to say—" We will come to
the Bible, and practically carry out the principles that we

believe, and we will let the oppressed go free." They have
stood by, looked on, and have been glad when they thought
they saw any indications of failure, and have carried away
foolish and ridiculous reports—aye and carried away our
hard cash too, leaving salt-fish in exchange. No one has
had more substantial proofs than the Yankees themselves
that the abolition of slavery in these islands is not a failure.
Then look at the French. Great changes have taken place
with them; their former system of government is entirely
overthrown; they have formed themselves into a Republic,
and they have let the oppressed go free. Well, here is
something done. England took the lead, and she can look
back on other countries now following in her wake; and
this is what the resolution states. But while there is something very complimentary admitted, there is also something
very suspicious implied; namely, that she has stopped short
in the work, when she should have gone forward. We have
to put her in mind that she must not relax her efforts to
extend the blessings of freedom to every part of the world.
It implies that there is some fear she will relax—that the
glory will wax dim, even if the crown do not ultimately fall
from her head. We are to look at the signs of the times.
These have been alluded to by a previous speaker, and in
his remarks I fully concur. The ladies of England, in the
greatness of their zeal for abolition, gave up their luxuries,
because they would not, in an indirect way, give encouragement to slavery. There is something noble in this self-de-
nying, self-sacrificing zeal; but those who were ready then
to sacrifice themselves on the altar of benevolence, seem
now to bow down at the shrine of Mammon. We are sorry
to speak thus of Britain, but it seems to be the truth. I
speak with fear and trembling, but facts are stubborn things.
To drive a good bargain seems to be now the great object of
Britain and of the British Government; and what has been
the consequence? The slave-trade has increased in its horrors, because Britain must have cheap sugar. To emancipate her slaves she paid £20,000,000, and to compensate for
this she must have cheap sugar. Now, I thought benevolent

persons did not look for any remuneration—not even cheap sugar—for their deeds of justice; as for the reward of such deeds, that matter would be decided another day. But England has come down from her high standing; and if she is to drive a good bargain, do not let her do it at the expense of her own children. They have a right to look to her for protection—protection to person, property, trade, and commerce. There·are signs of a retrograde movement on the part of England, and this, certainly, must be a cause for lamentation. But the resolution urges that she should not go back. It is well known that perseverance is essential to success. In learning, in invention, in statesmanship, as well as in religion, there must be a continual advance in order to realise success. Let Britain, then, maintain what she has done. So long as a bondman is on the face of the earth, England has something to do. The people of England have committed themselves to this great principle. They dared not go back; if they do, they will become the ridicule of all Christian nations. If the scheme is carried out, other nations will be obliged to follow; if England relaxes, evil will be perpetuated. But, in the present case, it is only if the British people come around the British throne and say, our judgments, and principles, and efforts, are with you in this cause, that the Sovereign is in circumstances to maintain unimpaired the honour and dignity of her Crown. I anticipate the day, which, I trust, is not far distant, when such will be the language of the Christian people of England, and if nothing else will do, they will cheerfully endure a peaceful siege—a siege of ten years, if needful, in securing the honour of the Crown on behalf of the oppressed—a siege in which the nation will protect herself, not against bombs and bullets —for these, I trust, will never come nigh her—but against hogsheads, and puncheons, and bales, bearing on their front the forbidden brand of slavery. And if, through the Christian efforts of England, you in the meantime should be warmed and comforted, and enriched, I trust you would aid her during the straits of the siege to the full extent of your ability. You assisted Ireland in her famine, and would

you not aid England (Ireland and Scotland, too) in such
an honourable emergency? Once England has resolved to
occupy this ground—the only ground which will make her
influence of any avail—freedom will begin to advance
with graceful and rapid steps. The peaceful weapons by
which one victory has been gained will not be laid aside till
every remnant of slavery be destroyed. Then, as the certain
approach of freedom is announced by the organs of their
respective Governments, the planters of Cuba, Porto Rico,
and Brazil, yielding to the generous impulses of our common
nature, will follow the example of our own planters, and
receive the tidings with joyful acclamation—then the seeming
unkindness which now crushes our spirits, and the uncer-
tainty as to the future which embarrasses our plans, will be
taken away—the load which now weighs heavily on the
agriculture, trade, and commerce of the country, and ob-
structs, to a fearful extent, the instruction and elevation of
our liberated population, will be removed—then a happy and
powerful impulse will be given to the cause of freedom
throughout the whole of the western world, and no small
progress made in the coming of the day when "judgment
shall dwell in the wilderness, and righteousness remain in
the fruitful field; when the work of righteousness shall be
peace, and the effect of righteousness quietness and assurance
for ever."

The Rev. John Cowan then rose to propose the third
resolution, and spoke nearly as follows:—Your Honour,
ladies, and gentlemen, by an unavoidable circumstance, the
resolution I have the honour to propose did not reach me
till I came here to-day. I hope, therefore, that in calling
your attention to the important subject which the resolution
embraces, you will favour me with some degree of indulgence. I feel, and from the countenances of those around
me I perceive that you feel, that by uniting together in
efforts for the good of those who enslave others, or who are
themselves enslaved, we are pursuing a course fitted to have
a happy influence on our own minds. The exercise of the
benevolent feelings with which God has endowed us is a

proper and profitable exercise. For this reason, while I
deeply sympathise with my neighbours on the evils which of
late have befallen them, it is some alleviation to my regret,
both that they have borne them with equanimity, and that
our present circumstances, although distressing in themselves, have been the means of leading us to give special
attention to the good work of preventing the brand of
bondage from being put upon our fellow-men, and of taking
off the fetters from the slaves. In this good work you
reasonably expect the valuable co-operation of the Christian
people of Great Britain, and it is of no small importance
that you have confidence in them, as well as that they have
confidence in you. Late events have weakened, but, I trust,
they have not destroyed your confidence. England has not
wearied in her other Christian and philanthropic efforts—
but unfounded statements and specious arguments have been
put forward by influential, but interested or erring men,
which, through the multitude of other engagements, the
Christian minds of England have not as yet sufficiently
examined, and of which, indeed, in most cases, they had not
the means of forming a correct judgment. The question of
the slave-trade has in a great measure been overlooked—
but it has only been overlooked. Once the path of duty is
plainly seen, and the question cleared of the mists that have
been thrown around it, the Christianity of England will
show to the world that it is what it ever was, indomitable
in its opposition to oppression and injustice. In regard to
the treaties, of which my resolution speaks—in 1817, Spain
agreed "to abolish all slave-trade throughout her dominions" in May, 1820. In 1826, Brazil signed a treaty, by
which it would be " unlawful for the subjects of the Emperor
of Brazil to be concerned in the slave-trade, under any pretext or in any manner whatever." This treaty was to be in
force at the end of three years, after the exchange of ratifications. Ratifications were exchanged in 1827. According
to these treaties, the slaves introduced into Cuba and Porto
Rico during the last twenty-nine years, and those introduced into Brazil during the last nineteen years, are entitled

to their freedom. Britain agreed to pay to Spain £400,000 as an indemnification for the losses she might sustain by the abolition of the slave-trade. The Brazilian treaty was virtually in confirmation of a treaty previously agreed to by Portugal, in which Britain agreed to pay to Portugal about £600,000. The money in both instances has been well and truly paid. It has been given by one party and received by the other. But the men, on whose behalf these treaties have been made, have been imported as slaves, in late years, at the rate of 60,000 annually. Such are the treaties and such their fulfilment—treaties made by the Ministers of the British Crown. When we think of that Crown, preserved as it has been amidst the storms of ages, made sacred and blessed by means of the prayers of many Christians, do we not speak the language of truth and soberness when we say that the hitherto untarnished fame of the British Crown, worn by our honoured and beloved Sovereign, is seriously implicated in these treaties, particularly as they have been made with the strong on behalf of the oppressed, and as the violation of them is a violation of the law of humanity, of the common moral tone which permeates and engrosses the whole British nation? I have very great pleasure in submitting the resolution just read for your adoption this day.

The resolution was seconded by Patrick Morgan, Esq., and carried unanimously.

Mr. Litherland, in seconding the resolution, said—I feel myself inadequate to add almost anything to what has been said, and so well said; but there is one observation I feel justified in making, that if the cause had had none but avowed opposers to contend with—none behind the scene—we should not now have had to-day the trouble of advocating it. Ere now it would have triumphed. I am quite sure, that the philanthropic principles of the people at home would have carried it through without us. But the parties to whom I refer as our opponents are not here. They are British merchants in England—these are the opposers of the emancipation of those unfortunate slaves. When our death-

blow was served out to us, what was said by these free-
traders, what was it they advocated? It was, that they
required a trade to the Brazils, a great mart for all their
goods, that would give bread to the poor people at home—
all that they might live and thrive. What does it consist of,
Sir, this trade? It consists, Sir, of Manchester cotton and
Birmingham hardware, and Sheffield hardware. These go
to the Brazils, and what becomes of them then? All go, Sir,
to support the slave-trade. Of the poor victims of that
traffic, one out of five survives the passage, and then his
heart's blood is worked out of him—for what? for the sake
of our very fine and philanthropic and humane men in
Britain. These parties have influence with the venal press
to say to your resolutions—" the Jamaica people are rousing
themselves to get protection—it is protection they are fighting for!" I tell these gentlemen, and all the world, that
such protection as they talk of we never had. If taxing our
community for the produce of the island one hundred per
cent., and in some cases six, if that is protection, then we
had it. That was a prohibitory duty—so far prohibitory,
that when the poor people of England could not afford to
buy our produce, the surplus was sent to a foreign continental market, there to compete with all foreign produce ;
and it is a well-known fact, that this surplus ruled the
market of Britain. What, then, became of our protection?
It is also a well-known fact, if these gentlemen would own
it, that there is nothing else to pay them there (in Brazil)
for their manufactures, but the slave-trade. On the other
hand, it is well-known that a ton of sugar, manufactured by
a freeman, brings a far better return than one manufactured
by a slave. I mean, the working freeman requires more
from the manufacturer than the slave will. If honest, they
would find that honesty, after all, would be their best policy.
But their market is the coast of Africa. With these
observations I would conclude, only by saying further,
when I see the beaming eyes of the ladies (here the speaker
turned to the jury box, which this day was turned to a
happy use in accommodating that portion of the audience),

it ought to rouse our energies, dissipate our fears, and
encourage our hopes; and now I will say, give Jamaica a
fair field, and she asks no favour. Mr. Litherland sat down
amidst a burst of applause.

Mr. A. J. Lindo moved the fourth resolution, and said—
Ladies and gentlemen, the resolution I have the honour to
present for your consideration, is one which opens to view
the great cause of the deep distress which has overtaken our
beautiful island.

"That so long as the planters in Cuba, Porto Rico, and Brazil
are allowed illictly to fall back upon the slave-trade for the reple-
nishment of their labour lists, it is impossible for Jamaica, thinly
peopled as she is, ill supplied with continuous labour, and reduced
to the very brink of hopeless ruin, much longer to survive the
unfair and unjust competition with those countries, to which she
is exposed by the extraordinary Sugar Bill of 1846."

We who feel so deeply the practical result of the illegal
and unjust traffic alluded to in this resolution, need no explanation from me of the dire effects; but if any observations
I may make tend in any way to strengthen our desire to aid
in the suppression of this traffic, I most willingly lend my
feeble aid. In the words of this resolution, it is hopeless for
us much longer to survive the unfair and unjust competition
with the Spanish colonies and Brazil: and must not England now begin to feel the injustice she is doing her colonies
by not enforcing those treaties, which would at once and
for ever do away with slave traffic ? Can it be denied that the
greatest encouragement is given to slave trading by the
extraordinary Act of 1846 ? I call it extraordinary, because
it is notorious that just before the passing of this Act, it was
a matter of deep deliberation in Cuba, whether, in order to
obtain the British markets for her sugars, it would not be
politic to free her slaves. I often wonder what has become
of the boasted philanthropy of England, aided as it was by
the powerful influence of the softer sex, who held their meetings, entered into subscriptions, and by the more powerful
impetus than all, made their loves the bond by which they

bound their husbands, fathers, and brothers, to carry out the abolition of slavery in the British dominions ; and the lovely maiden, no doubt, in giving her heart, made the abolition of slavery a condition with her anxious suitor—and where, I ask, can there be more powerful influence? Since their success with the British colonies we hear no more of the English ladies. But I see here a strong indication of that influence being once more aroused, and I cheerfully tender my thanks for the attendance of ladies here to-day, to aid us in so just a cause. It is needless for us to hope that the people of England will give us credit for humanity in our endeavours to press on Ministers the necessity of enforcing the treaties for the suppression of the slave-trade ; but we may very justly retort, by asking, what motive induced Mr. Milner Gibson's motion in the House of Commons for the repeal of the act which makes Brazilians, found in the traffic, guilty of piracy, supported as that motion was by the interest of Manchester, Birmingham, and Sheffield? Was it humanity that dictated it—although it was declared to be so, alleging as they did that it operated to aggravate the horrors of the middle passage? Well, then, if they will not believe our motive to be that of humanity, let them, if they can, deny that it is founded on justice. Let us, then, call on Ministers to do us justice—to do justice to themselves, for it is most surprising to see England permitting her statutes, founded on treaties, to be violated as they are. In the course of the debate on Mr. Gibson's motion it was urged, that the Act sought to be repealed increased the horrors of the middle passage, for Mr. Hume, in support of the motion, stated, " He believed the means adopted for the suppression of the slave-trade by the maintenance of a squadron on the coast of Africa, instead of effecting that object, only tended to aggravate the evils of that abominable traffic." In answer to which, Lord Palmerston replied, " I deny, in the first place, that the means which have been adopted have entirely failed. They have done immense good ; they have prevented enormous evil. I deny, in the next place, that opinion which has passed from mouth to mouth, and is taken up without examination, that

the methods of suppression we have adopted have aggravated
the horrors of the middle passage; whenever we come to
discuss that question, I will show that it is not the case—that
the horrors of the middle passage were greater in former
periods than at the present time." I think my Lord Palmerston might, with justice, be asked, not whether the
horrors of the middle passage exist in a modified form, but
why they exist at all. Do ministers require proof of the
existence of the slave-trade by Spain and Brazil? Why it is
so notorious, that here we have it illustrated in a paper
largely circulated throughout the British dominions (the
Illustrated London News), where it is shown not to be a
chance trading, but a regularly organised system ; for in this
account of the destruction of a factory, with barracoons, &c.,
it is stated, " The premises destroyed were the residence and
factory of Don Jose Louis, a Spanish dealer." And speaking
of the loss of property, it states, " The amount of loss sustained by the slave dealers must have been very great, as
they were quite unprepared for such a visit, and their stores
were full of goods." The general idea is, that from £100,000
to £200,000 worth of property was burned, perhaps more.
And who supplied the property? No doubt the manufacturers of Manchester, Birmingham, and Sheffield can answer
that ; is it, therefore, to be wondered at, that they also desire
free trade in slaves ? What led to the conquest of this very
island ?—was it not the non-observance of a treaty with England and Spain?—was it not because Spain, in contravention
of her treaty, took British vessels in these seas, and committed acts of cruelty on her seamen? And, although Great
Britain at that period had no acknowledged settlement in
the western world, she avenged the cruelties inflicted on a
handful of her subjects, by sending an expedition to St.
Domingo; failing there, they made a descent on this island,
and captured it. Will England in the present day, (if I may
use the expression) omnipotent as she is, permit her subjects
in this and the other West India Islands to be utterly ruined
from the non-observance of treaties entered into for our
protection? I trust not. I hope we shall yet have justice

dealt out to us, and our utter ruin averted. Let but the slave-trade be put an end to, and I am sure I speak the sentiments of every planter around me when I say, we can, and are ready and willing to compete with any foreign colony in the sugar market; and the stoppage of the slave-trade, there cannot be a doubt, will ultimately put an end to slavery. I take leave of the subject, looking to the future with hope, not fear.

Mr. G. B. Da Costa seconded the resolution, which was unanimously carried.

The Rev. Mr. Teall, in seconding the fourth resolution, said —Looking round on the large assemblage of people gathered here to-day, seeing the deep interest taken by all classes in the subject which brings us together, and looking at the variety of talent brought to bear on it, we cannot but be impressed with the fact that it is all in keeping with these times. I suppose Port Maria never witnessed before a meeting like this; and I am heartily glad that the people of Jamaica can lay aside their differences, and come together to discuss such a subject. If anything is fitted to give a character to the age in which we live, it is the bringing together of extremes. Places, at one time viewed as so distant that they could not be reached, people can go to and return from, and not be missed from their neighbourhood. So in the political world, if you look to various distinctions that at one time existed, they are now lost; parties have been broken up—their identity is gone. The opposition benches are occupied with those who vote with Ministers, and Government men are found opposing Government men; and who can say that the change in Jamaica is not in keeping with the times? So in the religious world. Religious differences are apt to excite more animosity, more strife, more wrangling, than any other; but we have lived to see the time when Christians of every creed can meet together amicably, and give up their sectarianism, and do this without for one moment risking their denominational distinctions. We can meet as churchmen or dissenters, without a cross word or angry look. The change is one for the better. And among the various classes of men a great change has taken place, and this meeting is characteristic of it. We have lived to see the time when men of all classes and professions can express their opinions fully and freely, upon any and every subject in the country. If we extend our view, and look abroad on the various families of the earth, do we not see signs that the times are rapidly advancing when all men shall meet as brethren? We see the fraternal visits now going on between France and England. At one time Englishmen hated the French: Frenchmen now come over to England, and they receive a hearty welcome. By-and-by, there shall be one bond of brotherhood, when all men shall live in peace, and as members of one family. I am glad, as an Englishman, to second this resolution, because I like to say something in praise of England. The resolution speaks of the policy Great Britain has followed with the view of extirpating slavery from the earth, and gives her credit for having exhibited great wisdom, foresight, and justice, in the course she took of entering into treaties with other powers, and particularly with Spain and Brazil. But it is notorious that the treaties are quite disregarded, and matters, instead of mending, are growing worse and worse. Yes, your Honour, we speak of the foresight of England, and men may be as far-seeing as others, and yet an honest man cannot see so far as a rogue. The Spaniard has not the courage to refuse the treaties and the bribe ; he pockets the treaties and the cash, that he may have both hands to work iniquity with greediness. Four hundred thousand pounds were paid to Spain—that would fit out some ships to send to the coast of Africa. Who can tell what have been the horrors caused indirectly by these very treaties? And if Britain were to stand still in the face of them, we would say—Why you have done mischief, and only mischief. There was a time when slavery was legalised, and it was an offence against the law if the captain of a slaver carried more than the ship was chartered to carry. But what is the case now ? They give the poor people no room to sit. Will the vessel sail well? how does she behave before a stiff breeze? will she cope with the cruiser? These are the questions they ask ; nothing at all is cared for, or inquired about, as to accommodations ; they think only how they may stow plenty of people, though it should be at the expense of losing many lives—the value of those they save is so much increased, it becomes worth their while to carry on the traffic, in a money point of view, at every risk, because their slave sugar is now brought to compete with our free sugar. We shall cry out shame on Britain, if she do not come to the help of the injured—yea, to the help of the weak against the mighty. One thing is exceedingly pleasing ; we are unanimous in this matter. In former times, when a cry of ruin was made, another party sprang up, and said, " They are not so bad." Here all cry, " Ruin, ruin ! help, help ! " There is poverty everywhere ; and although poverty is not in itself a blessing, it is not unaccompanied with blessings. It has broken down barriers to union—made men forget their differences. It has concentrated their energies, that they may seek, as one man, the good of Jamaica. When we look at the spirit that has been awakened, we do not despair for the cause of humanity. We believe the time will very soon come, when there shall not be a slave left on the face of the earth.

The Rev. R. Robinson being called upon, in the absence of Henry Westmorland, Esq., to propose the fifth resolution, spoke as follows :—Mr. Chairman, ladies, and gentlemen, I rise, I must confess, with some little hesitation, to propose the next resolution, which had been entrusted to one whom it would so much better have become to undertake the task. I will read it to you—

" That whilst the inhabitants of the British possessions in the West Indies have, notwithstanding untold difficulties and disheartening trials, willingly, loyally, and faithfully performed their allotted part in the great and godlike work of abolishing the abominable traffic in human beings—and the mother country is annually spending her wealth, and the lives of her brave seamen and marines, in maintaining a costly squadron in the unwholesome region of the African coast, with a view to suppress the heartless contraband—our rulers are bound, by every principle of humanity, not less than of justice to England herself and her suffering colonies, to enforce, by all available means, the observance of the solemn treaties already entered into with the Governments of Spain and Brazil for the same noble object."

I have said, Sir, that I rise with some hesitation to move this resolution, which I would much rather have contented myself with simply seconding; not because I feel myself so much out of place on an occasion like the present, but because all that has been so boldly said on the subject has utterly failed to convince me that we may trust ourselves at all times safely in the arena of popular controversy. When the clergy, Sir, contrary to their accustomed habits, are coming forth from the retirement of the holy place—from their more immediate and peculiar duty of ministering in holy things, of guarding well the bulwarks of our holy Zion—and are taking an active part in a great public movement, there are persons, I doubt not, to whom it will not be unacceptable to hear why we think ourselves justified in doing so, and why I think myself, this once, at least, perfectly within the line of duty in maintaining each position set forth in the resolution which I have just read. We act as we are doing, Sir, because the question about which we are now concerned is one involving, on the one hand, the first principles of humanity—the very essence of charity—much of morality—many of the highest and best interests of man. Then, again, on the other hand, our time and agency can hardly be thought to be ill-used, in lending all the strength of our intellect and influence in the hallowed and hallowing cause of freedom against slavery—of honour against perfidy—of afflicted and struggling honesty and obedience against rampant wickedness—against the meanest, basest, and most heartless of all theft and outrage—against the painful profligacy of the man-stealer—against the illicit oppression and bondage of myriads who should be free. These, Sir, are some of the reasons convincing to myself, and I should hope, also, to this meeting, which induce us, after the bright example of our respected Bishop, to join your righteous and deserving cause; and, as the features of the case are now strikingly altered from what they were even a few years ago, I apprehend that not here alone, but in England also, the body of the clergy will be roused to a determined advocacy, which shall so increase the " pressure from without," that it may, we hope, be more quickly felt ; and your cry for relief and justice will be so loud, and so effectually rendered, that, whilst the friends of humanity shall again buckle on their sacred armour, and echo back the thunder of your complaint, new champions shall be enlisted, and all be cheered on to fresh vigour and fresh action, until not alone the degrading and accursed contraband trade in human beings shall be abolished, but the time be hastened when the plague-spot of slavery itself shall be wiped away and healed ; then England's honour shall be vindicated—her sincerity no longer questioned—her prowess no longer defied ; then the rights of her languishing colonies will have been duly weighed and enforced, and we shall hear no more of the anomaly of the produce of slave labour being mixed up in the jumbled category of free trade, for the best and most effectual of all reasons, that the shackles of oppression and injustice will have been struck off the limbs of thousands now robbed of their liberty, in spite of solemn treaties, and the plighted troth of kings and princes ; then, in a word, humanity itself shall be dis-enthralled, and restored to its rightful honours and privileges. So much for the general question. And who shall doubt, then, either the reason or the sense of duty which has led myself and others of my sacred calling, to take our stand with our fellow-colonists in the enunciation of their wrongs— in the proclamation of their blighted prospects and fast-vanishing hopes—in the maintenance of the moral truth, that even a true principle may be pushed too far, and that it is so, whenever a large section of a great and enlightened empire is sacrificed and blighted for the benefit of another section, or for the whole? And this doctrine is pre-eminently true, when the freed and free-born children of that empire are sacrificed at the shrine of the worthless god, Mammon, who has no benign smiles for us, and whose favours are all showered into the lap of the alien, who will not care, in the end, to sting the generous hand of England, who, in her mistaken policy only, I do believe, has been

cajoled into fostering him in his very wickedness. I may be
permitted to say a word or two on some of the points stated
in this resolution before I have done. Right loyally, and
(as far as I have seen) I can bear witness, right willingly
and faithfully has this colony, at least, borne its allotted part
in the great work of abolishing slavery. To the difficulties
which you have so patiently encountered, I know not well
how I may bear sufficiently strong testimony; nor know I
how to describe the melancholy picture of ruin which meets
us at every turn, in every class, of every pursuit; or of the
unhappy change which has come upon the land in the ten
short years during which I have resided amongst you.
Were it not, indeed, that we have the knowledge and belief
that "God will protect the right," actual despair might well
take place of—what shall I call it?—of the general con-
sternation, which is relieved only by very rare tints of
brighter prospects, and lingering anticipations of better
times. Yes, Sir, the rose of our Sharon is blasted—the
heart of Jamaica is very sad. "Men's hearts are everywhere failing them for fear" of the terrible results which
must ensue upon hope and succour much longer deferred.
Who that rides through this magnificent island and sees the
thorns and briars now occupying the plains that were so
lately covered with a waving harvest of canes, or the hill-side
on which once bloomed the fragrant coffee, now a neglected
waste—who, in short, that beholds the surface of the land
thus defaced, commerce destroyed, our social system un-
hinged, can help feeling his heart sicken at the prospect?
Who can contemplate Jamaica as she was but recently,
smiling in prosperity and her newly-gained freedom, and as
now she is—dejected and care-worn—a very wreck struggling with the breakers—her men unmanned and her case
desperate — without apostrophising the unhappy country,
still beautiful even in her decline, somewhat after the manner
that Byron did prostrate Greece, whose greatness he only
recognised in its ruins :—

> " Shrine of the mighty! can it be
> That this is all remains of thee?"

Surely, Sir, when this description of things, which is unfortunately over-true, is made known to our Queen, to our rulers, and amongst the friends of humanity at home, with one voice, and one purpose, as it will be now, England will see the necessity of a speedy and determined course of remedial action. She will not let it be longer asserted by a sneering world (as I have heard it asserted in more than one foreign land), that her philanthropy has grown cold—that hypocrisy would be a far more fitting motto for her shield—that she has spent her millions of gold, and risked the energy and credit of her navy for naught—that her work is not accomplished, because she lacks either the will or the moral courage to effectuate the great purpose of benevolence, which, foremost among the nations, she so worthily began, and has, up to a certain point, so well carried on. But no!—These things must not be said of her. England is willing, for she would not otherwise have done what she has at so great cost and pains. And if, after the peaceful machinery of diplomacy and the restrictions of commerce have been tried in vain, her moral courage and her prowess (which heaven forefend!) must be tried to the limit against the perfidious nations who are feeding on the bread which falls from England's table, and rightfully belongs to England's own children; if, after all, the strong right arm of truth and honour must be raised to strike the blow that shall let in the full, bright flood of freedom on the world— then " God's will be done!" Our prayers, in such a case, may well ascend for the Lord's host, going forth, not for the first time, in a righteous cause; and He will be with them, until, in his own good time, the cry of gladness and triumph that greets your returning commerce and prosperity shall proclaim to the world that the conflict is over—that your temporary difficulties have passed away—and that, under God, the victory and its glorious effects are for yourselves and the free.

The Rev. Mr. Simpson, in moving the sixth resolution, said—It would not be proper to occupy the attention of this respectable audience with any lengthened remarks, but I may be allowed to offer a few words in support of the resolution entrusted to my care. There is one feature in our present movement which, I think, is worthy of notice, as auguring well for its success. It is this: that among the various interests which happen to be involved in it, a due proportion of regard is given to each, and none is overlooked. It is remembered that money is not the all of man, and that the commercial and agricultural interests, allowedly of vast and necessary moment, are not the only interests we are looking to, or set a value upon. There are considerations why we should render a helping hand in this great movement which respect us as men, as citizens of the great world, as well as those which affect us as members of interesting communities in these western isles, that have just entered on a new era in their history. These are the interests of humanity, in relieving our fellow-men from the sorest evils that can afflict them, and obtaining for them the first rights of our common nature. The movement is of a most expansive character and of corresponding magnitude—to rescue a large portion of the human family from crying ills under which it is groaning, and to assail and batter down those walls which inhumanity, goaded on by avarice, has reared against the improvement of the human species. It involves in it immediately, or by consequence, all that is comprehended in the great cause of universal liberty to man. But while it calls into exercise the general affection of respect and regard for the great human brotherhood, and sympathy for a peculiarly degraded and afflicted portion of it, it looks also to the state of our own suffering communities, and the manifold evils which late measures seem to be entailing upon them. Our changed position, as communities now seeking to attain our right place in the scale of social improvement, is kept prominently in view. Hence the interests of education, morality, and religion, are all looked to, it being rightly considered that these form the only solid and enduring basis of the prosperity of this or any land. These highest interests are largely suffering in the general calamity. And it is this view of our situation we wish to hold up and press on the attention of that land which has shown by deeds, and not words only, that she understands better than any other of the nations of the earth at what price to rate these interests, being herself the parent of them to us. For this we honour her, and now, when these are hazarded, we make our appeal to her on their behalf. Of late years, England contributed largely to the religious and educational improvement of the emancipated part of the population; but just at the time when the continuance of her help would have been the measure of wisdom, as well as mercy, it was in a great degree withdrawn. At the same time a course of declension had begun among the people, attributable to various causes. And now, from the new cause which has been operating, the distress which prevails and affects every class, matters are assuming their most serious aspect. The country is disabled, and friends are withdrawing their wonted assistance. That ignorance and irreligion, heathen practices and superstitions, and their inseparable concomitants, vice and immorality, are rife in many quarters, it is impossible to deny. That a general profligacy of manners prevails among that large class that are either attached to no Christian society, or attached only by name, is too apparent, and, alas! the number is not small to whom the Christian pastor may turn and say, "Ye did run well, who did hinder that you should no more obey the truth?" There are, doubtless, means within ourselves of ameliorating our moral and spiritual condition, and I may be allowed, without being called an accuser of any, to notice what is too patent, that the claims of religion are not inquired into, and, consequently, not regarded by the more influential portion of the community to the extent that might be expected. This makes a large item still in the account against our social improvement, though we have of late years to hail symptoms of a changed state of feeling, and of respect for the claims of religion, among the higher classes, attended with a corresponding good influence on the lower. Even the presence of the ladies in our public meetings is a token for good, while it imparts strength to our cause. The discipline through which we have passed has

not been without its advantage. It has been a sifting time
to churches, to separate the chaff from the wheat; and, were
it duly considered, it might be seen to be, after all, a providence of mercy, and its proper fruit would be a reforming
tide setting in where its influence would be powerfully and
most beneficially felt, which would give new power for bearing the trials of the evil day should it be prolonged, and
prepare us for turning to right account the day of prosperity
when it arrived. But that to which the resolution points
attention, is the failing of the agency whose direct work it is
to arrest the progress of moral declension, and to seek, in
the use of the divinely appointed means, the moral and
spiritual regeneration of the country. It is not to be overlooked that all classes have been doing their part, more or
less, of late years, to support religion and its institutions. I
can at least assert this of the inhabitants of our own parish,
who have contributed (including every class) not a small
portion of what has built our chapels, and who would continue to assist as they have done, but for the want of means.
No doubt, many take advantage, from low views, of a time
of depression to withhold what they might give. But this
is an evil which works at all times; in the day of prosperity
as in our worst days, though after a different form. The
agency in the work of moral and religious reformation is
necessarily suffering; some of them from the withdrawal of
aid from friends at a distance, and (which is the case of all)
the inability of their own people to do as they have done in
supporting religious ordinances. Should this agency be
withdrawn, the work will either totally fall away, or go into
other hands, the least fitted for it, and the responsibility
involved in such an issue is such as the friends of religion in
another land will surely not rashly or inconsiderately incur,
whilst the consequences are such as it is fearful to contemplate. These things we wish to urge before the conscience
of Christian England,—a tribunal where they will surely not
be disregarded. If they can do nothing else, they can lift
their united voices for the enforcement of violated treaties,
and for delivering honest men from the competition of the

worst contraband that could possibly exist. In the spirit in which the present movement has been conceived, and taken up, and is now carrying on, I hope we discern a rainbow of hope arching the cloud which has settled over us, and is darkening our sky with its gloom ; we have, I think, touched chords which vibrate in the breasts, not only of all true Britons, but of all true philanthropists, whether in the eastern or western hemisphere. What is there on the one side of the cause but truth and honesty, and manly independence (for even protection is not asked, and is not wanted)? It is to turn our industry to the account of good, and not of evil—to produce and foster a healthy state of our own community, and thereby to foster trade and commerce of a legitimate kind with England and the world, whilst those against whom the crusade is making, rank among their agents the veriest miscreants on the face of the earth, the foulest dregs of this evil world's scum, and with whom all who have the smallest regard for a pure reputation ought to scorn connection, even the most remote. We can appeal to the God of truth and rectitude, and mercy, for the goodness of our cause, humbly under a sense that we have all come short, but with confidence that the cause is His as well as ours. And as England has won laurels already in this same field, we hope laurels await her again, by a general rise of Britons in the cause of her own suffering colonies whom she made free, and of universal emancipation; and that our good Queen's reign, auspiciously begun by the manumission of her own slaves, will yet be rendered more signal and illustrious by the angel of fame, whose voice has been heard through the breadth and length of her wide empire, proclaiming liberty to the slave, carrying the tidings to the earth's utmost bound, north and south, east and west, sounding with the silver trumpet of peace, liberty,—liberty to every slave; proclaiming in the ear of Africa—poor, stricken, bleeding Africa—look up! for thy redemption, long sighed and prayed for, is now at length come; and England will earn the name, not of the conqueror, but (what is unspeakably better fame) the deliverer of the world!

The Rev. John Campbell then rose and said—I have much pleasure in seconding the resolution which has now been proposed by my friend and brother, Mr. Simpson, and, in doing so, I do not deem it necessary, after what has been said, and especially at this advanced hour of the day, to detain the meeting with any lengthened remarks. The resolution, however, is a most important one, and I cannot refrain from saying a few words in connection with it. That this island is at present in a very depressed and almost ruined condition, so far as its temporal interests are concerned, is a truth which I believe no one, who knows anything of the facts of the case, will venture to deny ; and that the religious and educational interests of the country, to which the resolution refers, are now imperilled, and that, unless some remedy be speedily devised and applied, these interests—the interests of religion, education, and morality in the land—must greatly, perhaps irreparably, suffer, all who are capable of thinking on the subject will at once admit. That it is, therefore, our solemn duty to contemplate these greatest of all evils, to state the consequences which we foresee, the fears by which we are alarmed, and the convictions which we entertain, in reference to the responsibility of the people and government of England in this matter, is abundantly obvious. And, Sir, I would ask, are we not warranted in entertaining the fears of which the resolution speaks, in reference to the interests of religion and education in this island ? Is not our trade diminishing ? Are not our difficulties increasing ? Is not the competition into which we have been unjustly brought with slave labour in other lands, ruinous and destructive ? Are not the industrious habits, which our population were beginning to form, in danger of receiving a fatal blow from the abandonment of cultivation ? Is not the ability, in short, of all classes of the community to support institutions of every kind, small, indeed, compared with what it must be, before these institutions can be efficiently supported for any length of time ? Yes, Sir, our fears are warranted ; and it is my solemn conviction that unless the voice of our warning and remonstrance is speedily heard and attended to, our worst fears will, ere long, be realised.   It is well known, Sir, that several Christian churches in England and Scotland have long looked upon this land with the deepest interest, and that these Christian churches have manifested their interest in the cause of religion and education in this country, by sending hither and supporting many ministers of the Gospel, and many teachers of the young, who have laboured with just fidelity and with marked success amongst the population of the island.   Large sums of money and many valuable lives have thus been expended for the advancement of the cause of Christ in this land; and, assuredly, those who have thus contributed of their substance for this purpose have not been weary in well doing.   They expected, however, and were certainly entitled to expect, that the people of this country, when they came to know and appreciate the value of the religious privileges which they enjoy, would, agreeably to what many of us believe to be the law of Christ in this matter, do what they could to support among themselves the ordinances of the Gospel.   This expectation has hitherto been to a great extent realised; but such is now the wofully altered state of matters, in regard to the ability of the people generally, that I think they cannot in present circumstances be reasonably expected to contribute very much either for religious or educational institutions.   What may be the consequence of this, I cannot tell; but when I consider what the Christian Churches and Societies to which I have referred have already done for Jamaica, and when I consider, also, that new and more interesting fields of missionary enterprise are opening up in other parts of the world, I think it more than probable that assistance will be diminished, if not altogether withdrawn, and that thus what has been gained will be irrecoverably lost.   Sir, this is a result, the faintest prospect of which every Christian heart must bitterly deplore.   And permit me to say, that the present state of matters affects not Jamaica only; it affects and deeply affects Africa, too.   Africa now lies in her blood. The balm for the bleeding wounds of Africa is found in the

Gospel of Christ. The Bible and the Missionary of the Cross, and these only, by the Divine blessing, will regenerate the sons and daughters of Ethiopia. "But how shall they hear without a preacher, and how shall he preach except he be sent?" And if those institutions which have been founded in this land for the express purpose of training up descendants of Africans for preaching the Gospel to the teeming millions of Africa, who are now perishing for lack of knowledge—if these institutions, I say, should be necessarily abandoned for want of support, how awfully dark will be the prospect for degraded and blood-stained Ethiopia! But, Sir, I am persuaded that better things than these are in store for us, and things which shall yet make our hearts to rejoice, though I thus speak. The resolution speaks of Christian England; and, Sir, if we make our appeal to the Christianity of England, in connection with this accursed slave-trade and its effects upon this country, I have no fear that our appeal will be in vain. Can we forget what the Christianity of England has already done? It was the Christianity of England which aroused that spirit of abhorrence to slavery—awakened by Clarkson and Wilberforce, both eminent disciples of the Saviour—which rested not until 800,000, held in bondage, stood erect and free. It was the Christianity of England which hesitated not for a moment to sacrifice twenty millions of money in order that the glorious result might be gained. And, Sir, what the Christianity of England has already done, it will again accomplish; for if I am persuaded of one thing more than another in connection with this matter, it is of this—that when the Christian mind of England and of Scotland has become fully enlightened on this subject; when it is clearly seen that the slave-trade, with all its horrors, is directly encouraged—that slavery is directly countenanced and maintained—that the cheapness on which so many are insisting, and of which some are boasting as the result of their efforts, is the "price of blood" and the price of souls—then, I say, I am well persuaded that no sacrifice will be deemed too great, no self-denial too painful, in order that the British

nation may be freed from this awful responsibility, and that
the curse of God may, by God's mercy, be averted from that
highly-favoured land. Sir, this cause is ours, but it is also
God's. It is the cause of humanity, it is the cause of
morality, it is the cause of religion, and therefore it is the
cause of God himself. Whilst we express our feelings, then,
and demand our rights, let us pray for a blessing on our
efforts, and we must and we shall succeed. It has been said
by a previous speaker, and said well and forcibly, that we
are strong in the justice of our claims ; but, oh, let us see,
above all, that we are strong in the purity of our motives,
and in the piety of our desires, and in the earnestness and
importunity of our entreaties to Him, whose faithful promise
it is to break every yoke, and to let the oppressed go free.
Then, assuredly, shall our hearts be made to rejoice. The
sigh of the needy and the cry of the destitute shall be heard
and answered—the last slave shall heave the last sigh, and
the last chain shall be trodden beneath the heel of triumphant freemen ! I beg to second the resolution.

The Rev. John Davidson rose to propose the seventh
resolution—

"That this meeting cordially approves of the resolutions and
general line of proceeding adopted at the influential meeting held
in Spanish Town, on the 24th day of May last"—

and spoke as follows :—In submitting to you a resolution,
expressing approbation of the results of the great meeting
held in Spanish Town, I shall not attempt to add to the
information or to emulate the eloquence which has been
brought to bear upon their and our common object. Influential as that meeting deserves to be, on account of the rank,
the talents, the number, and the unanimity of those who
composed it, it is not chiefly on these grounds that I claim
your concurrence, but because I am convinced that the
opinions and feelings of all here present are in unison with
theirs. We all see and lament that the upper and middle
classes of the community are tending to poverty—the lower,
to pauperism with its attendant evils—ignorance, irreli-

gion, and barbarism. We all attribute these evils to the unequal competition into which our agriculturists have been forced with the products of countries still polluted by the presence of slavery. In seeking relief, we ask no favour, no protection, from the mother country. We ask a measure of bare justice. We ask her not to consummate the ruin of her colonies, by encouraging foreigners to perpetuate a system which she has denounced as unchristian and long striven to abolish. We ask her to vindicate her own honour, by enforcing the observance of treaties—the observance of which would put us on a parity with those who have held an unjust advantage over us. In the name of humanity, of Christianity, of patriotism, we implore our mother country not to abdicate her high rank among the nations—not to frustrate her past efforts in the cause of freedom—not to rivet tighter those chains which she has loosened—which it is her mission, and I trust, under God's blessing, it will be her glory to burst asunder.

Mr. Henry Rigg rose to second the resolution, which was unanimously carried.

Mr. J. W. Gray then proposed the following resolution :—

"That a committee be appointed to draw up a respectful memorial to her most gracious Majesty the Queen ; also petitions to the right hon. the House of Peers and the House of Commons. The memorial to be transmitted by the Chairman to his Excellency the Governor, to be forwarded in the most dutiful and proper manner to her Majesty. That the Right Hon. Lord Brougham and Vaux be requested to take charge of the petition to the House of Lords, and Benjamin D'Israeli, Esq., M.P., of that to the House of Commons. Committee—His Honour the Custos, Rev. D. Day, Rev. J. Simpson, the Rector, and A. J. Lindo, Esq."

Seconded by Mr. A. De Souza, and carried unanimously. The next resolution was moved by Mr. W. Litherland.

"That this meeting earnestly invites the co-operation of benevolent and philanthropic societies and individuals, in all parts of the world, for the accomplishment of the objects contemplated in the preceding resolutions."

Mr. Kelly seconded it.

The greatest unanimity prevailed throughout the day, and the meeting separated at five o'clock.

We close these reports with that of the meeting held on the 4th of July, in Metcalfe, the youngest of the twenty-two great parishes into which the island of Jamaica is divided.

In pursuance of a requisition to his Honour the Custos, to convene a public meeting for the purpose of co-operating with the other parishes, for the total suppression of the odious traffic in slaves, the same was held at the Court-house, Annotto Bay, on the day we have named. The meeting was very well attended, and was also graced by the presence of the ladies.

Patrick C. Crichton, Esq., was unanimously called to the chair.

The Chairman—Gentlemen, the unexpected honour which has been conferred upon me, in calling me to take the chair at this meeting, I was totally unprepared for. You may, however, rest assured I will, to the utmost of my abilities, fulfil the duties which you have so kindly imposed on me. I came down to attend the meeting, in order to join in any measures that might be adopted to ameliorate the condition of the suffering African slave. I can only express, gentlemen, my cordial co-operation in your proceedings, and trust that your endeavours may attain the desired end. I shall not detain you any longer, as I know there are several gentlemen who wish to address you. I will therefore call upon Dr. Clarke to move the first resolution.

T. Clarke, Esq., M.D., rose and said—Sir, in rising to speak to the resolution which it has fallen to my lot to propose on the present occasion, I confess, Sir, that I approach the subject not altogether without that sense of weariness which arises from hope deferred. Not that I have any doubts, still less any despair, of the ultimate success of the movement in which we are engaged—(a movement begun by us some years ago) — for " freedom's battle once

begun "—and it is the battle of freedom that we are now
fighting—

> " Freedom's battle once begun,
> Bequeathed from bleeding sire to son,
> Though vanquished oft—is ever won."

And it by no means follows that because the end and aim of
our efforts may be still distant, they have been altogether
useless in preparing the way for their accomplishment. But
were I still less inclined than I am to re-enter upon this
agitation, the recent assemblage held with the same views
in the legislative metropolis of this island, under the highest
auspices which rank, station, and character could confer upon
a meeting—were I much less inclined than I really am, the
prestige of that great meeting furnishes an encouragement
which it would be treason to humanity not to respond to.
(At this moment some ladies entered the Court-house.)
And, Sir, if still further encouragement were wanting, the
auspicious entrance at this moment of that sex, ever true to
us in the sure hour of desolation and trial—true, I say, to the
sufferings of humanity as the needle to the pole—the happy
omen, I say, would nerve me with a lion's heart, in a cause
even less worthy and noble than the one we are engaged in.
But, to return to the subject of the Spanish Town meeting,
I cannot help remarking upon it, as somewhat curious, that
gentlemen who had up to that period, or nearly so, stood
aloof from all agitation against the iniquitous and ruinous
competition to which the Act of 1846 had doomed us—who
held it to be something like treason to condemn that Act—
who mocked at the loud cry of financial ruin as a delusion
and a snare—should now come forward to sympathise with
the public voice, and that for the first time during the late
remarkable legislative recess. Sir, it is a patent and striking
fact, and not less striking as a coincidence, that up to that
time there had been no practical interference on the part of
the representatives of the people with the beatitudes of quarter-
day. Up to that time there was still an " oasis ; " amid the
wreck of fortune all around them, there was still a paradise
of punctual payment for them.

" In the desert a fountain still springing,
    In the wide waste they still had their tree,
    And a bird in the solitude singing,
    Which warbled, dear Barclay,* of thee !"

Now their sympathies are awakened, they begin to see, and
admit, and deplore the general distress ; I will not be so
ungenerous as to say that " Timeo Danaos et dona ferentes,"
because, from the pure, elevated, and justly-esteemed
character of the source whence this great movement is generally supposed to have originated, it is entirely out of the
question to suppose that any unbecoming motives could have
had place in it ; but whilst we cordially and frankly accept
the powerful aid which that movement furnishes, it is due to
the exertions which we have so long been making—it is due
to our own honest and earnest, though humble efforts, to
ask—it is due to our country and to freedom that we should
ask, where were those voices, when they might happily have
stayed or averted the downfall of Jamaica ?   Where were
they all, great officers of State as they are, when the mortal
blow was levelled ? When the deep damnation of that accursed
deed first waked the echoes of coming woe, disaster, and
ruin, where were they ?   Silent still, and silent all ; nay,
many of them were worse than silent.   If the competition
involved the guilt of human blood and the ruin of Jamaica,
and to that they have now set their hand and seal, why not
have denounced it, as we did, at the onset, and on the same
principle ?   Mistake me not, Sir.   In commenting on these
circumstances I would seriously guard myself against joining
in any Jacobin cry against official men.   I believe the high
places of Jamaica to be filled, for the most part, by men who
are an honour to their office and ornaments to society, and I
for one should bitterly bewail the day (if come it must) when
such men should be wanting to her offices and in her society.
But with all this free tribute of respect and homage, it is due
to the welfare of the island to bear in mind that they are but
men, and that our views for that welfare must not be sacri-

* Receiver-general.

ficed to the mere prestige of rank and station. The age of patriots is past, and we live in an era when it seems that every sentiment which ennobles men and nations is to be sacrificed at the shrine of a sordid or a greedy lust; and I am sorry to say that the melancholy moral which past events in this island seem to point to, is—that if we wish to carry the weight of official names with us, it must be by showing them, in a homely and practical way, that their fortunes depend upon the general welfare of Jamaica. But, Sir, at that great meeting there was much of eloquence. I was, in particular, struck with the forcible address of one reverend gentleman, a visitor, and a stranger on these shores, in painting, in dark but true colours, our fallen fortunes. The hand of heaven, I think he said, had done everything for you. "The sense of vision might exhaust itself in taking in all the loveliness and beauty of your landscapes! How is it that, with all this, you present the moral aspect of a land smitten by famine or pestilence? Where are all your great families?" Oh, Sir, I could not, in reading these striking expressions, but recall those memorable lines of the poet, which you are no doubt familiar with — the invocation addressed by the shade of Troy's departed hero to the sleeping son of Anchises—

> "Heu fuge, nate Deâ, teque his (ait) eripe flammis.
> Hostis habet muros, ruit alto à culmine Troja:
> Sat patriæ Priamoque datum: si Pergama dextrâ
> Defendi possent, etiam hâc defensa fuissent."

"Hostis habet muros!" Slavery has got possession of the sugar markets. The marts of England are the great ulcer where all its guilt and corruption gather, and find an issue! Many is the ruined father of a family who, in the abandonment of the island, or of his patrimonial acres, could have said, with drooping head and broken heart—"Sat patriæ Priamoque datum: si Pergama dextrâ defendi possent, hâc defensa fuissent.—If the vigour and energy of an honest right hand could have saved me and mine from ruin, it had not been wanting." I have sunk my capital in improved modes of cultivation, and in modern and scientific implements of agriculture. I have combined industry and economy with the most ardent enterprise, and have imported all into the management of my estate; but what avails it? " Hostis habet muros!" Not the stranger, nor my country's enemy—not the foes of my nation, but the foes of man—have been let loose and harked on against me! Hell-hounds! whose occupation it is to rend in sunder every human tie!—to sear every human sympathy!—to wade, shoulder-deep, through crime and human blood in pursuit of their unhallowed gains!—these have been competitors, this the competition beneath which I have sunk; aye! and at which humanity has shrieked and freedom trembled. And at whose hands have I suffered this cruel wrong? Severe as was the cost to me, I sympathised with— nay, I gloried in—the high morality of my fatherland, which, as I thought, had doomed slavery to extinction. I trusted to her promise to cherish me in my sacrifice. I trusted to her promise to requite me for that surrender by her support, shelter, and protection. How has she kept that pledge? " Hostis habet muros!" She, to whom I clung in faithful reliance—she, the land of my loyalty and love, broke her pledge—mocked at my trust in her, and left me helpless— a prey to the very crime which, denounced in me, she had invoked against me. I have no great expectations of the success of any appeal to the present Cabinet. Haply Lord Palmerston may have a grudge to gratify against the Duke of something or other (I forget his name), and the violation of these treaties may furnish a convenient handle for a new quarrel. It will be well for us if it is so. But I cannot see how the Russell Cabinet, of all others, can with any face invoke the fulfilment of the obligations of national faith. Can I imagine them making an appeal of this kind— " Spain! you must keep the faith of those treaties: your hands are stained still with the life-blood of the human race, and that in defiance of national treaties." What is the obvious answer:—" We are not without regard for the obligations of good faith; we know all you say to be just and true, and might have respected it; but you have taught us a different lesson. How have you kept faith with your own colonies? We know our hands are stained with blood, but you have clutched those bloody hands in base and greedy welcome. Boasting of your preference for the chaste sweets of freedom, you have yourselves wantoned in the embrace of slavery! Away with you—for base, unblushing hypocrites!" But without this, Sir, I am confident that these appeals must ultimately rouse the British nation, in whose high honour and humanity, and sense of justice, I have the utmost confidence, and in that confidence I propose with pleasure the first resolution :—

" That, true to the principles which have ever animated the inhabitants of Metcalfe to protest, in often-repeated public meetings, against the ruinous consequences of the Sugar Bill of 1846, to the interests of the British West Indies, of free labour, and of humanity, this meeting cordially co-operates with the great public assemblage which has been held in Spanish Town, in invoking the suppression of the slave-trade."

Mr. Edward Bond seconded the resolution, and it was carried unanimously.

Mr. Westmorland, being called upon to move the second resolution, said—After the numerous, able, and eloquent speeches which have been delivered at the meetings in Spanish Town and Kingston, and other parishes, on the same subject as we are met here, to-day, to discuss, and especially after the brilliant and soul-stirring address of Dr. Clarke, he felt that he might content himself with simply proposing the resolution placed in his hand by the chairman, without detaining them with remarks which must almost necessarily be repetitions of what had already been said. He could not, however, be wholly silent on a subject of so much interest. He agreed with his friend, Dr. Clarke, in deprecating the dilatoriness of the officials in Spanish Town in coming forward, as they should have long ago, in so righteous a cause; but the clergy were, however, to be excepted from this charge, for he (Mr. W.) believed the delay on their part arose from no lukewarmness or absence of philanthropic feelings, but from their disinclination to appear at public meetings. He rejoiced that the clergy, with our esteemed Bishop at their head, had come forward so manfully to fight the battle of the injured African race, and to aid the ruined planters, who had met for years and years without getting their grievances redressed. No taunt of self-interested motives could be thrown out at their endeavours to put an end to a traffic so universally execrated. He had never seen slavery in this island, still he felt, that connected as he had been from his birth with Jamaica, when its social position was so very different, that an appeal from him, on behalf of the victims of the slave-trade, did not come with such force as from his friend, Dr. Clarke, and others, who had ever been the advocates of universal freedom for the African race, though he yielded to none in his horror of this traffic, and in his anxious desire to see it put an end to. The resolution he held in his hand principally referred to the unfortunate state of this island, in consequence of the success of slavery, and on this point he would say a few words. He would ask them to contrast the present condition of Jamaica and its inhabitants with what it was, only four or five years ago. No man can shut his eyes to the misery and want which exist among a large class of the inhabitants, and the ruin and despair staring in the faces of the majority of them. Let them look at the "Gazette," and see, for the last two years, how many hard-working planters, who had invested their all since freedom in the cultivation of the soil, had been brought to bankruptcy; let them look at the steady march the bush was making to the sea shore, from the rapid abandonment of cultivation; let them go into the interior parts of the parish, and see what ruin had overtaken the middling classes — once comfortable plantations and happy homes were now wildernesses, and scarcely tenantable habitations; let them see the father, once moving in a respectable sphere of life, now obliged to toil in the mid-day sun, to raise a few eddoes that perhaps formed the sole subsistence of his unfortunate family; let them see the wife, pale and emaciated from hard work and scanty food, striving to hide her ill-clad children, with a mother's pride, from the gaze of a stranger. He could relate a few more of these harrowing scenes, did he not know they were all aware too painfully of their existence; and when he reflected that these scenes of misery and distress had been brought about by the effects of the encouragement given by England to the growth of slave sugar, he asked himself if this could be the great and noble nation he was from his youth taught to believe it? Could he, with the same hearty will, and national pride, exclaim—

" England, with all thy faults, I love thee still!"

Where, he would ask, were those feelings of philanthropy that were once so powerful?—are they for ever to be stifled for motives of gain?—is slavery to flourish and our colonies to be ruined, simply because you must have your sugar a little cheaper? He hoped not, and believed that the same noble feeling still existed in British hearts, though it had long lain dormant—that a few sparks remained unextinguishable, which only required the bellows of agitation to kindle into a flame, bright, pure, and strong. Let us, then, fan the flame, and if successful, we shall not only have the satisfaction of feeling that we have assisted in delivering thousands of our fellow-creatures from their present miserable condition, but that we have also been instrumental in rescuing a large portion of the inhabitants of this island from that misery and ruin which is now threatening them. Mr. Westmorland then proposed the second resolution :—

" That in consequence of the unnatural competition the productions of this island are exposed to with those of the slave colonies, cultivation is rapidly ceasing, trade is entirely paralysed, and ruin and despair are staring in the face a majority of its inhabitants."

Mr. Wm. Espeut seconded it, and it was carried by acclamation.

The Hon. R. C. Burke, being called upon to propose the next resolution, said :—Mr. Chairman, ladies, and gentlemen, when the celebrated Edmund Burke was returned for

Bristol, he sat down after a very able and eloquent speech.
His colleague, a man of facts and figures, but few words,
rose and said, "I say ditto to Mr. Burke—ditto to Mr.
Burke." After all that has been said, and so well said—
after the thrilling denunciations against slavery we have just
listened to from my friend Dr. Clarke, and other gentlemen
who have addressed you—perhaps it would have been acting
discreetly if I had followed such a good example; but the
subject is one of such interest to the agriculturists of this
island, I cannot sit down without a few brief remarks.   After
a manner, I have been myself a voyager; I have visited the
estates in Cuba and on the banks of the Mississippi.   In the
first-named place I remained three weeks, and had good
opportunities of noticing how the slaves were worked and
fed.   About three o'clock, a.m., their sleeping-rooms were
unbarred, they received their breakfast, already prepared
for them, and eating it, walked to the field, where they
remained at continued labour till night, when they again
made their appearance at the manager's door, and received
a second meal of great corn, boiled with some inferior salt
fish; they then returned to the barracoons, or sleeping-
prisons, where they were locked up, without regard to age or
sex, or health, until they were again summoned to labour at
the usual hour.   On Sunday they did not go to the field, but
worked about the buildings till noon, when they were allowed
from that hour to supper, to wash their clothes and persons.
Sometimes, on the Sabbath, a single negro would approach
the manager, and, prostrate on the ground, ask permission
to visit some sick or dying shipmate on a neighbouring property, and it was considered an indulgent act to grant this
request.   A written pass was indispensable, and I have witnessed it given and returned in some four hours.   A priest
(shame on that priest!) regularly attended this plantation, but
it was not to soothe the sufferer in his afflictions, to impart the
consolations of religion to poor, injured, suffering humanity; it
was not to intercede for some unfortunate defaulter, but to
collect his quarter's dues which the law allowed, and the
owner was compelled to pay, for the performance of duties

never thought of. This is a single instance; but I could give you a hundred, of the manner in which the Cuban slave drags his chain through a short but horrible life. This is the state of things in a country abounding in riches of soil equal to any in the world, and not more than twelve hours' passage in a steamer from where we stand. I call on all who hear me—I call on all Christians of every denomination, by the sanctity of their creed—I call on my fellow-subjects of the Mosaic faith, by the ancient grandeur of their church—I call on the sons of Africa and their descendants, by the blessings of freedom which, under the British constitution, they enjoy —and though last, not least, I call on that sex, powerful in everything, invincible in good. I call upon each and all fervently, unitedly, to aid us in this good work. England may boast of its living heroes, its Wellingtons, its Hardinges, and its Goughs—its poets may sing in praise of its Marlborough and its Moore—its annalists may point with pride to its sages in the names of Locke, and Newton, and Bacon, and More; but its brightest page, in after-times, will be that in which is recorded—"This year, through the influence of Queen Victoria, a Sovereign who lived in the hearts of her subjects, and ruled over the greatest nation in the world, slavery ceased to exist on earth." I beg, Mr. Chairman, to move the third resolution :—

" That although treaties have been long ago entered into by England with Spain and Brazil for the total suppression of the slave-trade; that notwithstanding a large blockading squadron stationed on the coast of Africa for the interception of slaves, which not only involves an enormous expense to the British nation, but a sad mortality among our officers and seamen; it has been incontestibly shown by the clearest evidence, that since the admission of slave-grown sugar for consumption in England, the slave-trade had been prosecuted with increased vigour, and with an unparalleled augmentation of misery and suffering to its unfortunate victims."

Mr. W. Bell rose to second this resolution, and it passed unanimously.

Mr. H. J. Jacobs, being called upon to move the next

resolution, said, Mr. Chairman, ladies, and gentlemen—It affords me much pleasure to address this meeting, based as it is on the pure principles of philanthropy, and therefore equally incumbent upon men in all situations to lend a helping hand in carrying out that great boon to humanity, which, if it had been granted in sincerity, would have been a lasting monument to the glory of the British nation. The subject has been so ably handled by the gentlemen who have preceded me, that it leaves me little to say; yet callous must that heart be, when roused to action by the glorious cause which those great and good men, Clarkson, Wilberforce, Macaulay, and many others had illustrated, if it did not vibrate with feelings of emotion, when called upon to join in, I hope, the final accomplishment of the downfall of the most nefarious traffic which ever cursed the earth. When we review the years that have passed by, when this traffic was sanctioned by the legislature, we are led to the conclusion that much has been done, and had it not been for the false policy which has pervaded the British Government for these last few years, we would have indeed had cause to rejoice over the total extinction of this horrid traffic. That Government cannot now impute our endeavours to romance, enthusiasm, or fanaticism, for, alas! evils have overcome us, they have borne us down to the very verge of destruction, and in bitterness of heart do we exclaim—" How have the mighty fallen!" I can, Mr. Chairman, ladies, and gentlemen, as an Israelite, the more readily enter into the true spirit of this meeting; for when I reflect, as a descendant of those who were once held in bondage by the wicked Egyptian king, on the sufferings they were made to undergo, on the heavy tasks that were imposed on them, and how they were delivered by an outstretched Almighty arm, and made to enjoy equal rights and privileges with their fellow-men—I can, I say, Sir, the more readily exert my humble abilities in striving to ameliorate the condition of the suffering slave; for, with the poet, can I exclaim—

" My ear is pained,
My soul is sick with every day's report

Of wrong and outrage with which earth is filled.
There is no flesh in man's obdurate heart,
It does not feel for man ; the natural bond
Of brotherhood is severed as the flax
That falls asunder at the touch of fire.
He finds his fellow guilty of a skin
Not coloured like his own ; and having power
To enforce the wrong, dooms and devotes him as his lawful prey.
Thus man devotes his brother, and destroys,
And worse than all, and most to be deplored,
As human nature's broadest, foulest blot,
Chains him and tasks him, and exacts his sweat
With stripes, that Mercy, with a bleeding heart,
Weeps when she sees inflicted on a beast.
Then, what is man ? and what man, seeing this,
And having human feelings, does not blush
And hang his head, to think himself a man ? "

—" Oh Slavery, thou art a bitter draught !"—but more bitter still will the stings of conscience be to those by whose acts the chains of the slave are more firmly riveted than ever. Those men who, by their wicked and short-sighted policy, have caused, and still cause, thousands of their fellow-men to languish and die in chains and slavery ; those men, Sir, who, to save a penny in the pound on sugar, partake of the blood and sinews of their fellow-man ! Out, I say, on such mawkish philanthropy ; 'tis, indeed, a bitter mockery of the justice of the British nation ! The principal steps, Mr. Chairman, to be taken towards the accomplishment of this great and noble cause, is that which we, in conjunction with the other parishes, are now doing. It is our bounden duty, as well for our own protection as for the cause of humanity, to call upon the British Government to enforce those treaties made with Spain and the Brazils for the total suppression of this nefarious traffic. Let petition upon petition be piled upon the table of the House of Commons—let the British Government be made aware of the premium she is holding out to slavery, and of the deep injury she is inflicting on her own colonies. If these treaties are enforced, we may once again hope to see Jamaica regain her pristine vigour, and resume her wonted station as the queen of the Antilles. Let

us, then, join heart and soul in this cause—let no petty
jealousies disunite us in carrying out this great principle—but
let us, with one accord, give a long pull, a strong pull, and a
pull altogether, for the hurling to destruction this curse of
the earth! And now, Mr. Chairman, the following is the
resolution which I have the honour to propose:—

" Resolved—That this meeting calls upon her Majesty's Government at once earnestly to enforce the terms of the treaties
referred to, and thus for ever extinguish the horrid traffic in human
flesh at present being carried on ; or, should such a course be
deemed politically inexpedient, then we call upon the British
Parliament to exclude from the English market all sugar produced
by slave labour, thereby discontinuing the direct encouragement
given to the man-stealer, and the enriching of a trade so universally and justly execrated."

Mr. Wm. Dixon seconded the resolution, and it was
carried by acclamation.

Mr. A. J. Schoburg, to whom was entrusted the next resolution, submitted the same as follows:—

" That a memorial to the Queen, embodying the substance and
spirit of the foregoing resolutions, be prepared and signed by the
chairman on behalf of the meeting, and that his excellency the
Governor be requested to forward it through the usual channel."

Mr. Da Costa seconded it, and it was carried unanimously.

On motion of Mr. H. J. Jacobs, it was then resolved, that
the resolutions passed should be published in the Kingston
daily papers.

Thanks were voted to the Chairman in the customary
manner, and the meeting separated.

From the answers of Viscount Palmerston and Earl Grey
to the communications from Jamaica, on the subject of
the present movement, it is not to be doubted that what we
have been doing is in perfect accordance with the views of
her Majesty's Government. In order to show that the two
Houses of Parliament are, at least, not at variance with us,
we subjoin an abridged report of the debate in the Lords on

the Bishop of Oxford's motion, together with that in the Commons, on the motion of Mr. Milner Gibson; and, that the fourth estate may not be left out of consideration, there follows a leading article or two from the *Times* and the *Jamaica Despatch.*

HOUSE OF LORDS, FEB. 22, 1849.

The Bishop of Oxford rose, in pursuance of his notice, to move for "the appointment of a Select Committee to consider the best means which Great Britain could adopt for the final extinction of the African slave-trade." He commenced by saying that it became their lordships to examine carefully the plan on which the British Government was now acting, to investigate the objections which were urged against it, and to consider the possibility of retracing or maintaining any portion of the career on which we had entered; and it was upon that sense of the duty of their lordships that he now asked them to appoint the committee of which he had given notice. It was also his conviction that the result of that examination would show that, without the maintenance of a blockading squadron on the coast of Africa, any other measures which we might adopt for the furtherance of our object would be futile and insufficient. Whether any alterations should be made in the management of those squadrons of blockade, and whether they ought to be maintained in some other shape, was a point into which he most anxiously wished their lordships to inquire. He confessed that it appeared to him, after a careful perusal of the evidence which had been taken by a committee of the other House of Parliament, that, except in the evidence of those persons who had recently been engaged, according to general suspicion, in that trade which was now declared by Act of Parliament to be piracy, there was a remarkable concurrence of opinion that just in proportion to the efficiency of the blockading squadrons on the African coast had been the diminution of the slave-trade, and just in proportion to its inefficiency had been its renewal, and, he might almost say, revival. He was anxious that their lordships should appoint a committee to go fairly and fully into every portion of this part of the question—to examine both sides—to hear whether the objections urged against the great principle for which he contended were idle or valid—and to devise what measures ought to be adopted to carry out successfully the greatest moral and social experiment which had ever been undertaken by any nation in the history of the world. Just in proportion to his conviction of the expediency of such an inquiry was his desire that their lordships should enter into it carefully and dispassionately ; for there was no change, he was sure, in the public mind of England, on the necessity of suppressing the slave-trade. Any change of opinion, if change there were, was merely transient, and was founded upon other motives. To hear of men confined between decks, in layers three deep, and carried near the Equator under a burning sun,—to hear that they were packed so closely that they could not, on their first embarkation, move from side to side, except by a general agreement among the unfortunate negroes,—to hear that it was only by their subsequent attenuation on their voyage, and by the sure but gradual diminution of their numbers by death, which afterwards ensued, that room could be granted for them to turn in—these were facts (if the mind of England were directed to them, instead of looking at the mere abstract question of Brazilian trade) sufficient to convince all men of ordinary humanity that no secondary consideration of temporal advantage ought to make us swerve from, much less abandon, the system which we had adopted to exterminate such crying evils. In his opinion there could not be a question more worthy of their lordships' attention than this. It was with nations as with men. It was a fearful thing for either to decline from the high standard of excellence to which they had been accustomed, and to take up with a lower. It was one thing to prohibit the slave-trade along the whole coast of Africa, and to declare that you do so because you would not allow the regions in the centre of Africa to be filled with rapine and conflagration, and murder, in order that the

Brazilian plantations should be cultivated by slave labour, and it was a fearful thing to shrink from the enforcement of that prohibition, when God had given you the power and the means to suppress the horrors which you prohibited. On evidence it was known that the slave-trade was the most lucrative traffic under the sun. There was not a tittle of evidence to show that it was a trade likely to wear itself out; on the contrary, there was evidence in abundance to show that it was a trade likely to increase to an unprecedented amount. For, though the papers on the table showed that, in the years 1846 and 1847, 65,000 was the number of slaves imported from Africa into the Brazils, it was impossible to stand by the demand of the Brazilian market in that year, and to affirm that it would not be exceeded; for there was an immense amount of virgin soil of the greatest fertility in the Brazils, which by slave labour could be brought immediately into lucrative cultivation. Moreover, the price of a slave at present in the Brazilian market was £50; but it was apparent from the evidence given over and over again, that, if the trade in slaves were thrown open, slaves could be carried to that market from Africa at so low a cost as £10 a head. To say that such a trade would wear itself out, was altogether to forget the deep lust of gain, and the utter carelessness of human life, which went together in that degraded portion of our common nature which engaged in its atrocity. There was one part of this subject upon which, however reluctantly, he must still briefly touch. England was more particularly bound to interfere for the suppression of slavery, although there might be some inconsistency in its interference, because it had recently given a considerable stimulus to the slave-trade by opening the British market to slave-grown sugar. Attached as he was, upon mature deliberation, to the principles of free trade, he must be permitted to observe, that in applying its doctrines to this particular case, we had been committing one of the grossest crimes which it was possible for a nation to commit, for we had entangled ourselves again in that accursed trade which we professed, and had taught the world to believe, that we had abandoned

for ever.   In the evidence given before the House of Commons, by those parties who could not be described as pre-
judiced, the great stimulus recently given to the Brazilian
slave-trade was attributed to our Sugar Act of 1846.   He
was quite sure that those who proposed that Act never contemplated any such result.   He was likewise quite sure that
the people of England, for the miserable advantage of saving
a penny in the pound in the price of their sugar, did not
intend to stimulate the slave-trade.   If, at a time when the
people thought that economical considerations were by no
means to be neglected, Parliament had forgotten the stern
dictates of justice, morality, and religion, it was high time
that it should now reflect that there were paramount duties
with which no economy should be permitted to interfere;
and it was, therefore, the bounden duty of their lordships
not to flinch now, even if it should be found necessary to
increase largely the expenditure, to stop an evil which Parliament had recklessly and needlessly inflicted.   He, therefore, called upon them, as legislators and Christians, to
examine whether they could not prevent, for the future, the
evil which had resulted of necessity from their legislation.
He then moved the resolution.

The Marquis of Lansdowne did not anticipate any intention to oppose the motion of the right rev. prelate.   It would
be painful to him even to express his assent to this motion,
if he were to found that assent upon any notion that it was
necessary to convince the people of England that they
ought to maintain, with resolution and firmness, that course
on which they had been so long engaged, on the highest
principles of duty and conscience.   For his own part, he did
not believe that there had been any alteration on this subject
in the public mind of England.   If there had been any, it
had not been on the importance of the duty to be performed,
nor on the value of the exertions made, efficiently or ineffi-
ciently, to put down the slave-trade.

The Earl of Aberdeen, having expressed his concurrence
in the motion, said that he took share in this debate in consequence of the observations which the right rev. prelate had

made on the misapprehension entertained by our naval officers on the coast of Africa with respect to the instructions issued to them. He was happy that this inquiry was to be instituted; for he trusted that one of its main objects would be to ascertain the efficacy of the step which the late Government had taken in increasing the force on the coast of Africa for the suppression of the slave-trade. He considered himself as mainly responsible for the means now employed on that coast. When he first took office, in 1841, he found 800 or 900 men employed there; when he quitted office he left 3000 men there. He was, therefore, more interested than any other person in ascertaining the real efficiency of the squadron which was employed, and how that efficiency could be increased, if increased efficiency were possible. He then reminded the House that as to the blockading squadron on the coast of Africa we were not free agents. We were bound by treaties with foreign powers to maintain a certain force, and till we were relieved from those treaties we could not make any alteration in the amount of that force. He trusted, at any rate, that our squadron would not be entirely withdrawn.

Lord Stanley most cordially concurred in the wish so eloquently expressed by the Bishop of Oxford, for the final extinction of slavery, and as cordially concurred in the noble marquis's observation, that the present was a fitting time to inquire into the efficacy of the means which we had adopted for that object. While he agreed with the noble earl (the Earl of Aberdeen) that the principal point of inquiry should be the efficacy of our means to suppress the slave-trade by a squadron of blockade, he must observe, that in his opinion the proposed committee would fall short of its duty, if the members of it shrank from a full inquiry into the obstacles which that squadron had to encounter. That was a matter of great importance; and he trusted that the committee would examine and report on the several stages of advance and retrogression, in the success and exertions of the blockading squadron, and that it would consider the state of the traffic in 1840, and the great success of the squadron from

1842 to 1846. He trusted, likewise, that their inquiries
would not terminate there; but that they would be extended
into the increase of the slave-trade, and into the aggravation
of its horrors in the years between 1846 and 1849, although
the vigilance and devotion of our squadron in those years
was not inferior to the vigilance and devotion which distinguished them in the years between 1842 and 1846. His
opinion on this question had often been stated before, and he
had no hesitation in now stating it again. Whilst he gave
every credit to, and placed all due stress upon, the measures
of coercion adopted by our squadron, he believed that whilst
we had increased the force of that squadron we had un-
knowingly and inconsistently neutralised the effects of that
increase by giving a fresh stimulus to the slave-trade, and
new and strong motives for embarking in it, by the alteration
of the sugar duties, which we had made in 1846, upon a
miserable plea of mistaken economy.

Earl Grey said he was in no degree shaken in the opinion
he originally entertained, that the measure of 1846 was a
wise measure, with reference (apart from all other considerations) to the ultimate extinction, not only of the slave-
trade, but of slavery. He was confident that when the real
results of that measure came before the House and the
country, they would be seen to afford no ground for these
premature taunts. Whenever that great question should be
regularly discussed, neither he nor his colleagues would
shrink from meeting the noble lord upon it.

Lord Brougham said, for himself, he did not require
further information before forming his opinion; he had
evidence enough, and to spare; but there were others to be
considered—there was Parliament, and the country, and the
executive Government; and therefore he thought the inquiry
most desirable. But he should go into committee with no
bias or prejudice; he should go to hear the truth and act
upon it. To be sure, the noble earl had said that the noble
lord (Stanley), with his characteristic impetuosity and disposition to come to a premature conclusion, was labouring to
bring out "a philippic" upon the sugar duties and the slave-

trade, in their unhappy and most calamitous connexion, as he (Lord Brougham) maintained it to be. The facts were not to be got rid of; and if the facts were as stated, they bore out all the gloomy prognostications of 1846, and showed, in immediate juxtaposition and necessary and indissoluble connexion, the policy of 1846 and the extension of the slave-trade. Now, with his characteristic perseverance and courage, the noble earl had said that he was quite satisfied with all that had happened since 1846, and that, instead of shaking, it only tended to confirm his former opinion. Really, if the facts since 1846 had only tended to confirm him in his opinion, he (Lord Brougham) would not say that he was unteachable—would not say that he was of the number of those upon whom all experience was thrown away; but he would say that the noble earl was happy in the possession of a sanguine temperament, and that defeat, the most manifest and glaring want of success, produced upon him the same effect that the most triumphant victory produced upon other men.

The motion was then agreed to, and the committee appointed, after a short conversation between the Earl of Ellenborough, the Marquis of Lansdowne, and the Bishop of Oxford, upon a doubt raised by the noble earl whether the terms of reference were quite sufficiently extensive.

HOUSE OF COMMONS, APRIL 24, 1849.

Mr. M. Gibson then called the attention of the House to the state of our relations with the empire of Brazil, and to submit a motion for the repeal of the Brazilian Act, 8 and 9 Vic., c. 122. Its object was to effect a complete and perfect abolition of the slave-trade, and if it was not effected in Brazil, it was not from want of will, but of power, on the part of the Brazilian Government. He was sorry to be deprived on this occasion of the services of the hon. member for Gateshead, in endeavouring to obtain the repeal of this Act. The grounds upon which he sought it were, that this country maintained it by violating international laws. The history of their treaty with the Brazilian Government was this :—In 1826, a treaty was entered into between Brazil and Great Britain, by which it was declared and agreed to, that all persons found engaged in the slave trade, if subjects of either country, should be declared guilty of piracy, and treated as such. That treaty was to last for fifteen years, and subjected the vessels of Brazil to the right of search, and the appointment of Mixed Commission Courts to try all cases which might be deemed necessary. In 1815, Lord Aberdeen declared, however, that they did not want the privilege of a right of search, or mixed commissions ; that by the first article of the treaty, Brazil agreed that persons guilty of slaving should be treated as pirates, and therefore, the sovereign of Great Britain was entitled to take every step she thought proper, to punish Brazilians, as such, who should be found guilty. But who ever heard that the declaration in a treaty created a criminal law, or the offence of piracy ? An Act of Parliament was, however, passed, founded on his lordship's construction of that article, which declared Brazilian or British subjects, engaged in slaving, guilty of piracy. By that Act it was declared that the subjects of an independent country should be governed by a certain number of Acts of Parliament, passed in England, which were law before that period ; and it was contended that they were liable to the punishments inflicted by those statutes. But it should be recollected that a Brazilian ship, sailing under a Brazilian flag, was, to all intents and purposes, Brazilian territory, so that they were legislating for the subjects of an independent empire. Before this was done, however, the opinions of Mr. M. D. Hill, and the hon. and learned member for Youghal—who was well known to possess an extensive knowledge of the laws of nations—were taken, and they decided that the treaty entered into with Brazil gave no right to treat the subjects of a foreign state as pirates ; that the 8th and 9th Victoria, cap. 192, was founded on an erroneous assumption of power, and therefore inoperative ; and, therefore, the seizure and condemnation of Brazilian ships by British cruisers, or British authority, was unlawful. It would also be recollected that at that time the present Lord Chief Justice of the Common Pleas brought the attention of Parliament to the subject, and that eminent personage had recently informed his (Mr. Gibson's) hon. and learned friend the member for Gateshead, and authorised him to state so, that had he continued a member of that House, he would have deemed it an imperative duty to seek the repeal of that act of the legislature. In the communication to his hon. friend, dated in March of the present year, his lordship stated that he always thought the conduct pursued towards Brazil a national disgrace ; that it was manifestly done, either in ignorance of the law of nations, or by reason of an immense assumption, calculated to lead to war, or to render this country contemptible ; for if redress were demanded by a foreign nation, and refused, it would be a just cause of war. The question, continued his lordship, was, what constituted piracy? Piracy was a spoliation and violence committed on the high seas, not against one nation, but against all, and therefore any one nation may punish it ; but particular treaties entered into would not authorise the contracting parties to punish as criminals the subjects of the other, for neither of them were justified in legislating against the subjects of an independent state. That was clear, and, indeed, such a principle as enunciated in the Act he (Mr. Gibson) referred to, was plainly contrary to the dictates of common sense. It went so far as to say that the Government of Brazil authorised the British Government to punish its subjects as pirates, because of a treaty which was entered into. Let them recollect that the municipal law required in Brazil for the proper execution of the treaty was never carried into effect ; and although his noble friend, now at the head of the Foreign Department, was not responsible for that Act, he would ask him would the following case be lawful or just, which was exactly similar with the position in which the executive Government of Brazil was placed? Suppose the noble lord had entered into a treaty with Brazil—which Parliament subsequently refused to ratify—but the execu-

tive Government of Brazil, in executing it, blockaded
British ports, and watched the Channel, heedless of what
was done in this country. Would that be just, or proper, or
politic?—And yet that was the conduct now pursued by
England towards Brazil. When he thus brought before
them the opinion of Mr. Hill, and of the hon. and learned
member for Youghal,—when he brought before the House
the solemn protest of the Duke of Wellington, of Lord
Lyndhurst, in the House of Lords, in the case of the
Portuguese, which was exactly similar,—he thought he
exonerated himself from the charge of having brought the
subject lightly before the attention of the House. They
were bringing Brazilians before a tribunal which they did
not recognise; trying them in a language which they did
not understand, and before judges who had no *locus standi*
as regarded them ; and all that, too, contrary to the rights
and privileges of an independent state. Was not such a
course more likely to defeat than to accomplish the object
they had in view, to create irritation and bad feeling, and to
extend the evil for the suppression of which such great
sacrifices had been made by this country? Now, with
regard to the engagements of Brazil, if the treaty was not
fulfilled, it was for them to inquire into the matter—to
proceed in the business in the same manner as when an
ordinary dispute occurred, and not take the matter into their
own hands. They ought to recollect that it took thirty-two
years to carry the abolition of the slave-trade in England—
and why should they expect that the Brazilian Government
could carry such a measure all at once through their legislature, and in the face of innumerable difficulties? The slave-
trade was abolished by the slow progress of public opinion ;
and he was confident that if, while that opinion was in progress, they had had an enemy on their shores, seizing their
ships and committing other acts of hostility, they never would
have had that slave-trade abolished. He believed that the
present policy was not a sound one. When this Act was
passed, distinct declarations were made by the Foreign
Secretary, that nothing would give him greater pleasure

than to repeal this Act; and since that time, as he was informed, the Brazilians had submitted such a project as would have satisfied Lord Aberdeen. The project submitted, he was informed, was satisfactory to both parties, but was not carried out, in consequence of a change of administration, when Lord Palmerston wrote a despatch, which immediately put an end to the whole negotiation. Lord Palmerston promised to prepare a draft of a treaty, but his intimation was that it was not to be questioned, and that they had nothing to do but to sign it. Ten months afterwards came out this draft, and in June, 1847, it was forwarded. Lord Howden was instructed that he was not to alter a letter in that treaty. (The right hon. gentleman read the despatch.) He ventured humbly to say that these instructions, affording no ground for negotiation, were not calculated to be successful. The plan, as might have been anticipated, had entirely failed, and to that Sir Charles Hotham, the commander of the squadron there, had borne his testimony. His opinion was that they should be met half-way, particularly as there was a party, especially among the younger men, who were favourable to this project. But Lord Palmerston's instructions had armed against us the whole population. He had stated sufficient reasons, he hoped, to induce the House to agree to a Bill, which he wished to bring in to repeal so much of the present law as was obnoxious to the renewal of amicable relations with the empire of Brazil. He moved for leave to bring in a Bill to repeal the Act 8 and 9 Vic., c. 122.

Mr. Urquhart said, that if the Government of this country was anxious to find new channels to advance the trade of this country, nothing could more facilitate that object than opening up amicable relations with the southern continent of America, and especially with the Brazilian empire. Yet that was the empire with which, from the clear and explicit statement they had just heard, they had the worst understanding. Our measures, from the testimony of Sir C. Hotham, were the chief support of the slave-trade in that country. The Portuguese Government had been treated in a similar

manner.   The hon. member concluded by saying, that for
the reasons he had stated, he felt pleasure in seconding the
right hon. gentleman's motion.

Sir F. Thesiger trusted the house would give no encouragement to the motion of the right hon. member for Manchester.   Were they to follow his recommendation they
would not only destroy all means of giving efficiency to
the most important treaty with Brazil, concluded in 1826,
but would also exhibit a weakness and vacillation on
the part of the legislature of this country which would
not tend to enhance its character and estimation among
foreign nations.   The right honourable gentleman had
introduced the question to the House with great clearness
and force ; but he had fallen into one or two errors.   He
appeared to understand the Act 8th and 9th of Victoria
as if it gave power to the courts of this country to deal with
the persons of Brazilian subjects.   But the Act gave power
only to the Admiralty to adjudicate with respect to the
vessels of Brazilian subjects and the cargoes of those vessels.
The treaty with Brazil of November, 1826, incorporated all
the clauses of the treaty with Portugal of 1817 ; and by the
first article of the treaty of 1826 it was provided that within
three years after the exchange of the ratifications the slave-
trade should be utterly abolished, and that any subjects of
the Brazilian Government who should traffic in slaves after
that period should be guilty of piracy.   The ratifications
were exchanged on March 13, 1827.   The three years expired in 1830 ; but under the additional treaty with Portugal,
in 1817, it was provided that after the slave-trade should be
utterly abolished, the Portuguese treaty should subsist for
fifteen years ; and, that article being incorporated into the
Brazilian treaty of 1826, the treaty of fifteen years, from
March 13, 1830, continued to subsist, and expired on March
14, 1845.   Mixed Commission Courts had been established,
which had the power of adjudicating with respect to vessels
which were engaged in the slave-trade ; and the 7 and 8
George IV. was passed to give effect to the treaty of 1826.
By a clause of that Act, parties were prohibited from pro-

ceeding in the Courts of Admiralty against any vessels or persons engaged in the · slave-trade, and they were compelled to resort to the Mixed Commission Courts, in terms of the treaty of 1826. So stood the law up to March 13, 1845, when the treaty came to an end. Then it was obvious, as the 6 and 7 Geo. IV. was existing, and prohibited proceeding in the courts of this country, and the Mixed Commission Courts had come to an end with the treaties on which they were founded, that, though the stipulations of the convention of 1826 were binding and conclusive on the part of the Brazilian Government, with respect to the termination of the slave-trade in 1830, there was no possibility of enforcing the provisions of the treaty, in consequence of there being no Mixed Commission Courts in existence. When a Sovereign entered into a treaty, it was not necessary to consider what was the municipal law of the State which he represented; it was a binding treaty which might be enforced. The treaty of 1826 placed this country in a position in which it was entitled to legislate on the subject, and to substitute for the Mixed Commission Courts other tribunals which might enforce the performance of that treaty. Such was the view taken by the Chevalier de Mattos, who, on October 4, 1830, stated that the slave-trade being totally forbidden to Brazilian subjects, from March 13, 1830, and those who thereafter should engage in it being liable to punishment by the ordinary tribunals of the contracting parties, he had been directed to negotiate the dissolution of the Mixed Commission Courts as absolutely superfluous. The opinion of the Lord Chief Justice of the Common Pleas had been introduced in a somewhat unusual and irregular way. It was not right that a letter addressed to the hon. member for Gateshead by his right hon. and learned friend, as he hoped he might still venture to call him, should be used to influence that House; and it was surprising that if that learned person thought the act a disgrace to the country he should not have opposed or divided against it, when he was a member of that House. The right hon. member for Manchester had referred to the decision of thirteen of the

judges, in the case of "the Queen v. Serva and others," as
favourable to his argument. In that case, there being no
slaves on board the "Felicidade," there was no right of
seizure given by the treaty; and the only question was,
whether the "Felicidade" was in the lawful possession of
the captors—in which case she would have been within the
jurisdiction of the British Government. There was no
authority for the view urged by the right hon. gentleman.
The case of Portugal had no bearing on the question; and,
with all deference to Mr. Hill, he could not agree with his
opinion. Were the House to repeal the Act of Parliament
the stipulations in the treaty of 1826 would become a dead
letter, because this country would then possess no means of
enforcing them. In 1845 the Brazilian Government received a distinct intimation from this country that, unless
they carried the stipulations of the treaty into effect, a Bill
would be passed by the British Parliament, under which the
ordinary tribunals of the country would be substituted for the
Mixed Commission Courts. After the sacrifices which we
had made for the purpose of putting an end to the abominable
traffic in human beings, and the endeavours we had used to
induce other countries to concur with us in that object, surely
it would be very irrational to repeal the Act of Parliament and
to leave the stipulations of our treaty with Brazil a dead letter.

Mr. Bright travelled over the ground which had been
previously trodden by his colleague, contending, like him,
that this country was not justified in exercising over
Brazilian subjects a power to which their own Government
could not subject them—that the Brazilian Government had
failed to carry into effect the stipulations of the treaty of
1826, not from bad faith, but from inability, in consequence
of those stipulations being opposed to the public opinion of
Brazil; and that we would not have ventured to enforce the
provisions of the Act of Parliament against any country
whose power equalled or approached our own. The state
of our relations with Brazil had thrown our commercial
treaties as well as our slave treaties into disorder, and that
was a matter of some importance, seeing that not less than

between £4,000,000 and £5,000,000 of British capital was invested in various commercial undertakings in the Brazils, whilst we annually exported there not much less than £3,000,000 worth of manufactures. Our commercial treaties with Brazil expired in 1834, and the Brazilian Government refused to renew them, except upon the condition that their sugar should be imported into this country on the same terms as those on which our manufactures were admitted into Brazil. Since that time, therefore, we had had no commercial treaty with Brazil, and the consequence was that British goods, which used to pay fifteen per cent. duties, now paid duties amounting to twenty-six, and even thirty per cent. The unsatisfactory state of our relations with Brazil was productive of another disadvantage to British subjects. If a British subject died at Brazil intestate, his property, even if he had a partner, was obliged to go through a Brazilian Court, or, he should rather say, to go into it, for very little ever came out again. The Anti-slavery Society had issued a circular, stating that the slave-trade had increased since the abolition of the sugar monopoly, in 1846, but he believed the averment to be incorrect. What, after all, availed the efforts which we made for the suppression of that trade? In addition to the annual waste of life and treasure on the African coast, we were in danger of losing one of the best customers for our manufactures, by our attempts to dragoon her into the adoption of a course which we ourselves would never have taken if it had been dictated to us. The noble lord at the head of the Foreign Department had a benevolent crotchet on the subject of the slave-trade, but there was hardly a man out of doors who was not opposed to his policy.

Mr. Anstey contended that the account which the hon. member for Manchester had given, of the decision of the judges in the case of the Brazilian pirates, was correct. When questions of the nature of that which had given rise to the present debate came before the fifteen judges, the decision which they pronounced upon it was always in the nature of a recommendation to the Crown, and not in the manner of an award, as though they had themselves any authority or jurisdiction in the case. Amongst the objections taken was this, that the slave-trade, as carried on by the Brazilians, was not piracy; that the men engaged in it had been wrongfully and illegally captured; and that the homicide which they did commit was an act done not within the Queen's jurisdiction. Mr. Baron Alderson was understood to hold, that if guilty of a crime, and though brought within the Queen's jurisdiction by an illegal act, it was not competent to the tribunals of this country to try them for such crime. It appeared to many by whom this question had been attentively considered, that the crime he referred to was not committed by them, but by their captors; and, assuming that to be the true state of the case, he affirmed that they were at liberty to rise upon their captors and put them to death. The result had shown that the Court of Admiralty in Brazil had taken this view of the question, for they upheld the doctrine that Brazilians captured under the alleged authority of an Act of the British Parliament were entitled to turn on their captors and treat them as pirates. Looking at the decision of the fifteen judges, he felt himself warranted in saying that they declared the opinion on which his hon. and learned friend had proceeded, to have been an erroneous opinion. They seemed to entertain no doubt that the law did not treat or recognise the acts of slave trading committed by the Brazilians, as cases not covered by the treaty, or as offences of which any court of justice could take cognisance, still less could they visit them with punishment. Further, he must observe that there were some important documents not noticed in the course of the present discussion—he alluded to the Brazilian protest of 1847, in which the Brazilians declared, as an excuse for their so long omitting to carry into effect their treaty with this country, that that omission was owing to the treaty of 1826, which could not be imputed to them, but to the noble lord opposite, who neglected to proceed in the matter, or to invest our representative at Rio Janeiro with the necessary powers. Then came the question regarding the prerogative of the British Crown. Now, he believed that in all treaties of authority on the law of prerogative, it was held that the municipal law of every other country formed an exception to its effect and operation. If the treaty of 1826 had been adopted, it would have made the slave-trade a crime; but, not having been adopted, not having been incorporated in the treaty of 1830, it had not that effect; and he did not hesitate to say, that if the noble lord had intended to induce the Brazilians to reject every proposition for the accommodation of those differences, he could not have taken any steps more calculated to produce that result than the course which he had pursued ever since he came into office; nor could he have selected a better instrument for effecting that purpose than Lord Howden, although he said this without the least knowledge of the noble lord, beyond the information which his public acts furnished; for he could know nothing of the noble lord other than what related to his public career. There was not a treaty for the suppression of the slave-trade that he would not gladly see repealed tomorrow, because he did not see why we should make ourselves the policemen of the world, for the purpose of contributing a very doubtful service to humanity. Whether the House agreed to this motion, or not, the Act of Parliament would be a dead letter, for it was in itself a gross and wicked infraction, not only of the principles of natural justice, but of international law.

Sir E. Buxton would not enter into the legal question, but he would take the more general and popular view of the subject, as it related to the great question of the opposition of this country to the slave-trade. He regretted that the right hon. member for Manchester had brought this motion forward at the instigation of his constituents; because he believed it was a notorious fact that the goods by which the slave-trade was fed, were nearly all produced in Manchester, and that it was the desire of some of those who had suggested this motion, that all restrictions upon the slave-trade should be withdrawn, in order that their trade with the Brazilians might be increased.

Mr. M. Gibson—Substantiate the charge.

The right hon. gentleman would have an opportunity of replying to him, but he thought his right hon. friend would not deny that a great proportion of the goods bartered for slaves originally came from Manchester. He considered that a great and fatal step towards increasing the slave-trade had been taken in 1846, by admitting Brazilian sugar into this country, because they had thus given a great stimulus and impetus to that abominable traffic. He believed that the object of this motion was to throw difficulties in the way of carrying into effect our treaties with Brazil. By those treaties we had the power to capture Brazilian vessels engaged in the slave-trade, but without such an Act as that to which the motion referred, we had no power to adjudicate and condemn them, and therefore the repeal of that Act would render the cruisers almost entirely useless. He looked upon this as a preliminary motion to one which he feared was likely to be made by the hon. member for Gateshead (Mr. Hutt), the chairman of the committee now sitting on the slave-trade, for altogether removing our cruisers from the African coast.

Mr. Hume expressed his surprise at the charges made by the hon. baronet against the manufacturers of Manchester. Why, if they were to bring all the distillers and brewers in the country to book, they might be charged with encouraging intoxication, and if the hon. baronet were judged by a committee of teetotallers, he might be condemned for making deleterious drinks injurious to the health of the people. He believed the means adopted for the suppression of the slave-trade, by the maintenance of a squadron on the coast of Africa, instead of effecting that object, only tended to aggravate the evils of that abominable traffic; and that opinion was now entertained by many humane persons, who were most anxious that the slave-trade should be put down. Besides the sacrifice of life entailed by the maintenance of the squadron, its cost to the country amounted to £1,000,000 a-year. He was glad his right hon. friend had brought this subject forward, because, by thus meddling with the affairs of other countries, they created much irritation and ill-feeling, and placed themselves almost beyond the pale of commercial intercourse.

Mr. J. O'Connell thought the hon. member for Montrose had not succeeded in clearing the Manchester manufacturers from the charge which had been made against them by the hon. member for Essex. Indeed, the charge had been almost admitted by the hon. member for Manchester (Mr. Bright). The Manchester argument seemed to be, " in order that we may have free trade in goods let us have free trade in slaves." He regarded this motion as another attempt at a retrograde movement, and he considered they ought now to make a stand, or next year another and more decided step might be taken. The question had been argued as if there were only two parties concerned—the British and the Brazilians; but there was a third party interested, the Africans, who seemed to be altogether lost sight of. With regard to what had been said as to the African squadron, he might remind the House that their retrograde movement, admitting slave-grown sugar, had increased the premium upon slaves, and had offered an additional inducement to slave dealers to endeavour to avoid the vigilance of the cruisers.

Sir R. Peel would postpone till some other opportunity the discussion on the general question connected with Africa, and relating to the question of what measures it might be desirable to adopt for the suppression of the slave-trade; understanding that the whole of that question would be brought forward at no remote period in the report of the committee, before which important evidence had been adduced. He did not think the argument of the hon. member for Montrose to be conclusive, that, because in our efforts to suppress the slave-trade we aggravated, in some degree, the sufferings of the slaves in the middle passage, those efforts should therefore be abandoned. There could be no doubt that if England were to lend Brazil her vessels to carry slaves to Brazil, the middle passage would be rendered more comfortable; but would any one advise that this country should submit to the discredit and disgrace of taking an

active part in carrying on the slave-trade, merely in order
to promote the comfort of the slaves in the passage? He
should be sorry if the house were disposed to apply to the
slave-trade the general principles which governed our commercial policy. Some years since the general impression
was, that the Christian and white population owed a deep
debt to the African race, on account of the misery which had
been inflicted on them for the base purpose of pecuniary
gain; and there was a general determination on the part of
Christian nations to co-operate for the purpose of reforming
the laws regarding slavery, and for suppressing the slave-
trade; and it was on the execution of one of the treaties
made by two Christian countries—this country and Brazil—
that the particular Act under consideration was introduced,
in 1845, to give effect to the convention voluntarily entered
into by Brazil with this country. It was said that that Act was
a manifest violation of the clear principles of international
law; but, if that were so, it was strange that every great
authority on the principles of international law was consulted
by the Government, and expressed the opinion that there
was nothing contrary to those principles in seeking, by intervention of Parliament, to give effect to the convention.
The Bill passed the House of Lords unanimously, and no
one discovered the objection at present relied on; and the
House of Commons, which was now invited to repeal that
Act by a single vote, passed the measure, in 1845, without a
division. Some reference had been made to a Chief Justice
calling the Bill a scandal, but that learned individual, then
in that House, only offered some objections to the third
clause, but did not oppose the Bill on the second or third
readings. The Bill, he repeated, passed both Houses unanimously, and if it were now said to be at variance with international law, and if it were on that account to be now
repealed, then never let the House attempt to persuade the
people that its decisions were entitled to respect. The right
hon. member for Manchester had argued that the offence of
the slave-trade, whatever they might call it by convention,
clearly was not that species of piracy ordinarily understood

by the law of nations as piracy. Nevertheless, if two nations by convention agreed to make a certain act piracy, then, by virtue of that convention, one of the countries might undertake to execute that which the other ought to execute, if it neglected to discharge its obligations. There was nothing contrary to the principles of national equity in that proceeding. Had, then, the subjects or the Government of Brazil any right to insist on our forbearance in this respect? He said that a more constant and flagrant violation of all promises had never been committed than that which Brazil had committed on this subject, and if Brazil had not the power to execute what she had promised, that was a just reason why we should step in. The following was the account given by Lord Aberdeen, upon moving the second reading of the Bill in question, of what Brazil had done :— "With rare and short exceptions the treaty had been by them systematically violated, from the period of its conclusion to the present time. Cargoes of slaves had been landed in open day in the streets of the capital, and bought and sold like cattle, without any obstacle whatever being imposed upon the traffic. Our officers had been waylaid, maltreated, and even assassinated, while in the execution of their duty; and justice, in such cases, if not actually denied, had never been fairly granted. No doubt much had happened, in the course of the last ten or twelve years, which would have justified, and almost called for, an expression of national resentment; but her Majesty's Government had no wish save to provide for the effectual execution of the treaty as stipulated for by the first article." If the House repealed the existing Bill, it would substantially proclaim to the world that all the efforts made to prevent the slave-trade, or to mitigate its horrors, were now at an end; and, if that should be done, his advice was that the next thing that the House should do, should be to determine how best to encourage and sanction it, permitting Cuba and Brazil to carry it on to their hearts' content without opposition, and publicly proclaiming to the nations of the world that the Parliament was determined to employ neither actual force nor authority for the purpose of rescuing the African race from misery.

Mr. P. Wood thought that no one could doubt that England would never retrace the steps she had taken in the way of promoting that great object of humanity to which the right hon. baronet had alluded, but he considered that the Act now in question did not carry out the treaty. The treaty, be it observed, did not rest with declaring the slave-trade piracy; it provided a special tribunal, a mixed tribunal, for the trial of the offence. It might be argued that that was a temporary provision, and the declaration was a thing of a permanent nature; but the Act of 8 and 9 Victoria did not provide for dealing with the offenders as pirates. The right hon. baronet (Sir R. Peel) had said that Parliament was asked to stultify itself by a single vote; but that was not so; the proposition was to bring in a Bill. He (Mr. Wood) trusted he should not be suspected of giving the slightest indication of any disposition to encourage the slave-trade.

Lord Palmerston.—I certainly shall follow the recommendation of my friend, the hon. member for Essex, by not entering, at present, at large into the question of the means for the suppression of the slave-trade. Indeed, I must do my right hon. friend (Mr. M. Gibson) the justice to say, that there was nothing in his speech which rendered such a discussion necessary. He felt no doubt that, as a committee was sitting which had this matter under consideration, he was better performing the duty he had undertaken by confining himself to arguing the motion he made, and not going into the other more large and extended question. My hon. friend, the member for Montrose (Mr. Hume), certainly launched at once into his favourite topic; and I am accused by the other member for Manchester of having a benevolent crotchet. The hon. member (Mr. Hume) must excuse me for saying that he has a crotchet to which I cannot apply the same epithet. For myself, I acknowledge a "crotchet." I believe it is shared by a very large proportion of the people of this country; for, however

hon. members may give out, for the purpose of their argument, that public opinion is changed, and that the people of
England are indifferent to the abominable and atrocious
crime of slave-trading, they may depend upon it, if the people
of England thought this House likely to retrace the steps
which for so many years have been followed, in deference to
the opinions of all the most eminent men, of whatever side
of politics, who have adorned this House and this country,
the hon gentlemen would find themselves under a grievous
mistake.   I shall content myself upon that point with saying
that I totally differ from the assertions that are made with
regard to it. I deny, in the first place, that the means which
have been adopted have utterly and entirely failed.   They
have done immense good; they have prevented enormous
evil.   I deny, in the next place, that opinion which has
passed from mouth to mouth, and is taken up without examination, that the methods of suppression we have adopted
have aggravated the horrors of the middle passage.   Whenever we come to discuss that question, I will show that that
is not the case ; that the horrors of the middle passage were
greater in former periods than at the present time.   But I
pass all that by, as a matter too large to be dealt with at
present, and not belonging to the present question—at least,
not to the argument of my right hon. friend.   But I must
be allowed to say one word in reference to what has fallen
from the hon. member (Mr. Wood), that he would not vote
for this motion, if he thought by doing so he was giving the
slightest indication of a disposition to encourage that atrocious
and abominable crime.   Why, nobody is consistent that I
have yet heard, except my hon. friend (Mr. Hume), who
avows—at least I think he is not prepared to deny—that he
does wish to set the slave-trade free.   What would be the
effect of repealing this law ?   It would entirely exempt the
Brazilian flag from all molestation in the pursuit of the slave-
trade, and therefore you would have the ocean covered, the
coast of Africa swarming with slave-traders sailing under the
protected flag of Brazil, and exercising their violent and
cruel occupation from one end of that continent to the other.

And, therefore, when the honourable and learned gentleman
says that he would not wish to do anything that should indicate
that disposition, I must say, that in voting for this motion he
will be giving, not an indication, but infinitely more—proof
that, as far as his vote can go, he is ready to let loose the
slave-trade upon Africa.   With regard to the law itself, the
statements made by the right hon. baronet (Sir R. Peel) and
the honourable and learned gentleman seemed to me to place
the matter upon the clearest and most satisfactory ground.
I have heard arguments, founded, I think, upon a jumble of
ideas, arising from gentlemen dealing with matters with
which, perhaps, they are not quite familiar; and a great deal
of the argument which I have heard to-night has been
founded upon a confusion of international piracy and conventional piracy.   At one moment, gentlemen argue this
matter as if they were dealing with international piracy—
piracy by the law of nations; and then, all on a sudden, they
change their ground, and treat it as conventional piracy, and
then again go back to international piracy, and the confusion
of their ideas leads them to think that their argument is
sound.   Now, what is the state of things ?   There is a piracy
which is, by the law of nations, cognisable by all nations
without any conventional arrangement; piracy, I may say,
consisting in acts of violence and plunder upon the high
seas, which is proved by an overt act; but which, when
committed, and the parties taken in the fact, is punishable
summarily, without any international convention.   But that
is not the case.   The slave-trade is not a high crime of that
description; it is not piracy by the law of nations; it may
be made piracy by convention, or by the law of any particular country.   Now, in this case, two countries agreed
that it should be piracy; Great Britain and Brazil made a
convention, by which any act of slave-trading committed by
subjects of Brazil should be deemed and treated as piracy.
That convention gave, therefore, to both parties the right of
so dealing with and treating an act of piracy by a subject of
Brazil.   And when, by reason of the interpretation which
had been put upon it, the Portuguese convention was held

to have ceased, and all that machinery of mixed commissions was put an end to, then the late Government was justified in passing that Act, by which the act of piracy, and the crimes committed by Brazilian subjects, were brought to the cognisance of British tribunals. Notwithstanding (continued the noble lord) what the hon. and learned gentleman had said, he could not help thinking that the silence of the authorities in the House of Lords was a strong presumption that the objections sought to be urged, on the ground of international law, had no foundation whatever. The hon. and learned gentleman appeared to object, not that the law went too far, but that it did not go far enough. His argument was, that they ought to have dealt with the subjects of Brazil; and that they had only dealt with their ships. If it was conceived that the Government of this country had gone beyond the treaty, he could understand the argument; but he could not see that the assertion that they had not taken the full extent of the power vested in them, was a reason to show that they had gone beyond what they had authority to do by the convention of 1826. It was said that there were no parties to watch the passing of the Act, but was not the Brazilian minister aware of the passing of the Act? [Sir R. Peel here made a remark.] He was reminded by the right hon. baronet that there was the three years' notice, and that the Brazilian Government were perfectly warned beforehand that if they persisted in the course complained of, something of this sort would be adopted. It was not controverted, that not only from the time of the actual passing of the convention, but from the time of the passing of the law in Brazil in virtue of the convention, the Government of Brazil had pursued one uninterrupted course of violation of that treaty. It was said that the British Government had assumed a power of dealing with Brazilian subjects that was not warranted by the laws of that country. Now, the law of that country did not, he (Lord Palmerston) admitted, make the slave-trade piracy; but the Brazilian Government passed a law in 1831, which, if carried into execution, would have had a very great effect in checking it.

It was true, that after he came into office, in February, 1847, the Brazilian minister did communicate to him a draft of a treaty, but which he said had been drawn out and prepared by a Government which was not then in office, and therefore he was not authorised to propose the treaty to him (Lord Palmerston) in any official way. That was the only proposition that had come from the Government of Brazil, and it was liable to great objection. Accordingly, he sent out by Lord Howden a draft of a treaty such as would, if agreed to by the Brazilian Government, justify the Government at home in proposing the repeal of the present law to Parliament. That treaty had not been accepted by the Brazilian Government. They said they would send a counter-proposition, but it had not been made. A verbal communication had been made by the Brazilian minister, that he expected shortly to receive such a communication, but, as yet, no such communication had been made to him (Lord Palmerston.) It was now said by some parties that this question of the slave-trade was the cause that no commercial treaty was made with Brazil, and he understood his right hon. friend to say that it was on account of this slave-trade controversy that the Brazilian Government refused to continue the expired treaty of commerce. The fact was not so. The former treaty of commerce with Brazil was an example of the bad effect caused by trying, in commercial transactions, to get an undue advantage. It was a treaty by which the import duties on British goods imported into the Brazils were very low in amount, and these low duties were felt to be very irksome by the Brazilian Government, who groaned under the restraint, and they longed for the day when they could fix that tariff according to their own convenience. It must not, therefore, be supposed that the raising of the duties upon the import of British goods, from thirteen to twenty-five or thirty per cent., was owing to the slave-trade. It was the natural re-action from the restraint which they were compelled to observe, from the treaty made many years before, and under different circumstances; and if the Government abolished the Act complained of, and let the slave-trade loose upon Africa, it would not be found that the Brazilians were ready again to enter upon the tariff with this country from which they had escaped. Practically he did not think that our commerce with Brazil suffered from inconvenient restrictions. It was perfectly true that there existed a law of Brazil which inflicted great inconvenience and injury on British subjects, as well as other foreigners in Brazil—namely, the law by which the estates of persons dying intestate were administered by the Court of Orphans, but that law was practically modified by arrangements made between the two countries. He was convinced that even those who were of opinion that everything that had been done was wrong, and that this country should retrace her steps, and let the slave-trade be freely carried on,—that even those persons ought to suspend any effort to carry their opinions into effect at present, until the committee had reported and had stated to the House whether they saw any other measures better calculated to accomplish the object, and what those measures were. On these grounds, he certainly resisted the motion of his right hon. friend; and, notwithstanding the feeling that seemed to exist in the minds of some persons of indifference to the slave-trade, he could not allow himself to think that the majority of that House would declare themselves adverse to those principles which had so long done honour to this country, or that they would, now that they had made great progress in putting it down, give their sanction to the opinion that this country was indifferent to the continuance of that atrocious and abominable traffic.

Mr. Roundell Palmer contended that the Government of Brazil had declared that we should be entitled, as between them and ourselves, to deal with Brazilians engaged in the slave-trade as outlaws from the law of nations, as public enemies of mankind, and therefore as outlaws from the law of Brazil and enemies to that empire as much as to ourselves. They never could complain, then, of this country, if she proceeded to legislate concerning those persons, and to deal with them in the same manner as she would be justified in dealing with any other pirates. There could be no *bonâ fide* complaint of the Brazilian Government, that this country was insincere in the policy which directed the treaty in question, and if the house believed that that treaty had a tendency to carry out that policy, let them not be frightened by any technical legal objections about the law, for he believed that no lawyer could say there was anything in doing so inconsistent with the recognised rules of law.

Mr. Cobden said he should not have spoken at all, but for a remark of the noble lord, the Foreign Secretary, which, in his opinion, was calculated to place this question on a false issue. The noble lord attempted to do great injustice to his hon. friend the member for Montrose, and those who concurred with him in condemning the present system of repressing the slave-trade ; for the noble lord argued as if those who opposed the present system were in favour of renewing the slave-trade. If there was one thing more universally admitted than another, it was the disastrous failure of putting down slavery by armed cruisers. The little tract which had been placed in their hands that morning by the Anti-slavery Society, stated that the number of slaves exported averaged more now than in 1807, when the trade was carried on by the United States, and England too, and that the horrors of the middle passage were increased in the same proportion. It was somewhat cool, then, for the noble lord, or the right hon. baronet, who put the question on a similar issue, to assume that those who were for doing away with the system of armed cruisers were advocates for a return of the slave-trade. Would the noble lord say that Mr. Scoble and the Anti-slavery Society to which he was secretary, because they denounced the system of armed cruisers, were in favour of returning to the old system of the slave-trade ? And yet, if the argument of the noble lord were good against the honourable member for Montrose, it was good against Mr. Scoble. He believed that the failure had arisen from the system of coercion, and why he quarrelled with the Anti-slavery Society of the present day was because they had departed from their old principle of attempting to influence mankind by appeals to humanity and religion, and had attempted to do their work through statesmen and politicians. He spoke not of modern times only; he believed that every effort made at the Congress of Vienna, and in Paris in 1814, had had the same injurious effect. The Duke of Wellington, writing from Paris in 1814, said that the French nation gave England no credit for sincerity in the abolition of the slave-trade, but attributed it to some selfish object. If they wished to convert other nations, they must leave them to the operation of the same principle they had acted on in this country. He believed that they were pursuing a course towards Brazil which they would not dare to do towards France or the United States; and the opinion of the statesmen of Europe and the *corps diplomatique* of the whole world was against it.

Colonel Thompson said, that even if they were to concede that the Anti-slavery Society was right in its assertion that there wás more slave-trading now than ever was known in history, it did not follow that all endeavours to diminish it were useless, but that, on the contrary, if no effort had been made, the slave-trade would have been greater. There was a parallel case which his honourable friend, who had alluded to him, might be ready to answer. Suppose it was urged that that great change in the commercial policy of this country, strongly affecting powerful interests, had not done many and certain things—which some would say it was very desirable should not have happened—how ready would his honourable friend have been to say that there was not much in that argument that was effectual and conclusive. During his whole life he had supported the object of the Anti-slavery Society, but he could not help suspecting that their intellect was under some cloud. He was not bound to explain the *rationale* of their proceedings, but when he heard his honourable friend talking of a benevolent crotchet, it led him seriously to expect that his honourable friend would be executing an office at the Horse Guards, or perhaps taking the command of the Channel fleet. He implored the gentlemen to suspend their judgment until they had a perfect opportunity of judging ; and he was confident that they who had passed their lives in glorying in the repression of the slave-trade on the coast of Africa would see that this country did not take part against them in the end.

After a few words from Mr. Bright in explanation,

Mr. Gibson briefly replied.

The House then divided, when the numbers were—

For the motion...................................	34
Against it	137
	———
Majority..................................	103

The motion was accordingly lost.

From the " Times," April 27.

There never was any public object that excited such enthusiasm in England as the suppression of slavery and the slave-trade. With all deference to Mr. Cobden, we may assert that neither the repeal of the Corn Laws, nor Financial Reform, nor any popular movement of later years, was so assiduously prosecuted, so enthusiastically supported, had so great, so powerful, and so religious an organisation among all classes of the community, as that which was directed against the traffic in slaves. Now that many of the inducements which formerly existed have lost their charm, and that the real consequences of that great measure stand forth, stripped of the illusions with which not only philanthropy and piety, but imagination and credulity, once invested them, it may be difficult for us of a later and soberer generation to realise the intensity of purpose, the stubbornness of will, and the prodigality of labour which the first disciples of Wilberforce and Clarkson exhibited fifty years ago. But there are men now living whose pride it is to have assisted those earnest and single-hearted champions of freedom—who commenced public life by voting with Grenville for the abolition of the British slave-trade—whose most eloquent speeches were devoted to the extirpation of colonial slavery, and whose official abilities have been engaged in attempts to suppress, on every sea, the cruel traffic which still supplies the labour-markets of Cuba and Brazil. To men of this stamp, blessed with such recollections, and exulting in such triumphs, it is hopeless to address a word on the vanity of the schemes which they have planned, or on the fruitlessness of the negotiations in which they have shared. They seem too proud, or too sanguine, or too blind, to be corrected by facts, or to be taught by experience. The consciousness of an exalted principle, and the animation of an ardent hope, blind them to the dark realities upon which they can hardly fail to stumble. To doubt of the success of their policy is, in their opinion, to doubt the sanctity of their principles,— to throw a slur upon the memories of Pitt, Canning, Grenville, Wilberforce, and a host of other worthies. They are convinced,—or rather, they cherish a belief which proceeds from intuition rather than conviction,—that the course which they have planned and pursued so long, is one which has other and higher recommendations than success, and is neither to be disparaged for its failures nor abandoned for its hopelessness.

We can thus well understand why statesmen like Sir R. Peel and Lord Palmerston so eagerly resist any proposal for deserting a policy which they were among the first to recommend, and so stoutly deny the inferences which are easily deducible from its effects.—But we question whether the world at large takes the same views of the subject. We do not, indeed, know what an Exeter-hall agitation might do; nor are we at all anxious to bring such machinery to bear. But, as far as we can judge, the prevalent opinion, out of doors, is very nearly this :—We have gone on year after year expending vast sums of money, and what is of far greater moment than money, the lives of brave men, in unavailing efforts to put an end to the slave-trade; the number of slaves exported from the coast of Africa is greater than it was in 1807; the horrors of the middle passage are more than doubled; the loss of life, both among the slaves themselves and our own crews, is frightful; and we have gained nothing but the certainty of continual bickerings and disputes with foreign states, who pertinaciously refuse to understand the treaties which they have made with us, and cavil also at our resolutions to abide by them.

We fear that in this instance the popular belief is not very far from the truth. No one doubts that the slave-trade is carried on, in spite of our schooners and steamers. The very value of the risk of exportation has been reduced to calculation; out of so many slavers that quit the African shore, so many will get clear off and reach their proposed destination; out of so many slaves crammed between the hatches and on deck, so many will escape the shot of the frigate in chase; only such or such number will be cast overboard, or suffocated, or shot; and on this worse than fruitless policy—this cruel and barbarous philanthropy—we expend something like a million sterling every year, to say nothing of the suffering, debility, and mortality to which we expose the lives and constitutions of English sailors, in a harassing service and a pestilential climate. Whatever may be the advantages that the committee now sitting will bring to light, our treaties with Portugal, Brazil, and the United States, relative to the slave-trade, have certainly borne no ostensible and appreciable fruits save those of burdening the country with a vast expense and unnecessary obloquy. We have not even succeeded in impressing foreign powers with a belief in the honesty of our intentions —Exeter-hall labours under the imputation of driving a religious bargain.

Nations who hear only of the fabulous wealth of England give no credit to our benevolence or disinterestedness. They see what efforts England makes to control and coerce foreigners, they pay no heed or credence to the sacrifices she has extorted from her own subjects. They denounce the "grasping ambition," which under the guise of liberty fills remote seas and hugs unwholesome shores with audacious and privileged buccaneers. They do not know that the same men that uphold this armed aggression have consigned the colonial plantations of England to poverty, degradation, and despair. If they are told to look at Jamaica, Trinidad, or Guiana—to witness the distress and dismay which a suicidal philanthropy has wrought among English planters—they retort, with a sneer, that English statesmanship is refined beyond the usual limits of a Machiavelian craftiness; that she ruins a helpless body of her own citizens, in order that she may have a pretence for ruining the colonies of her neighbours; that her energies are inspired by the malevolence of jealousy and the lust of power, not by the love of liberty or mercy. "For how comes it," they ask, "that, after all the brave words which her orators, preachers, and statesmen have thundered forth against slavery and slave-owners, her statesmen and people, after the show of a temporary delay, have resolved to deal only with the slave-owner, and purchase the sugar made by the unholy toil of the oppressed slave? If the philanthropy of England is sincere, let her cease to soil her hands with the produce of slavish labour. If her economy is sincere, let her put an end to expensive armaments, which succeed only in annoying and worrying foreign States, but which do not succeed in stopping the exportation or diminishing the misery of slaves." Such language is not uncommon in Paris, Madrid, Rio, or Havanna, and to us it seems not very unreasonable.

Amid the failures of costly armaments and unintelligible treaties, we are compelled to fall back upon a hope which the lapse of time will probably realise; and the realisation of which can only be retarded by violent acts or hot-headed counsels.

We believe, for our own part, that an event of startling importance will, within a very few years, give an entirely new aspect to the condition of the slave-trade. Already the American papers have announced that it is in the contemplation of some leading statesmen of the Republic to introduce a modification of slavery. When once slavery has been modified, our own experience warns us it will soon be destroyed. With the abolition of slavery in the United States will come the suppression of slavery elsewhere. The Americans, when they have won that most hard-fought of victories, the victory over the interests and the selfishness of their own slave proprietors, will have really stricken the most fatal blow at slavery and the slave-trade throughout the whole western hemisphere. The negroes of British West India free, the negroes of the United States free, and the slaves in Mexico free,—what power in the western world will be so rash as to import Africans within the dangerous contiguity of their liberated countrymen ? We say nothing of the occupation of Cuba. Were the design of annexing that most fertile of the Antilles carried into execution, it could only be done by the consent and under the auspices of the abolitionist party in the States. And if Cuba were not annexed, still the proximity of the southern States and the British West Indies would itself be fatal to any attempt at importing negroes into that island. In either case the slave traffic must, before a few years, become a perilous undertaking within view of American or English possessions ; and even now, it seems to us, nothing would be so dangerous to those who carry on the traffic as the wholesale and unlimited exportation of slaves to countries within purview of Governments which have abolished or are abolishing slavery, and within the vicinity of a great multitude of human beings just rising up from the protracted torpor of a loathsome and detested bondage. Let the free blacks of the British West Indies be but doubled in numbers—let the negroes of Virginia, Carolina, and Alabama, be emancipated, and a very few years would suffice to create a negro party in the colonies of England and the States of America, which would be a far more formidable obstacle to the slave-trade than the fleetest of steamers, the lightest of schooners, or the most adventurous of cruisers.

From the " Jamaica Despatch" of June 13th, 1849.

While Jamaica, under the auspices of her clergy, is urging on the Government its paramount duties with respect to the suppression of the slave-trade, the magnates of the Anti-Corn Law League are engaged in a praiseworthy effort to

extend British commerce by conceding international immunity to the spoilers of Africa.   It is a matter of history that
when, in the year 1774, the Assembly of Jamaica passed a
law for the suppression of the slave-trade, as far as she was
concerned, the merchants of England—the calico-printers
and cotton-spinners of Manchester—treated the question as
one of " vested rights," and succeeded in obtaining the rejec-
tion of the measure, as calculated ruinously to injure British
commerce.   Lord Somers' notable observations on this head
will live as long as English annals exist; and the celebrated
instructions to colonial Governors, that they should consent
to no act restricting a trade so important to the merchants
of England as the slave-trade with Africa, are emblazoned
in letters too substantial to be rubbed out by a subsequent
forced and spurious philanthropy.   Mr. Milner Gibson is
the mouth-piece of the mammon of the present day, as my
Lord Somers was of that of 1774.   We have, in the late
debate on the Brazilian slave-trade question, an index to the
motives which have dictated the Free-trade Sugar Bill of
1846.   If Mr. Milner Gibson himself had not revealed those
motives, they were abundantly exposed by Sir E. Buxton.
Rem quocunque modo rem, was the motto of the calico-men
three quarters of a century ago, and their moral escutcheon
has not yet changed its scroll.   The "Assiento Treaty,"
which gave the monopoly of the slave-trade to England, is
no longer in force; but the same interest that dictated the
terms of that blood-stained parchment has done its worst to
confer a chartered monopoly on the Brazilian slave-trader,
that Manchester cotton-spinners may profit by the traffic.

Of what do Mr. Milner Gibson and his free-trade constituents complain?   They aver that " the commercial relations between Great Britain and Brazil have for some years
been placed in a most unsatisfactory position by the intervention of the British Legislature; and that the Act 8 and 9
Vict., c. 122, for the suppression of the slave-trade, was not
only exceedingly offensive to Brazil, BUT MOST INJURIOUS TO
THE COMMERCIAL INTERESTS OF THIS COUNTRY."   We have no
doubt that Mr. Milner Gibson spoke plain truth here for

once. The fact is, that the Act complained of runs counter to the objects of the free-trade party. Their sole purpose in urging the admission of foreign slave-grown sugars into the British market, on equal terms with those produced by free labour in our own colonies, was to open fresh markets for the produce of the ten towns. They knew that Manchester goods afforded a sterling medium of exchange between the Brazilian pirate and the slave-dealer of the coast, and they looked for a corresponding increase in the consumption of those goods, in proportion as increased consumption of Brazilian sugar might stimulate the traffic in slaves. The Act of Parliament of which they complain has interfered to stay the consummation of this selfish desire. Brazilian sugars are admitted at a duty scarcely distinctive, but the firmness of Lord Palmerston has held Brazil to her treaties for the suppression of the slave-trade, and Brazil has interposed a hostile tariff. The truth has now come out that the slave-trade is as lucrative to the cotton-spinners now, as it was to what was called British commerce, in the days of Lord Somers. And they know it. Sir Edward Buxton hit the mark well when he said that the Manchester men suggested the motion, in order that their trade with Brazil might be promoted, because "*a great quantity of the goods paid for slaves originally came from Manchester.*"

Mr. Milner Gibson, with an hypocrisy which is natural to him, and which his treachery to the Conservative constituency of Ipswich has attached to his name for ever, has the effrontery, in the face of all this, to say that the petitioners whom he represented "yielded to none in their detestation of slavery and the slave-trade," whilst, in the same breath, he was seeking legislative immunity for the Brazilian slave-trader, in order that the same petitioners might profit by the iniquitous trade. This is the morality of the League, in which Mr. Gibson was supported by Mr. Richard Cobden and Mr. Quaker Bright! It says something for the House of Commons, ill as it is at present constructed, that only THIRTY-FOUR members could be got to back up this hypocrisy.

The merits of the question have been so well discussed, and Mr. Gibson's sophistry so well answered, that we need only on this head refer our readers to the debate.

From the " Times" of August 18th.

Amongst the advantages enjoyed by the country at this moment, that of a cheap and liberal supply of sugar must certainly be reckoned. Great authorities have expressed their convictions, that we owed to the law which gave us cheap bread, no small share of those exemptions from political disturbance which have made us, for the last twelvemonth, the envy of Europe. The circumstances of the two transactions are not, it is true, altogether parallel ; but, omitting for the moment any reference to the measures which induced such result, we may, perhaps, really say that one of the conditions which have combined to modify, in this country, the virulence of the raging epidemic, is the abundant supply of good sugar, which has been placed within the reach of all classes above the level of actual pauperism, and by which the commonest and least wholesome fruits of the season are converted into pleasant and nutritious alteratives. It must be recollected, however, that even if this state of things had been fairly brought about, it could not be lasting. We are living, as it was well expressed, on bankrupts' stocks, and after this resource has been exhausted, we shall find but small favour in the eyes of the slaveholding planters, whose machinery we attempt to demolish with one hand, while we quietly take its produce with the other.

As the question is one of such intimate and universal interest, perhaps the reader would like to see more minute details than are generally given respecting the production of an article, which may be now fairly classed among those of the first necessity. What are called the " *Gazette* averages per cwt." are, indeed, often quoted ; but it is hardly probable that their technical figures supply the ordinary inquirer with even an explanation of the price he himself pays per pound. The great question, it will be recollected, is between free and slave labour—terms which must be understood as relating not merely to the advantages derivable from labourers working without pay, but to those which depend upon a continuous and safe supply of labour always at command. What is often urged respecting the superiority of voluntary over involuntary work is perfectly true, as far as it goes ; but the argument is nullified by the fact that voluntary work, of such a character as to be of any service, has never yet been obtained, and is declared by good judges to be absolutely unattainable, from an enfranchised African. If the free negro could be induced to work steadily and industriously for hire, like the native of any other country, our own colonists might have a chance of righting themselves; but such is not the case, and it is this which constitutes the substantial difference between the planters of Brazil and the planters of Jamaica. The former can reckon with perfect certainty on an adequate supply of labour at that particular season of the year when the whole produce of the twelve-month is at stake. The latter can repose on no such assurance, for the work at "crop time" is necessarily so severe, even with a full supply of hands, that it is far beyond the resolution of the lazy " squatters" of the district. Slaves at this season are, we believe, worked unremittingly for eighteen hours in the day, and the consequence is, that the sugar is fairly got in and manufactured ; but there is no such chance for the British colonist. In England, where the inducements to free industry are so different, thousands of men could be obtained, at a moment's warning, to work, for a due consideration, eighteen hours out of the twenty-four ; but in the West Indies, where the negro has neither taxes to pay nor need of clothes to cover him, no such exertions can be purchased by any reasonable offers. This is the real point of difference between free and slave labour, as practically affecting our colonies ; otherwise, as will be seen, the slave-holder has heavy liabilities to counterbalance his advantage.

In the old days of West Indian prosperity, when planters suffered no penalties save those of surfeits and extravagance, the cost of an ablebodied slave was, we believe, about £80.

At this figure he was expected to be some twenty-five years of age, and to have ten years' honest work in him, and the number of his working days throughout the year was usually set at 310 out of the 365. This was not a very rigorous proportion, perhaps; but, then, for a proportion of this period, he was worked at " crop time" hours, and during the rest of the year a respectable twelve hours' labour was expected from him. This, to be sure, is no more than what an English labourer gives—from six to six—allowing for mealtime in both cases, nor was the work always very laborious, but still the total amount performed was considerable. Its results were estimated by some such calculations as the following :—A good healthy slave would cultivate two acres annually, and an acre was ordinarily expected to produce about one ton of sugar and a due proportion of rum, that is, about sixty gallons to a ton. Or, putting the estimate in another form, the estate was considered to be doing pretty well, if one hogshead of sugar of 17 cwt., with its proportion of rum, was produced for every head of slave stock upon it, reckoning old and young together. The cost, then, of an ablebodied slave would have stood thus against his earnings—

	£	s.	d.
10 per cent. on his original price	8	0	0
Food, clothing, &c. (almost exactly that of a Russian soldier)	5	0	0
Depreciation and mortality on ten years, at 10 per cent.	8	0	0
Total annual cost...........	21	0	0
2 tons of sugar, say.................................	50	0	0
120 gallons of rum	18	0	0
Total annual earnings.........	68	0	0
	21	0	0
Profit £47		0	0

Now, when the experiment is made with "free labour," that is, as it should be always remembered, with such labour as an emancipated negro can be brought to give in a country where he has no natural or artificial wants to supply, the results found are these :—Say that he works the same number of days, 310, yet the average duration of his labour will certainly not be above six or eight hours a-day, and the total average produce cannot be calculated at more than one-half that of the slave. So that if his wage—one shilling a-day—be compared with his work, the following will be the conclusion—

	£	s.	d.
One ton of sugar	25	0	0
60 gallons of rum	9	0	0
	34	0	0
Deduct wages, 310 days	15	10	0
	18	10	0
Profit of slave over free labour	£28	10	0

These calculations indicate the true point of our planters' disabilities, viz., the deficiency of effective labour. The annual cost of a slave exceeds by more than 20 per cent. the wages of a free labourer, but so ineffective is the work of the latter that this advantage is soon neutralised, and the difference rises above the compensation of any moderate differential duty. The great object, then, if we would still retain sugar at its present reasonable rates, is to furnish our own plantations with better supplies of labour, and seek out, at the same time, fresh fields of action, where this indispensable auxiliary to success is readily procurable. We have now a statement before us containing proposals for establishing a sugar plantation in the British settlement of Malacca, the soil and climate of which are said to be eminently favourable to such culture, while the all-important commodity of labour is poured in abundantly by the Chinese immigrations from Singapore. The Straits' Government, it is stated, has granted liberal tracts of land, rent-free for five years, for the purposes of the undertaking, and has expressed every desire to promote it by encouragement and aid. A Chinese "contract labourer" is estimated to be worth, wage and work being compared together, fully £12 5s. per annum more than an ablebodied negro slave, and the calculations of the proprietors are intended to prove that the Brazilian and Cuban planters could be fairly undersold by the produce of our own possessions raised by free labour. We pronounce no opinion upon the soundness of these conclusions, but it is only too clear that if we do not by some means obviate what will soon become the monopoly of slaveholding sugar-growers, we shall expiate our injustice to our own colonists in a very appropriate but extremely unpleasant manner.

In the course of the observations to which the present movement has given rise, the mere slave dealer has been treated with suitable severity. Neither have the Spanish and Brazilian authorities, who derive a disgraceful profit from their connivance in the traffic, escaped without reproach. But there are still other classes, some among our fellow-subjects at home, and others of our kith and kin at the western side of the Atlantic, without whose active assistance the trade could not be carried on so successfully, who must not be allowed to pass unnoticed.

If you ever entered into conversation with a lady or gentleman from New England, on the subject of the African slave-trade, perhaps you have twitted them with the skill which the Maryland ship-builders have acquired in the construction of fast-sailing clippers. And it would be very extraordinary if you did not meet with the "*tu quoque*" by way of retort, calling your attention to the cheapness of negro shackles at Birmingham, and the easy terms on which you can supply yourself at Manchester with any quantity of that class of soft goods known to commerce by the convenient generality of "Domestics." For ourselves we find it difficult to discover the benefit of this sort of

national recrimination, unless in the course of it we could
discover the means of drawing a clear and intelligible line of
distinction between the honest manufacturer, who prepares
his bandanas for the market with a conscience as clear as
Wilberforce himself could desire, and his nearest neighbour
who, not knowing or not caring about their ultimate destination, contents himself with the fact that there is a brisk
demand in the market for his cheap domestics, and takes
especial care not to trouble himself with other men's affairs,
and to ask no questions.

The delicate shades which separate the innocent from the
guilty, it would not be easy to fix and discriminate by Act
of Parliament. It might be difficult, even for the man who
reflects in his moments of leisure on the nature of his
employment, and the purposes to which the product of his
labour may ultimately be applied, to detect in his own breast
the nice distinction between a state of absolute unconscious-
ness and the first uncertain and passing shadow which
crosses his mind. From this undefinable point, through
every deepening tint of doubt, suspicion, and awakening
consciousness, down to guilty knowledge, and its attendant
remorse, how, if we could even probe him to the quick, and
read his thoughts, in the innermost recesses of his bosom,
are we to arraign him at the bar of any tribunal which does
not pretend to judge the secrets of the heart ?

In England, it is true, the influence of public opinion
may often be brought to bear on a doubtful transaction,
since no man could show his face among his fellows, if he
were known to be a manufacturer or an exporter of leg-
irons. But as the scale of inward consciousness is gradua-
ted, so, also, is the public test by which it is adjudged. As
far as the slave question is concerned, public opinion does
not work in the same way at either side of the Atlantic.
Perhaps it was your injudicious taunt which roused the

nationality of your friends from New England, and provoked them to defend what they did not exactly approve. But, whatever may have been the state of public feeling in Maryland,—from the time when the lines of the " Venus" or the " Socorro," two of the most successful of that beautiful class of vessels which the ship-yards of Baltimore have produced, were first laid down on the floor of the building loft, until, after the last hand had been put to her equipment, she was hauled out from the wharves of the prettiest of the Atlantic cities, to proceed to her murderous and piratical destination, amidst the shouts of admiring thousands,—it is very certain that, in the old country, at least, we have the grace to be ashamed of the dirty work that some of us are content to engage in, and if we have soiled our fingers, we resort to the wash-hand bason before walking out into the street.

But take your passage in the craft you have been admiring, on her first trip down the Chesapeak, with the star-spangled banner at her main, and proceed in her to that stage in her criminal career, the isle-besprinkled bay of Rio, or that of Todos los Santos. If you have the courage to walk into the counting-house of the consignee, and are not suspected of being either a New Englander or a Britisher, you will meet with a frank and hospitable reception. You will find your new acquaintance at the head of a large establishment; and if you accept his invitation to dinner, you will sit down, any day in the week, with a party consisting of several scores, or at least dozens, of persons of respectable exterior, among whom,—after running your eye down the sides of the table, and observing the long rows of clerks belonging to the establishment, with the junior partners at proper intervals, and here and there an American ship-master, who having disposed of his cargo of lumber, or his assortment of notions, is now looking out for a cheap load of muscovado, with its due proportion of browns and yellows, to carry to St. Petersburgh or New York,—you will be able, all unpractised as you are, to distinguish another class of men, of sallow complexion and sinister aspect, with a bold and reckless deportment, and an indescribable expression of countenance, in which the astute and the cunning are strangely associated with the open and the frank.   The dress of those men is in the extreme of the mode, the beard is cut, the moustache pointed, and turned up in the most approved fashion ; and every one of them is decked out with as much finery as can well be disposed about his person, in the shape of finger rings, diamond brooches, and massive gold chains, with the addition, perhaps, of some precious amulet, or a crucifix, to protect him from the perils and in the hair-breadth escapes in which he delights.   The profession of these men you have discovered at a glance, and you hardly need be told that they have all been more or less deeply engaged in the traffic of which men, women, and children are the staple; that one is fitting out the " Arrogante" for a fresh expedition to the coast; or that another is an aspirant for the command of the clipper from which you have just landed, whose raking masts and broad-spread canvas, whose lines of symmetry and rate of sailing, are the sole subject of admiring conversation at the table that day.

You must not imagine that this is a mere fancy sketch. At all events, here is a little anecdote which is strictly historical, and which, if you be, as we expect, a sturdy John Bull, you will acknowledge to be stranger than fiction.

There is a great house of business in Birmingham, whose name, as everybody will tell you, is not only good on 'Change, but against whose commercial character, or the personal reputation of its members, not a whisper has ever been heard ; and yet, strange to say, this respectable body of men, who will sell you anything in the way of their business, from a pair of handcuffs to a steam engine,—having become the acknowledged agents and representatives of one of the most notorious houses at the Havanna, who have acquired immense wealth by large transactions in slave-trade,—consented in the year 1840, for the sake of obliging such a valuable connection, to travel out of their peculiar line of business, which is that of wholesale ironmongers and bankers, and to cause to be built in a distant English sea-port, under the inspection and subject to the orders of an experienced Spanish navigator, sent to England for that purpose from the Havanna, a vessel which turned out to be of such doubtful character that the able and honest ship-builder, Mr. Moore, of Plymouth, on hearing that on her first voyage she had been cleared out at the port of Liver-pool for the Havanna, thought it his duty to address a letter to the Consular representative of her Majesty's Government in that part of the world, declaring that the vessel he had constructed, which had been named the " Antonio," deserved to be closely watched, as from her unrivalled sailing quali-ties, and the number and extent of her openings, she was peculiarly well adapted to the purposes of the slave-trade, for which, in the opinion of the builder, she was clearly designed.

With this suicidal declaration on board, the " Antonio" arrived in due course at the Havanna, under the nominal command of an Englishman, Captain Wallen, with a certi-ficate of British registry, establishing the fact that Messrs. Rabone, Brothers, and Co., of Birmingham, were the sole owners; with a crew containing the exact proportion of British-born subjects imperatively required by British law; and with a certain Señor Menguaga on board, in the capa-city of supercargo, the same who had so carefully superin-tended her construction.

Not long after this arrival had been reported at the Custom-house, and the muniments of the ship had been deposited by Captain Wallen, according to law, at the office of the British Consul, a Spanish gentleman presented himself in the same public place, and producing a bill of sale, purporting to have been executed for a valuable consideration by the registered owners, at the port of Liverpool, in favour of Messrs. Fernandez Pozo and Co., of the Havanna, demanded that the deed of transfer should be recognised, and entered on the archives of the consulate, and that the certificate of British registry should be cancelled ; the effect of which would have been to alter the "Antonio's" nationality, deprive her of the British flag under which she had arrived, and entitle her to wear that of Spain.

The applicant having announced himself as a member of the firm in whose name he made the demand, met the question which was proposed to him, *in limine,* as to the fact of his house being largely engaged in slave-trade, with a frank acknowledgment; but added, in a tone of some solemnity, and it may be added, of great apparent sincerity, that it was not the intention of his house to send the "Antonio" to the coast of Africa ; that, in fact, she was far too valuable for that branch of their business, having cost more than 30,000 dollars ; and that her true destination was to ply as a regular trader between the Havanna and the port of Liverpool.

On the suggestion that no vessel of so high a class had ever been engaged in the Liverpool trade ; that she was far too sharp to stow well; and that she could evidently go to windward of the fastest clipper in the harbour, Señor Pozo admitted that she was a beautiful vessel, and possessed of fine sailing qualities, but stated that she was the fancy of the senior partner of the house, who had a perfect right to please himself in the orders he had given regarding her construction ; and persevered in his denial of the imputation which this course of interrogation suggested.

Then, as to the unusual size and number of the hatchways, and the openings, like port-holes, ahead and astern, Señor Pozo was prepared with a ready explanation ; which was, that his house was largely engaged in the importation of steam machinery and sugar-making apparatus on the largest scale, and that the main hatchway had been made so large for the purpose of admitting vacuum pans and steam boilers, which were constantly in demand, of increasing power and capacity ; and with regard to the port-holes, it was as well to be prepared for the very possible case of her being required, some day or other, to carry spars or timbers of large dimensions.

This was all very plausible, but it appears that it did not satisfy the Consul, who, after a vast deal of discussion and correspondence, and after causing the ship to be inspected by the commanders of several of her Majesty's cruisers, determined definitively to refuse the application, and to refer it to the decision of her Majesty's Government, on the return of the "Antonio" to Liverpool, which, according to the voluntary declaration of Señor Pozo, was, at all events, to be her destination.

In due course, the "Antonio" was cleared out for Liverpool, and returned, by-and-by, to the Havanna, on her second voyage, followed very closely by one of the partners of the house at Birmingham, in whose name she stood registered.

It so happened that, in the course of the year 1840, when preparing to proceed to the Havanna in his official capacity, the Consul had paid a visit to a very dear friend of his at Birmingham, a distinguished member of that enlightened and benevolent Society, who have taken to themselves the name of the Friends, not only of each other, but of the whole human family. While showing the Consul-elect the lions of the place, his friend took an opportunity of carrying him into the great hardware establishment of Messrs. Rabone, Brothers, and Co., where it turned out that his kind-hearted object was to select for his friend, on the eve of his departure, some token of remembrance, which presently assumed the shape of a very nice chest of working tools. The name of the house had not been mentioned, or had been forgotten; but when the partner who came to the Havanna presented himself at the consulate, on the business of the "Antonio," he was at once recognised as the same person who had been acting a few months before as the head of the house in Birmingham. In addition to this accidental recommendation, Mr. Lloyd brought with him a letter of introduction from the late Sir Thomas Fowell Buxton, another dear friend of the Consul, in which the gentleman is described as his cousin.

At the close of this first interview, in the hope of being able to do due honour to the introduction he had received, the Consul inquired of Mr. Lloyd at which of the hotels in the city he had taken up his abode; when, to his inexpressible surprise and mortification, he learned that the cousin of Sir Thomas Fowell Buxton had established himself under the roof of Messrs. Fernandez Pozo and Co., at whose well-spread table it is known, to all the little world of the Havanna, that it is impossible to avoid the contamination of associating with slave-captains and other miscreants, the refuse of the human race. Thus, from one blunder to another, this English gentleman, so respectably connected, had contrived to flounder into a position as mistaken and as false as it is possible to conceive; and from which it became daily more difficult to escape. He was in the hands of the slave-traders, who, doubtless, owed him large sums of money; and it was not, therefore, quite convenient to quarrel with them. For, although they might be good on the Bolsa, their virtue, in any other sense, was not to be relied on—as, in order to enforce his co-operation, they plied him with threats of repudiating the debt; and in order to work more directly in other quarters, they did not scruple to insinuate, in a manner alternately corrupt and truculent, that the Vice-consul (Mr. Cocking) might make his fortune if he procured the recognition, and that the life of his chief would not be safe if he persisted in refusing it.

Finding that cajolery and intimidation were equally unsuccessful, the slave-trading firm made the further mistake of supposing that they could bring the influence of the Captain-general to bear on the mind of the Consul, to whom they proposed an interview in his Excellency's presence.

To this the Consul made no sort of objection. The audience was appointed, and the parties were ushered into the cabinet of the Viceroy, when the Consul perceived that, instead of reading the usual presentation in form, his countryman had already found an opportunity of stating his case in person to that gallant old soldier, the pure and high-minded General Valdez, who, however, had kept his own counsel, and had left the slave-trading firm, as well as their English victim, in the most profound ignorance of his views and intentions on the subject.

After a conference, which lasted more than two hours by the Cathedral clock, in the course of which the same arguments and protestations were repeated *ad nauseam,*—and the whole were listened to by his Excellency with the most imperturbable gravity,—a direct appeal was made to the Consul, who observed to his Excellency that he had reported the whole case, many months before, to the Government of the Queen his Sovereign, who had not seen fit to alter his decision; that Messrs. Rabone, Brothers, & Co., had had an opportunity of appealing against that decision, if they thought proper,—of which it was their own fault if they had not availed themselves ; and that he had heard nothing that day to justify him in altering the judgment he had already formed on the subject.

On hearing this statement, his Excellency rose, and with the evident intention of bringing the audience to a close, but to the equally manifest disappointment and dismay of the majority of his hearers, he stated in a very few words that even if the Consul had freely consented to cancel the British registry of the "Antonio," it would not have been in his power to allow that vessel to assume a Spanish nationality, or to wear the Spanish colours, because he had received an express order to that effect from the Government of her Catholic Majesty.

This brief declaration was so forcible and so clear, that further controversy became impossible; and the Consul received no further annoyance beyond the mere formal repetition of the threat of Mr. Lloyd, that his house would hold him liable for the great loss and damage they were about to sustain by his refusal to comply with their request, and that he might expect to receive their notice of action, as soon as they heard of his landing in any part of her Majesty's dominions. The subsequent history of the "Antonio" is lost in obscurity. She entered the port of the Havanna from Liverpool, on her second voyage, under the command of a Maltese captain, named Babbe, but she was never known to sail from it,—if the records of the Havanna Custom-house speak the truth,—and it was whispered that a vessel named the " Triumphante," which had never entered the Havanna, and had not been built there, had soon afterwards taken her departure under the flag of one of the Hanse Towns, bearing a striking resemblance to the ship which had so mysteriously disappeared.

It was not more than a year after these last transactions that the Consul returned to England, and having landed at

Liverpool, he made a halt at Birmingham, for the express purpose of letting his arrival be known to Messrs. Rabone, Brothers, and Co., because his stay in the country was to be limited, and it would be much more convenient to have the judicial proceedings, which had been threatened so boldly, put to a test as speedy and conclusive as possible.

Had the affair ended here, it might have been supposed that Mr. Lloyd, who by this time was observed to have donned a coat of a form peculiar to himself, with a beaver of doubtful dimensions, was preparing, as the French say, to play the comedy, but it will be seen that in the sequel it degenerated into the broadest farce. One good end had already been achieved as the result of his inconsiderate proceedings. It is not perhaps quite certain that all our English ship-builders are as jealous of the national honour as that excellent person, Mr. Moore, of Plymouth; but the exposure of this case, in all its truth and simplicity, will make it more difficult, if not impossible, to convert Plymouth, Hull, or Sunderland, or any of our mercantile sea-ports, into so many Baltimores for the construction of fast-sailing clippers, with which to arm the Spanish and Brazilian slave-traders against the risk of capture by her Majesty's cruisers; some of which, it is to be feared, are not quite so fast as the " Antonio," although the skill of her enlightened architect is not unknown to her Majesty's Government, for whom he has executed many beautiful specimens of his craft, without the assistance of any slave captain from the Havanna.

The Earl of Aberdeen having decided to rely on the fragile pledges of the Spanish Government for the voluntary suppression of the slave-trade, which, when made, were evidently designed to be broken, found it necessary in strict consistency to withdraw the Consul, who had been selected by Viscount Palmerston for the express purpose of watching over the execution of that very simple system of slave-trade suppression which it is the object of the present movement in Jamaica to recommend to the attention of the people of England, and to press once more on the notice of her Majesty's Government.

On reaching Downing Street, the Ex-consul, who still held the office of Superintendent of liberated Africans at the Havanna, received from the hands of Viscount Canning the duplicate of a private letter from Lord Aberdeen, proposing to him, in terms of great kindness and consideration, to proceed directly from the Havanna to Jamaica, to place himself at the head of a Court of Mixed Commission about to be established in that island, in virtue of a new treaty for the suppression of the slave-trade, which had recently been negotiated with Portugal.

The other members of this new Commission had thought it necessary to remain in England until the Secretary of State should receive an answer to the proposal which his lordship had thus transmitted to Cuba, and which was at once acceded to, when renewed in person by Lord Canning, who represented how very desirable it was that the gentlemen concerned should be on the spot, to open the Court with as little delay as possible. The senior member being tied, of course, by no English engagements, declared his readiness to embark at the shortest notice; and, with his colleagues, he received notice that her Majesty's steam-ship "Thunderbolt" was under orders to carry them to Jamaica; but, unhappily for the second member, and his interesting family, he was not quite ready. The "Thunderbolt" was withdrawn from that service to go to the Cape of Good Hope on a similar errand; the Jamaica Commissioners were directed to find their way to their destination by the steam-packet, as might best suit their several convenience; and thus poor Mr. Fitzjames, with his wife, four young children, and two servants, for the want of a little promptitude, were carried off, at one fell swoop, in the catastrophe of the "Solway," by which so many lives were lost off the harbour of Corunna.

The Mixed Commission had not been long established in Jamaica, when Mr. Lloyd of Birmingham arrived there, under feelings, apparently, of great irritation, in consequence, perhaps, of the difficulties which had supervened, in obtaining a satisfactory settlement of accounts with his slave-trading connections at the Havanna. The first intimation which her Majesty's Commissioners received of the whereabouts of the ex-member of the Society of Friends, presented itself in the form of a letter from Mr. Macpherson M'Niel, an eminent solicitor in Kingston, declaring that Mr. Lloyd felt aggrieved by the late Consul's proceedings at the Havanna in relation to the "Antonio." The tone and expression of this lawyer's letter, like the habiliments of his client, were somewhat ambiguous in their nature. The redress required might either mean a renewal of the threat of judicial proceedings held out at the Havanna, but not followed out in England ; or it might be construed, by a very determined belligerent, into a demand of personal satisfaction. Inasmuch, however, as the missive reached its address by the hands of a servant in livery, which is not the customary mode of inviting your friend's adversary to meet him in mortal combat, the Commissioner treated it, in the simplicity of his heart, not as a sanguinary cartel, but as a demand for a pecuniary indemnity, in consequence of the losses Mr. Lloyd had sustained, through his connection with the "Antonio," and his inability to pass her in a legal manner to Messrs. Fernandez Pozo and Co., which he had always ascribed to the act of her Majesty's Consul.

Under that impression the reply was written, and it was conceived in terms which were calculated to deter an upright man of business, which Mr. M'Niel is universally acknow-

ledged to be, from advising his client to embark on a course
of litigation, which could only end in disappointment and
defeat.

The Commissioner heard no more from Mr. M'Niel;
but on the following morning there arrived at his residence
in the country another friend of Mr. Lloyd, Mr. John
Mulholland, now of Belfast, but then of Kingston, who had
held the rank of Custos Rotulorum, or chief magistrate of
the city, and who presented a letter of credence from his
principal, in the most approved belligerent form, together
with a verbal explanation, that the purport of Mr. M'Niel's
communication had been quite misunderstood, which was
not by any means intended to be in the nature of a lawyer's
letter, but had for its object the healing of the wounded
honour of Mr. Lloyd, who was reported to have been
charged by the Commissioner with having aided and abetted
in the practice of the slave-trade.

Mr. Mulholland having committed this explanation to
writing, the Commissioner returned an answer, protesting
against the claim of Mr. Lloyd to any sort of redress, legal
or personal, for acts which had been called for in the con-
scientious performance of a public duty, for which he was
responsible to her Majesty's Government, and to no one
else whatever. But he assured Mr. Mulholland, as he
had previously assured Mr. M'Niel, that he had never
accused Mr. Lloyd of anything beyond the most grievous
indiscretion, which, if not checked as it had been, might
have brought disgrace on the national character, and
have reduced the masters of our dock-yards to the same
level, in point of morality, with that of the clipper-builders of
Baltimore.

With this explanation Mr. Mulholland was perfectly contented, and in the name and behalf of his principal declared,
in writing on the spot, that the Commissioner had done no

more than his duty, that Mr. Lloyd had no further claims upon him, and ought to be satisfied.

It might have been supposed that here the affair would have ended ; but with a pertinacity which would have done honour to a better cause, Mr. Lloyd, on the third morning, sent a third friend to the Commissioner, in the person of Captain John William Seymour, a magistrate for the city of Kingston, who declared that Mr. Lloyd was more deeply aggrieved by the explanatory letter addressed to Mr. M'Niel, the lawyer, than by anything else, and that, waiving all other grounds of complaint, he insisted on its being withdrawn. To this the Commissioner demurred ; on which Captain Seymour assumed a warlike attitude, and required a reference to a friend, to arrange the usual preliminaries to a hostile meeting. Not admitting that Mr. Lloyd had any just claim on him, the Commissioner, from motives of courtesy to Mr. Seymour, referred him to his nearest neighbour, the Baron Von Ketelhoot, who possessed his confidence, and was already acquainted with the circumstances of the case ; and that gentleman succeeded, at the first interview, in convincing Captain Seymour that Mr. Lloyd had no sort of claim on her Majesty's Commissioner, either for the withdrawal of the letter in question, or for anything else.

As if to cover the whole of Mr. Lloyd's proceeding with ridicule, Mr. Mulholland thought himself aggrieved by the step thus taken by Captain Seymour, and deemed it necessary to demand satisfaction, not only from that gallant officer, but from his former principal, Mr. Lloyd. The whole affair became a nine day's wonder among the *quidnuncs* of Kingston ; and in the meantime, the unsatisfied Mr. Lloyd took his departure from the scene in which he had so strangely distinguished himself.

We conclude by referring our readers to Mr. Turnbull's volume, entitled, "Travels in the West, Cuba," &c. ;

Longman and Co., 1840, pp. 340 — 360; and to the following documents :—

1. Despatch from Mr. Turnbull to Lord Aberdeen, dated Havanna, November 6th, 1841, transmitting memorials relative to the proposed Convention of Lord Palmerston.—*Slave-trade Papers*, 1841, *Class B., pp.* 363, 364.

2. Circular of Captain-general Valdez.—*Ibid. p.* 365.

3. Report of the Junta de Fomento to the Captain-general, on the Draft of the Convention relating to slave-trade, proposed to Spain by Great Britain.—*Ibid. p.* 365, 375.

4. Report of the Conde de Santo Venia to the Captain-general, dated Havanna, October 3, 1841.—*Ibid. pp.* 375—380.

5. Report of Don Wencenslao de Villa Uriueta, on the Draft Treaty proposed to Spain by Great Britain, dated Havanna, October 21, 1841.—*Ibid. pp.* 388—402.

6. Report of the Licentiate Don Bernardo Maria Navarro, on the Draft of the Convention regarding slave-trade, proposed by the British Government.—*Ibid. pp.* 402—409.

7. Report of the Marquis de Santiago y San Felipe, on the Convention proposed by the British to the Spanish Government regarding the slave-trade, dated Havanna, October, 1841.—*Ibid. pp.* 409—412.

8. Report of the Royal Patriotic Society on the proposed Convention for the fulfilment of treaties for the abolition of the slave-trade.—*Ibid. pp.* 412—423.

9. Memorial addressed by the Junta de Fomento to the Regency of Spain, on the abolition of slavery and the slave-trade. —*Ibid. pp.* 285—289.

10. Memorial of the Municipal Council of Havanna to the Regency of Spain, on the abolition of slavery and the slave-trade. —*Ibid. pp.* 289—292.

11. Memorial of the Tribunal of Commerce.—*Ibid. pp.* 292—298.

12. Memorial of the Conde de Santo Venia to the Captain-general.—*Ibid. pp.* 298, 299.

13. Memorial of the inhabitants of Cuba to the President Governor and Captain-general of Cuba.—*Ibid. pp.* 263—265.

DATE DUE

FE 14 71			
DE 13 72			
OC 20 75			
GAYLORD			PRINTED IN U.S.A.